DEATH NATION

The Experts Explain American Capital Punishment

Matthew B. Robinson
Applachian State University

PEARSON

Prentice
Hall

Upper Saddle River, New Jersey 07458

Library of Congress Cataloging-in-Publication Data

Robinson, Matthew B.
    Death nation : the experts explain American capital punishment / Matthew Robinson,
        p. cm.
    Includes index.
    ISBN-13: 978-0-13-158693-2
    ISBN-10: 0-13-158693-9
    1. Capital punishment—United States. I. Title.

    KF9227.C2R63 2007
    345.73'0773—dc22

                                2006100846

Editor-in-Chief: Vernon R. Anthony
Senior Acquisitions Editor: Tim Peyton
Associate Editor: Sarah Holle
Editorial Assistant: Jillian Allison
Marketing Manager: Adam Kloza
Production Editor: Connie Strassburg, GGS Book Services
Production Liaison: Barbara Marttine Cappuccio
Managing Editor: Mary Carnis
Manufacturing Manager: Ilene Sanford
Manufacturing Buyer: Cathleen Petersen
Senior Design Coordinator: Christopher Weigand
Cover Design: Jill Little
Cover Image: Dave Cutler/Images.com
Composition/Full Service Project Management: GGS Book Services
Printer/Binder: R.R. Donnelley & Sons

Pearson Education Ltd.   Pearson Education Australia Pty. Limited
Pearson Education Singapore Pte. Ltd.   Pearson Education North Asia Ltd.
Pearson Education Canada, Ltd.   Pearson Educatión de Mexico, S.A. de C.V.
Pearson Education–Japan   Pearson Education Malaysia, Pte. Ltd.

10 9 8 7 6 5 4 3 2 1
ISBN-13: 978-0-13-158693-2
ISBN-10: 0-13-158693-9

Dedication

This book is dedicated to the death penalty experts who participated in this study, and those who did not. This work would not have been possible without your participation and your scholarship. One day, America will be a better nation because of what you do.

Contents

Preface

For a long time, like most Americans, I thought of myself as a supporter of capital punishment. I didn't see anything wrong with using the most severe punishment to rid the nation of the most severe criminals. In fact, I won debates in school arguing in favor of capital punishment.

I recall a debate in a sixth-grade social studies class in my St. Petersburg, Florida, middle school where my opponent argued that electrocution was cruel and unusual punishment. He had glossy posters that illustrated the effects of electrocution via "Ole Sparky" (Florida's electric chair) on the human body. At the age of only 11 years, my response seems even now to be somewhat witty: "All my opponent has demonstrated is that the electric chair is undeniably messy.[1] This has nothing to do with whether capital punishment is right or wrong." Somehow I remember I said it with a smirk.

And I won the debate. In all likelihood, given their young age and unfamiliarity with the realities of capital punishment, most of my classmates were already in favor of capital punishment, too. Support for capital punishment at an emotional level is a no-brainer.

My discussions about the death penalty since my middle school years taught me that supporters of capital punishment are not easily swayed, even with graphic descriptions of what happens when a human being is put to death. We are talking about convicted murderers after all.[2]

Up until graduate school, I really did not spend much time thinking about the death penalty, even though I majored in criminology and criminal justice at Florida State University.[3] Most Americans probably do not spend much time thinking about capital punishment either. Why should they? Capital punishment is so rarely used that the likelihood it will directly affect any given person in any given year is slim to none.

Some numbers bear this out. Between 1977 and 2004, there were 558,745 murders and nonnegligent manslaughters in the United States, or an average of 19,955 killings per year.[4] During this time, 6,806 people were sentenced to death, or an average of 243 death sentences per year. Further, 944 people were executed, or an average of 33.7 executions per year. This means only 1.3% of killings from 1977 to 2004 led to death sentences, and only 0.17% of killings led to executions (so far).[5]

Not all people sentenced to death end up on death row. And most are not executed. The odds of receiving a death sentence and ending up on death row or being executed for a murder or nonnegligent manslaughter between 1977 and 2004 were only 0.8%.[6] If you added in all the deaths caused by corporate crimes, then it becomes clear that American states kill a minuscule, seemingly meaningless fraction of all killers through capital punishment.[7]

Although it is true that only those that commit *death-eligible murders* can be sentenced to death and be executed, the likelihood that we will execute any given aggravated murderer is far less than 5%.[8] For example, one study showed that the death sentencing rate, or the ratio of death sentences in a state to the number of murders in that state, between the years of 1977 and 1999 was 0.022 (meaning 2.2% of murders led to death sentences).[9] And, the death sentencing rate, which is "the number of death sentences divided by the population," was 0.048 per 100,000 people in 2003, "the lowest rate since the reinstatement of the death penalty in 1976."[10] This means that, controlling for population size, death sentences generally have gotten rarer in the United States.

The point is that the death penalty is rarely administered in this country. Figure A shows the average number of murders in the United States in the 1990s, versus the average number of arrests for murder, average number of prosecutions for murder, average number of homicide convictions, an estimate of the average number of death-eligible defendants, average number of death sentences imposed, and average number of executions per year.[11] With each step of the criminal justice process, from the commission of the crime, until the final disposition of the case, individuals are screened out in a process called *filtering*, which occurs for several reasons.[12] This is the most important reality of American capital punishment—it is extremely rare relative to the number of murders that occur each year in the United States.

The rarity of capital punishment may lead one to question whether an entire book on the subject is called for. It is. And the reason is simple. The more rarely we use the punishment, the less likely it will achieve its goals of *retribution, incapacitation,* and *deterrence.* That is, the less we execute murderers, the less we get even with murderers and achieve justice for murder

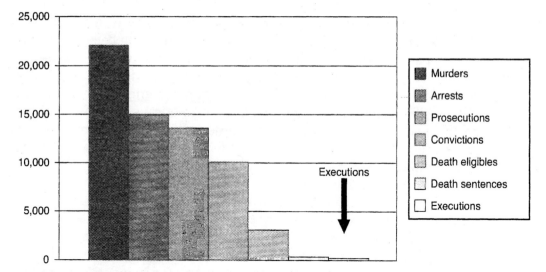

FIGURE A   Comparing Murders and Criminal Justice Processing of Murderers (1990s)
Source: The Contradictions of American Capital Punishment, by Franklin Zimring, 2003, New York: Oxford University Press.

victims, and the less able we are to prevent future murderers by ending the lives of murderers and causing fear in would-be murderers. Clearly, the death penalty in the United States has become so rare that even supporters (who also know about the rare nature of the punishment) are concerned about our ability to achieve our goals through capital punishment.

This says nothing about the many alleged serious problems with the application of capital punishment in the United States. Critics assert that America's death penalty system is plagued by race, class, and gender biases, that it is excessively costly and inefficient, and that it is occasionally used against the innocent.[13]

Further, much of the world views America's continued practice of capital punishment with disdain and even disbelief. The cover on this book—with Uncle Sam standing in a dark corner, as if ashamed—is not meant to suggest that Americans should be ashamed of being the only industrialized Western nation to still practice the death penalty. Instead, it is meant to suggest that citizens of many other nations, including most of our allies, view America's continued capital punishment practice in a negative light. After all, the United States of America is supposed to stand as a beacon to the world—a place that exists "with liberty and justice for all."

To some, the reality of capital punishment, as actually practiced in the United States, flies in the face of liberty and justice. To others, America's death penalty, as is actually applied, is nothing more than a farce, an expensive, political folly that—if it was not so serious—would be laughable. But, are these accurate characterizations of our death penalty system?

Apparently, Americans are either unaware or unmoved by such sentiments. In spite of growing worldwide rejection of the death penalty, most Americans say they still support capital punishment. For example, an October 2005 Gallup poll found that 64% of Americans say they favor the death penalty for those convicted of murder (although this number drops to between 50% and 55% when respondents are given the option of life imprisonment without the possibility of parole).[14]

Is the death penalty plagued by significant problems, or is it an effective, nonproblematic punishment that should enjoy the support of a majority of Americans? The primary goal of this book is to answer this question: to discover and present an honest examination of the realities of capital punishment in America. I achieve this through a survey of expert opinion about the realities of American capital punishment. I attempt to show what scholarly experts think about capital punishment in the United States. Do the experts agree that there are significant problems with the administration of capital punishment, or do they feel the penalty is fair, efficient, effective, and consistent with liberty and justice? Additionally, do experts support capital punishment or alternative punishments such as life imprisonment without the possibility of parole? Finally, why, according to the experts, do states in the United States of America continue to practice capital punishment, even though they do so only rarely?

Using empirical evidence, I answer each of these questions. Throughout *Death Nation*, I emphasize the empirical realities of capital punishment in the United States. The focus is on how the death penalty is actually practiced in America, not on some ideal notion of capital punishment. For reasons better explained later in the book, I deemphasize moral and philosophical issues of capital punishment in hopes of establishing some key empirical truths of the death penalty as it is actually carried out within the United States. As my colleague and friend Robert Bohm (who also happens to be a leading capital punishment scholar) once said to me: "The death penalty does not exist in theory, but exists in reality." And that is how capital punishment should be evaluated, not in some idealized form but instead as it is actually practiced in the United States.

WHY *DEATH NATION*?

Some might wonder why I chose the title *Death Nation* for this book. After all, there is not a national system of capital punishment in the United States, nor is there an "American pattern" or "single national profile."[15]

Our system of *federalism* has allowed huge variation in death penalty practice across states. This led capital punishment scholar Franklin Zimring to conclude: "There are huge differences in policy and in execution risk among the states of the Union, differences so great that it seems foolhardy to talk of 'an American policy' on the death penalty."[16]

In spite of this truism, when people think of the death penalty, they typically do not think of the tremendous variation in policies across states. In my experience teaching classes in criminal justice and on the death penalty, students are unaware that 13 states do not have capital punishment laws on the books and that most states rarely carry out executions (the 13 states without capital punishment include New York, whose state Supreme Court recently struck down its death penalty statute). Instead, they are either supportive or not supportive of continuing with executions anywhere within the United States.

This is one reason I chose the title *Death Nation* for the book. Because 37 states, the federal government, and the U.S. military allow executions, we are a "death nation"—one of only 73 countries that practices executions in the world (as opposed to 123 that do not).[17] Further, we are in the top five nations in the world in terms of the number of executions we carry out each year. The Death Penalty Information Center explains: "In 2005, there were at least 2,148 executions in 22 countries around the world. China, Iran, Saudi Arabia, and the United States were responsible for 94 percent of these known executions."[18] As shown in Table A, China led with at least

TABLE A	Nations With the Most Executions, 2005
China	1,770
Iran	94
Saudi Arabia	86
United States	60
Pakistan	31
Yemen	24
Vietnam	21
Jordan	11
Mongolia	8
Singapore	6

Source: The Death Penalty: An International Perspective, Executions Around the World, by the Death Penalty Information Center, 2006. Retrieved from http://www.deathpenaltyinfo.org/article.php?did=127& scid=30#ar

1,770 executions, followed by Iran (with at least 94), Saudi Arabia (with at least 86), and the United States (with 60). The remaining top 9 countries included Pakistan (with 31), Yemen (with 24), Vietnam (with 21), Jordan (with 11), Mongolia (with 8), and Singapore (with 6). That we are in the same company as some of the world's leading human rights abusers is another reason why I chose the cover image for this book. Prior to the U.S. invasion and occupation of Iraq—which led to the removal of Saddam Hussein from power—Iraq also ranked in the top 10.[19]

ORGANIZATION OF THE BOOK

The book is organized into six chapters. In Chapter 1, I discuss important issues in America's history of capital punishment, including key events; differences in the capital punishment systems of local, state, and federal governments (and the military); and different methods of execution in the United States. In this chapter, I cover some of the most important basics of the death penalty, which forms a foundation for understanding issues discussed in later parts of the book.

In Chapter 2, I examine death penalty law, including laws that define acts as capital offenses, and court cases that specify how and when the death penalty is appropriate and can be used. In this chapter, I give special focus to four U.S. Supreme Court cases that most shaped America's capital punishment practice, focusing on why the Supreme Court has not been consistent in its capital punishment jurisprudence over the years.

In Chapter 3, I discuss the methodology of the study of capital punishment experts that forms the heart of the book. Here, I discuss what I did, how I did it, and identify and discuss limitations of the data. Perhaps the most important thing in this chapter is the discussion of how I think the death penalty (and all criminal justice policies) should be evaluated. I also include a copy of the survey instrument used in the study.

In Chapters 4 through 6, I present the findings of the survey of death penalty experts. In Chapter 4, I lay out arguments in favor of capital punishment and discuss the justifications for capital punishment— vengeance and retribution, incapacitation, and deterrence. In this chapter, I provide a brief summary of each justification for capital punishment, identify the main issues of contention, and present the views of the experts with regard to whether capital punishment achieves its goals. Finally, I offer my own "fact check" of the experts based on the available empirical evidence.

In Chapter 5, I lay out arguments against the death penalty and discuss alleged problems with American capital punishment—arbitrariness and discrimination, innocence (mistaken convictions and executions), and other problems (including politics, problems with capital juries, and costs). In this chapter, I provide a brief summary of each alleged problem with capital punishment, identify the main issues of contention, and present the views of the experts with regard to whether capital punishment is plagued by such problems. Finally, I again offer my own fact check of the experts based on the available empirical evidence.

Finally, in Chapter 6, I discuss issues related to American opinion on the death penalty and expert opinion of capital punishment, including whether the experts favor or oppose capital punishment, what sentence they feel is most appropriate for convicted murderers, and whether they support a moratorium on executions and complete abolition of the death penalty. After identifying policies justified by the findings of the book and barriers to bringing about these policies, I examine the issue of why capital punishment persists in America and make an effort to predict the future of America's death penalty experience. Will capital punishment continue to be practiced indefinitely, or will America's death penalty experiment soon end?

ACKNOWLEDGMENTS

This book would not have been possible without the assistance and support of several people. First and foremost, I want to thank my wonderful wife, Holly, who supported me through the research and writing of this book. It is not a stretch to say that every minute I spent conducting the research reported in this book and writing the book is a minute I could have spent helping her with other important things—including caring for my two amazing children, Bella and Marley.

Second, I want to thank my supportive family—the Robinsons (especially Mom and Brandt), Chiodos, Johnsons, Clements, and Kings—for your encouragement and curiosity of my work. Nothing I do would be possible without you.

Third, I want to thank Frank Mortimer of Prentice Hall who offered me a contract on the spot one morning at breakfast after hearing about my planned book. It has been a true pleasure writing books for the Prentice Hall team and it's an honor to be part of your list. I also want to say thank you to Sarah Holle at Prentice Hall who handled all the behind-the-scenes issues related to the production of this book. Thank you for sticking with the project and making it a reality!

Fourth, I want to thank Dr. Richard Dieter of the Death Penalty Information Center whose responses to my queries regarding my proposed study were helpful as I finalized my plans for this study. Also, his

Web site remains an enormous resource for those of us who need information about capital punishment. I relied on information from the Web site throughout the book.

Fifth, I offer my sincere appreciation to Bob Bohm and Stuart Banner. Bohm's thorough text on capital punishment has been crucial to my thinking about the death penalty, and his treatment of death penalty law has also been quite helpful. Banner wrote an excellent book on the history of capital punishment in the United States. Banner's work allowed me to better understand vital realities of America's death penalty experience, often through the stories of the real people who lived it.

Sixth, I owe the reviewers of this book a great thanks. Your comments and suggestions were essential to making the book a reality: Mary Atwell, Radford University; Susan Brinkley, University of Tampa; Christine Ludowise, Georgia Southern University.

Seventh, thank you to Connie Strassburg and the staff of GGS Book Services. Your hard work on the page proofs of the book is greatly appreciated.

Eighth, I want to thank my colleagues and friends in the Department of Political Science and Criminal Justice at Appalachian State University for supporting my request for leave from the university so I could write this book. Thanks also to the university officials for granting my leave. Additionally, thank you to my student assistant—Bryan Thompson—who helped me identify experts and locate them in order to send them the surveys. Thanks for all your hard work!

Finally, thank you to Dr. Daniel Murphy. Your encouragement of and interest in my work means a lot to me. You'll notice that all of the articles you provided me about the death penalty have been cited and discussed in the book! It's great to have a colleague and friend like you.

ENDNOTES

1. I might have said "gross" rather than "messy."
2. With regard to the execution of convicted murderers, there are three important points to consider: First, in our nation's history, we have executed people for offenses less than murder (e.g., burglary, rape), but it is generally accepted that the U.S. Supreme Court will no longer allow an execution for any offense other than murder. Second, not all executed murderers were legally convicted—some were lynched—but these are not counted as authorized executions by most capital punishment scholars. Finally, it is certain that not all people we have executed—including the legally convicted murderers—were actually guilty of the charges against them. Had I known these facts, this might have affected my opinion about the death

penalty (but I doubt it, given my age, low level of education, and low exposure to facts about the death penalty).

3. I never took a death penalty class at the undergraduate or graduate level in college.

4. Murder and nonnegligent manslaughter is defined as "the willful (nonnegligent) killing of one human being by another." See Federal Bureau of Investigation. (2005). *Crime in the United States 2004*. Retrieved from http://www.fbi.gov/ucr/cius_04/offenses_reported/violent_crime/murder.html

5. The average time of stay on death row is now about 11 years.

6. This was calculated by adding the total number of people on death row at the end of 2004 (3,503) and the total number of people executed from 1977 to 2004 (944), and then dividing by the number of murders and nonnegligent manslaughters from 1977 to 2004 (558,745).

7. For example, tobacco kills 430,000 Americans every year, poor diet and inactivity kill 300,000 per year, more than 100,000 people die from adverse reactions to legal and approved drugs, hospital errors kill another 100,000 people, 60,000 die each year due to toxic chemicals, occupational diseases and hazards kill 35,000, and defective products kill more than 20,000 people. In the case of tobacco, civil juries have recognized that it is a defective product and that corporations have acted negligently and recklessly in selling this product. See Robinson, M. (2005). *Justice blind? Ideals and realities of American criminal justice*. Upper Saddle River, NJ: Prentice Hall.

8. See Bohm, B. (2003). *Deathquest II: An introduction to the theory and practice of capital punishment in the United States* (2nd ed.). Cincinnati, OH: Anderson.

9. Blume, J., Eisenberg, T., & Wells, M. (2004). Explaining death row's population and racial composition. *Journal of Empirical Legal Studies, 1*(1), 165–207.

10. Death Penalty Information Center. (2005). *Rate of death sentencing at its lowest point since reinstatement*. Retrieved from http://www.deathpenaltyinfo.org/article.php?did=840&scid=64

11. These numbers are taken from Bedau, H. (2004). An abolitionist's survey of the death penalty in America today. In H. Bedau & P. Cassell (Eds.), *Debating the death penalty: Should America have capital punishment? The experts from both sides make their case*. New York: Oxford University Press, pp. 26–27.

12. Robinson (2005).

13. For information on such problems, see J. Acker, B. Bohm, & C. Lanier (Eds.). (2003). *America's experiment with capital punishment: Reflections on the past, present, and future of the ultimate penal sanction* (2nd ed.). Durham, NC: Carolina Academic Press; Bedau, H. (1998). *The death penalty in America: Current controversies*. New York: Oxford University Press; Costanzo, M. (1997). *Just revenge: Costs and consequences of the death penalty*. Cranbury, NJ: Worth; Liebman, J., Fagan, J., & West, V. (2000). *A broken system: Error rates in capital cases, 1973–1995*. Columbia University Law School. Retrieved from http://www2.law.columbia.edu/instructionalservices/liebman Martinez, M., Richardson, W., & Hornsby, B. (2002). *The Leviathan's choice: Capital punishment*

in the twenty-first century. Lanham, MD: Rowman & Littlefield; Prejean, H. (2004). *The death of innocents: An eyewitness account of wrongful executions.* New York: Random House; Radelet, M., Bedau, H., & Putnam, C. (1994). *In spite of innocence: Erroneous convictions in capital cases.* Boston: Northeastern University Press; Sarat, A. (2001). *When the state kills: Capital punishment and the American condition.* Princeton, NJ: Princeton University Press; Zimring, F. (2003). *The contradictions of American capital punishment.* New York: Oxford University Press.

14. Death Penalty Information Center. (2005). *News and developments—public opinion.* Retrieved from http://www.deathpenaltyinfo.org/newsanddev .php?scid=23

15. Zimring (2003), p. 7.

16. Zimring (2003), p. 84.

17. Death Penalty Information Center. (2006). *The death penalty: An international perspective, Abolitionist and retentionist countries.* Retrieved from http:// www.deathpenaltyinfo.org/article.php?did=127&scid=30#ar

18. Death Penalty Information Center. (2006). *The death penalty: An international perspective, Executions around the world.* Retrieved from http://www.death penaltyinfo.org/article.php?did=127&scid=30#ar

19. McAllister, P. (2003). *Death defying: Dismantling the execution machinery in the 21st century U.S.A.* New York: Continuum International Publishing Group.

CAPITAL PUNISHMENT FACTS AND HISTORY

INTRODUCTION

The death penalty, or capital punishment, is the ultimate punishment imposed by any society. The punishment has been practiced for thousands of years in virtually every society on the planet,[1] although the first written death penalty laws are from the Code of Hammurabi, in 18th century BC Babylon.[2] This law classified 25 crimes as capital offenses, including "sorcery and the fraudulent sale of beer."[3]

Primitive societies executed people for all sorts of crimes, many of them minor, and did so through brutal and excessive methods that included crucifixion, burning alive, drowning, and impalement.[4] Our British brethren executed hundreds of thousands of their citizens in their long history, typically for minor crimes and in inhumane ways, such as boiling, burning at the stake, and drawing and quartering.[5] By the 1700s, there were more than 200 crimes for which a person in Britain could be executed, including minor theft.

More than any other country, it is Britain that most affected America's capital punishment system.[6] Britain became an abolitionist country after centuries of experimentation with the death penalty. America also has a long history with this criminal sanction, including both state-sanctioned killings and the murders of mostly African American men through lynchings carried out in the name of "punishment" for alleged wrongdoings.

In this chapter, I introduce key facts of the death penalty in America, including an examination of our history with the punishment; important facts about death penalty practice at the local, state, and federal levels of government, and in the military; and methods of execution in the United States. This chapter provides an important foundation on which to evaluate the empirical realities of the death penalty in the United States today.

WHAT IS CAPITAL PUNISHMENT?

Capital punishment is the extinguishing of the life of a human being by the government for a criminal act defined as a capital offense. In the United States today, the only crime for which a person will likely be executed is a capital murder. The meaning of capital murder varies by jurisdiction, and the process for administering capital punishment also varies by state.[7] As noted in the preface of this book, there is no capital punishment system in the United States, as each state has the right to create its own death penalty scheme (or not). Death penalty scholars James Acker and Charles Lanier explain:

> Shorthand references to "the death penalty" can obscure the profoundly significant differences in capital-punishment statutes that have existed historically and that continue to exist today. Death-penalty statutes define who is eligible for the capital sanction, designate the crimes that qualify as capital offenses, create the criteria and procedures used to select offenders who are sentenced to death, and regulate many other important administrative issues ranging from the qualifications of capital jurors, to the processing of appeals, through establishing the method of carrying out executions.[8]

State variation in capital punishment matters because it means to speak of the death penalty or capital punishment broadly, thus misses the fact that what is true of one state death penalty system may not be true of others. At the same time, it is true that states generally must meet some minimum legal standards in order to carry out executions.

States generally require that individuals accused of capital crimes (e.g., aggravated murder) be convicted beyond a reasonable doubt in a guilt phase that is separate from the sentencing phase in a *bifurcated trial*. Further, in order to be sentenced to death, a jury must find that *aggravating factors* outweigh *mitigating factors* in "guided discretion" and "structured discretion" statutes, both of which are defined by state or federal statute.[9]

Aggravating factors tend to focus on *offender characteristics* (e.g., the defendant's prior criminal history, degree of future dangerousness, whether the offender was incarcerated at the time of his or her offense), the *manner of the offense* (e.g., motive for the crime, whether the crime was committed during the commission of another felony, and whether the murder was "especially heinous, atrocious or cruel, manifesting exceptional depravity,") and *victim characteristics* (e.g., killing of a public servant, witness, children, elderly person, pregnant woman, etc.).[10] Similarly, mitigating factors can include offender characteristics (e.g., no prior record or little involvement with violent behavior, low level of future dangerousness) and manner of the offense (e.g., committed in the heat of the moment), among many other possible factors that might lessen one's culpability and degree of blameworthiness. Table 1.1 shows the aggravating and mitigating factors for my state of North Carolina.

TABLE 1.1   Aggravating and Mitigating Factors in North Carolina

Aggravating factors

(1) That the Defendant Was "Lawfully Incarcerated" When the Homicide Occurred;

(2) That the Defendant Had Previously Been Convicted of Another Capital Felony;

(3) That the Defendant Had Previously Been Convicted of A Violent Felony;

(4) That the Homicide Was Committed to Avoid or Prevent an Arrest, or to Escape From Custody;

(5) That the Homicide Was Committed During Another Homicide, Robbery, Rape, Arson, Burglary, Kidnapping, etc.;

(6) That The Homicide Was Committed "For Pecuniary Gain";

(7) That The Homicide Was Committed To Disrupt or Hinder Government or Law Enforcement;

(8) That the Homicide Victim was a Law Enforcement Officer, Judge, Prosecutor, Etc.;

(9) That the Homicide Was "Heinous, Atrocious, or Cruel";

(10) That The Defendant "Knowingly Created A Great Risk of Death To More Than One Person By Use of a Hazardous Weapon or Devise";

(11) That The Homicide Was Part of a Course of Conduct Involving A Crime of Violence Against Another Person.

Mitigating factors

(1) That the Defendant Had No Significant History of Prior Criminal Activity;

(2) That the Homicide Was Committed While the Defendant Was Under The Influence of Mental or Emotional Disturbance;

(3) That the Victim Voluntarily Participated in the Defendant's Homicide;

(4) That the Defendant Was Only An Accomplice And His Participation Was Relatively Minor;

(5) That the Defendant Acted Under Duress or the Domination of Another Person;

(6) That the Defendant's Capacity to Appreciate That His Conduct Was Criminal, or to Conform His Conduct to the Law, Was Impaired;

(7) The Age of the Defendant;

(8) That the Defendant Aided the Prosecution in Apprehending Another Capital Felon, or Testified Truthfully to Assist the Prosecution at Trial;

(9) That the Defendant Shows Any Other Circumstances That the Jury Deems to be of Mitigating Value.

Source: Race and the Death Penalty in North Carolina: An Empirical Analysis: 1993–1997, by I. Unah and J.C. Boger, 2001. Retrieved from http://www.unc.edu/~jcboger/NCDeathPenaltyReport2001.pdf

In North Carolina, like other death penalty states, juries must unanimously agree that aggravating factors are present and that they outweigh mitigating factors. All possible mitigating factors can be considered by juries (whether they are in the criminal statutes or not), unanimity among jurors is not required to consider mitigating factors, and states can use a "preponderance of evidence" standard for accepting mitigating factors (as opposed to the more stringent "beyond a reasonable doubt" standard). Generally, states where capital punishment is legal also provide automatic appellate review of convictions and sentences and proportionality reviews in an attempt to ensure that death sentences are justified relative to other murders.[11]

Guided discretion statutes list and define aggravating and mitigating factors, and before a jury can impose death, they must agree that aggravating factors outweigh mitigating factors. This is the type of statute present in my state of North Carolina. Texas, the state that leads the nation in the number of executions each year, has a structured discretion statute that does not define aggravating or mitigating factors and that allows both the prosecution and defense to present any evidence relevant to aggravation and mitigation. Then, if all the jurors agree that the defendant committed the crime for which he or she is accused, that he or she may commit violent criminal acts in the future and be a danger to the community, and that there is not enough mitigating evidence to justify sentencing the defendant to life imprisonment instead of death, the death penalty will be imposed. The state of Georgia has an aggravating-only statute that requires jurors to find that at least one of the aggravating factors listed in the statute is present and that this factor (and any other present aggravating factor) outweighs any and all mitigating factors presented to the court (although they are not listed in the statute).

The use by most states of aggravating factors (in aggravating-only statutes) and mitigating factors (in guided discretion and structured discretion statutes) to determine which murders are eligible for death generally began in the 1970s after the U.S. Supreme Court struck down statutes that did not provide guidance to capital juries. These guided discretion statutes, as well as postconviction appeals and proportionality review, were aimed at fairness in death penalty practice and eliminating arbitrariness and discrimination that allegedly existed up to the 1970s.

The administration of capital punishment throughout most of America's history has been characterized by significant problems such as arbitrariness, so that it is typically difficult to distinguish between those murderers that receive the death penalty and those that do not. This is but one important lesson that a history of the death penalty in the United States teaches us.

A HISTORY OF CAPITAL PUNISHMENT IN AMERICA

Scholars typically examine the history of capital punishment by time period. There are at least four eras of capital punishment that have been identified.[12] They include the

1) colonial period
2) 19th century
3) Progressive Era (early 20th century)
4) late 20th century

Each period is marked by significant changes in capital punishment law, practice, and public attitudes. The four periods are examined in this chapter, beginning with a synopsis of American capital punishment today.

The Present: The Death Penalty Today

States With and Without the Death Penalty in the United States

Today, the death penalty is legal in 39 jurisdictions within the United States. This includes 37 states, the federal government, and the military (the Supreme Court of New York recently declared its death penalty statute to be unconstitutional). States without the death penalty thus include New York, plus Alaska, Hawaii, Iowa, Maine, Massachusetts, Michigan, Minnesota, North Dakota, Rhode Island, Vermont, West Virginia, and Wisconsin. The District of Columbia also does not have capital punishment.

Regionalization of Capital Punishment

Death penalty practice in America is highly regionalized. Most modern executions occur in the South, "from Virginia and the Carolinas west through Texas to Arizona." Capital punishment scholar Hugo Adam Bedau asserts that in the South, "the death penalty is as firmly entrenched as grits for breakfast."[13] Some numbers bear this out. Between 1976 and 2005, there were 1,004 executions. Of these, 355 occurred in Texas (35%), 94 in Virginia (9%), 79 in Oklahoma (8%), 66 in Missouri (7%), and 60 in Florida (6%). No other state has executed 50 people since 1976. Of the states that have executed at least 20 people since 1976, all but 2 are in the South (North Carolina and Georgia with 39, South Carolina with 35, Alabama with 34, Louisiana with 27, Arkansas with 27, Arizona with 22, and Ohio with 20).[14] Thus, since 1976, 82% of executions have occurred in the South, followed by 12% in the Midwest, and 6% in the West. Only

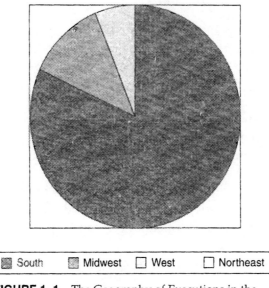

FIGURE 1–1   The Geography of Executions in the
United States (1976–2005)

Source: Death Penalty Information Center (2006). Number
of Executions by State and Region Since 1976. http://www
.deathpenaltyinfo.org/article.php?scid=8&did=186#region

4 executions have occurred in the Northeast since 1976. Figure 1–1 illustrates the geographic breakdown of executions.

Such numbers are used by some to charge that the death penalty
in America is plagued by a geographic bias.[15] This charge, revisited
in Chapter 5, ignores that in our system of federalism, each state has the
right to set its own laws and carry out its own punishments, including
executions. Thus, although a murderer may be more likely to be executed in Texas, Virginia, and Oklahoma than in any other state (since
53% of all executions have occurred there since 1976), this does not
make capital punishment itself unfair. It simply means that some states
react to murders more harshly than others.[16] In fact, some counties in
some states are far more likely to utilize capital punishment than other
counties in the same state.[17] Perhaps prosecutors in these counties take
murder more seriously and have more resources to pursue death
penalty cases.

In terms of execution rates per capita, the top 15 states most likely to
carry out death sentences through the end of 2005 were Oklahoma,
Delaware, Texas, Virginia, Missouri, Arkansas, South Carolina, Alabama,
Louisiana, Nevada, Georgia, North Carolina, Arizona, Florida, and
Indiana.[18] Again, the South leads the way, as 11 of the top 15 states are in
the South.

Looking at the numbers a bit differently—focusing instead on the ratio of death sentences to the number of murders—only 7 of the top 15 states from 1977 to 1999 are in the South. The states that lead the way here are Nevada (which sentences 6% of its murderers to death), followed by Oklahoma (5.1%), Delaware (4.8%), Idaho (4.7%), Arizona (4.3%), Alabama (3.8%), Mississippi (3.5%), Florida (3.4%), Ohio (2.8%), North Carolina (2.6%), Pennsylvania (2.4%), Missouri (2.4%), Nebraska (2.3%), Georgia (2.2%), and Oregon (2.2%). The national average of the ratio of death sentences to murders is 2.2%.[19]

What this does suggest is that the death penalty is not really something that exists throughout the United States. The fact that 37 states can carry out executions, along with the federal government and the U.S. military, probably signifies to most that the death penalty is widely practiced and supported in the United States. This is not the case. With the exception of just a handful of states, the vast majority of places in America, including the federal government and the military, do not carry out executions in large numbers. In fact, in the 30-year period between 1976 and 2005, only nine states carried out at least one execution per year. These include Texas (12 per year), Virginia (3 per year), Oklahoma (2.6 per year), Missouri (2.2 per year), Florida (2 per year), North Carolina (1.3 per year), Georgia (1.3 per year), South Carolina (1.2 per year), and Alabama (1.1 per year).[20]

Texas, the only state that has executed more than 10 murderers per year, had 51,729 murders between the years 1976 and 2002. This means it averaged 1,915 murders per year over the 27-year span.[21] Texas, the state that has executed 35% of all murderers since 1976, executes roughly only 12 out of 1,915 murderers per year, or 0.63% of murderers per year. Further, between 1977 and 2004—a 28-year period—Texas sentenced to death 878 murderers, or only 31 per year.[22]

So, even in states that are thought to be active in death sentences and executions, such as Texas, the death penalty is pretty rare relative to the number of murders that occur there.[23] This is an important point to remember throughout this book. Yes, the death penalty persists in the United States, but it is an extremely rare phenomenon. This rarity is a sign to many that the death penalty in the United States may be on its last legs. Bedau says that "the death penalty in America today is but a shadow of its former self."[24]

Capital Punishment Worldwide

The United States is now the only Western, industrialized country still practicing the death penalty. We are also "one of the very few nations with a representative government which still uses the death penalty, and the only one where the laws regarding its implementation are not uniform throughout the nation but vary widely in different parts of the country."[25] Most of our European allies abolished capital punishment after the horrors of World War II.[26] This may suggest either that American respect for life is less or more than in other countries, depending on how one feels about capital punishment. And we are far different than other close allies. According to death penalty scholar Franklin Zimring, "the United States and the developed nations of Europe and the former Commonwealth nations [are] further apart on the question of state executions than on any other issue."[27]

Worldwide practice of capital punishment has slowed as more and more countries have abolished capital punishment over the years. Currently, 84 countries in the world are without the death penalty for all crimes, 12 countries are without the death penalty for ordinary crimes, 24 have not executed someone in so long that they are without the death penalty "in practice," meaning there are 120 countries that currently do not utilize the death penalty. Only 76 countries can be considered retentionist countries, or countries that retain and actually use the death penalty.[28]

The divergence of the United States from the rest of the world when it comes to capital punishment is a recent phenomenon: "Up until the 1970s, emerging policy trends toward capital punishment seemed similar throughout the developed world, and the United States did not seem out of step with the general trend. In the quarter century after 1975, however, policy in both the United States and the rest of the developed West has been changing rapidly and in opposite directions."[29] This is likely due to the landmark decisions by the U.S. Supreme Court in the 1970s (see Chapter 2).

Declining Executions and a Ballooning Death Row

Although we continue to use the death penalty, its use began to decline after World War II as our allies moved to abolish it. For example, 1,289 people were executed in the 1940s, but only 715 were executed in the 1950s. From 1960 through 1976, only 191 were executed.[30] After the moratorium on executions ended in 1977, 120 people were killed through 1989. In the 1990s (through 1999), the United States witnessed a rebirth of capital punishment, as 478 people were executed. Finally, from 2000 until 2005, 406 people were executed, but the number of executions has recently begun to decline. Figure 1–2 shows the number of executions over the years in the United States.

During the past 30 years, whereas executions grew and then declined, the size of death row skyrocketed. Figure 1–3 illustrates the number of

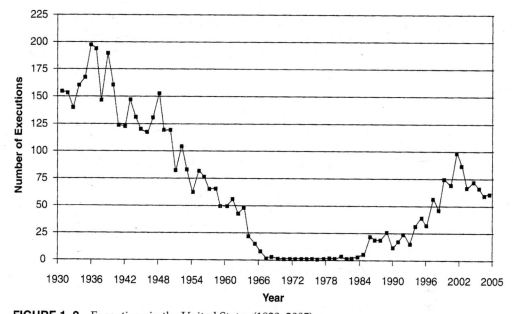

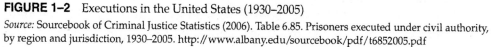

FIGURE 1–2 Executions in the United States (1930–2005)

Source: Sourcebook of Criminal Justice Statistics (2006). Table 6.85. Prisoners executed under civil authority, by region and jurisdiction, 1930–2005. http://www.albany.edu/sourcebook/pdf/t6852005.pdf

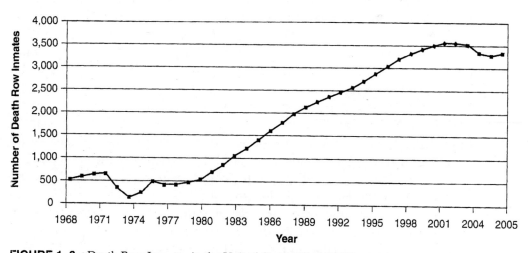

FIGURE 1–3 Death Row Inmates in the United States (1968–2005)

Source: Bureau of Justice Statistics (2005). Number of persons under sentence of death, 1953–2004. http://www.ojp.usdoj.gov/bjs/glance/tables/drtab.htm; Death Penalty Information Center (2006). Size of Death Row by Year (1968–2005). http://www.deathpenaltyinfo.org/article.php?scid=9&did=188#year

inmates on death row over the past four decades. Although death rows have grown consistently during this time, a very large majority of the inmates on death row have yet to be executed and likely will not for decades.

A Sustainable Punishment?

In the 21st century, several events have cast serious doubt on the sustainability of America's capital punishment system. Here are some examples. In 2000, Governor George Ryan ordered a moratorium on all executions in the state of Illinois after serious problems were discovered with the state's capital punishment system. One inmate's case, in particular, troubled Governor Ryan—that of Anthony Porter—who had come within 48 hours of his execution date prior to being released after an investigation by a group of journalism students identified the real killer.

Governor Ryan discovered that since 1977, the state had executed 12 people. During the same time, however, the state had released 13 people from death row. Believing there to be a serious problem with the state's capital punishment system, Ryan established the Commission on Capital Punishment to study the state's death penalty system. The commission put forth 85 specific recommendations that it said should improve the accuracy and fairness of Illinois's death penalty system, and a narrow majority of members said they believed the death penalty should be abolished in the state. Some said so due to moral objections, others because no system could reasonably guarantee total fairness and a lack of error, and others because the resources spent on the death penalty outweighed the benefits.[31] In 2003, the Illinois legislature took action on some of the recommendations but not others. Further, Governor Ryan commuted the sentences of every person on death row just before he left office.

Other states have taken actions toward moratoria, including Maryland, North Carolina, and New Jersey. In 2000, Maryland governor Parris Glendening imposed a moratorium on capital punishment in the state after a study found widespread racial disparities in the state's use of capital punishment.[32] In 2001, a bill to enact a moratorium in Maryland was passed by the House of Delegates, but was blocked by a filibuster in the Senate. In 2002, the governor enacted a moratorium on executions but in 2003, new Governor Ehrlich lifted it, even after the study finding racial and geographic disparities in the punishment was released.

In 2003 the Senate of the state of North Carolina voted to institute a moratorium on executions, but the House never brought the bill to a vote despite support by more than 150 prominent state residents and a call by the American Bar Association (ABA) for a 2-year moratorium on executions.

A study in North Carolina, first published in 2001, also found racial disparities in capital punishment.[33] Recently, North Carolina became the first state to establish an Innocence Commission which will review claims of innocence by those awaiting execution.

In New Jersey in 2006, Governor Richard Codey signed legislation to halt executions and create a commission to conduct a study of the state's death penalty system. New Jersey became the first state to legislatively enact a moratorium. Earlier in 2003, only a month after New Jersey's legislature passed a bill calling for a commission to study the state's death penalty system, Governor James McGreevey vetoed the bill. A study by the New Jersey Supreme Court found evidence of racial disparities in its use of capital punishment.[34]

Other states have recently introduced moratorium legislation, including Alabama, California, Connecticut, Florida, Georgia, Kentucky, Louisiana, Maryland, Missouri, Mississippi, New Mexico, Oklahoma, South Carolina, Texas, and Virginia.[35] The ABA's Death Penalty Moratorium Implementation Project recently called for a moratorium on capital punishment in Georgia and Alabama.

Among the problems noted in Georgia were inadequate jury instructions with regard to mitigating evidence (so that jurors did not understand that any mitigating evidence could be considered and mistakenly believed that mitigating evidence had to be proved beyond a reasonable doubt), and racial disparities in death sentences (so that killers of whites were 4.56 times more likely to be sentenced to death than those who killed blacks).[36] Among the problems in Alabama include inadequate indigent defense services at trial and on direct appeal, lack of defense counsel for state postconviction proceedings, lack of a statute protecting people with mental retardation from execution, lack of a postconviction DNA testing statute, inadequate proportionality review, overly vague aggravating factors, and capital juror confusion.[37]

In its study of Arizona, the ABA did not call for a moratorium, yet it still outlined some notable problems with the death penalty in Arizona. The problems were similar to those in other states, including a lack of a centralized system of assigning defense attorneys to indigent defendants, poor compensation for defense counsel, lack of effective proportionality review, and the use of a vague aggravating circumstance ("especially cruel, heinous, or depraved" homicides).[38]

The ABA is currently studying other states as well, including Arkansas, Florida, Indiana, Louisiana, Mississippi, Nevada, Ohio, Oklahoma, Pennsylvania, Tennessee, South Carolina, Texas, and Virginia.[39] It is expected that the ABA will call for moratoria in at least some of these states. I return to the moratorium issue in Chapter 6.

Other states, including Massachusetts and Michigan, rejected reimposition of the death penalty in the past 2 years. Both of these states, without the death penalty for many years, had the opportunity to reinstate the punishment but voted not to.

Several other states are conducting studies of capital punishment to examine alleged problems with the application of capital punishment, including Arizona, Connecticut, Delaware, Kansas, Maryland, North Carolina, Illinois, Indiana, Nebraska, Nevada, Ohio, Pennsylvania, Tennessee, Virginia, and the federal government.[40] Part of the reason so many states are taking action to study the application of the death penalty is the recent flurry of activity calling the fairness, effectiveness, and infallibility of the punishment into question. Significant concerns include issues of racial bias, executing the innocent, financial costs, and others.

An Associated Press study published in 2005 of Ohio's death penalty system found evidence of racial and geographic disparities in the use of the death penalty.[41] Also, a study of the federal death penalty system published in 2000 found both racial and geographic disparities in its use of the death penalty,[42] although a more recently published study found no evidence of racial bias in the federal death penalty from 1995 to 2000.[43] I return to the issue of racial bias in Chapter 5.

Although 36 of the 37 states that still practice the death penalty provide an automatic appeal of all death sentences,[44] the use of appeals does not necessarily make it less likely that a death sentence will be inappropriately handed down. Automatic appeals do not apparently lessen the likelihood that an innocent person will be wrongfully executed, for evidence pointing to the defendant's innocence may arise or be discovered only years later. Contrary to popular belief, many discretionary appeals initiated by defendants are not frivolous. In fact, since 1976, there have been nearly 2,000 cases in which defendants have either had their convictions overturned or had their sentences reduced by appeals courts.[45]

Using such statistics, death penalty scholar Robert Bohm asserts that approximately 21% to 32% of imposed death sentences "have been found faulty" by appeals courts, for reasons such as ineffective counsel, prosecutors referring to defendants' refusal to testify (as if this is a sign of guilt rather than a constitutional right), denial of an impartial jury, and use of bad evidence such as coerced confessions of guilt.[46] A more recent report shows an even higher incidence of serious reversible error.[47]

A 2000 study that reviewed 4,578 capital appeals between 1973 and 1995 found that capital trials end up placing people on death row who do not belong there (either because serious errors were made during their cases or because they were innocent of the crimes of which they were charged). According to the findings of this report, "American capital sentences are so persistently and systematically fraught with error" their reliability is seriously undermined. The study found an overall rate of prejudicial error of 68%. That is, "courts found serious, reversible error in nearly 7 of every 10 of the thousands of capital sentences that were fully reviewed during the period."[48] I return to the issue of error in Chapter 5.

Further, in 2002, a New York federal judge, Jed Rakoff, ruled that the federal death penalty did not achieve due process because of the clear risk of executing an innocent person. This ruling was overturned on appeal.[49] Amazingly, more than 100 people have been released from death rows in the United States since 1976. I return to the issue of innocence in Chapter 5.

Studies from the 1990s into the early 21st century have also found that the practice of capital punishment is financially more costly relative to alternatives to the death penalty. Studies have been conducted in California, Indiana, Kansas, New Jersey, North Carolina, Tennessee, and Texas. The North Carolina study, considered the most comprehensive death penalty study in the country at the time, found that capital punishment costs North Carolina $2.16 million more per execution than a life sentence would have cost.[50] I return to the issue of costs in Chapter 5.

States, in the past 20 years, have also taken steps to forbid the execution of people with mental retardation and juveniles. These issues ultimately reached all the way to the U.S. Supreme Court. The result was a restriction of the use of the punishment. For example, in the case *Atkins v. Virginia* (2002), the Court ruled by 6–3 that the execution of people who are mentally retarded constituted cruel and unusual punishment under the Eighth Amendment. Also, in the case of *Roper v. Simons* (2005), the Court held 5–4 that the Eighth and Fourteenth Amendments to the U.S. Constitution forbid executing people who committed crimes when they were under the age of 18 years.

Although the U.S. Supreme Court has not recently ruled on the other issues being dealt with by states, the point is that there seems to be a groundswell of concern about the way in which capital punishment is being utilized in many states within this country. That is one significant reality of the death penalty in the United States today.

But how did a country like ours, which has executed people for hundreds of years, get to this point? An examination of our nation's death penalty history—from its earliest history—allows us to discover the answer.

The Past: The Death Penalty Yesterday

The Colonial Period

The First Execution

America's death penalty history goes back as far as 1608, when Captain George Kendall, a member of the Virginia colony, was executed for the crime of spying for Spain. This is the earliest recorded execution in America.[51] Since that time, about 23,000 people have been executed in America.[52] This includes at least 7,000 people executed in the 20th century.[53] Other scholars suggest the first execution in the United States was in 1622, when Daniel Frank was executed for theft in Virginia.

American Colonies Versus England

In early America, executions were usually carried out by local governments. In fact, most people executed in U.S. history were killed under the authority of local governments. Each colony had the authority to set laws and execute individuals for offenses deemed wrong and worthy of death by local citizens. Thus, practice varied widely by locality. Early American settlers agreed that the death penalty was acceptable, but the degree of punitiveness varied between Puritans and Quakers.[54] Generally, Puritan law was more strict and thus capital punishment was more common among Puritan colonies. In Quaker colonies in Pennsylvania and New Jersey, even manslaughter was not a capital crime.[55]

Early death penalty laws in America called for capital punishment for crimes as mundane as striking a parent, denying God, stealing grapes, killing chickens, and trading with Indians. Crimes against morality were often capital crimes in early American northern colonies, including blasphemy, idolatry, adultery, sodomy, and bestiality.[56] Other capital crimes varied across the colonies, and included piracy, perjury, smuggling tobacco, stealing a hog, receiving a stolen horse, and burning timber intended for building a house.[57] Often, capital punishment was mandatory for certain crimes.[58]

Early American practice was quite different than in England.[59] For one thing, England developed a list of 350 capital crimes, referred to as the "Bloody Code," that was much more extensive than the crimes for which early Americans could be executed.[60] England's history is obviously much longer than America's, but England's experience clearly has influenced ours.[61] Bedau explains: "No one should be surprised that the colonists embraced the death penalty (along with other corporal punishments, such as flogging, branding, and the pillory); the Mother Country itself put extensive reliance on such punishments to control an unruly public."[62]

In northern American colonies, the laws regulating property were more lenient than in England. For example, burglary and robbery did not lead to death sentences in Connecticut, Massachusetts, Plymouth, or Pennsylvania, and led to death sentences for third offenses only in New York, New Hampshire, and New Haven.[63] Even crimes against the person were not always capital crimes in northern colonies. For instance, rape did not lead to death sentences in Massachusetts, New York, or Pennsylvania.[64]

Southern colonies typically did not enact new laws and thus followed English law. This meant more capital crimes for offenses against property but less for crimes against morality. There were generally more capital crimes in southern colonies than northern colonies, in part due to less even property distribution in southern colonies and to the fact that many southern settlers came from more violent parts of England. Southern colonies also had more capital punishment laws aimed only at black slaves, in part due to the perceived need to control them as they were not only a captive workforce, but also made up significant portions of the populations of many southern states.[65] In the 1700s, far more slaves were executed than whites in the South.

Executions of Juveniles

During this time, a significant number of juveniles was executed. The year 1642 represents the first recorded execution of a juvenile in America, when Thomas Graunger was executed for bestiality in Plymouth Colony. The year 1786 marks the period in American history when the youngest ever juvenile was executed. Ocuish Hannah, only 12 years old, was executed for murder in Connecticut.[66]

Purpose of Early Capital Punishment

During the 18th century, a primary purpose of capital punishment was deterrence—instilling fear in citizens through punishment so that they would not violate the laws. Thus, it had to be carried out in public, in a large space so that many people could witness it, and during the day. Historian Robert Johnson writes: "Colonial executions were well-attended, featuring high officials and common citizens. The behavior of the crowd was generally restrained, though an air of celebration—of confirmation of one's righteousness—would be apparent."[67] The punishment was also meant to be a solemn event, to achieve maximum effect on those who watched or who merely observed the long procession from the jail to the place of execution.[68] Capital punishment during this time, according to historian Stuart Banner, was an "emphatic display of power, a reminder of what the state could do to those who broke the laws."[69]

In the late 17th and early 18th centuries fake executions were also used (e.g., false hangings), executions were halted at the last minute by clemency, and many executions were "intensified" through extreme methods such as burning at the stake, dismemberment, dissection, and public display of bodies after death. All of this was aimed at deterring others. Methods like burning at the stake were aimed at making sure death was slow and painful, making it worse to contemplate and ideally increasing its deterrent effect.[70]

Burning was reserved only for slaves who committed crimes against their masters or plotted revolts, and women who murdered their husbands. Such offenses were considered disruptive to the social order, meaning burning was a method aimed at maintaining oppressive institutions such as slavery and even marriage. Treason, perhaps the one offense most threatening to the social order, was subjected to the most severe forms of capital punishment, including dismemberment preceded by disembowelment. Dissection replaced these forms of punishment by the end of the 18th century, although typically it was reserved for the worst offenders and was only discretionary.[71]

The death penalty in 18th-century America was also meant to serve as *incapacitation*—punishment aimed at taking away the offender's freedom so that he or she could not offend again. Given that prisons were not developed until the next century, and since jails were meant only as holding cells for those awaiting trials, capital punishment was the primary mechanism of incapacitation at the time.[72]

Retribution—correcting the harms caused by offenders through punishment—was also a goal of capital punishment in the 18th century. It was deemed not only appropriate, but also necessary to impose retribution for capital crimes. In part, this can be understood by the strong beliefs of people at the time in biblical verse. The death penalty not only achieved justice for harms inflicted by offenders but also allowed opportunity for expiation, repentance, and chance for eternal salvation.[73]

Repentance was important because criminals were viewed as no different than "normal" citizens; anyone could conceivably end up facing a death sentence. In modern America, criminals are viewed as different than "us" and thus undeserving of any pity or chance at repentance.[74] Additionally, the separation of religion from public policy makes repentance less important today.[75] In the 18th century, executions were preceded by lengthy speeches and sermons that focused public attention on sin and renunciation of it. Although it may seem strange when judged through today's lens, the execution ceremony provided the condemned with a chance at reintegration into society, even if it was only for a short time before his or her execution.

Death penalty practice in the 18th century was remarkably efficient. Individuals were frequently tried, convicted, and sentenced to death in one day. Sometimes, however, executions were delayed weeks or months to allow time for offenders to repent their sins in order to have hope of acceptance into heaven upon death.[76] A quick process is consistent with the deterrent and incapacitative goals of capital punishment, but surely many innocent people were executed during this time when capital trials were not even adversarial in nature.

Early Abolitionist Activity

The origins of abolition were seen in the 1760s and 1770s, when Americans began questioning the use of capital punishment against property offenders.[77] In 1786, Pennsylvania became the first state to abolish capital punishment for crimes such as robbery, burglary, sodomy, and buggery.[78] Part of this was simply a change in morality—no longer would some tolerate execution as a form of retribution for acts committed against property.[79] Twenty years later, even killing murderers "was a bitterly contested issue."[80] Banner points out: "Some rising political figures, such as James Madison and the future governor of New York DeWitt Clinton, favored abandoning capital punishment altogether. Others, such as Thomas Jefferson and Benjamin Franklin, advocated eliminating the death penalty for all crimes other than murder."[81]

Significant proponents of abolition eventually included Dr. Benjamin Rush (a signer of the Declaration of Independence), Benjamin Franklin, William Bradford (who would become attorney general of the United States), and Thomas Jefferson.[82] A bill written by Thomas Jefferson and presented to the Virginia House of Delegates in 1785 to revise the death penalty so that it would be applicable for only two crimes was defeated by one vote!

Italian Cesare Beccaria's *Essay on Crimes and Punishments* (1764) argued against the death penalty on philosophical grounds, including that the state had no right to take a life and that imprisonment was a more effective means of deterrence. The book was widely read in Europe and in America by influential figures such as George Washington, Thomas Jefferson, and John Adams.[83]

The abolitionist movement was part of more widespread penal reforms, rejection of other social institutions such as slavery, and efforts internationally to make punishments more humane.[84] For example, in the 1790s, abolition efforts were spreading in Europe. Efforts to do away with or restrict capital punishment were mostly concentrated in northern states.

In the 1790s, "five states abolished the death penalty for all crimes other than murder, and three of the five even abolished it for certain kinds of murder.[85] These include Pennsylvania, New York, New Jersey, Virginia, and Kentucky for nonslaves. States that abolished the death penalty apparently questioned the justifiability and necessity of capital punishment, along with its purported deterrent and repentant values.[86]

During the late 1700s, the first prisons were established in Pennsylvania, New York, Massachusetts, New Jersey, Virginia, and Kentucky.[87] Penitentiaries were intended to give offenders the opportunity during incarceration to give penitence for their wrongdoings without killing the body.[88] The creation of penitentiaries signified a movement away from capital punishment.

The movement away from capital punishment in the late 18th century is also partially attributed to a change in the perceived causes of crime. As the believed etiology of crime slowly shifted from individual factors such as a lack of virtuousness to environmental factors such as poverty and poor upbringing, the retributive justification for the death penalty made less sense: "If crime was a disease, the retributive justification for capital punishment . . . virtually disappeared."[89] Benjamin Rush went as far as to suggest that capital punishment could actually increase murder by lessening the horror of taking away human life.[90] This would much later be referred to as *brutalization*.[91] I return to the issue of brutalization in Chapter 4.

Other successes of the abolitionist movement included the creation of degrees of murder and discretionary death penalty statutes. Pennsylvania in 1793 was the first state to distinguish between degrees of murder.[92] This represented the growing sentiment that not all murderers were worthy of death.

First Federal Execution

The federal government first executed someone on June 25, 1790, when Thomas Bird was hanged in Maine for murder. Since then 340 people have been executed by the federal government, including only 4 women[93] (currently, 43 people sit on federal death row, including only 1 woman).

The 19th Century

A Somber Hanging

In the 19th century, the most common method of execution was hanging, and hangings were originally carried out in public. Hangings, as well as other types of public executions, were somber events, like church. Yet, "the hope for dignified hangings before a tidy group was not realized. Inevitably, scores of uninvited guests attended, representing the influential and well-to-do, who now could observe the execution without the distraction of a disorderly mob or the fear that the condemned prisoner might find some favor in the crowd."[94]

Because executions were community events aimed at expressing disapproval of wrongful behavior, they included ceremonies that often took hours—a procession, speeches, prayers, and finally the actual execution.[95] The importance of executions for everyday life in the 19th century can be understood when one considers that executions generally grew larger crowds than any other type of event.[96] Whereas in modern America one might suspect that, were executions public, we might forbid children and women from witnessing them, in the 19th century public executions were seen as wholesome events suitable for even children.[97]

Further, it was standard for witnesses to develop and express sympathy for the condemned. This sympathy did not translate into opposition to the punishment; it likely strengthened support of the death penalty. This did eventually change, as sympathy for condemned offenders led to increased abolition efforts.[98] Public executions in early America were meant to amplify fear, reinforce order, and separate illegitimate, unacceptable violence by individuals from legitimate, acceptable violence committed by the state.[99]

Discretionary Death Penalty

Originally, death sentences were mandatory for many crimes, including murder, but this began to change in 1838 when the state of Tennessee enacted a discretionary death penalty statute.[100] Soon after, 20 more states enacted discretionary death penalty statutes. By 1939, only 4 states and the District of Columbia had mandatory death sentences on the books for first-degree murder.[101] This was in an effort to make the death penalty more acceptable to the public, which often refused to convict offenders when convictions would lead to mandatory death sentences.[102]

Some Abolitionist Success

Laws in the northern states were "all in the direction of abolition" from the 1820s through the 1850s.[103] During these decades, many northern states considered legislation to abolish capital punishment altogether. In 1837 Maine required a 1-year waiting period between death sentence and execution; after this time, the governor still had to sign a death warrant. The state executed no one between 1837 and 1863. Such laws were also passed in Vermont, New Hampshire, Massachusetts, and New York.[104]

In 1846, the first state to abolish the death penalty for all crimes except treason was Michigan. In 1852, the first state to abolish the death penalty for all crimes was Rhode Island. Wisconsin followed in 1853. By the 1860s, every state in the North had removed capital punishment for crimes except murder and treason.[105] In the 1870s, Iowa and Maine also abolished capital punishment, although both restored it within 10 years. Maine then abolished it again only four years later.

Meanwhile, in southern states, capital punishment was still used for crimes related to spreading discontent among free black people, insubordination among slaves, and even attempted rape by a black person against a white person.[106] No southern states abolished capital punishment completely, but every southern state did eliminate it for some crimes committed by whites.[107] Further, there was no large, sustained movement of people to abolish the death penalty in the South. This owed itself partly to the institution of slavery, which was firmly in place in the South until after the Civil War. In spite of the successes in the North, abolition of capital punishment by a state was typically followed by a restatement only a few years later.[108]

The abolitionist movement was short-lived because of politics, fear, and other social conditions.[109] And the record of successes and failures of abolitionists was mixed:

> They had persuaded the legislatures of three small states to abolish the death penalty. Five other states had established a one-year waiting period between conviction and execution. The abolitionists' biggest success was in abolishing capital punishment for crimes other than murder. In 1800, capital punishment had been common throughout the North for rape, robbery, burglary, and arson; by 1860 it was gone. But along with these achievements had come a consistent string of failures. Year after year, in state after state, they had been unable to convince legislatures to repeal the death penalty completely.[110]

Toward Private Executions

The nature of public executions changed in the 19th century. From the late 1700s and early 1800s to the 1850s, public executions went from a wholesome, moral experience to be enjoyed by all, to something to be avoided except by those commoners only out for a good time. Perhaps this is why from 1830 to 1860, every Northern state, led by Connecticut in 1830, moved its public hangings indoors to smaller spaces within jails. Pennsylvania hid its executions in 1834, followed by New York in 1835. Executions also became private because of a belief that public executions increased violent crime, even though most eyewitness accounts of public executions mention nothing about unruly behavior by those in the audience.[111] In the 19th century, "it was common knowledge that execution day crowds were often mischievous, with alcohol consumption and pickpockets regularly associated with public hangings. Rioting at public hangings also was not uncommon."[112]

Historian John Laurence writes: "Executions in the times when they were universally public, were occasions for rioting, revelry and ribaldry, and seldom was the demeanor of the crowd decorous in the face of death."[113] Yet, Johnson observes that the

> enlightened elite, of increasingly civilized and refined sensibilities, studiously avoided executions. Those who rallied around the scaffold

were of a more coarse and vulgar nature; ironically, many were outsiders to the community who would travel to executions for the entertainment value. Their behavior often closely resembled the unruly English mobs . . . and was quite unlike the quiet and penitent—even if smugly self-righteous—community members much-praised for their decorum and restraint by Puritan ministers over the preceding two centuries.[114]

Perceptions of unruly crowds meant public executions were no longer perceived as legitimate exercises of state power nor mechanisms to deliver a message of lawful retribution.[115] Further, the deterrent and incapacitative effects of executions were likely hindered by the fact that executions became private events. Over the next 100 years, every state hid its executions. Capital punishment historian John Bessler claims that executions became private "only in response to a movement in the 1830s to abolish capital punishment, and to a growing concern among civic leaders that public executions were unwholesome spectacles."[116] Further, "executions were seen as acts of violence that were likely to reflect badly on the larger community, harden the public, and demean the condemned."[117]

In the South, abolition of public executions took longer, but by the end of the 19th century, public executions had been abolished in at least seven states, including Kentucky, Louisiana, Maryland, Missouri, South Carolina, Tennessee, and Virginia, although Kentucky brought it back for rape and attempted rape in 1920. When the electric chair was adopted by Florida, North Carolina, Oklahoma, and Texas in the early 1900s, the new method of death necessitated indoor executions.[118]

The last public execution in the United States was in 1936 in Owensboro, Kentucky.[119] Between 10,000 and 20,000 people turned out to witness this public hanging, which was described by the press as a carnival-type atmosphere.[120] Decades after executions moved indoors, they still drew sizable crowds outside the jail. Eventually, however, the masses got their information from other sources, most notably the new "penny presses," which meant people no longer had to attend executions to experience the details.[121] However, some states even passed laws barring the press from attending executions and/or printing details about them in the papers.[122]

Banner explains the meaning of the shift from public to private executions:

> Executions lost much of their symbolic meaning. The community no longer gathered to make its statement of condemnation. There was no more ritual to reinforce communal norms proscribing crime, no more ceremony at which to display one's participation in a collective moral

order . . . with executions conducted behind closed doors, before a small group of the well connected, out of the public eye, the *people* were no longer punishing the criminal. Now the government was doing the punishing, and the people were reading about it later.[123]

Johnson adds:

> From this crucial transition—moving from passionate public executions to cold, clinical private ones—we can trace the beginnings of the bureaucratic regimen of modern private executions. Today, psychological dehumanization born of social isolation—on death row or in the death chamber—serves as the anesthetic that facilitates efficient, impersonal executions that are virtually devoid of human sentiment.[124]

Today, executions are very different from executions of the past. They are

> always conducted in secluded areas within prisons. Only a limited number of spectators attend and most do so for professional reasons; these witnesses maintain a discreet silence, though many are reportedly shaken by what they see. . . . Neither death nor killing is any longer a familiar part of daily life for the population at large; killings by officials are especially rare events, and are drained of their emotional import by secrecy (hardly anyone sees them) and euphemism (hardly anyone calls an execution a killing).[125]

The outcome of this move to make executions private is our current system of executing inmates in the middle of the night and early morning hours. According to Bessler:

> Executions in America, conducted behind prison walls, are cloaked in added secrecy because they frequently occur in the middle of the night. Of the 313 executions that took place in the United States from 1977 to 1995, over 82 percent of them were carried out between 11:00 pm and 7:30 am, and more than half of them happened between midnight and 1:00 am. Because television audiences are largest when people return home from work or school—viewership levels peak from 8:00 to 11:00 pm—many executions occur after most Americans are already sound asleep.[126]

It is state laws that typically require executions to be held at night. Yet, "even when executions are not mandated by statute, prison wardens or governmental officials frequently schedule executions for the middle of the night."[127] This is often done because midnight (and later) is the safest time in the prison where troublesome behaviors are least likely to occur. Further, midnight executions help "avoid unwanted protestors" and "ensure that enough time exists, because of possible last-minute stays and appeals, to carry out a death warrant—the legal document that lists a specific date on which the execution must occur."[128] Apparently, this practice started in 1885 in the state of Ohio.[129]

States Take Over

The first record of a person executed by a state government was in 1864, when Sandy Kavanagh was put to death in Vermont. After this time period, state governments began to take over capital punishment, typically in a central place located far from the municipalities where the crimes occurred that led to the death sentences. Earlier, "as far as possible it was customary for an execution to take place as near as possible to the scene of the crime, an old idea which died hard. Little by little executions were held in more or less fixed public places, later in front of prisons, and finally, on the abolition of public executions, within the prisons themselves."[130]

The Progressive Era (Early 20th Century)

New Methods of Death

In the early 20th century, states began adopting methods such as death by electrocution and by lethal gas. These methods required a single, fixed location for either the electric chair or the gas chamber. Perhaps this development, more than any other, is responsible for the distance that now typically exists between the place of the punishment and the capital crime that led to the death sentence. Modern methods used by states for their executions include hanging, the gas chamber, the electric chair, the firing squad, and lethal injection. Each of these is discussed later in the chapter.

Short-Lived Reforms

The early part of the 20th century is known as the Progressive Era because of the numerous (but short-lived) reforms of capital punishment laws in the United States. Between 1907 and 1917, six states abolished capital punishment and another three limited it to treason and murder of a law enforcement officer. The reforms were short-lived because five of the six states reinstated capital punishment by 1920 due to fear of revolution and class conflicts that threatened capitalism and America's way of life.[131] From 1920 to 1935, due in part to fear of gangsters and widespread media coverage of the Lindbergh kidnapping, there was a brief resurgence in death penalty statutes and executions.[132]

Still, activity aimed at abolition was high in prisons, churches, among legislatures, and in the press. Many famous cases kept the issue in the news, including Nathan Leopold and Richard Loeb, Gerald Chapman,

Nicola Sacco and Bartolomeo Vanzetti, the "Scottsboro boys," and Bruno Hauptmann.[133]

Executions Peak and Decline

Further, executions declined in the first half of the 20th century, and would not rise again until the 1980s and 1990s. As noted earlier in the chapter, 1,289 people were executed in the 1940s, 715 were executed in the 1950s, and only 191 were executed from 1960 through 1976.[134] From 1977 to 1989, only 120 people were executed. This decline has been described as an "administrative abolition"—"the slow erosion of capital punishment not by legislation or court decision but through a gradual change in the output of the criminal justice system."[135] Essentially, juries were just not sentencing people to death as frequently.

In the 1930s, the U.S. government began keeping detailed statistics of capital punishment. This was also the decade that saw the largest number of executions, when the average number of executions per year was 167.[136] The year 1935 is the year when the most people were executed in the 20th century, as 199 people were put to death. The 1930s saw so many executions likely because of "anxiety over the 'crime wave' generated by the Great Depression (1929–1940) and Prohibition (1916–1932)."[137] That is, a moral panic during tough times led to a "get tough" on crime outcome, which included a greater willingness to carry out executions.

After these peaks, executions declined in the United States for decades. For example, the last year with more than 150 executions was 1947, the last year with more than 100 executions was 1951, and by 1968, there were zero executions for the first time in U.S. history.[138] In fact, no one was executed again in this country until 1977. Cases heard by the U.S. Supreme Court about racial discrimination in the administration of capital punishment, particularly cases of alleged rapes of white women by African-American men, led to an "unofficial suspension" of the death penalty after June 1967.[139]

By 1950, 70% of the states that had abolished capital punishment had now reinstated it. Yet, its use actually began to decline in this decade.[140] There were at least three reasons for this. First, European countries were also moving away from capital punishment. In 1948 the United Nations General Assembly passed the Universal Declaration of Human Rights which proclaims a universal right to life. In the 1950s and 1960s further international treaties were signed, including the International Covenant on Civil and Political Rights, the European Convention on Human Rights, and the American Convention on Human Rights, each of which states a basic right to life.[141]

Second, the belief in free will was slowly being replaced with a greater acceptance in environmental and biological determinism—the belief that environmental and biological factors play significant roles in human behavior. To the degree that people attributed criminality and murder to causes beyond the control of individuals, executing them made little sense.

Third, social conditions turned public opinion against capital punishment. Four states abolished capital punishment and others reduced the number of death-eligible crimes.[142]

The Death Penalty Under Attack

The death penalty was attacked by numerous influential individuals. One was convicted kidnapper Caryl Chessman, who was on death row for kidnapping from 1948 to 1960. While incarcerated and awaiting death, Chessman wrote four books and was interviewed numerous times. Because of this, "he became an international celebrity—a literate, intelligent, white man believed to be innocent, who in any event, had not killed anyone."[143] His case was discussed all over the world and kept criticisms of capital punishment alive. Numerous religious organizations issued statements against capital punishment and vigorous debate inspired students to write letters to state governors and legislatures. During this time, Alaska and Hawaii abolished capital punishment (1957), as did Delaware (1958), as well as New York, Iowa, Vermont, and West Virginia (1965).[144]

An editorial published on May 3, 1966, in the *New York Herald Tribune* read, about Chessman's death:

> Caryl Chessman died well, as befitted a man well aware that the world's eyes were on his dying. Other nobler men have also died well, but few deaths have so dramatized the ugly absurdity of capital punishment in a society that should have outgrown it. . . .
>
> He may or may not have been guilty, twelve years ago, of robbery and sexual assault (called kidnapping by a strange quirk of California law). The courts found him guilty; to the end he maintained his innocence, and the germ of doubt thus left will continue to cloud the case. But certainly the man killed yesterday by the sovereign state of California was not the same man whom that state's court originally sentenced. . . .
>
> California sentenced a young thug; it killed a man who had learned law, and probably citizenship, the hard way.
>
> Californians are not safer today than before Chessman died, and respect for the law—which is different from fear of its power—is no stronger.
>
> The law should inculcate respect for life itself respecting the sanctity of life. The state should not, as California did yesterday, put itself in the position of the errant father telling his wayward son, "Do as I say, not as I do."

> Death is final. It leaves no room for second thoughts, or for correction of the errors that are a mathematical certainty in a system of justice based on fallible human judgment. And the quintessential premeditation which judicial killing represents makes it more coldly vicious than a crime of passion.[145]

In 1961, the law professor Gerald Gottlieb wrote that "the death penalty was unconstitutional under the Eighth Amendment because it violated contemporary moral standards, what the U.S. Supreme Court in *Trop v. Dulles* . . . referred to as 'the evolving standards of decency that mark the progress of a maturing society.'"[146] In 1966, support for the death penalty hit an all-time low (42%) and in 1969, New Mexico abolished it.

In the wake of all this activity, both the number of executions and the rate of executions per capita declined significantly. Not only were there fewer death sentences but also there were more and more successful appeals. Neutral observers from outside the United States likely thought that capital punishment would finally go away inside America. This perception would be reinforced in 1972 when the U.S. Supreme Court invalidated death penalty statutes.

The Late 20th Century

Supreme Court Intervention

The Supreme Court formally prohibited capital punishment with *Furman v. Georgia* (1972) but ruled it constitutional only 4 years later with the case of *Gregg v. Georgia* (1976). *Furman v. Georgia* (1972) decided by a 5–4 vote that existing death penalty statutes were "cruel and unusual" because they violated the Eighth and Fourteenth Amendments of the U.S. Constitution. In essence, the Supreme Court found that capital punishment was being imposed "arbitrarily, infrequently, and often selectively against minorities."[147] So, it was not the death penalty itself that was at issue, it was how this penalty was being applied arbitrarily and disproportionately to some groups of people.

The Supreme Court did not conclude that the death penalty per se was unconstitutional. It was only unconstitutional to the degree that is was imposed arbitrarily and unfairly. Thus, almost all of the 40 death penalty states began writing and adopting new death penalty statutes designed to meet the Court's objections.[148] States, concerned with their image as much as with the public safety of their citizens, quickly passed death penalty laws that would be considered constitutional by the Supreme Court and also began sentencing people to death under the new laws. Nearly one third of states enacted mandatory death sentences for some crimes, taking the issue of discretion of judges and juries out of the picture.[149] Most states passed guided discretion statutes that would give juries and sentencing judges some guidelines to follow when considering death sentences.[150]

The mandatory death sentence statutes were rejected 5–4 by the Supreme Court as unconstitutional in *Woodson v. North Carolina* (1976), but in the case of *Gregg v. Georgia* (1976), the Court ruled by a 7–2 vote that guided discretion statutes were acceptable in death penalty cases. The Court also upheld the use of bifurcated trials, where guilt or innocence would be decided in the first phase and sentencing decided in the second, as well as automatic appellate review of convictions and sentences, and, finally, proportionality reviews to compare sentences of some cases against similar cases to ensure just sentencing practices. Thus, suggestions made in 1959 by the American Law Institute's Model Penal Code and aimed at making the death penalty more fair were finally put into place.[151]

The *Furman* and subsequent cases meant no more mandatory death sentences, no more death sentences for crimes other than murder, and no more executions without review of the conviction and sentence by a state appellate court.[152] Ultimately, the length of inmates' death row stay also increased dramatically, as did costs associated with actually using the capital punishment system.

The last time guided discretion statutes themselves were seriously challenged, the Court failed to abolish capital punishment once and for all. In *McCleskey v. Kemp* (1987), the Supreme Court heard testimony from a sociologist (Dr. David Baldus) who showed that the death penalty was applied disproportionately to African Americans in Georgia. The study utilized a multiple regression analysis including 230 variables likely to affect the outcome of death penalty cases in order to test the hypothesis that race of defendant and race of victim played a role in death penalty sentences. This study found that only 1% of Caucasians received the death penalty in homicide cases between 1973 and 1979, whereas 11% of African Americans received the death penalty. Additionally, the study found that 22% of African Americans who killed Caucasians received death sentences, versus only 3% of Caucasians who killed African Americans.

The Court recognized the validity of these findings and even acknowledged a clear pattern of disparity in the application of death sentences in Georgia. Yet, the Court held that an individual defendant must demonstrate discrimination in his or her specific case in order for the case to be considered unconstitutional. That is, he or she must be able to demonstrate that the prosecutor acted in a discriminatory fashion in the individual case or that the legislature intended to make discriminatory law.

Capital punishment scholar Robert Bohm reviewed executions in Georgia since the *McCleskey* decision and found that racial disparities still exist. Specifically, killers of whites are far more likely than killers of African-Americans to be sentenced to the death penalty, especially when African-Americans are convicted of killing whites.[153] I return to each of these cases in Chapter 2.

Executions Resume

The first person executed after the death penalty was reinstated in 1976 was Gary Gilmore, who waived all his appeals and requested to be killed by the state of Utah.[154] Gilmore insisted that he be put to death by the state, and he was in 1977 by shooting squad. Gilmore's brother now discusses how ironic it is that his brother's last gift to humankind, created by his own push to be executed as rapidly as possible, was a return to capital punishment in the United States.

Federal Death Penalty

After the 1972 case *Furman v. Georgia*, the federal death penalty was not reinstated until 1988, and there had not been a federal execution since 1963. Thus, there was a 26-year period without any executions under federal jurisdiction. Between 1988 and 2005, the federal government killed only three people, all since 2001, and beginning with the execution of Timothy McVeigh for deaths caused by the bombing of a federal building in Oklahoma City.[155]

The bottom line with regard to the federal death penalty is that executions by the U.S. government are extremely rare, even more so than executions by states. Perhaps the federal death penalty system merely serves as "symbolic approval" for states that practice capital punishment.[156]

Since 1988, Congress has enacted several laws in an effort to expand the federal death penalty. This has led to what some experts call the "nationalization" or "federalization" of the death penalty. In the late 1880s, the federal government reduced the number of death-eligible crimes from 60 to 3, but in the 1990s, it increased that number from 3 back to more than 60. All but 3 of the crimes involve murder, and they are espionage, treason, and major drug dealing.

The 1988 Drug Kingpin Statute allows for death sentences for murders committed in the course of a drug-kingpin conspiracy. The 1994 Omnibus Crime Bill expanded the death penalty to 60 different offenses. These offenses included murder of some government officials, kidnapping resulting in death, murder for hire, fatal drive-by shootings, sexual abuse crimes resulting in death, car jacking resulting in death, and even some crimes that do not result in death, such as operating large-scale drug enterprises.

The 1996 Antiterrorism and Effective Death Penalty Act

amends federal habeas corpus law as it applies to both state and federal prisoners whether on death row or imprisoned for a term of years by providing: a bar on federal habeas reconsideration of legal and factual issues ruled upon by state courts in most instances; creation of a general 1 year statute of limitations; creation of a 6 month statute of limitation in death penalty cases; encouragement for states to appoint counsel for indigent state death row inmates during state habeas or unitary appellate proceedings; and a requirement of appellate court approval for repetitious habeas petitions.[157]

Essentially, this law makes it much more difficult to appeal death sentences at the federal level.

According to the Death Penalty Information Center,

There is only one appeal granted to the defendant as a matter of right and that is an appeal of the sentence and conviction to the U.S. Court of Appeals for the Circuit in which the case was tried. There is also one chance to present any facts which were overlooked or unavailable at the time of the trial. All other review, such as Supreme Court review, is discretionary and can only be requested once, except under the rarest of factual situations requiring both clear proof of innocence and certain constitutional violations.[158]

Still, the federal government provides numerous protections.

- Two attorneys must represent a capital defendant, at least one of whom has capital experience.
- Timely notice of intention to seek the death penalty must be given.
- A list of aggravated circumstances must be presented before the trial.
- Aggravated circumstances must be proven beyond a reasonable doubt.
- The jury must unanimously agree about aggravated circumstances.
- Weighing of aggravated and mitigating circumstances is required.
- No death sentence may be imposed unless at least one aggravating circumstance is present.
- Only one juror has to find mitigating circumstance to be considered.
- The defendant must be granted a right to appeal conviction and sentence.
- Jurors cannot consider race, color, religion, national origin, or sex of the defendant or victim.
- Each juror must sign his or her name swearing that no discrimination occurred.[159]

In 2004, President George W. Bush signed into law the Justice for All Act. It provides funds for training of lawyers in death penalty cases and expands access to DNA testing for death row inmates who want to challenge their convictions based on new evidence.[160]

Military Death Penalty

The U.S. military has executed the least number of people of all levels of government. The U.S. Army has executed 135 people since 1916, although a list discovered by the Pentagon shows that 169 people were executed by the U.S. military between 1942 and 1962.[161] At least another 267 people were executed during the Civil War by the Union.[162] The last execution by the U.S. military was in 1961, when a man was hanged for rape and attempted murder.

The place of execution for the U.S. military is the U.S. Disciplinary Barracks in Fort Leavenworth, Kansas. Methods used in the past by the U.S. military to carry out its executions include hanging and the shooting squad. The current method is lethal injection.

The U.S. military's death penalty statute was struck down in 1972, and a 1983 case, *U.S. v. Matthews* (U.S. Armed Forces Court of Appeals), held that military procedures were unconstitutional because no specific aggravating factors were listed. In 1984, President Reagan created them and the U.S. military once again had a workable death penalty system. Currently, only nine individuals, all men, sit on the U.S. military's death row.

Only the president can commute a sentence of death in the U.S. military, and no one can be executed without personal confirmation by the president. The military has 15 different death penalty offenses, many at time of war, and it provides numerous barriers to imposing death. For example, the decision to seek death must come from a convening authority (commanding officer); a unanimous conviction is required on a capital offense; aggravating factor(s) must be proved beyond a reasonable doubt; unanimous agreement is required that aggravation outweighs mitigation; there must be unanimous agreement on the sentence; a record of the trial is sent to an intermediate appellate court for the branch of the military, and if the death sentence is affirmed, it then goes to the Court of Appeals of the Armed Forces (five civilian judges). If the sentence is affirmed again, it is eligible for Supreme Court review; if affirmed there (or not reviewed) it then goes to the president; if denied, the individual can then seek relief from an Article III Judiciary.[163] New military regulations streamline military death penalty procedures, allow other locations to be used for executions, and make other changes to military death penalty law.[164]

Summary

In spite of the resurgence of capital punishment in the 1990s, an analysis of the four main eras of capital punishment shows that America has moved from

- brutal displays of excess carried out in public to clean, detached executions carried out in private;
- many death-eligible crimes to few death-eligible crimes;
- many executions to few executions; and
- greater efforts to ensure that death sentences are imposed fairly and rationally.

These trends suggest to many that the United States may be evolving away from capital punishment, albeit very slowly.[165] Similarly, some capital punishment scholars have claimed that the beginning of the end of the death penalty in the United States has already begun.[166] It is also possible that there will be another resurgence in death sentences and executions in the near future, as was seen in the 1990s, perhaps in response to a horrific crime or set of crimes. However, the terrorist attacks of September 11, 2001, did not prompt an outcry for increased executions, as some had expected (this could simply be due to the fact that Americans sought revenge through war instead).

Whatever happens in the future, the fact remains that America's death penalty experience ultimately led to a system of capital punishment where executions are extremely rare and only a handful of states regularly carry out executions. Further, executions are carried out in private and typically without the knowledge of the majority of Americans, but over the objections of many who continue to see serious problems with the way in which capital punishment is carried out in the United States.

METHODS OF EXECUTION IN THE UNITED STATES

According to one scholar, methods of death used in the world at one time or another included

- "crouching death, met on one's knees: as in a beheading, at the guillotine or a stoning";
- "death met upright: crucified, burned at the stake, impaled on a sharp object that splits the body up the middle, or strangled on a garrote, an iron collar, or stood up against a wall, with or without a blindfold, to be gunned down by a firing squad";

- "death met while still moving—walking the gauntlet, or stuffed into a bag and thrown from a cliff, or hanged on a gallows tree";
- "death met seated: in a chair, head back—suffocated by a combination of water and cloth, or by molten lead poured into one's mouth, or, in our modern age, strapped into an electric chair or in a gas chamber, waiting for cyanide pellets to poison the air";
- "death met lying down: dismembered on a rack, stretched until torn apart, or crushed by heavy weights such as boulders or elephants, or strapped to a gurney in a sterile room while lethal chemicals are injected through a syringe—one, two, three."[167]

Current execution practice is hardly this exciting. In fact, the only method widely used today is the last one described—lethal injection.

Lethal Injection

Currently, the only method that will likely be used in the near future to execute a human being is lethal injection. Of 37 states with the death penalty, lethal injection is authorized in 36. Nebraska stands alone as the only state to authorize a single method of execution other than lethal injection—it uses electrocution.

As evidence that lethal injection is virtually the only method of execution used in the United States, consider Table 1.2. As shown in the table, all 60 of the executions that took place in the United States in 2005 were conducted by lethal injection. Of the 59 executions in 2004, all but 1 were achieved through lethal injection; one individual was electrocuted in South Carolina. In 2003, of the 65 total executions, 64 were by lethal injection and 1 was by electrocution, in the state of Virginia. In 2002, of the 71 total executions, 70 were by lethal injection, and 1 was by electrocution, in Alabama. In 2001, all 66 executions were by lethal injection. In 2000, 80 of the 85 executions were by lethal injection, and only 5 were by electrocution (4 in Alabama and 1 in Virginia). Thus, so far in the 21st century, more than 98% of people executed have been executed through lethal injection,

TABLE 1.2   Method of Recent Executions in the United States

	2000	2001	2002	2003	2004	2005	Total
Lethal injection	80	66	70	64	58	60	398
Electrocution	5	0	1	1	1	0	8

Source: Executions in the United States, by the Death Penalty Information Center, 2006. Retrieved from http://www.deathpenaltyinfo.org/article.php?did=414&scid=8

as only 8 of 406 people have been executed by a method other than lethal injection; all of these were electrocuted.

The most recent execution, at the time of this writing, is of 27-year-old Brandon Hendrick for the rape and murder of a 23-year-old woman. Hendrick was executed in Virginia in the electric chair, the method he chose over lethal injection because of a fear of death by lethal injection.

The only method of execution for federal prisoners is lethal injection, except for those offenses committed under the Violent Crime Control and Law Enforcement Act of 1994. For those inmates, the method of execution will be that of the state in which the conviction took place. If that state has no death penalty, the judge can choose the method of another state. Finally, the only authorized method by the U.S. military is lethal injection.

In the past, the federal government used hanging, electrocution, and the gas chamber for its executions. All federal executions are carried out in Terre Haute, Indiana. Originally, federal executions were carried out in the state where the crime occurred, using the authorized method in that state. This changed in 1995 when the federal government added a death chamber. Most federal inmates were executed for murder but some inmates have been executed for other crimes such as piracy, rape, rioting, kidnapping, spying, and espionage.[168]

Oklahoma was the first state to adopt lethal injection in 1977. Yet, the first person executed by lethal injection was in Texas in 1982. The process typically works like this: The inmate is strapped to a gurney and "a member of the execution team positions several heart monitors on the skin. Two needles (one is a back-up) are then inserted into usable veins, usually in the inmate's arms. Long tubes connect the needle through a hole in a cement block wall to several intravenous drips. The first is a harmless saline solution that is started immediately." Next, "the inmate is injected with: 1) an anesthetic for sleep (sodium thiopental); 2) a muscle relaxant to paralyze and stop breathing (pancuronium bromide); and 3) cardiac arrester to stop heart (potassium chloride)."[169]

The benefits of lethal injection are that it appears to be a humane death, and it is an inexpensive method. The drawbacks are that medical ethics preclude doctors from participating in executions, and there is still the potential for error that may lead to immense suffering by paralyzed inmates who cannot express pain.[170]

Functional problems and image problems with the electric chair and lethal gas likely encouraged the development of lethal injection.[171] As a result, "the institutionalization of lethal injection has neutralized the reputation for brutality and anachronism associated with the electric chair and the gas chamber. While organized medicine is not party to executions, the physical apparatus of medicine—syringes and gurneys—have rapidly become the dominant physical representation of the execution process."[172]

Why Lethal Injection?

The move to lethal injection—deemed by most to be the most humane method of death ever devised—was prompted by problems with and challenges to other methods of execution. The U.S. Supreme Court does not allow cruel and unusual punishment under the Eighth Amendment to the U.S. Constitution. Historically, the Court interpreted the Constitution literally so that only the most barbaric and torturous punishments were not allowed.

From the 1800s to the present day, when particular methods of death were challenged, the U.S. Supreme Court has never found a specific method of death to be unconstitutional. This issue is discussed further in Chapter 2.

Legal scholar Deborah Denno summarizes the definition of "cruel and unusual" according to significant U.S. Supreme Court cases. She says there are

> four interrelated criteria for determining the constitutionality of an execution method: (1) "the unnecessary and wanton infliction of pain" (*Gregg v. Georgia* 1976: 173, *Louisiana* ex rel. *Francis v. Resweber* 1947: 463); (2) "nothing less than" human dignity (*Trop v. Dulles* 1958: 100) (for example, "a minimization of physical violence during execution" (*Glass v. Louisiana* 1985: 1085); (3) the risk of "unnecessary and wanton infliction of pain" (*Farmer v. Brennan* 1994: 842); and (4) "evolving standards of decency" as measured by "objective factors to the maximum extent possible" (*Stanford v. Kentucky* 1989: 369, *Coker v. Georgia* 1977: 592), such as legislation passed by elected representatives or public attitudes (*Atkins v. Virginia* 2002).[173]

Clearly, judged by today's standards, previous methods used in the United States and in the rest of the world would be deemed by most to be cruel and unusual punishments. These methods included flaying and impaling, boiling in oil, crucifixion, pulling asunder, burying alive, sawing in half, beheading, pressing to death, drawing and quartering, breaking on the wheel, drowning, burning at the stake, and so forth. Further, electrocution—still legal in 10 states—is cruel and unusual because it represents "unnecessary and wanton infliction of pain," constitutes "physical violence" and offends "human dignity," constitutes the risk of "unnecessary and wanton infliction of pain," and contravenes "evolving standards of decency" (because states have moved against it and moved to lethal injection, and only the United States maintains it). Perhaps this explains why Georgia's Supreme

Court—in the case *Dawson v. State* (2001)—declared electrocution cruel and unusual punishment in the state.

Relative to these methods, our primary method of execution is mundane, although no less serious. Yet, lethal injection is now under attack by abolitionists and human rights activists, and with at least some justification. Death row inmates have recently challenged the constitutionality of lethal injection, contending that lethal injection constitutes cruel and unusual punishment because the chemicals used in the execution process can cause pain.[174] An editorial by *The New York Times* explains:

> In lethal injection, three different chemicals are administered in sequence. The first is an anesthetic, another paralyzes the muscles and stops breathing, and a third stops the heart. Improper administration of the anesthetic can have the ghoulish effect of leaving the prisoner able to feel the tremendous pain of being killed by the poison that is injected into him while rendering him unable to communicate his agony by sound or gestures. [175]

In North Carolina, Willie Brown Jr. was put to death by lethal injection for the 1983 killing of Vallerie Ann Roberson Dixon. He was the first person executed in the United States using a "bispectral index (BIS) monitor, that measures brain waves and ranks . . . level of consciousness from a scale of zero to 100."[176] The BIS monitor was used in an attempt to alleviate concerns raised by Brown's attorneys that if he was not fully sedated before the second and third drugs were injected into his body he might be awake to experience an excruciating death.

Brown's appeal that the BIS monitor was inappropriate for this purpose was denied by a U.S. District Court judge and affirmed by two federal appeals court judges. One of the federal judges ruled in Brown's favor. When Brown's lawyer asked the full court of 14 judges to consider their appeal, it was not considered. The U.S. Supreme Court also refused to hear his case.[177]

One of the inmates challenging lethal injection, whose case is before the U.S. Supreme Court at the time of this writing, is Clarence Hill, who killed police officer Larry Bailly in Pensacola, Florida, in 1982. He was already strapped to a gurney and was awaiting his execution in April 2006, 24 years after his crime. The U.S. Supreme Court granted Hill a stay of execution, causing Governor Jeb Bush of Florida to stop signing death row warrants until the case is resolved.[178] According to one media account, the Court will "decide whether a federal appeals court was wrong to prevent Hill from challenging the lethal injection method. The justices could, however, spell out what options are available to inmates with last-minute challenges to the way they will be put to death."[179]

The Court did decide not to determine whether lethal injection itself is unconstitutional, consistent with its shirking of this issue for many years.[180] Denno explains that the Court has completely disregarded "how inmates are executed. While the Court continually recognizes the Eighth Amendment hazards associated with prison conditions . . . it has never reviewed evidence on the constitutionality of execution conditions despite repeated, horrifying, and entirely preventable mishaps." The Court did agree to hear challenges from California and Florida in the 1990s, "only to drop the cases after state legislatures . . . changed their methods of execution." [181]

Another inmate, Marvin Bieghler, was executed in Indiana in January 2006 for killing Tommy Miller and his pregnant wife Kimberly Jane Miller in 1981. The U.S. Supreme Court overturned a stay of execution granted to him by a lower federal court just 90 minutes earlier. Bieghler, unlike Hill, had already unsuccessfully challenged the execution method at the state level. When about to be executed, Bieghler said: "Let's get it over with." [182]

Then, in May 2006, Joseph Clark was executed in Ohio for the 1984 murder of David Manning as part of a drug-induced robbery (Clark also killed another man, Donald Harris, during the same crime spree). After officials worked to find a suitable vein in one arm for 90 minutes, the lethal injection process started, but one of Clark's veins collapsed, prompting Clark to sit up and tell prison officials: "It's not working. It's not working." Clark did not challenge his execution or ask for it to be stopped. Instead, Clark was executed after officials inserted the needle into his other arm.[183]

The point of these three cases is that even lethal injection—probably the most humane method ever devised of killing murderers—is not perfect, nor is it free from legitimate legal challenges. In fact, one inmate successfully argued to the U.S. Supreme Court (in a unanimous decision in the case of *Nelson v. Campbell*)[184] that he should be able to challenge a procedure known as a "cut-down procedure" as cruel and unusual punishment. Because Nelson's veins are badly damaged, it is likely impossible to insert a vein into his arm without first cutting into his arm, which could cause him pain, bleeding, and even problems with his heart.

Denno, who has testified numerous times in trials dealing with lethal injection, raises the possibility that lethal injection itself might meet the definition of "cruel and unusual punishment." She notes: "Sodium thiopental—an 'ultra short' acting drug . . . —typically wears off very quickly; other similar drugs, such as pentobarbital, endure far longer. The 'fast acting' aspect of sodium thiopental can have horrifying effects if the inmate awakens while being administered the other two drugs." Yet, since the inmate is paralyzed there is a "calm scene" even though the "inmate may be conscious and suffering." [185]

Further, because prison officials typically have discretion about capital punishment procedures and they may "ignore each prisoner's physical characteristics (for example, age, body weight, health), even those factors strongly affect an individual's reaction to the chemicals as well as the condition of their veins." [186] Individual physical characteristics are related to the amount of sodium thiopental an inmate would need to be asleep, and if the amount is insufficient, the inmate would be awake through his or her own death, which could lead to excruciating pain as the other drugs flow through the body.

Another interesting issue with lethal injection is that doctors have resisted participating in capital punishment through this "medical" method. In response to a challenge to lethal injection in Missouri, state officials sent letters to 298 certified anesthesiologists that resided near the state's death chamber in Boone Terre, and all of them turned down the state's offer to participate in executions. Both the American Medical Association and the American Society of Anesthesiologists have issued statements saying that doctors should never participate in executions because it is a violation of their basic oath to do no harm. The challenge was initiated in response to reports of a dyslexic Missouri surgeon who participated in lethal injections in Missouri and often improvised the process of executions by giving the condemned smaller doses of the anesthesia used to reduce the pain of the lethal drugs than required by state policy. As noted above, this could lead to intense pain on the part of the condemned inmate who is paralyzed and thus cannot react to the pain.[187]

Previous Execution Methods

Hanging

Two states still authorize hanging (in spite of the conclusion a century earlier that hanging was barbaric and cruel), including New Hampshire and Washington. However, New Hampshire authorizes hanging only if lethal injection cannot be given. Washington gives inmates the choice of hanging.

Until the 1890s, death by hanging was the primary method of execution used in the United States. One scholar writes: "Hanging was the method of choice in America for hundreds of years, a 'compassionate' alternative to stoning, burning, or beheading. If all went well, when the trapdoor opened and the prisoner dropped, death came quickly." [188] It was a relatively easy method of execution, requiring no expertise other than knowing how to tie a knot.[189] Inmates were often weighed the day before their executions, and rehearsals were done using sandbags of the same weight as the prisoners. This was to determine the length of "drop" necessary to ensure a quick death.

Experience showed that if the rope was too long, the inmate could be decapitated and if it was too short, the strangulation could take as long as

45 minutes. The rope (3/4 inch to 1 1/4 inch in diameter) was usually boiled and stretched to eliminate spring or coiling and the knot was often lubricated with wax or soap "to ensure a smooth sliding action," according to the 1969 U.S. Army manual.[190]

The process works like this: The inmate's hands and legs are tied, and he or she is "blindfolded or hooded." The noose is "placed around the neck with the knot behind the left ear." The execution occurs when a trapdoor is opened and the prisoner falls through. The goal is "to see that the prisoner's weight [will] cause a rapid fracture-dislocation of the neck (called a 'hangman's fracture') and thus, instantaneous death." However, instantaneous does not always occur.

If the "inmate [has] strong neck muscles, [is] very light, if the 'drop' [is] too short, or the noose [is] wrongly positioned, the fracture-dislocation [is] not rapid and death [will] result from slow asphyxiation." If this happens, the face becomes "engorged, the tongue protrudes, the eyes [may pop], the person defecate[s], and violent movements of the limbs [occur]."[191] Clearly, death by hanging can be very inhumane. This led to rejection of the punishment in the mid to late 1800s because pain was not supposed to be part of executions. Yet, no other method of execution was known to be painless and so hangings continued until the early 20th century when death by electrocution was developed.[192]

Firing Squad

Three states authorize the firing squad, including Idaho, Oklahoma, and Utah. Oklahoma authorizes the firing squad only if lethal injection and electrocution are held to be unconstitutional. Idaho authorizes the firing squad only if lethal injection is "impractical." In Utah, the firing squad has been banned except by those inmates who chose this method of execution prior to the passage of the legislation.

The firing squad was developed in Nevada and Utah as "a consequence of the Mormon doctrine of blood atonement, the concept that some sins are so heinous that the offender can atone only by literally shedding his blood." [193] In Utah, its laws in the late 1800s gave inmates the choice of being hanged, shot, or beheaded, and in Nevada a similar choice was given to inmates in 1912.[194]

The process works like this: Inmates are "bound to a chair with leather straps across their waists and heads, in front of an oval-shaped canvas wall. The chair [is] surrounded by sandbags to absorb the inmate's blood. A black hood [is] pulled over the inmate's head and a doctor . . . locate[s] the inmate's heart with a stethoscope and pin[s] a circular white cloth target over it." Five gunmen "armed with .30 caliber rifles loaded with single rounds" are standing 20 feet away in an enclosed structure, and "one of the shooters is given blank rounds." The prisoner dies "as a result of blood loss caused by rupture of the heart or a large blood vessel and tearing of the lungs." If not killed instantly, the inmate loses "consciousness when shock causes a fall in the supply of blood to the brain. If the shooters missed the heart, by accident or intention, the prisoner would simply bleed to death slowly." [195]

The firing squad is humane in the sense that death often results quickly, but botched executions are common and the method is brutal to the body and messy.[196] Nevertheless, one criminologist who has witnessed several executions and written a book about the execution process claims: "If I had to choose a method of execution, I believe I would choose the firing squad as being the fastest, most painless, and most humane—as well as being appropriate to the justice system." [197]

Electrocution

Ten states authorize electrocution, including Alabama, Arkansas, Florida, Illinois, Kentucky, Nebraska, Oklahoma, South Carolina, Tennessee, and Virginia. However, Illinois and Oklahoma authorize electrocution only if lethal injection is found to be unconstitutional. Alabama, Florida, South Carolina, and Virginia use lethal injection unless inmates request electrocution. Arkansas allows inmates who committed their offenses before July 4, 1983, to select electrocution. Kentucky allows inmates who committed their offenses before March 31, 1998, to choose electrocution. Tennessee allows those sentenced prior to January 1, 1999, to choose the electric chair.

Death by the electric chair was developed in competition between Thomas Edison's direct current systems and George Westinghouse's alternating current systems. Edison's systems were more expensive to use, making alternating current a preferable method for electricity in the home. An engineer named Harold Brown conducted experiments where dogs were killed using lower amounts of alternating current than direct current, suggesting that direct current was safer for home use. Edison invited Brown to his laboratory for the purpose of designing an electric chair that would use alternating current to kill the condemned. Edison even met with state officials in 1888 to persuade them to adopt alternating current for use in executions by electricity.[198]

After evidence suggested that animals were being mercifully killed using electricity, the first state to allow it was New York in 1888. John Laurence explains:

> There was great opposition by electrical companies to the use of electricity as a method of capital punishment, on the score that it would lead the public to believe that electricity was too dangerous for

ordinary use. One company which made use of the innocuous direct current, as against the admittedly more risky alternating current, gave public demonstrations of killing animals to show the dangers of using any other system than their own.[199]

New York adopted electrocution after it had commissioned a study of death by electricity and 34 other methods. After concluding that the method was clean, affordable, painless, and humane, the first person executed using the electric chair was William Kemmler in New York in 1890. Kemmler's execution was described in *The New York Times* headlines as "FAR WORSE THAN HANGING" and "KEMMLER'S DEATH PROVES AN AWFUL SPECTACLE." [200] Kemmler survived the initial jolts of electricity and continued to breathe after the electrodes were removed. After a subsequent shock for more than one minute, the capillaries in his face ruptured and blood appeared on his face. Kemmler's flesh and hair burned, filling the room with the smell of a burning human being.[201]

Nevertheless, the state of New York electrocuted four more inmates on the same day a year later, and all appeared to be clean and painless executions. Over the next several years, Ohio, Massachusetts, New Jersey, Virginia, North Carolina, Kentucky, and South Carolina adopted electrocution as its means of execution. Between 1888 and 1923, 15 states adopted the electric chair.[202] By 1950, 11 more states and the District of Columbia had also adopted it. Electrocution was the most common method of execution of the 20th century.

The process works like this: The inmate is "shaved and strapped to a chair with belts that cross his chest, groin, legs, and arms." A metal skullcap-shaped electrode is "attached to the scalp and forehead over a sponge moistened with saline. The sponge must not be too wet or the saline short-circuits the electric current, and not too dry, as it would then have a very high resistance." An additional electrode is "moistened with conductive jelly (Electro-Creme) and attached to a portion of the prisoner's leg" that has been "shaved to reduce resistance to electricity." The prisoner is blindfolded and a "jolt of between 500 and 2000 volts, which lasts for about 30 seconds" is administered. The current is then turned off and the body relaxes. Doctors wait "for the body to cool down and then check to see if the inmate's heart is still beating." If it is, more electricity is applied until the prisoner is dead.[203]

"The prisoner's hands often grip the chair and there may be violent movement of the limbs which can result in dislocation or fractures. The tissues swell. Defecation occurs. Steam or smoke rises and there is a smell of burning." [204] U.S. Supreme Court Justice William Brennan said that

the prisoner's eyeballs sometimes pop out and rest on [his] cheeks. The prisoner often defecates, urinates, and vomits blood and drool.

The body turns bright red as its temperature rises, and the prisoner's flesh swells and his skin stretches to the point of breaking. Sometimes the prisoner catches fire. . . . Witnesses hear a loud and sustained sound like bacon frying, and the sickly sweet smell of burning flesh permeates the chamber.[205]

After death, "the body is hot enough to blister if touched, and the autopsy is delayed while the internal organs cool. There are third degree burns with blackening where the electrodes met the skin of the scalp and legs." And the brain is turned to mush.[206]

The benefits of death by electrocution are that it is a cheap method to use, and it typically leads to instantaneous death. The drawbacks include numerous botched executions, and a disgusting mess to clean up afterward.[207] Another drawback is that the stationary electric chair meant a single, centralized location for executions, often far from the location of the crime for which the person was convicted and sentenced to death. This meant that people most affected by crimes such as murder would be less likely to witness executions. Further, until very recently, only two photos of people being executed were circulated in the press, meaning most people could never see what an electrocution looked like.

Lethal Gas

Five states authorize the gas chamber, including Arizona, California, Maryland, Missouri, and Wyoming. However, Wyoming authorizes the gas chamber only if lethal injection is found to be unconstitutional. In Arizona, those sentenced before November 15, 1992, may select lethal gas. In Maryland, inmates who committed their offenses before March 25, 1994, can choose lethal gas. In California, inmates can choose lethal gas. In Missouri, both lethal injection and lethal gas are authorized. According to the Death Penalty Information Center: "The statute leaves unclear who decides what method to use, the inmate or the Director of the Missouri Department of Corrections." [208]

Lethal gas was originally intended to kill inmates in their cells. Nevada was the first state to authorize lethal gas, in 1921. Nevada officials believed gas would be more humane than either hanging or the firing squad, which were Nevada's current methods of execution.[209] Another 11 states adopted the gas chamber by 1955, apparently in part because of Nevada's successes in executing offenders painlessly using the method. Of the 11 states, all but 3 were without the electric chair.[210] North Carolina, Mississippi, and New Mexico switched from the electric chair to the gas chamber.

The use of cyanide gas was introduced as Nevada sought a more humane way of executing its inmates. Like with electrocution, gas had previously been used successfully to kill animals. Gassing inmates in their cells proved to be impractical and thus the gas chamber was born.

The process works like this:

> Inmates are strapped to a chair in an airtight chamber. Below the chair rests a pail of sulfuric acid. A long stethoscope is typically affixed to the inmate so that a doctor outside the chamber can pronounce death. Once everyone has left the chamber, the room is sealed, and the executioner flicks a lever that releases crystals of sodium cyanide into the pail. This causes a chemical reaction that releases lethal hydrogen cyanide gas. The prisoner is instructed to breathe deeply to speed up the process. Most prisoners, however, try to hold their breath, and some struggle. Inmates typically do not lose consciousness immediately, and according to former San Quenton, California, Penitentiary warden, Clifton Duffy: "At first there is evidence of extreme horror, pain, and strangling. The eyes pop. The skin turns purple and the victim begins to drool."[211]

As it turns out, lethal gas is also not so humane after all.[212] Botched executions are also common.[213]

Further, gas was not intended to kill instantly, making it far less impressive than electrocution as a means to kill human beings. Many early executions using gas, as well as some of the last ever conducted, caused horrible pain and prolonged death, and were horrific to watch.

CONCLUSION

This chapter showed that America's history of capital punishment is long and varied. From the colonial period to the middle of the 20th century, fewer crimes led to death sentences; executions became more rare; executions became private events; methods of execution changed from brutal and violent methods to clean, medical methods; and states instituted numerous procedures and protections in an effort to ensure that death sentences were imposed fairly and rationally. In spite of all this, the practice of capital punishment is being challenged on grounds that it is still unfair and irrational, and that even lethal injection is not a humane method of death.

Currently, the death penalty is legal in 37 states, the federal government, and the military, making the United States the only Western, industrialized country that practices capital punishment. Yet, executions are extremely rare events in the United States, as only nine states have executed at least one person a year since 1976, and almost all of those are in the South. Critics maintain that the death penalty is thus plagued by a geographic bias based on legal and cultural differences between American states.

In the next chapter, I examine capital punishment law, including substantive criminal laws that define which crimes are eligible for death, procedural criminal laws that specify the procedures for capital punishment systems in the United States, and case laws that interpret and set limits on the substantive and procedural criminal law. I also examine how and why capital punishment is still legal in the United States, in spite of its alleged problems. I achieve this by discussing in depth four of the most significant cases ever decided by the U.S. Supreme Court pertaining to capital punishment.

ENDNOTES

1. Banner, S. (2003). *The death penalty: An American history.* Cambridge, MA: Harvard University Press.
2. Death Penalty Information Center. (2006g). *History of the death penalty.* Retrieved from http://deathpenaltyinfo.org/article.php?did=199&scid=15
3. McAllister, P. (2003). *Death defying: Dismantling the execution machinery in the 21st century U.S.A.* New York: The Continuum International Publishing Group.
4. For an excellent summary of ancient executions, medieval executions, and early modern executions, see Johnson, R. (1998). *Death work: A Study of the modern execution process.* Belmont, CA: Wadsworth.
5. Death Penalty Information Center (2006g).
6. As noted in the preface, there is actually not an "American system of capital punishment," nor is there an "American pattern" or "single national profile." See Zimring, F. (2003). *The contradictions of American capital punishment.* New York: Oxford University Press, p. 7. Our system of *federalism* has allowed huge variation in death penalty practice across states. Thus, "There are huge differences in policy and in execution risk among the states of the Union, differences so great that it seems foolhardy to talk of 'an American policy' on the death penalty" (p. 84).
7. For a detailed discussion with examples across states, see Acker, J., & Lanier, C. (2003). Beyond human ability? The rise and fall of death penalty legislation. In J. Acker, B. Bohm, & C. Lanier (Eds.), *America's experiment with capital punishment: Reflections on the past, present, and future of the ultimate penal sanction* (2nd ed.). Durham, NC: Carolina Academic Press.
8. Acker & Lanier (2003).
9. For an excellent summary of recent capital punishment activity at the state level, see Lifton, R., & Mitchell, G. (2000). *Who owns death? Capital punishment, the American conscience, and the end of executions.* New York: William Morrow.
10. Acker & Lanier (2003).
11. For more on these issues, see Bohm, B. (2003). *Deathquest II: An introduction to the theory and practice of capital punishment in the United States* (2nd ed.). Cincinnati, OH: Anderson.

12. Bohm (2003).
13. Bedau, H. A. (1997). *The death penalty in America: Current controversies*. New York: Oxford University Press, p. 21.
14. Death Penalty Information Center. (2006j). *Number of executions by state and region since 1976*. Retrieved from http://deathpenaltyinfo.org/article.php?scid=8&did=186
15. Bohm (2003); Zimring (2003).
16. Scheidegger, K. (2004). Smoke and mirrors on race and the death penalty. *Engage*, 4(2), 42–45.
17. Bohm (2003).
18. Death Penalty Information Center. (2006k). *State execution rates*. Retrieved from http://deathpenaltyinfo.org/article.php?scid=8&did=477
19. Death Penalty Information Center. (2006d). *Death sentencing rate by state, 1977–1999*. Retrieved from http://www.deathpenaltyinfo.org/article.php?scid=67&did=915
20. Death Penalty Information Center (2006k).
21. Bureau of Justice Statistics. (2006). *Results from state-level homicide characteristics database, number of homicides in Texas by year*. Retrieved from http://bjsdata.ojp.usdoj.gov/dataonline/Search/Homicide/State/RunHomTrendsInOneVar.cfm
22. Death Penalty Information Center. (2006c). *Death sentences in the United States from 1977 to 2004*. Retrieved from http://www.deathpenaltyinfo.org/article.php?scid=9&did=847
23. For the definitive examination of the Texas death penalty system, see Sorensen, J., & Pilgrim, R. (2006). *Lethal injection: Capital punishment in Texas during the modern era*. Austin: University of Texas Press.
24. Bedau, H. (2004). An abolitionist's survey of the death penalty in America today. In H. Bedau & P. Cassell (Eds.), *Debating the death penalty: Should America have capital punishment? The experts from both sides make their case*. New York: Oxford University Press, p. 24.
25. McAllister (2003), p. 21.
26. Zimring, F., & Hawkins, G. (1986). *Capital punishment and the American agenda*. Cambridge, UK: Cambridge University Press.
27. Zimring (2003), p. 5.
28. Death Penalty Information Center. (2006b). *The death penalty: An international perspective*. Retrieved from http://www.deathpenaltyinfo.org/article.php?did=127&scid=30#ar
29. Zimring (2003), p. 5.
30. Bedau, H. (1982). *The death penalty in America*. New York: Oxford University Press.
31. State of Illinois. (2002, April). *Report on the Commission on Capital Punishment*. Retrieved from http://www.idoc.state.il.us/ccp/ccp/reports/commission_report/
32. Paternoster, R., Brame, R., Bacon, S., Ditchfield, A., Biere, D., Beckman, K., et al. (2003). *An empirical analysis of Maryland's death sentencing system with*

respect to the influence of race and legal jurisdiction. Retrieved from http://www.newsdesk.umd.edu/pdf/finalrep.pdf

33. Unah, I., & Boger, J. (2001). *Race and the death penalty in North Carolina: An empirical analysis: 1993–1997.* Retrieved from http://www.unc.edu/~jcboger/NCDeathPenaltyReport2001.pdf

34. Baime, D. (2001). *Report to the Supreme Court Systematic Proportionality Review Project 2000–2001 term.* Retrieved from http://www.judiciary.state.nj.us/baime/baimereport.pdf

35. Equal Justice USA, Quixote Center. Retrieved from http://www.quixote.org/ej/

36. Pollak, S. (2006). *Stop Ga. death penalty until problems solved, report says.* Law.com. Retrieved from http://www.law.com/jsp/article.jsp?id=1138701911792

37. American Bar Association. (2006). *Evaluating fairness and accuracy in state death penalty systems: The Alabama Death Penalty Assessment Report.* Retrieved from http://www.sentencing.nj.gov/downloads/pdf/articles/2006/Jun2006/document2.pdf

38. American Bar Association. (2006). *News release: Arizona legal team urges reforms of state death penalty system, identifies broad problem areas.* Retrieved from http://www.abanet.org/media/releases/news071706.html

39. American Bar Association. (2006). *Death Penalty Moratorium Implementation Project.* Retrieved from http://www.abanet.org/moratorium/

40. Death Penalty Information Center. (2006a). *Changes in death penalty laws around the U.S.: 2000–2005.* Retrieved from http://www.deathpenaltyinfo.org/article.php?did=236&scid=40#AL

41. Death Penalty Information Center. (2006i). *News and developments—arbitrariness. The difference between life and death: Comprehensive Ohio study concludes that who lives and who dies depends on race, geography and plea bargains.* Retrieved from http://www.deathpenaltyinfo.org/newsanddev.php?scid=71&scyr=2005

42. U.S. Department of Justice. (2000). *Survey of the federal death penalty system.* Retrieved from http://www.usdoj.gov/dag/pubdoc/dpsurvey.html

43. Klein, S., Berk, R., & Hickman, L. (2006). *Race and the decision to seek the death penalty in federal cases.* Rand Corporation. Retrieved from http://rand.org/pubs/technical_reports/TR389/

44. Bonczar, T., & Snell, T. (2005). *Capital punishment, 2005.* Retrieved from http://www.ojp.usdoj.gov/bjs/pub/ascii/cp04.txt

45. Robinson, M. (2005). *Justice blind? Ideals and realities of American criminal justice* (2nd ed.). Upper Saddle River, NJ: Prentice Hall.

46. Bohm, B. (1999). *Deathquest: An introduction to the theory and practice of capital punishment in the United States.* Cincinnati, OH: Anderson, p. 45; also see Freedman, E. (1998). Federal habeas corpus in capital cases. In J. Acker, B. Bohm, & C. Lanier (Eds.), *America's experiment with capital punishment: Reflections on the past, present, and future of the ultimate penal sanction.* Durham, NC: Carolina Academic Press.

47. Liebman, J., Fagan, J., & West, V. (2000). *A broken system: Error rates in capital cases, 1973–1995.* Columbia University Law School. Retrieved from http://www.law.columbia.edu/instructionalservices/liebman

48. Liebman, Fagan, & West (2000).

49. United States District Court, Southern District of New York, *U.S. v. Quinones* S3 00 Cr. 761. Retrieved from http://www.nysd.uscourts.gov/rulings/quinones.pdf

50. Cook, P., Slawson, D., & Gries, L. (1993). *The costs of processing murder cases in North Carolina.* Retrieved from http://www-pps.aas.duke.edu/people/faculty/cook/comnc.pdf

51. Espy, M., & Smykla, J. (1987). *Executions in the United States, 1608–1987: The ESPY file* [machine-readable data file]. Tuscaloosa, AL: John Ortiz Smykla (producer). Ann Arbor, MI: Inter-university Consortium for Political and Social Research, University of Michigan (distributor).

52. Espy, personal correspondence. Reported in Bohm (1999), p. 2.

53. Bedau (1997).

54. Bohm (1999), p. 1.

55. Banner (2003), p. 6.

56. Banner (2003), p. 6.

57. McAllister (2003), pp. 18–19.

58. Bedau (1997).

59. Bohm (1999), p. 2.

60. McAllister (2003), p. 18.

61. For an excellent summary of the English experience, see Laurence, J. (1960). *A history of capital punishment.* New York: Citadel Press.

62. Bedau (2004).

63. Banner (2003), p. 6.

64. Banner (2003), p. 6.

65. Banner (2003), pp. 7–9, 137.

66. Bohm (2003). Executions of people who committed crimes up until the age of 18 were permissible until 2005 when the U.S. Supreme Court decided the case of *Roper v. Simmons* (2005).

67. Johnson (1998), p. 28.

68. Banner (2003), p. 11.

69. Banner (2003), p. 13.

70. Banner (2003), pp. 54, 70.

71. Banner (2003), pp. 71, 75, 76.

72. Banner (2003), p. 13.

73. Banner (2003), p. 14.

74. Robinson (2005).

75. Banner (2003), p. 22.

76. Banner (2003), p. 18.

77. Since the earliest days of America to the current day, abolitionist activity has gone through numerous historical cycles. The first was in the late 1700s (when some states abolished capital punishment for some offenses); the

second was in the 1830s (which led to the end of mandatory death sentences); the third occurred in the last years of the 19th century (which helped end public executions); the fourth took place in the late 1960s (which helped temporarily halt executions in the United States); the last is currently under way (which is chipping away at the number of death sentences and executions over time). See Haines, H. (1996). *Against capital punishment: The anti-death penalty movement in America, 1972–1994*. New York: Oxford University Press.

78. Banner (2003), p. 97.
79. Banner (2003), p. 90.
80. Banner (2003), p. 88.
81. Banner (2003), p. 88.
82. Bohm (2003).
83. Banner (2003), pp. 91–92.
84. Banner (2003), p. 89.
85. Banner (2003), p. 98.
86. Banner (2003), pp. 113–114.
87. Banner (2003), p. 99.
88. Banner (2003), p. 102.
89. Banner (2003), p. 103.
90. Banner (2003), p. 104.
91. Bohm (2003).
92. Bedau (1997).
93. Death Penalty Information Center. (2006e). *The federal death penalty*. Retrieved from http://www.deathpenaltyinfo.org/article.php?scid= 29&did=147
94. Lifton & Mitchell (2000), p. 31.
95. Banner (2003), p. 24.
96. Banner (2003), p. 25.
97. Banner (2003), p. 28.
98. Banner (2003), pp. 30–31.
99. Banner (2003), pp. 51–52.
100. Acker, J., Bohm, B., & Lanier, C. (1998). *America's experiment with capital punishment: Reflections on the past, present, and future of the ultimate penal sanction*. Durham, NC: Carolina Academic Press.
101. Banner (2003), p. 215.
102. Beginning in 1976, with the Supreme Court case *Woodson v. North Carolina*, mandatory death sentences became unconstitutional in a 5–4 decision. The Court ruled that mandatory death penalty statutes were "cruel and unusual" because they violated the Eighth and Fourteenth Amendments to the U.S. Constitution.
103. Banner (2003), p. 131.
104. Banner (2003), p. 134.
105. Banner (2003), p. 131.
106. Banner (2003), pp. 112–113.
107. Banner (2003), p. 139.

108. Bedau (1997).
109. Bohm (1999), pp. 6–7.
110. Banner (2003), pp. 134–135. Still, one noted abolitionist outlines the successes of the abolition movement thus far in the United States. They include degrees of murder, an end to public executions, the introduction of discretion into jury deliberations, a humanizing of execution methods, an increase in federal appellate intervention, and outright abolition of the death penalty in some states. See Bedau (2004), pp. 16–24.
111. Banner (2003), pp. 146, 149, 152.
112. Bessler, J. (1997). *Death in the dark: Midnight executions in America*. Boston: Northeastern University Press, p. 4.
113. Laurence (1960), p. 183.
114. Johnson (1998), pp. 29–30.
115. Banner (2003), p. 154.
116. Bessler (1997), p. 206.
117. Johnson (1998), p. 40.
118. Banner (2003), p. 155.
119. Ryan, P. (1992). *The last public execution in America*. Retrieved from http://www.geocities.com/lastpublichang
120. Banner (2003), p. 156.
121. Banner (2003), p. 162.
122. Bessler (1997).
123. Banner (2003), p. 168.
124. Johnson (1998), p. 31.
125. Johnson (1998), p. 41.
126. Bessler (1997), p. 81.
127. Bessler (1997), p. 82.
128. Bessler (1997), p. 82.
129. Bessler (1997), p. 84.
130. Laurence (1960), p. 169.
131. Death Penalty Information Center (2006g).
132. Banner (2003), p. 223.
133. For more on these cases, see Bohm (2003).
134. Bedau (1982).
135. Banner (2003), p. 227.
136. Schneider, V., & Smykla, J. (1991). A summary analysis of "Executions in the United States, 1608–1987: The ESPY File." In B. Bohm (Ed.), *The death penalty in America: Current research*. Cincinnati, OH: Anderson.
137. Bedau (1997), p. 9.
138. Banner (2003), p. 108.
139. Bohm (1999), p. 13.
140. Bohm (1999), p. 7.
141. Death Penalty Information Center (2006g).
142. Bohm (1999), p. 10.
143. Banner (2003), p. 241; also see Bohm (1999), pp. 9–10.

144. Banner (2003), p. 244.
145. Quoted in Laurence (1960), pp. xxv–xxvi.
146. Bohm (1999), p. 11.
147. Bohm (1999), p. 23.
148. Bohm (1999), p. 24.
149. Acker, Bohm, & Lanier (1998).
150. Bohm (1999), p. 25.
151. Bohm (1999).
152. Bedau (1997), pp. 15–16.
153. Bohm (2003).
154. Bohm (1999), p. 13.
155. Death Penalty Information Center. (2006f). *Federal executions 1927–2003.* Retrieved from http://www.deathpenaltyinfo.org/article.php?scid=29&did=149
156. Zimring (2003), p. 188.
157. Doyle, C. (1996). *Antiterrorism and Effective Death Penalty Act of 1996: A summary.* Retrieved from http://www.fas.org/irp/crs/96-499.htm
158. Death Penalty Information Center (2006e).
159. Bohm (2003).
160. Death Penalty Information Center (2006e).
161. Death Penalty Information Center (2006l). *The U.S. military death penalty.* Retrieved from http://deathpenaltyinfo.org/article.php?did=180&scid=32
162. Bohm (2003).
163. Bohm (2003).
164. U.S. Army. (2006). Army Regulation 190-55, *U.S. Army corrections system: Procedures for military executions.* Retrieved from http://www.fas.org/irp/doddir/army/r190_55.pdf
165. Costanzo, M. (1997). *Just revenge: The costs and consequences of the death penalty.* New York: St. Martin's Press, pp. 13–15.
166. Zimring (2003).
167. McAllister (2003), pp. 37–40.
168. Death Penalty Information Center (2006e).
169. Death Penalty Information Center. (2003). *Description of execution methods.* Retrieved from http://www.deathpenaltyinfo.org/article.php?scid=8&did=479
170. For more on this method of execution, see Denno, D. (2003). Lethally humane? The evolution of execution methods in the United States. In J. Acker, B. Bohm, & C. Lanier (Eds.), *America's experiment with capital punishment: Reflections on the past, present, and future of the ultimate penal sanction.* Durham, NC: Carolina Academic Press; Gillespie, L. (2003). *Inside the death chamber: Exploring executions.* Upper Saddle River, NJ: Prentice Hall; Lifton & Mitchell (2000).
171. Zimring (2003), p. 50.
172. Zimring (2003), p. 51.
173. Denno (2003), p. 701.

174. Wilson, C. (2006, January 30). Indiana inmate executed amid federal court drama. Law.com. Retrieved from http://www.law.com/jsp/article.jsp?id=1138356402268

175. *The New York Times*. (2006, April 26). Lethal cruelty. Retrieved from http://select.nytimes.com/gst/abstract.html?res=F40E15F7395B0C758EDDAD0894DE404482

176. Weigl, A. (2006, April 21). North Carolina first to monitor consciousness of inmate during lethal injection. *The News & Observer*. Retrieved from http://www.constitutioncenter.org/education/TeachingwithCurrentEvents/ConstitutionNewswire/16062.shtml

177. *Mainichi Daily News*. (2006, May 9). North Carolina man executed in U.S. for 1983 killing. Retrieved from http://mdn.mainichi-msn.co.jp/international/news/20060421p2g00m0in044000c.html

178. Word, R. (2006, April 25). High court to consider appeal on last-minute challenges to injection executions. Law.com. Retrieved from http://www.law.com/jsp/article.jsp?id=1145885163985

179. Wilson (2006), p. 2.

180. Holland, G. (2006, April 28). Supreme Court refuses to broaden death penalty review. Law.com. Retrieved from http://www.law.com/jsp/article.jsp?id=1141047296548

181. Denno (2003), p. 698.

182. Wilson (2006).

183. Cable News Network. (2006, May 2). Killer executed the hard way. Retrieved from http://www.cnn.com/2006/LAW/05/02/lethal.injection.reut/index.html

184. *Nelson v. Campbell*, 541 U.S. 637 (2004).

185. Denno (2003), p. 715.

186. Denno (2003), p. 721.

187. Davey, M. (2006, July 15). Missouri says it can't hire doctor for executions. *The New York Times*. Retrieved from http://www.nytimes.com/2006/07/15/us/15lethal.html?ex=1310616000&en=a36c6cb76aa3ccc3&ei=5088&partner=rssnyt&emc=rss

188. Lifton & Mitchell (2000), p. 44.

189. Banner (2003), p. 44.

190. Bohm (2003).

191. Death Penalty Information Center (2003). For more on the drop, and other innovations in hanging over the years, see Laurence (1960).

192. For more on this method of execution, see Denno (2003); Gillespie (2003); Lifton & Mitchell (2000).

193. Banner (2003), p. 203.

194. Banner (2003), p. 203.

195. Death Penalty Information Center (2003). For more on this method of execution, see Denno (2003); Gillespie (2003); Lifton & Mitchell (2000).

196. Borg, M., & Radelet, M. (2004). On botched executions. In P. Hodgkinson & W. Schabas (Eds.), *Capital punishment: Strategies for abolition*. Cambridge, UK: Cambridge University Press.

197. Gillespie (2003), p. 56.
198. Banner (2003), pp. 181–182.
199. Laurence (1960), p. 64.
200. Banner (2003), p. 186.
201. Banner (2003), p. 186.
202. Banner (2003), p. 169.
203. For more on this method of execution, see Denno (2003); Gillespie (2003); Lifton & Mitchell (2000).
204. Death Penalty Information Center (2003).
205. *Hindustan Times*. (2004). Execution methods around the world. Retrieved from http://www.hindustantimes.com/news/181_854462,001600690000.htm
206. Death Penalty Information Center (2003).
207. For more on botched executions in the United States, see Borg & Radelet (2004). These authors identified 34 total botched executions from 1977 through 2001, or 4.5% of all executions during this time period. The most botched executions were for lethal gas (18.2%), followed by electrocution (6.7%) and lethal injection (3.8%). Botched executions included noninstantaneous death, evidence of a painful death, and evidence of a lingering death.
208. Death Penalty Information Center. (2006h). *Method of execution*. Retrieved from http://www.deathpenaltyinfo.org/article.php?scid=8&did=245
209. Banner (2003), p. 196.
210. Banner (2003), p. 199.
211. Death Penalty Information Center (2003).
212. For more on this method of execution, see Denno (2003); Gillespie (2003); Lifton & Mitchell (2000).
213. Borg & Radelet (2004).

DEATH PENALTY LAW

INTRODUCTION

As noted in Chapter 1, the practice of capital punishment was temporarily halted in the United States from 1972 to 1976. In this chapter, I explain how and why this happened, and also discuss other important death penalty laws. I differentiate substantive criminal laws (that define which crimes are eligible for death), procedural criminal laws (that specify the procedures for capital punishment systems in the United States), and case law (that interprets and sets limits on the substantive and procedural criminal law). Most important is a discussion of the issue of consistency in death penalty case law by the U.S. Supreme Court. This final section of the chapter might just explain how and why capital punishment is still legal in the United States, in spite of its rare implementation and the problems that allegedly characterize its use. This chapter, like the last, forms a solid foundation on which to base an evaluation of the death penalty as it is actually practiced in the United States.

DEATH PENALTY LAW

There are three important types of death penalty law. First, *substantive law*, which is created by state legislatures and the U.S. Congress, defines the crimes that are eligible for death and sets forth the punishment as death or some other sanction. Second, *procedural law*, which is also created by state legislatures and the U.S. Congress, sets forth the procedures that must be followed in order to carry out the law. For example, as discussed in the last chapter, in order to execute a person, certain conditions must be followed, depending on the level of government. Finally, *case law*, which is made by courts when they hear and decide cases, interprets the meaning of the substantive and procedural law. Here, U.S. Supreme Court cases are most relevant, telling us which criminal laws are constitutional and which are not. The procedures of capital punishment were discussed in the last chapter.

Statutory Law

As explained in the previous chapter, 39 jurisdictions authorize the use of capital punishment. This includes 37 states, the federal government, and the U.S. military. The crimes for which a person may be executed depend on the laws of each jurisdiction. Table 2.1 shows the crimes for which a person can be executed if convicted in various states.

Every state allows a person to be executed for *aggravated murder*. In some states, this includes *felony murder* and murders committed in furtherance of a narcotics conspiracy or during commission of a crime of terrorism. Yet, some states legally permit citizens to be executed after conviction for other crimes, including treason; train wrecking; capital drug trafficking; capital sexual battery; aggravated rape of a victim under age 12; perjury causing execution or death; aircraft hijacking or piracy; and aggravated kidnapping.

Table 2.2 illustrates the crimes for which a person can be executed by the U.S. government if convicted in a federal court.

The federal government also permits executions of people convicted of capital murder, as well as for the crimes of espionage; treason; trafficking in large quantities of drugs; and attempting, authorizing, or advising the killing of any officer, juror, or witness in cases involving a continuing criminal enterprise (CCE), regardless of whether such killing actually occurs.

You might be wondering if it is possible for a person to be executed for a crime other than murder. From 1977—when the U.S. Supreme Court held in *Coker v. Georgia* that capital punishment is an excessive punishment for rape (of an adult woman)[1]—until 2003, no person had been sentenced to death for a crime other than murder. In fact, no one has been executed in the United States for a nonhomicide offense since 1964.[2]

However, a Louisiana man was sentenced to death in 2003 for raping his 8-year-old stepdaughter. Apparently, the Louisiana Supreme Court plans on allowing this execution because in 1996 it held that the 1995 statute passed constitutional muster.[3] According to the Court, the *Coker* precedent did not apply because this case dealt with a child victim.

TABLE 2.1 Capital Offenses, by State, 2004

Alabama—Intentional murder with 18 aggravating factors (Ala. Stat. Ann. 13A-5-40(a)(1)-(18)).

Arizona—First-degree murder accompanied by at least 1 of 10 aggravating factors (A.R.S. sec. 13-703(F)).

Arkansas—Capital murder (Ark. Code Ann. 5-10-101) with a finding of at least 1 of 10 aggravating circumstances; treason.

California—First-degree murder with special circumstances; train wrecking; treason; perjury causing execution.

Colorado—First-degree murder with at least 1 of 17 aggravating factors; treason.

Connecticut—Capital felony with 8 forms of aggravated homicide (C.G.S. 53a-54b).

Delaware—First-degree murder with aggravating circumstances.

Florida—First-degree murder; felony murder; capital drug trafficking; capital sexual battery.

Georgia—Murder; kidnapping with bodily injury or ransom when the victim dies; aircraft hijacking; treason.

Idaho—First-degree murder with aggravating factors; aggravated kidnapping; perjury resulting in death.

Illinois—First-degree murder with 1 of 21 aggravating circumstances.

Indiana—Murder with 16 aggravating circumstances (IC 35-50-2-9).

Kansas—Capital murder with 8 aggravating circumstances (KSA 21-3439).

Kentucky—Murder with aggravating factors; kidnapping with aggravating factors (KRS 532.025).

Louisiana—First-degree murder; aggravated rape of victim under age 12; treason (La. R.S.14:30, 14:42, and 14:113).

Maryland—First-degree murder, either premeditated or during the commission of a felony, provided that certain death eligibility requirements are satisfied.

Mississippi—Capital murder (97-3-19(2)MCA); aircraft piracy (97-25-55(1) MCA).

Missouri—First-degree murder (565.020 RSMO 2000).

Montana—Capital murder with 1 of 9 aggravating circumstances (46-18-303 MCA); capital sexual assault (45-5-503 MCA).

Nebraska—First-degree murder with a finding of at least 1 statutorily defined aggravating circumstance.

Nevada—First-degree murder with at least 1 of 15 aggravating circumstances (NRS 200.030, 200.033, 200.035).

New Hampshire—Six categories of capital murder (RSA 630:1, RSA 630:5).

New Jersey—Murder by one's own conduct, by solicitation, committed in furtherance of a narcotics conspiracy, or during commission of a crime of terrorism (NJSA 2C:11-3c).

New Mexico—First-degree murder with at least 1 of 7 statutorily defined aggravating circumstances (Section 30-2-1 A, NMSA).

New York—First-degree murder with 1 of 13 aggravating factors (NY Penal Law sec. 125.27).

North Carolina—First-degree murder (NCGS sec. 14-17).

Ohio—Aggravated murder with at least 1 of 10 aggravating circumstances (O.R.C. secs. 2903.01, 2929.02, and 2929.04).

Oklahoma—First-degree murder in conjunction with a finding of at least 1 of 8 statutorily defined aggravating circumstances.

TABLE 2.1   (Continued)

Oregon—Aggravated murder (ORS 163.095).

Pennsylvania—First-degree murder with 18 aggravating circumstances.

South Carolina—Murder with 1 of 11 aggravating circumstances (sec. 16-3-20(C)(a)).

South Dakota—First-degree murder with 1 of 10 aggravating circumstances; aggravated kidnapping.

Tennessee—First-degree murder with 1 of 15 aggravating circumstances (Tenn. Code Ann. sec. 39-13-204).

Texas—Criminal homicide with 1 of 8 aggravating circumstances (TX Penal Code 19.03).

Utah—Aggravated murder (76-5-202, Utah Code Annotated).

Virginia—First-degree murder with 1 of 13 aggravating circumstances (VA Code sec. 18.2-31).

Washington—Aggravated first-degree murder.

Wyoming—First-degree murder.

Source: Adapted from "Capital Punishment, 2004," by the U.S. Department of Justice, Office of Justice Programs, Bureau of Justice Statistics, *Bulletin,* November 2005 (NCJ 211349). Retrieved February 1, 2006, from http://www.ojp.usdoj.gov/bjs/pub/ascii/cp04.txt

TABLE 2.2   Federal Capital Offenses, by Topic

- Assassination or kidnapping resulting in the death of the President or Vice President.
  18 U.S.C. 1751
  [by reference to 18 U.S.C. 1111]

- Bank-robbery-related murder or kidnapping.
  18 U.S.C. 2113

- Civil rights offenses resulting in death.
  18 U.S.C. 241, 242, 245, 247

- Crimes against persons in the United States resulting in death, committed by a person engaged in conduct transcending national boundaries.
  18 U.S.C. 2332b

- Death resulting from aircraft piracy.
  49 U.S.C. 46502

- Death resulting from offenses involving transportation of explosives, destruction of government property, or destruction of property related to foreign or interstate commerce.
  18 U.S.C. 844 (d), (f), (i)

- Destruction of aircraft, motor vehicles, or related facilities resulting in death.
  18 U.S.C. 32, 33, 34

- Death resulting from aggravated sexual abuse, sexual abuse, sexual abuse of a minor or ward, or abusive sexual conduct.
  18 U.S.C. 2241, 2242, 2243, 2244, 2245

(continued)

TABLE 2.2   (Continued)

- Espionage.
  18 U.S.C. 794
- First-degree murder.
  18 U.S.C. 1111
- Genocide.
  18 U.S.C. 1091
- Mailing of injurious articles with intent to kill or resulting in death.
  18 U.S.C. 1716
- Murder by a Federal prisoner.
  18 U.S.C. 1118
- Murder by an escaped Federal prisoner already sentenced to life imprisonment.
  18 U.S.C. 1120
- Murder committed by the use of a firearm during a crime of violence or a drug trafficking crime.
  18 U.S.C. 924 (j)
- Murder committed during a drug-related drive-by shooting.
  18 U.S.C. 36
- Murder committed at an airport serving international civil aviation.
  18 U.S.C. 37
- Murder committed during an offense against a maritime fixed platform.
  18 U.S.C. 2281
- Murder committed during an offense against maritime navigation.
  18 U.S.C. 2280
- Murder committed in a Federal Government facility.
  18 U.S.C. 930
- Murder during a hostage taking.
  18 U.S.C. 1203
- Murder during a kidnapping.
  18 U.S.C. 1201
- Murder for hire.
  18 U.S.C. 1958
- Murder involved in a racketeering offense.
  18 U.S.C. 1959
- Murder involving torture.
  18 U.S.C. 2340, 2340A
- Murder of a court officer or juror.
  18 U.S.C. 1503
- Murder of a Federal judge or law enforcement official.
  18 U.S.C. 1114
- Murder of a foreign official.
  18 U.S.C. 1116
- Murder of a member of Congress, an important executive official, or a Supreme Court Justice.
  18 U.S.C. 351
  [by reference to 18 U.S.C. 1111]

TABLE 2.2

- Murder of a State or local law enforcement official or other person aiding in a Federal investigation; murder of a State correctional officer.
18 U.S.C. 1121

- Murder of a U.S. national in a foreign country.
18 U.S.C. 1119

- Murder related to a carjacking.
18 U.S.C. 2119

- Murder related to a continuing criminal enterprise or drug trafficking offense, or drug-related murder of a Federal, State, or local law enforcement officer.
21 U.S.C. 848 (e)

- Murder related to sexual exploitation of children.
18 U.S.C. 2251

- Murder with the intent of preventing testimony by a witness, victim, or informant.
18 U.S.C. 1512

- Retaliatory murder of a member of the immediate family of law enforcement officials.
18 U.S.C. 115 (b)(3)
[by reference to 18 U.S.C. 1111]

- Retaliatory murder of a witness, victim, or informant.
18 U.S.C. 1513

- Terrorist murder of a U.S. national in another country.
18 U.S.C. 2332

- Treason.
18 U.S.C. 2381

- Use of a weapon of mass destruction resulting in death.
18 U.S.C. 2332a

- Use of chemical weapons resulting in death.
18 U.S.C. 2332c

- Willful wrecking of a train resulting in death.
18 U.S.C. 1992

Source: Federal Capital Offenses by Topic, by the Capital Defense Network, no date. Retrieved February 1, 2006, from http://www.capdefnet.org/fdprc/contents/fed_cap_off/fed_cap_right_frame.htm

When the defendant appealed his case to the U.S. Supreme Court, the Court denied his petition for certiorari (cert.) on jurisdictional grounds because its review of state–court decisions is confined to the final decisions by the highest court of the state courts. The Court may ultimately hear another appeal from this individual if the state Supreme Court refuses to hear his appeal of the death sentence or denies his appeal.

The individual sentenced to death for this rape—Patrick Kennedy, an African American man—fits the pattern of people sentenced to death for rape in U.S. history. For example, between 1930 (the year the federal government began keeping statistics on capital punishment) and 1972 (the year the U.S. Supreme Court struck down prevailing death penalty statutes), 455 men were executed for rape. All but two were in the South, and 405 were African American.[4]

South Carolina and Oklahoma also recently signed laws allowing people to be executed for sex crimes against minors, meaning there are now five states that have such laws on the books.[5] Each of these two states requires that there be more than one sexual offense committed against a person below a certain age.

Case Law

There have been scores of U.S. Supreme Court cases that have specified who can be executed, how, and under what circumstances. Many of these cases have provided special protections to defendants charged with capital crimes. Some of the most significant cases decided by the U.S. Supreme Court that impact American capital punishment practice are briefly discussed below. The discussion is not meant to be exhaustive, but rather, illustrates some of the most important cases decided by the Court.

According to capital punishment scholar Robert Bohm, every case decided by the U.S. Supreme Court prior to 1968, with only one exception, dealt with the issue of the constitutionality of different methods of execution.[6] As noted in Chapter 1, no method of execution has ever been held by the Court to be in violation of the Eighth Amendment's ban on cruel and unusual punishment (although the Court has specified which methods of punishment would be considered cruel and unusual if they were actually being used). After 1968, the U.S. Supreme Court became intimately involved with nearly every aspect of capital punishment.

Methods of Execution

In the case of *Wilkerson v. Utah* (1878), the U.S. Supreme Court found no constitutional violation in inflicting death by public shooting. It held: "Cruel and unusual punishments are forbidden by the Constitution, but the authorities referred to are quite sufficient to show that the punishment of shooting as a mode of executing the death penalty for the crime of murder in the first degree is not included in that category, within the meaning of the eighth amendment."[7] According to the Court, for a punishment to be cruel and unusual, it must involve torture or unnecessary cruelty.

In the case of *In re Kemmler* (1890), the first challenge of New York's new electric chair, the Court found that electrocution was not cruel punishment. According to the Court: "The punishment of death is not cruel, within the meaning of that word as used in the Constitution. It implies there something inhuman and barbarous, something more than the mere extinguishment of life."[8]

In *Andres v. U.S.* (1948), the Court held that hanging did not constitute cruel and unusual punishment. This was largely due to the fact that the method was the most common method utilized in the United States for most of its history.[9]

So, if execution by shooting squad, electrocution, and hanging are not cruel and unusual, what method might the Court deem cruel and unusual? In *Weems v. United States* (1910), the Court held that the meaning of the Eighth Amendment changes with time. Although it is clear that the Eighth Amendment bans excessive punishments, the Court explained that the meaning of "excessive" changes with "evolving social conditions."[10] In the decision *Trop v. Dulles* (1958), the Court specified that the meaning of the Eighth Amendment is based on the "dignity of man," that the amendment bans punishments that interfere with human dignity, and that the "limits of civilized standards" are informed by "evolving standards of decency that mark the progress of a maturing society."[11] This means that when legislatures enact punishments, juries impose it, correctional facilities carry it out, and courts approve it, they are not cruel and unnecessary. Conversely, when punishments are not enacted, used, or approved by courts, they become cruel and unusual.

As explained in Chapter 1, the most common method used today in the United States—lethal injection—is currently being challenged on grounds related to the issue of cruel and unusual punishment. Although there is no case currently before the Court that makes this argument, the Court will likely decide key challenges in the near future that will touch upon issues such as whether pain during lethal injection is acceptable under the U.S. Constitution.

Crimes Eligible for Death

The only crime for which a person is likely to be executed in the United States is capital murder. This assumption is based on several cases. First, in the case *Coker v. Georgia* (1977), the Court held that the crime of rape of an adult woman cannot lead to a death sentence unless death results.[12] In the same year, in *Eberhart v. Georgia* (1977), the Court held that the crime of kidnapping cannot lead to a death sentence unless death results.[13] In the case of *Enmund v. Florida* (1982), the Court held that felony murderers are eligible for death.[14] Felony murder is typically any death that results from the commission of a felony, whether the death was intended or not. Felony murder typically differs from aggravated murder in that it is not intentional, although both are eligible in many states for capital punishment.

Classes of People Eligible for Death

Current death penalty practice in the United States is limited to certain classes of people. That is, some capital murderers cannot be executed due to major decisions by the U.S. Supreme Court. For example, in the case of *Ford v. Wainwright* (1986), the Court held that the legally insane cannot be executed.[15] This does not mean that people who are mentally ill cannot be executed. Insanity refers to the legal defense whereby an inmate does not know right from wrong or cannot appreciate the consequences of his or her behavior. In the case of executions, this generally means that a person cannot be executed if he or she does not understand that the execution is a result of past criminal behavior or what is going to happen to him or her as a result of the execution. In reality, people with serious mental illnesses are often executed in the United States.

As for the age of the offender, in the case of *Thompson v. Oklahoma* (1988), the Court held that no one can be executed for a crime committed while under the age of 16 years old.[16] In *Stanford v. Kentucky* (1989), the Court held that the execution of people who were 17 years old at the time of their offenses is permissible under the Constitution,[17] and in *Wilkins v. Missouri* (1989), the Court held that the execution of those who were 16 years old at the time of their crimes is permissible under the Constitution.[18]

However, in the case of *Roper v. Simmons* (2004), the Court recently overturned its own precedents, ruling that the execution of any person who committed the crime under the age of 18 years is not permissible under the U.S. Constitution.[19] The ruling was based on the element of the "evolving standards of decency" implicit in the Eighth Amendment to the U.S. Constitution. By 2004, at least 30 states prohibited the juvenile death penalty, including the 12 states that rejected the death penalty altogether. In this case, the Court inferred from state legislative activity that standards of decency had changed in the United States in less than two decades.

In the case of *Penry v. Lynaugh* (1989), the Court held that states could execute offenders who were mentally retarded.[20] Yet, in *Atkins v. Virginia* (2002), the Court overturned its own precedent and held that people who are mentally retarded cannot be executed.[21] This ruling, like the *Roper* case, was based on the issue of "evolving standards of decency." By 2002, at least half of the death penalty states had passed laws forbidding the imposition of the death penalty against people with mental retardation. In reality, they can still be executed if they fail to meet the legal standards required by states (which typically requires evidence of a certain IQ or lower and some form of dysfunction).

Validity of Capital Punishment Statutes

Over the years, various capital punishment statutes have been challenged. In the case of *United States v. Jackson* (1968), the Court found to be unconstitutional a provision of the federal kidnaping statute that allowed defendants to be coerced into pleading guilty so that they would avoid the death penalty.[22] In reality, prosecutors still regularly use the death penalty as a stick to coerce defendants to plead guilty to lesser offenses in order to avoid death sentences.

Two very significant cases, *McGautha v. California* (1971) and *Crampton v. Ohio* (1971), held that unfettered jury discretion is acceptable in death sentencing and that guilt and sentence can be determined in the same deliberations by a capital jury.[23] In these cases, the Court reasoned that even when juries were not provided guidance in their deliberations (e.g., no statutorily prescribed aggravating and mitigating factors), the death penalty was still permissible. Yet, in *Furman v. Georgia* (1972), decided just one year later, the Court held that death sentences handed down in capital trials that do not provide the jury with guidance are "cruel and unusual" because they violated the Eighth and Fourteenth Amendments to the U.S. Constitution.[24] The seeming inconsistency across these cases is examined later in the chapter.

Four years later, in *Gregg v. Georgia* (1976), the Court approved new capital statutes that guided jury discretion by specifying both aggravating and mitigating factors to jurors to assist their decisions of who should live and who should die by execution.[25] Yet, it rejected, in the case of *Woodson v. North Carolina* (1976), statutes that called for mandatory death sentences for capital crimes.[26] Each of these cases is also discussed in greater depth below.

The Supreme Court also respectively rejected, in the cases of *Roberts v. Louisiana* (1977) and *Sumner v. Shuman* (1987), mandatory death sentences for the crimes of killing a police officer and murder while incarcerated.[27] It is clear from these cases that the U.S. Supreme Court will not tolerate mandatory death sentences.

Mitigating and Aggravating Statutes

Many cases decided with regard to mitigating and aggravating factors in capital cases have been decided that have benefited capital defendants. For example, in the cases of *Lockett v. Ohio* (1978) and *Bell v. Ohio* (1978), the Court held that all mitigating factors can be considered by juries whether they are in the criminal statutes or not.[28] This ruling was supported by the decision of *Hitchcock v. Dugger* (1987) and *McKoy v. North Carolina* (1990), the latter of which held that jury instructions indicating that the jury cannot consider any mitigating factors are unacceptable.[29] Even good behavior by an inmate in jail can be considered by a sentencing jury, according to the ruling in *Skipper v. South Carolina* (1986).[30]

In the case of *Mills v. Maryland* (1988), the Court held that unanimity among jurors is not required to consider a mitigating factor. Thus, juries must consider a factor that mitigates the defendant's degree of culpability even if all the jurors do not believe the mitigating factor is true.[31] In *Walton v. Arizona* (1990), the Court held that it is permissible for states to adopt a "preponderance of evidence" standard for accepting mitigating factors.[32] That is, a mitigating factor must not be proven true beyond a reasonable doubt to be considered.

One case decided by the Court—*Godfrey v. Georgia* (1980)—held that broadly stated or vague statutory aggravating factors are unconstitutional if they are not explained by the sentencing judge to the jury.[33] In fact, many states contain broadly stated or vague aggravating factors, such as those that try to separate out the worst murders from "ordinary murders" by calling them especially heinous, cruel, or depraved (whatever that means). As long as this is explained to the jury, it is acceptable.

Other decisions have benefited the government. For example, the Court held, in *Barefoot v. Estelle* (1983), that a prediction of future dangerousness by a psychiatrist is allowed as an aggravating factor.[34] This is potentially problematic because many scholars agree that it is not possible to predict future dangerousness in the majority of cases. In the case of *Barclay v. Florida* (1983), the Court held that any aggravating factor can be considered whether it is in the criminal statutes or not, as long as one statutory factor is found.[35]

Procedural Issues

The one case decided by the U.S. Supreme Court prior to 1968 that did not deal with methods of executions was *Powell v. Alabama* (1932).[36] In the *Powell* case, which involved the "Scottsboro boys," nine African American males between the ages of 13 and 21 years were arrested for the alleged rape of two white women on a train (the rapes actually did not occur). The process of capital punishment in this case was very swift—all but one of the young men was arrested, indicted, tried, convicted, and sentenced to death in only one week. Yet, none of the accused was provided with a defense attorney until the morning of the trial.

The Alabama Supreme Court overturned the convictions of only one of the young men that was convicted and sentenced to death, but upheld the convictions of the other seven. The U.S. Supreme Court overturned the convictions because the defendants were not given their right to effective assistance of counsel required by the Fourteenth Amendment's due process clause. This was true because not only were the accused not provided with attorneys but also because of "the ignorance and illiteracy of the defendants, their youth, the circumstances of public hostility, the imprisonment and the close surveillance of the defendants by the military forces, the fact that their friends and families were all in other states and communication with them was necessarily difficult, and above all they stood in deadly peril of their lives."[37] According to Bohm, the significance of the case is that it was the first time "the U.S. Supreme Court applied the Fourteenth Amendment's due process clause to capital cases adjudicated in state courts" and "it was the first in a series of cases that would extend the Sixth Amendment right to the effective assistance of counsel."[38] Later, the Court ruled in *Murray v. Giarratano* (1989) that courts are not required to provide counsel to the indigent for discretionary appeals.[39]

In the case of *Witherspoon v. Illinois* (1968), the Court held that jurors cannot be excused from jury service simply for being opposed to capital punishment; they must be excused for cause (which includes being unwilling to impose a death sentence under *any* circumstance).[40] In *Adams v. Texas* (1980), the Court held that jurors can be excluded if their views on capital punishment would not allow them to obey their oath and follow the law without conscious distortion or bias.[41] Later, in the case of *Wainwright v. Witt* (1985), the Court held that jurors should be excluded in a manner no different from how they are excluded in noncapital cases.[42] The important issue is whether a person's view prevents or impairs the performance of his or her duties as a juror. One year later, in *Lockhart v. McCree* (1986), the Court held that jurors can be removed for cause if their views against capital punishment are so strong they would impair their duties as jurors in the sentencing phase of trials.[43] Finally, in *Morgan v. Illinois* (1992), the Court held that jurors can be removed for cause if they would automatically vote for the death penalty in every case.[44] Many of these cases are revisited in Chapter 5 when the issue of problems with capital juries is examined.

The case of *Strickland v. Washington* (1984) dealt with the issue of ineffectiveness of defense counsel. In order to prove that a defendant did not have effective counsel, he or she must make a two-pronged showing, demonstrating that defense counsel's performance was deficient (e.g., falling below "prevailing professional norms") and that this deficiency caused some prejudice (e.g., the outcome of the trial would likely had been different).[45] This standard is generally viewed as one that is extremely hard to meet. In Chapter 5, I show evidence that the courts have found acceptable the counsel of some clearly incompetent attorneys.

In *Antone v. Dugger* (1984), the Court held that defendants cannot raise last-minute appeals if they could have been raised earlier.[46] This is consistent with efforts later by Congress to restrict access to the courts for those facing death sentences.

Recently, in the case of *Ring v. Arizona* (2002), the Court held that juries rather than judges must determine eligibility for the death penalty.[47] Thus, death sentences imposed by judges without approval by capital juries are no longer acceptable. This contradicted the ruling in *Spaziano v. Florida* (1984), which held that a judge override of a jury sentencing recommendation is constitutional.[48] In *Schriro v. Summerlin* (2004), the Court clarified that the decision in *Ring* is not retroactive.[49]

Sentencing

Many cases have been decided by the Court that have dealt with issues of sentencing. For example, in the case of *Beck v. Alabama* (1980), the Court held that juries must be allowed to consider convictions for lesser crimes when the evidence supports it.[50] In *Payne v. Tennessee* (1991), the Court held that victim impact statements are allowed into sentencing consideration.[51] This decision overturned the ruling in *Booth v. Maryland* (1987) which held that no victim impact statements were admissible, and that of *South Carolina v. Gathers* (1989), which held that a detailed description of the victim violated the ruling in *Booth*.[52]

In the case of *Simmons v. South Carolina* (1994), the Court held that defendants have the right to tell juries that life sentences actually mean life (i.e., life imprisonment without parole) in cases where future dangerousness is being argued by the prosecution.[53] The ruling in *Shafer v. South Carolina* (2001) is consistent with this case.[54] However, this is not required in cases where life does not actually mean life without parole, as held in *Ramdass v. Angelone* (2000).[55]

Fairness

Many cases have also been decided with regard to the issue of fairness in the capital punishment process. For example, in the case of *Pulley v. Harris* (1984), the Court held that proportionality review of death sentences is not required by state appellate courts. As a result of this ruling, some states simply no longer conduct these reviews, aimed at distinguishing between those murders that receive death sentences and those that do not.[56]

In *Miller-El v. Dretke* (2004), the Court held that jurors cannot be excused based on race-specific factors if race-neutral explanations are invalid.[57] In the case, a prosecutor used peremptory challenges to excuse

African Americans from a jury pool and his explanation for the use of the peremptory challenges was not reasonable. This is consistent with the decision in *Batson v. Kentucky* (1986) which held that using peremptory challenges to exclude minorities is unacceptable.[58] Similarly, the Court held, in *Vasquez v. Hillery* (1986), that an indictment by an all-white grand jury where African Americans were systematically excluded was unconstitutional.[59] Further, in the case of *Turner v. Murray* (1986), the Court held that the defendant has the right to ask potential jurors about their possible racial biases.[60]

In *McCleskey v. Kemp* (1987)—considered by many to be the last serious challenge to the death penalty itself—the Court found that statistical patterns indicating racial disparities in punishment are not enough to determine that the application of capital punishment is discriminatory.[61] Because of this ruling, defendants must show that they were discriminated against as individuals or that the legislature of the state meant to enact discriminatory law (a burden that is impossible to meet). This case is discussed in greater detail below.

In the case of *Sawyer v. Whitley* (1992), the Court held that in order to show actual innocence in a habeas corpus writ, the defendant must show by clear and convincing evidence that no reasonable juror would have imposed a death sentence except for a constitutional error.[62] One year later, in *Herrera v. Collins* (1993), the Court held that a claim of actual innocence based on newly discovered evidence is not grounds for granting a new hearing in a federal court.[63] In 1995, the Court changed the standard to probable innocence in the case of *Schlup v. Delo* (1995).[64]

Consistency by the Supreme Court?

The term *inconsistent* means "lacking consistency; as not compatible with another fact or claim; containing incompatible elements."[65] Supreme Court activity regarding the death penalty has been very inconsistent over the years. Both insider accounts of Court operations[66] and analyses of private papers of Supreme Court justices[67] show wide inconsistencies across all stages of Court activity. Inconsistencies appear in Court decisions to grant or deny certiorari, in conference discussions among justices, in circulated drafts of preliminary opinions, in the final written opinions of the justices, and most surprisingly, in opinions across time. The brief review of the cases above illustrate several examples of inconsistency over time in the ruling of the U.S. Supreme Court.

One might wonder how Supreme Court activity could be "lacking [in] consistency; as not compatible with another fact or claim; containing incompatible elements," especially when lives hang in the balance as they do with the death penalty cases. Apparently, even among Supreme Court justices, capital punishment is such a contentious issue that it seems to breed inconsistency. Lazarus explains that

> the issue of the death penalty provides an especially revealing view into the Court's work as a whole. Death penalty cases, both now and in the past, cut to the root of the Court's ideological divisions. In the terrible context of a choice between life and death, these cases raise many of the issues that have divided the legal world since the Civil War, including issues about the Court's own role and authority.[68]

An examination of what are probably the four most important cases decided by the Supreme Court, cases that had the largest influence on the administration of capital punishment in the United States—*Furman v. Georgia* (1972),[69] *Gregg v. Georgia* (1976),[70] *Woodson v. North Carolina* (1976),[71] and *McCleskey v. Kemp* (1987)[72]—provides some understanding of how and why the Supreme Court is so inconsistent when it comes to the death penalty. These are the cases I refer to as the "Big Four."[73]

The Big Four

Of the many important cases decided by the U.S. Supreme Court with regard to capital punishment, four cases stand out as the most important because they determined how capital punishment is actually practiced in America. They are *Furman v. Georgia* (1972), *Gregg v. Georgia* (1976), *Woodson v. North Carolina* (1976), and *McCleskey v. Kemp* (1987).[74]

The Court invalidated all capital punishment statutes in effect in *Furman*, but failed to abolish it once and for all. By outlining the problems with the way that American jurisdictions practiced the death penalty, the Court set the stage for changes to state laws that would be accepted by the Court in *Gregg*, and others that would be rejected by the Court in *Woodson*. These three cases determined that (1) capital punishment itself was constitutional; and (2) that first-degree murderers could be executed only under certain circumstances. The case of *McCleskey* is viewed by many capital punishment scholars the last real challenge to America's death penalty experience.[75]

An analysis of these inconsistencies is critical to understanding why the death penalty is still legal in the United States. My experience teaching death penalty courses has shown me that it is these four cases that help students best understand why the Supreme Court has not invalidated death penalty statutes once and for all, in spite of the rare application of the punishment and the problems that allegedly characterize its use.

Between 1972 and 1987, a total of 12 justices were involved in deciding the constitutionality of capital punishment in the United States. These justices not only decided that the death penalty is not unconstitutional per se, thereby ensuring its continued practice, but also determined under which conditions it could or could not be used.

The Cases and the Main Justifications of Justices in Each Case

Furman v. Georgia, 408 U.S. 228 (1972)

William Henry Furman was convicted of the murder of a Coast Guard petty officer—the father of four children and the stepfather of six others. Furman was a 25-year-old African American with an IQ of only 65 who killed his victim in a failed burglary attempt.[76] This case was unusual because it did not fit the stereotypical killing in America. Because Furman was an African American and a stranger, and his victim was a white and a family man who served in the military, Furman's chance of *not* receiving the death penalty was slim, especially in a southern state with a history of racial unrest.

Furman's attorneys argued to the Supreme Court that capital punishment in Georgia was unfair because capital trials essentially gave the jury unbridled discretion about whether to impose a death sentence on convicted defendants. Consolidated with *Furman* were two cases (*Jackson v. Georgia*, No. 69-5030 and *Branch v. Texas*, No. 69-5031) that dealt with death sentences imposed against African American men for rapes of white women, a crime that has been a primary source of discriminatory punishment in American history.

The *Furman* case led to nine separate opinions by each of the justices of the Supreme Court, the longest ever opinion, and the ruling was 5–4 that the death penalty statutes in question were "cruel and unusual" because they violated the Eighth and Fourteenth Amendments to the U.S. Constitution. Justices Douglas, Brennan, Stewart, White, and Marshall wrote concurring opinions, and Justices Burger, Blackmun, Powell, and Rehnquist filed dissenting opinions. In essence, the Supreme Court found that capital punishment was being imposed "arbitrarily, infrequently, and often selectively against minorities."[77] So, it was not the method of death that was at issue; it was how the method was being applied arbitrarily and disproportionately to some groups of people.

Rohm writes: "A practical effect of *Furman* was the Supreme Court's voiding of 40 death penalty statutes and the sentences of 629 death row inmates." The Supreme Court, however, did not conclude that the death penalty per se was unconstitutional. It was unconstitutional only to the degree that it was imposed arbitrarily and unfairly. Thus, "36 states proceeded to adopt new death penalty statutes designed to meet the Court's objections."[78] States grappled to quickly pass death penalty laws that would be considered constitutional by the Supreme Court.

Nearly one third of states enacted mandatory death sentences for some crimes,[79] taking the issue of discretion of judges and juries out of the picture. Most states passed guided discretion statutes that would give juries and sentencing judges some guidelines to follow when considering death sentences. The validity of mandatory sentencing and guided sentencing approaches would be decided by the Court only 4 years later with the cases of *Woodson v. North Carolina* (1976) and *Gregg v. Georgia* (1976), respectively.

In *Furman*, each justice had a different view of what constitutes cruel and unusual punishment.

Justice Douglas defined punishment as cruel and unusual when it is discriminatory or selective in its application. He said that even though unfettered discretion was originally viewed as acceptable by the Supreme Court, even as recently as one year prior in *McGautha v. California* (1971),[80] that once a punishment is arbitrarily applied, it can be considered cruel and unusual. The death penalty as applied without juror guidance is arbitrary, which Douglas suggested was a violation of equal protection. Douglas wrote that providing no guidelines for a juror to decide who lives and who dies is unacceptable, especially given that it will ensure biases against the lower class, those with inferior attorneys, and so forth. Douglas suggested that the "discriminatory statutes are unconstitutional in their operation. They are pregnant with discrimination and discrimination is an ingredient not compatible with the idea of equal protection of the laws that is implicit in the ban on 'cruel and unusual' punishments."[81]

Justice Brennan suggested that although what is cruel and unusual is not clearly defined, to him it is something that does not comport with human dignity. Brennan developed four tests to assess whether a punishment comports with human dignity. First, any punishment that degrades human beings is offensive. Brennan wrote that the reason we outlawed brutal forms of punishment is that they violate human dignity because they treat humans as nonhumans. Second, he suggested that any arbitrary punishment, especially a severe one, is unusual: "When a country of over 200 million people inflicts an unusually severe punishment no more than 50 times a year, the inference is strong that the punishment is not being regularly and fairly applied. . . . The conclusion is virtually inescapable that it is being inflicted arbitrarily. Indeed, it smacks of little more than a lottery system."[82] Third, any punishment that is not acceptable to the public is cruel and unusual. Finally, a punishment is unnecessary if it is excessive. Brennan suggested that the death penalty is no more effective a deterrent than other punishments such as life imprisonment and thus it is unusual. Because the death penalty meets all these conditions, it is a violation of human dignity according to Brennan.

Justice Stewart also grappled with the issue of what is cruel and unusual punishment. He suggested that capital punishment is excessive because it goes beyond what states deem to be necessary and because it is arbitrarily applied. He wrote: "These death sentences are cruel and unusual in the same way that being struck by lightning is cruel and unusual . . . [they are] so wantonly and so freakishly applied."[83]

Justice White noted at the outset to his opinion that the death penalty is not unconstitutional per se and suggests that it is possible for a system of capital punishment to comport with the Eighth Amendment. He wrote that even though death is in theory a valid form of retribution and incapacitation, it does not serve either of these goals when it is used so infrequently. His main problem with the death penalty, it appears, is arbitrariness. White wrote "that the death penalty is exacted with great infrequency even for the most atrocious crimes and that there is no meaningful basis for distinguishing the few cases in which it is imposed from the many cases in which it is not."[84]

Marshall, the final justice in the majority, examined the issue of what is cruel and unusual punishment and related it to the evolving standards of decency in a maturing society. He suggested that a punishment can be cruel and unusual if it meets any of four conditions. First, a punishment is cruel and unusual if it causes too much physical pain or is excessive. Second, it is cruel and unusual if it has not been practiced prior. Third, it is cruel and unusual if it serves no valid purpose or it is unnecessary. Finally, it is cruel and unusual if popular sentiment is against it or it is immoral. Marshall attempted to shoot down all justifications for capital punishment by suggesting that the death penalty as practiced does not actually serve retribution, deterrence, or incapacitation. He also added that it is more expensive than life imprisonment.

The most significant part of the Marshall opinion is the statement of what has now been called the "Marshall hypothesis." He stated, "the question with which we must deal is not whether a substantial proportion of American citizens would today, if polled, opine that capital punishment is barbarously cruel, but whether they would find it so in the light of all information presently available."[85] Marshall put forth what he views as the reality of capital punishment and suggests that people would not support it if they knew this reality. He concluded by writing:

> I believe the following facts would serve to convince even the most hesitant of citizens to condemn death as a sanction: capital punishment is imposed discriminatorily against certain identifiable classes of people; there is evidence that innocent people have been executed before their innocence can be proved; and the death penalty wreaks havoc with our entire criminal justice system.[86]

In his dissent, Chief Justice Burger suggested that what is cruel and unusual is not clearly defined, but noted that what is unacceptable is not up to the Court but is up to legislatures of the states and to the U.S. Congress. He went on to show that the death penalty is widely supported in public opinion polls and that it is practiced in 42 jurisdictions, meaning it is not against our evolving standards of decency. Burger conceded that the death penalty is rarely applied but wrote that it would be "unrealistic to assume that juries have been perfectly consistent in choosing the cases where the death penalty is to be imposed, for no human institution performs with perfect consistency."[87] He appears to be saying that even though the death penalty is arbitrarily applied, this is acceptable because consistency is not humanly possible. Burger concluded the "claim of arbitrariness is not only lacking in empirical support, but also it manifestly fails to establish that the death penalty is a 'cruel and unusual' punishment."[88] Furthermore, Burger stated that it is not up to courts to decide the efficacy of punishment and that the U.S. Constitution does not demand that we follow informed principles of penology. He suggested that deterrence is simply not relevant to the Constitution.

He stated that the facts of majority are not supported and claims that the Court has exceeded its power in its ruling. Finally, it should be pointed out that Burger noted that decisions by a jury of our peers is crucial to our democracy and has been viewed by the Court as an advance from mandatory punishments, so to take away discretion of jurors in capital cases is a setback. Mandatory sentencing, according to Burger, gives too much power to the legislature to determine who lives and who dies.

Justice Blackmun began his dissent by noting that he is opposed to the death penalty personally but that what is right or wrong is not a Court issue. He wrote: "I yield to no one in the depth of my distaste, antipathy, and, indeed, abhorrence, for the death penalty, with all its aspects of physical distress and fear and of moral judgment exercised by finite minds. That distaste is buttressed by a belief that capital punishment serves no useful purpose that can be demonstrated."[89]

Despite these feelings, Blackmun conclusively demonstrated that society has not evolved, especially in the short time since previous cases have been decided by the Court. Blackmun suggested that the argument that society has evolved is "a good argument and it makes sense only in a legislative and executive way and not as a judicial expedient."[90] It is not a Court issue, then, but is an issue for the people to decide through its representatives. He concluded that the Court has simply exceeded its power.

Justice Powell wrote that the decision departs from the principles of stare decisis, federalism, judicial restraint, and separation of powers. He noted that the Constitution specifically says capital punishment is acceptable, that the Supreme Court repeatedly has said capital punishment is acceptable, and that legislative activity in the states refutes the evolution argument. Powell also set the stage for future challenges based on race by writing: "If a Negro defendant . . . could demonstrate that members of his race were being singled out for more severe punishment than others charged with the same offense, a constitutional violation might be established."[91] Finally, Powell predicted that only a constitutional amendment will change this ruling and said that the decision is undemocratic.

Finally, Justice Rehnquist succinctly argued that the majority's lack of judicial restraint in striking down the state statutes violates the checks and balances of the U.S. Constitution. Rehnquist offered little in the way of explanation for his dissenting opinion.

As explained earlier, after the *Furman* decision was handed down, states changed their laws in one of two ways. Some states passed mandatory death sentencing laws and some established guided discretion for jurors using bifurcated trials and a system of aggravating and mitigating circumstances to help determine which convicted murderers should be sentenced to death and which should not. The validity of these laws were decided in *Woodson* and *Gregg*.

Woodson v. North Carolina, 428 U.S. 280 (1976)

Four men were convicted of first-degree murder of a cashier as the result of their participation in an armed robbery of a convenience food store. James Tyrone Woodson, one of the participants in the crime, remained in the car with a rifle as a lookout during the robbery. He did not enter the store nor did he fire any shots. Further, Woodson claimed that he was coerced into participating in the robbery by Luby Waxton, the man who actually fired the fatal shot. Woodson, who had been drinking heavily on the day of the robbery, said that Waxton struck him in the face and threatened to kill him in an effort to make him sober up and come along on the robbery.

The two other robbery participants agreed to plead guilty to lesser charges and to testify for the prosecution and thus did not face the death penalty. During the trial, Waxton asked to be allowed to plead guilty to the same lesser offenses to which the others pleaded guilty, but he was not allowed to. Woodson maintained throughout the trial that he had been coerced by Waxton, that he was therefore innocent, and that he would not plead guilty. After his trial, Woodson was found guilty on all charges and sentenced to death under North Carolina's mandatory death penalty law.

Woodson's attorneys argued to the Supreme Court that mandatory death sentences upon conviction for murder are unconstitutional. The ruling was 5–4 that the death penalty statutes in question were "cruel and unusual" because they violated the Eighth and Fourteenth Amendments to the U.S. Constitution. Justices Stewart, Powell, Stevens, Brennan, and

Marshall were in the majority, and Justices White, Burger, Rehnquist, and Blackmun filed dissenting opinions. In essence, the Supreme Court found that mandatory death sentences violated the evolving standards of respect for human life implicit in the Eighth Amendment to the Constitution.

Justices Stewart, Powell, and Stevens, in a plurality opinion by Stewart, held that "two crucial indicators of evolving standards of decency respecting the imposition of punishment in our society—jury determinations and legislative enactments—conclusively point to the repudiation of automatic death sentences."[92] That is, society has evolved away from mandatory sentences.

The majority suggested that mandatory sentences do not eliminate arbitrariness because they do not give juries any guidance about which murderers should live and which should die (which offenders should be convicted of capital crimes and which should be convicted of lesser sentences). They also suggested that the respect for human dignity implicit in the Eighth Amendment requires

> consideration of aspects of the character of the individual offender and the circumstances of the particular offense as a constitutionally indispensable part of the process of imposing the ultimate punishment of death [and that the statute in question] impermissibly treats all persons convicted of a designated offense not as uniquely individual human beings, but as members of a faceless, undifferentiated mass to be subjected to the blind infliction of the death penalty.[93]

Justices Stewart, Powell, and Stevens found that juries often "find the death penalty inappropriate in a significant number of first-degree murder cases and refuse[] to return guilty verdicts for that crime."[94] They wrote:

> The history of mandatory death penalty statutes in the United States thus reveals that the practice of sentencing to death all persons convicted of a particular offense has been rejected as unduly harsh and unworkably rigid. . . . At least since the Revolution, American jurors have, with some regularity, disregarded their oaths and refused to convict defendants where a death sentence was the automatic consequence of a guilty verdict.[95]

Furthermore, were one to use only the actual decisions of death-qualified jurors, where most convicted murderers do not actually get sentenced to death, this would "suggest that under contemporary standards of decency death is viewed as an inappropriate punishment for a substantial portion of convicted first-degree murderers."[96]

With regard to the issue of whether there is an evolution in societal standards against capital punishment, these justices concluded that mandatory sentencing laws "reflect attempts by the States to retain the death penalty in a form consistent with the Constitution, rather than a renewed societal acceptance of mandatory death sentencing."[97] They went so far as to claim that these mandatory sentencing laws "have simply papered over the problem of unguided and unchecked jury discretion."[98]

Justice Marshall concurred in the judgment for the reasons stated in his dissent in *Gregg*, discussed below. Justice Brennan also concurred in the judgment for his reasons stated in his dissent in *Gregg*.

Justices White, Burger, Rehnquist, and Blackmun dissented in this case for reasons stated in other cases. Rehnquist's dissent is the longest and is the only one that offers any details as to the rationale for the dissent. Rehnquist suggested that the plurality of Stewart, Powell, and Stevens is simply mistaken in their assertion that society has evolved away from mandatory sentences for first-degree murderers. Rehnquist attacks the plurality by writing that the states'

> willingness to enact statutes providing that penalty is utterly inconsistent with the notion that they regarded mandatory capital sentencing as beyond "evolving standards of decency." The plurality's glib rejection of these legislative decisions as having little weight on the scale which it finds in the Eighth Amendment seems to me more an instance of its desire to save the people from themselves than a conscientious effort to ascertain the content of any "evolving standard of decency."[99]

Rehnquist also reaffirmed his belief that appellate review of sentences will remove any arbitrariness in jury decisions, and again asserted that the plurality is ignoring previous decisions such as *McGautha* which approved of unbridled jury discretion in 1971.

Gregg v. Georgia, 428 U.S. 153 (1976)

Tony Gregg was convicted of armed robbery and murder after killing two men who had picked up Gregg and fellow hitchhiker Floyd Allen. Gregg and Allen had been picked up in Florida and rode north toward Atlanta when the car broke down. The driver, Fred Simmons, was in possession of enough cash to purchase a new car. After purchasing this new car, the group picked up another hitchhiker who was let out in Atlanta. Apparently, Gregg and Allen decided to rob and kill the men after the other hitchhiker got out of the car. This hitchhiker, Dennis Weaver, contacted the police after reading about the murders in the newspaper. The next day, Gregg and Allen were arrested in North Carolina driving the victim's car and were in possession of the murder weapon.

Gregg's attorneys argued to the Supreme Court that the state's new guided discretion law was unconstitutional and asked the Court to overturn the death sentence. The ruling was handed down on the same day as *Woodson*, and was 7–2 that the death penalty statute in question was not unconstitutional because it provided guidance to jurors in deciding the fate of convicted murderers. Justices Stewart, Powell, Stevens, Burger, Rehnquist, White, and Blackmun were in the majority, and Justices Brennan and Marshall filed dissenting opinions. In essence, the Supreme Court found that the death penalty per se was not unconstitutional and the application of the death penalty under guided discretion laws was constitutional. In upholding the revised statute, the Court gave approval to the use of bifurcated trials where guilt or innocence was decided in the first phase and sentencing was decided in the second, as well as automatic appellate review of convictions and sentences, and finally, proportionality reviews to compare sentences of particular cases against similar cases to ensure just sentencing practices. Thus, suggestions made by the American Law Institute's Model Penal Code (in 1959), aimed at making the death penalty more fair, were finally put into place.

The Court actually decided five cases that day: *Gregg* (concerning Georgia's guided discretion law and use of bifurcated trials), *Woodson* (discussed above), *Roberts v. Louisiana* (1976)[100] (concerning the state's mandatory death penalty law that also allowed for lesser sentences when defendants were convicted of lesser crimes), *Jurek v. Texas* (1976)[101] (concerning the state's mandatory death penalty law which allowed jury consideration of future dangerousness of offenders), and *Proffitt v. Florida* (1976)[102] (concerning the state's guided discretion law and use of bifurcated trials). *Gregg* is discussed here because the Court issued the most specific opinion for this case.

Justices Stewart and White turned out to be the key votes in the *Gregg* decision, as each had voted to void capital punishment as practiced under *Furman* only 4 years earlier. Both of these justices concluded that Georgia's new sentencing laws would eliminate the arbitrary sentencing that gave them cause for concern in *Furman*.

Justices Stewart, Powell, and Stevens found that juries under the new laws were given guidance. They wrote:

> The concerns . . . that the death penalty not be imposed arbitrarily or capriciously can be met by a carefully drafted statute that ensures that the sentencing authority is given adequate information and guidance, concerns best met by a system that provides for a bifurcated proceeding at which the sentencing authority is apprised of the information relevant to the imposition of sentence and provided with standards to guide its use of that information.[103]

Further efforts to eliminate arbitrariness under the new laws include a state Supreme Court mandated review of the sentence, as noted by Justices White, Burger, and Rehnquist. The seven-justice majority also pointed out that juries are given the option of a lesser sentence, and that the death sentences under review were found not to be influenced by prejudice, suggesting the absence of arbitrariness.

The majority found that capital punishment is valid given that it is a democratically elected punishment, that it has a long-accepted use in the history of the United States, that there is no evidence of an evolution of standards away from the death penalty in society, and that newly passed statutes show it does not upset Americans. They explain that even though the evidence of deterrence is unclear, retribution is a valid measure of outrage over murder and thus capital punishment is justifiable.

In summary, the majority of justices quote Justice White's dissent in *Furman* by stating that with the new guidance given to jurors, "no longer should there be 'no meaningful basis for distinguishing the few cases in which [the death penalty] is imposed from the many cases in which it is not.'"[104] A similar sentence boldly claims: "No longer can a jury wantonly and freakishly impose the death sentence; it is always circumscribed by the legislative guidelines."[105]

Justice White, joined by Justices Burger and Rehnquist, discussed that life imprisonment is a possible option for juries, that juries must be unanimous in recommending the death penalty, and that the state Supreme Court provides a careful review to ensure that arbitrariness does not play a role in sentencing. Further, these justices claimed that any potential bias of prosecutors is not relevant for arbitrariness. They wrote that the

> argument that prosecutors behave in a standardless fashion in deciding which cases to try as capital felonies is unsupported by any facts . . . [the argument] that since prosecutors have the power not to charge capital felonies they will exercise that power in a standardless fashion . . . is untenable. Absent facts to the contrary, it cannot be assumed that prosecutors will be motivated in their charging decision by factors other than the strength of their case and the likelihood that a jury would impose the death penalty if it convicts.[106]

Justice Blackmun simply concurred in the judgment.

Justices Brennan and Marshall each dissented from the majority. Justice Brennan asserted again that standards of decency have changed. He wrote:

> This Court inescapably has the duty, as the ultimate arbiter of the meaning of our Constitution, to say whether, when individuals condemned to death stand before our Bar, "moral concepts" require us to hold that the law has progressed to the point where we should declare that the punishment of death, like punishments on the rack, the screw, and the wheel, is no longer morally tolerable in our civilized society. My opinion in [*Furman*] concluded that our civilization and the law had progressed to this point and that therefore the punishment of death, for whatever crime and under all circumstances, is "cruel and unusual" in violation of the Eighth and Fourteenth Amendments of the Constitution. I shall not again canvass the reasons that led to that conclusion. I emphasize only

that foremost among the "moral concepts" recognized in our cases and inherent in the Clause is the primary moral principle that the State, even as it punishes, must treat its citizens in a manner consistent with their intrinsic worth as human beings—a punishment must not be so severe as to be degrading to human dignity. A judicial determination whether the punishment of death comports with human dignity is therefore not only permitted but compelled by the Clause.[107]

In essence, Brennan concluded that it is a Court duty to regulate morality.

Justice Marshall claimed that new statutes are not informed by public opinion that is aware of the facts of capital punishment, and he even provided evidence from a study in support of his Marshall hypothesis from *Furman*. Marshall boldly claimed that the Court is wrong in concluding that death penalty is not excessive, and that the Court accepts a flawed study by Professor Isaac Ehrlich which claims a deterrent effect of the death penalty (for more on this study, see Chapter 4). He went on to refute the notion that the death penalty stops families of murder victims from taking the law into their own hands: "It simply defies belief to suggest that the death penalty is necessary to prevent the American people from taking the law into their own hands."[108] Marshall asserted that the death penalty is not necessary to stop killing and thus is excessive.

After the *Gregg* decision, capital punishment states passed new laws similar to Georgia's and began sentencing more people to death. In Georgia, the last serious challenge to the death penalty would be decided 11 years later in *McCleskey v. Kemp* (1987).

McCleskey v. Kemp, 481 U.S. 279 (1987)

Warren McCleskey joined three accomplices to rob a furniture store. McCleskey, an African American man, secured the front of the store by rounding up customers and the manager, while his accomplices entered the store from the rear. A silent alarm was tripped and a white police officer entered the front of the store. The officer was hit with two shots, killing him. McCleskey, while under arrest for an unrelated offense, admitted to the robbery but denied the shooting. Two witnesses testified at trial that McCleskey admitted to the shooting and evidence suggested that at least one of the bullets came from the type of gun that McCleskey carried during the robbery. Thus, two aggravating factors were determined beyond a reasonable doubt: that McCleskey committed a murder during the commission of an armed robbery and that he killed a peace officer engaged in the performance of his duties. No mitigating factors were offered for evidence, so the sentencing jury recommended death and McCleskey was sentenced to die by the judge.

McCleskey's attorneys argued to the Supreme Court that the administration of capital punishment in Georgia was racially biased against African

Americans. The Court heard testimony from Professor David Baldus and others who showed in a statistical study that the death penalty was applied disproportionately to African Americans in Georgia. The study utilized a multiple regression analysis including 230 variables likely to effect the outcome of death penalty cases in order to test the hypothesis that race of defendant and race of victim played a role in death penalty sentences. This study found that 11% of people charged with killing whites received the death penalty, but only 1% of those charged with killing African Americans received the death penalty. Furthermore, the death penalty was assessed in 22% of the cases involving African American defendants and white victims, versus only 3% of cases involving white defendants and African American victims. Prosecutors sought the death penalty in 70% of cases involving African American defendants and white victims, versus only 9% of cases involving white defendants and African American defendants.

After controlling for legally relevant variables, the Baldus study found that defendants charged with killing whites were 4.3 times more likely to receive a death sentence than defendants charged with killing blacks, or a disparity based on the race of the victim. The Court recognized the validity of these findings and even acknowledged a general pattern of racial disparity in the application of death sentences in Georgia. Yet, the Court held that an individual defendant must demonstrate discrimination in his or her specific case in order for the case to be considered unconstitutional. That is, he or she must be able to demonstrate that the prosecutor acted in a discriminatory fashion in the individual case or that the legislature intended to make discriminatory law. As noted by Haney:

> The practical implications of this requirement were obvious. Because persons who are most prejudiced often are least aware of their biases and, when they are aware, are least willing to disclose them, requiring clear proof of intentional discrimination meant that it would be difficult if not impossible for a future petitioner ever to succeed. Moreover, *conscious* prejudice . . . is merely one aspect of racially unfair treatment. A system of death sentencing could operate with little conscious awareness on any one person's part that he or she was bringing racial prejudice to bear on the discretionary criminal justice decisions being made. Yet structural, implicit, and nonconscious biases still could produce outcomes that were no less discriminatory or invidious.[109]

The ruling was 5–4 that statistical evidence of racial discrimination is not enough to demonstrate unconstitutional discrimination in violation of the Fourteenth Amendment's Equal Protection Clause or irrational, arbitrary, capricious sentencing under the Eighth Amendment. For capital punishment to be unconstitutional, a person must prove either that he or she was discriminated against as an individual and/or that the legislature intended for law to be discriminatory. Justices Powell, Rehnquist, White, O'Connor, and Scalia were in the majority, and Justices Brennan, Marshall, Blackmun, and Stevens filed dissenting opinions.

The evidence of racial bias presented in the Baldus study, discussed earlier, was dismissed by the five-justice majority: "The statistics do not prove that race enters into any capital sentencing decisions or that race was a factor in petitioner's case. The likelihood of racial prejudice allegedly shown by the study does not constitute the constitutional measure of an unacceptable risk of racial prejudice." The majority continued: "At most, the Baldus study indicates a discrepancy that appears to correlate with race, but this discrepancy does not constitute a major systemic defect."[110]

Justice Powell, joined by Rehnquist, White, O'Connor, and Scalia, suggested that the burden rests on the defendant to show purposeful discrimination by the prosecution. The Court assumed the validity of Baldus study but dismissed the findings as inconsequential and suggested that disparities "are an inevitable part of our criminal justice system."[111] It concluded: "In light of the safeguards designed to minimize racial bias in the process, the fundamental value of a jury trial in our criminal justice system, and the benefits that discretion provides to criminal defendants, we hold that the Baldus study does not demonstrate a constitutionally significant risk of racial bias affecting the Georgia capital sentencing process."[112] After discussing the numerous efforts to minimize bias in the system, and claiming that discrimination is an issue left for the legislature not the courts, the majority compared race to other possible disparities that could be demonstrated such as one based on different facial characteristics or attractiveness.

Justice Brennan, joined by Marshall, Blackmun, and Stevens, disagreed. They wrote: "Nothing could convey more powerfully the intractable reality of the death penalty: 'that the effort to eliminate arbitrariness in the infliction of that ultimate sanction is so plainly doomed to failure that it—and the death penalty—must be abandoned altogether," quoting an earlier decision by Justice Marshall'.[113] The dissent suggested that a demonstrated pattern of disparity based on race violates *Furman*, which said that even a *substantial risk* of arbitrary punishment is unconstitutional, and *Gregg*, which suggested a *pattern of arbitrary sentencing* would be unconstitutional. The dissent discussed the racial makeup of victims and those subjected to capital punishment since the *Gregg* decision and concluded that there is clear evidence of discrimination by prosecutors in Georgia. They concluded that McCleskey's sentence was likely based on race and thus he cannot be put to death.

The dissent also pointed out numerous times when the Court has previously ruled that evidence of race discrimination is not acceptable and that racial discrimination is a problem in other areas of the criminal justice system. They claimed that if juries consider race, their discretion should be taken away: "Reliance on race in imposing capital punishment, however, is antithetical to the very rationale for granting sentencing discretion."[114] The dissent concluded by asserting that the Court, by finding that disparities are meaningless given all the safeguards, relies on safeguards that obviously do not work.

Justice Blackmun, joined by Justices Marshall, Stevens, and Brennan, also asserted that the Court issues an opinion that is inconsistent with previous rulings that have set aside convictions when racial discrimination is illustrated and that have required the prosecution to prove that it is not race but some other relevant factor that can explain away the discrimination. That disparities were most prevalent in the midrange murder cases—where prosecutors and juries actually had discretion to decide which cases were or were not capital cases and which convicted defendants would live or die—seemed to illustrate clearly that prosecutors and juries were abusing their discretion. This argument, however, did not convince the Court.

DEGREE OF INCONSISTENCY ACROSS *FURMAN*, *WOODSON*, *GREGG*, AND *MCCLESKEY*

From the analysis of the opinions in these Big Four cases, it is clear that some justices were inconsistent in their opinions and that the Court is some cases was inconsistent with its previous rulings. Three forms of *inconsistency* are most significant:

1) Issuing an opinion that is contradictory to opinions issued in earlier cases (e.g., a justice rules in favor of capital punishment in one case and then against it in another, or vice versa).
2) Issuing an opinion that appears to be contradictory to statements made in written opinions in earlier cases (e.g., a justice votes in a way opposite to the principles he or she has put forth in previous cases).
3) Ruling in a way that appears to violate a precedent or rule of law.[115]

Table 2.3 illustrates the degree of inconsistency among justices across the cases of study. I have classified opinions into those that favor abolition of capital punishment as practiced or those that favor retention of the death penalty. These terms are misleading because the rulings in these cases apply

TABLE 2.3   Consistency of Justices in Major Supreme Court Cases Regarding the
Death Penalty

Furman	Woodson	Gregg	McCleskey
Favoring abolition in the case			
Douglas	Stevens (new)		Stevens[a]
Brennan	Brennan	Brennan	Brennan
Stewart	Stewart		
Marshall	Marshall	Marshall	Marshall
White	Powell[a]		Blackmun[a]
Favoring retention in the case			
Burger	Burger	Burger	
Blackmun	Blackmun	Blackmun	
Rehnquist	Rehnquist	Rehnquist	Rehnquist
Powell	White[a]	White	White
		Stewart[a]	O'Connor (new)
		Powell[a]	Powell
		Stevens[a]	Scalia (new)

[a]Indicates a switch of position from the earlier decision.

Source: Adapted from "Logical and Consistent? An Analysis of Supreme Court Opinions Regarding the Death Penalty," by M. Robinson and K. Simon, 2006, *Justice Policy Journal, 3*(1), pp. 1–59. Retrieved from http://www.cjcj.org/pdf/logical_and.pdf

only to the cases themselves and the laws to which they relate, not to the issue of capital punishment itself. Thus, I have labeled in Table 2.3 decisions as either "favoring abolition in the case" or "favoring retention in the case." As you can see, some justices did change their minds about the administration of capital punishment over time, depending on the specific issue being decided (a change in position is indicated with a footnote). The most important of these were justices White and Stewart, who opposed capital punishment in *Furman*, but who gained confidence in capital punishment after states passed laws to remove arbitrariness in death penalty sentencing (by passing mandatory sentencing laws, giving jurors guidance in death penalty sentencing, using bifurcated trials, and providing postconviction review). White voted to reinstate capital punishment in *Woodson* and *Gregg*, whereas Stewart voted only to reinstate capital punishment in *Gregg*.

Table 2.4 shows under which conditions each justice involved in these four cases determined that capital punishment is acceptable. The number in the last column of the table reflects the number of cases, out of the number participated in by each judge, that each justice ruled in favor of retaining capital punishment.

TABLE 2.4 Specifying When Capital Punishment Is Acceptable in Four Major Supreme Court Cases (*Furman, Woodson, Gregg, McCleskey*)

Justice	When is capital punishment acceptable?	# cases ruled
Rehnquist	under all conditions	4/4
Burger	under all conditions	3/3
O'Connor[a]	under all conditions	1/1
Scalia[a]	under all conditions	1/1
Blackmun	all except a pattern of racial disparity	3/4
Powell	all except mandatory death sentences	3/4
White	all except evidence of arbitrary sentences	3/4
Stewart	only with juror guidance, bifurcated trials, postconviction review	1/3
Stevens	only with juror guidance, bifurcated trials, postconviction review	1/3
Douglas[a]	never	0/1
Brennan	never	0/4
Marshall	never	0/4

[a]Involved in only one decision in the analysis.

Source: Adapted from "Logical and Consistent? An Analysis of Supreme Court Opinions Regarding the Death Penalty," by M. Robinson and K. Simon, 2006, *Justice Policy Journal, 3*(1), pp. 1–59. Retrieved from http://www.cjcj.org/pdf/logical_and.pdf

This review of all opinions of the justices in these cases seems to support the following findings:

1) Rehnquist and Burger were the Court's strongest proponents of capital punishment in these cases.
2) Brennan and Marshall were the Court's strongest opponents of capital punishment in these cases.
3) Only four justices who ruled in at least three of the cases issued opinions on the same side of the issue every time, either for retention of capital punishment or for its abolition (Rehnquist and Burger for retention, Brennan and Marshall for abolition).
4) There is evidence of what can be called inconsistency in the opinions of individual justices in these cases that can be detected only with careful review of opinions across time.

As noted earlier, specific examples of inconsistencies in opinions of justices could take three forms. First, there are those opinions that are contradictory to opinions issued in earlier cases (TYPE I inconsistency). Second, there are those opinions that appear to be contradictory to statements made in written opinions in earlier cases (TYPE II inconsistency). Third, the Court rules in ways that appear to violate precedents or rules of law (TYPE III inconsistency). Here are some examples of each type of inconsistency:

- The decision in *Furman* violated the precedent set only one year earlier in *McGautha* that approved of unbridled jury discretion (TYPE III inconsistency).
- White and Stewart opposed capital punishment in *Furman* in part because of the theoretical possibility of arbitrary sentencing, but gained enough confidence in capital punishment to vote to reinstate capital punishment in *Gregg* after states passed laws to remove arbitrariness in death penalty sentencing. (Given the lack of evidence of a lack of arbitrariness, this change in opinion is a TYPE I inconsistency.)
- Stewart left the Court prior to *McCleskey*, but White voted in *McCleskey* to retain capital punishment even after evidence showed a pattern of disparity based on race of victim, which is suggestive of arbitrary sentencing. (Because White's opinion in *McCleskey* contradicts his concerns expressed in *Furman* and *Gregg*, this is a TYPE II inconsistency.)
- Justices Stevens and Blackmun, who both voted to reinstate capital punishment in *Gregg*, each voted to end capital punishment in *McCleskey* based on the evidence of racial disparity. Blackmun had voted in each of the previous three cases to retain or reinstate capital punishment, and Stevens voted to reinstate capital punishment in *Gregg* (TYPE I inconsistency). It could be argued that social scientific evidence of disparities in the sentences convinced two justices to change their minds, but this evidence was seen as insufficient to provide proof of individual discrimination by the other justices.
- Blackmun accepted the Baldus study in *McCleskey* despite having rejected statistical evidence of racial discrimination in rape cases in *Maxwell v. Bishop* (1970)[116] (TYPE II inconsistency).
- Powell ruled to retain or reinstate capital punishment in all cases except for mandatory sentencing (TYPE I inconsistency). To Powell, juror discretion is fundamental to the American justice system, so removing it through mandatory sentencing is not acceptable even if it removes disparities. At the same time, disparities emerging from juror discretion are apparently acceptable because he voted to retain capital punishment in *McCleskey*.
- Powell in *Furman* claimed that a pattern of race discrimination could lead to a valid Eighth Amendment challenge, but he ruled against the validity of this very challenge in *McCleskey* (TYPE II inconsistency).

- Burger in *Furman* noted how jury discretion was superior to mandatory sentencing, but then voted to uphold mandatory sentencing in *Woodson* (TYPE II inconsistency).
- The standard from *McCleskey*, which places the burden on individual defendants to prove purposeful discrimination, is a different standard than in other situations such as the use of peremptory challenges to exclude minorities from juries (TYPE III inconsistency). For example, under *Batson v. Kentucky* (1986),[117] prosecutors are required to prove that race did not play a role in dismissal of potential jurors if the defendant alleges that race played a role in decisions for peremptory challenges. Peremptory challenges and the death penalty are two separate issues, but it is hard to justify different standards to prove racial discrimination.
- Strangely, Justice Powell authored the Court's opinion for the seven-justice majority in *Batson*. Had he stayed consistent in his reasoning, Powell would have seen the legitimacy of McCleskey's claims; yet, Powell voted against McCleskey with the five-justice majority (TYPE II inconsistency).
- Similarly, Justice White had written in his *Gregg* opinion: "Absent facts to the contrary, it cannot be assumed that prosecutors will be motivated in their charging decision by factors other than the strength of their case and the likelihood that a jury would impose the death penalty if it convicts."[118] When the facts were presented to the Court in *McCleskey* that suggested race of victim played a role in capital sentencing, it did not change his mind as to the guided discretion statutes (TYPE II inconsistency). Apparently, White was "persistently skeptical of claimants seeking to prove discrimination by showing unequal racial outcomes as opposed to more direct proof of intentional discrimination."[119] White reasoned that the findings of the Baldus study might be explained by some other factor, even though Baldus controlled for more than 230 other variables including all legally relevant ones.
- The ruling in *McCleskey*, which suggested that racial disparities could possibly be explained away by other factors, also was inconsistent with the ruling in *Bazemore v. Friday* (1986)[120] where "the Court had specifically stated that a statistical study need not take into account every conceivable variable to qualify as meaningful evidence of discrimination."[121] (The different standard for proving discrimination is again a form of TYPE III inconsistency).

These examples show that justices do change their minds over time and do not remain consistent in their interpretations even when confronted with seemingly identical issues. Although each case reviewed here is unique, with facts specific to each case, ideally the Supreme Court will not ignore its own precedents, nor should individual justices ignore their previous opinions or the reasoning used to arrive at previous decisions.

Factors That May Lead to Changes in Opinions Across Time: Explaining Supreme Court Inconsistency

One might wonder how the Court and its justices could be so inconsistent over time with respect to capital punishment or any given issue. It seems to the layperson that once a punishment is declared unconstitutional or constitutional, the issue is decided. In fact, "every issue is always open for reargument in later cases; changed parties, changed circumstances, and changed courts often lead to changed conclusions."[122] This is an apt description for the Supreme Court decisions in the death penalty cases examined here.

Potential explanations for inconsistencies in Court activity include (1) the ambiguous nature of the Constitution; (2) ideology or attitudes and political party affiliation of individual justices; (3) approach to interpreting the Constitution; (4) strategic rationality and bargaining; (5) changing justices over time; (6) evolving human standards; and (7) public opinion and state legislative activity.[123]

Ambiguous Nature of the Constitution

Part of the inconsistency problem seems to stem from the very nature of the Constitution itself. Lieberman describes it as "elusive, ambiguous, murky, sometimes quite opaque" such that its meaning could be known "only through some human, and fallible, means of interpretation."[124] Justices can make decisions by interpreting the Constitution literally, attempting to interpret the meaning of individual words in the Constitution, making logical inferences, and enforcing stare decisis.[125] In the case of capital punishment, a literal interpretation of the Constitution would suggest that it is acceptable: "In both Due Process Clauses, the Constitution itself recognizes the death penalty, in saying that a person may be deprived of life as long as in so doing the government acts with due process of law."[126] Justices in the cases analyzed here did generally acknowledge that capital punishment is permissible according to the Constitution.

When the justices used the approach of determining the meaning of key words (such as "cruel" and "unusual"), they disagreed about the meaning of these words and this affected their decisions. For example, in *Furman*, Justice Douglas said capital punishment would be cruel and unusual if it was discriminatory or selective in its application. Justice Brennan suggested that although what is cruel and unusual is not clearly defined, to him it is something that does not comport with human dignity, either because it degrades human beings, it is arbitrary, it is acceptable to the public, or it is unnecessary. To Justice Stewart, a punishment is cruel and unusual if it is excessive and/or arbitrary. To Justice White, a cruel and unusual punishment is arbitrarily applied. To Justice Marshall, a cruel and unusual punishment is one that violates the evolving standards of decency in a maturing society, either because it causes too much physical pain or is excessive, it has not been practiced prior, it serves no valid purpose or it is unnecessary, or if popular sentiment is against it or it is immoral.

Finally, justices in these cases also attempted to make logical inferences based on their reasoning abilities and referred to previous decisions of the Court to justify their opinions, but different justices reached different conclusions. For example, some justices inferred discrimination from clear disparities in *McCleskey* as they thought previous Court decisions called for. Others justices either refused to make such inferences or disagreed that such inferences were appropriate, despite the fact that such inferences had been encouraged in previous cases.

The ambiguous nature of the Constitution might account for TYPE I inconsistencies (issuing an opinion that is contradictory to opinions issued in earlier cases) or TYPE II inconsistencies (issuing an opinion that appears to be contradictory to statements made in written opinions in earlier cases). Justices may very well interpret the Constitution differently at different stages of their careers, based on their variable understanding of the Constitution, even when dealing with the same basic issues such as those that are common in death penalty cases. However, the ambiguous nature of the Constitution would appear to best account for TYPE III inconsistencies (ruling in a way that violates a precedent or rule of law), for as the Court is more conservative or more liberal, the approach to interpreting the Constitution would be significantly different. Thus, precedents might be more likely to be overturned when they were established by Courts with different political persuasions.

Ideology or Attitudes and Political Party Affiliation of Justices

The importance of ideology or personal attitudes of justices cannot be understated.[127] Justices in these cases simply disagreed about the proper role of the Courts in dealing with issues such as arbitrary sentencing and demonstrated disparities in punishment. Opposing ideologies led to opposing opinions even when justices agreed about the relevant facts in the cases reviewed.

Ideology logically affects one's political party affiliation and one's approach to interpreting the Constitution, so it is difficult to separate out the effects of these influences. It is clear in these cases that these factors played a role. Political party affiliation appears to have played a role in the opinions of justices in these four cases. In these cases, 12 justices wrote 36 opinions, 20 to retain capital punishment and 16 to halt its use. Justices identified as Democrats issued 10 opinions to halt capital punishment (83%) and only 3 to retain it (17%); all 3 to retain it were by the same justice (White). Justices identified as Republicans issued 17 opinions to retain capital punishment (74%) and only 6 to halt it (16%); 5 of these by Stevens and Stewart. Two of the four cases most clearly provide evidence of a relationship between political party affiliation and the opinion issued in the case: in *Furman*, four out of five Republican justices voted to retain capital punishment (80%), all four of which were nominated by President Nixon; and in *Gregg*, all six Republican justices voted to reinstate capital punishment (100%).

Justice Burger was chosen by Nixon because Burger opposed many of the advances made in the areas of individual rights and liberties during the Warren Court years. Justice Blackmun, a boyhood friend of Burger, was chosen to achieve Nixon's promise of turning the Court around.[128] Interestingly, Wagman noted many inconsistencies in Burger's record:

> But quite possibly no Chief Justice has come to the Court with a background so filled with contradictions. As a young lawyer in Minneapolis, Burger was known as a defender of individual rights, and at one time served as co-chairman of the Minnesota Commission on Human Rights. In his thirteen years on the court of appeals, he had developed a reputation as an expert in the area of court administration, and had exhibited a moderately conservative voting record. But he was also a sharp critic of the activism of the Warren Court. During his Senate confirmation, Burger put on his most moderate face and was easily confirmed. But it was clear he was Nixon's choice because the president believed Burger would move the Court back to the right.[129]

Burger did so in the death penalty cases reviewed here, voting all three times in the decisions he was involved with to retain or reinstate the death penalty.

Firm conclusions about the role of political party affiliation in death penalty cases cannot be made based on an examination of only four cases. However, in these cases, there is evidence of an association between political party affiliation of the justices and the opinions issued. Political party affiliation probably best accounts for TYPE III inconsistencies because conservative Courts tend to be more likely to overturn precedents established by liberal Courts, and vice versa.[130]

Approach to Interpreting the Constitution

Why would political party affect the decisions of the justices in these cases? Here is where basic beliefs about the proper role of the Supreme Court in American government come into play.[131]

Disagreements among justices about capital punishment often come down to disparate views of the proper role of the government in settling disputes among people and their government, and the appropriate role of the courts in resolving constitutional issues. The most important of these issues include federalism, the separation of powers, and individual rights and liberties versus government power.[132]

Federalism refers to the distribution of power between the U.S. federal government and its states. Certain powers are granted to the federal government by the Constitution, whereas others are reserved for the states, and some are denied to both the federal government and to the states.[133] The *separation of powers* refers to the endowment of different powers to different branches of American government (legislative, judicial, and executive branches), as well as constraints on those powers that can be exercised by other branches of government through a system of checks and balances.[134] Certain *individual rights and liberties* are guaranteed by the Constitution. Because of the Bill of Rights and the Fourteenth Amendment to the Constitution, neither the federal government nor the states are permitted to violate these rights and liberties without serious consequences.[135] The issues of federalism, the separation of powers, and individual rights and liberties versus government power affected rulings of justices in major cases dealing with capital punishment.

Republicans tend to favor less involvement of the federal government in state issues (federalism). In the cases reviewed here, Republican justices were more likely to temper their opinions by concerns of separation of power issues and judicial restraint. Democrat justices in the cases reviewed here were more inclined to extend the power of the Court and to engage in so-called judicial activism. Interestingly, justices on both sides cited case law to support their opinions while freely ignoring or violating precedents that could have or should have changed their own opinions (TYPE III inconsistency); thus stare decisis appears to be a matter of choice over which precedents should take precedence. This may be why Epstein and Walker claimed: "Many allege that judicial appeal to precedent often is mere window dressing, used to hide ideologies and values, rather than a substantive form of analysis."[136]

Data show that of the Warren, Burger, and Rehnquist Courts through 1995, the Rehnquist Court was the least "liberal" Court in the areas of civil liberties and federalism.[137] In civil liberties, nearly 79% of the Warren

Court decisions were liberal, versus approximately 30% for the Burger Court and only about 21% for the Rehnquist Court. In federalism cases, more than 73% of the Warren Court decisions were liberal, versus nearly 68% of Burger Court decisions but just over 39% of Rehnquist decisions. This means the Rehnquist Court was the least likely to decide cases in favor of individual defendants and most likely to decide cases in favor of state governments. Decisions of the Rehnquist Court tend to uphold the rights of states above all else. In fact, to Rehnquist

> the human error of wrongfully depriving a man of his constitutional rights was less severe than mistakenly striking down an otherwise constitutional statute. For the Court to thwart the will of the legislature was, in Rehnquist's view, to violate the rights of every individual in that state. That was a far greater wrong than allowing one man to die.[138]

This is why Rehnquist supposedly voted in *Furman* to uphold the death penalty as practiced (and in every case since).

The Rehnquist Court is associated, at least in part, with the strongly conservative nature of the chief justice himself. Rehnquist's successful efforts to limit federal habeas corpus appeals stems from his disgust over what he saw as abuses of such appeals by criminal defendants over his life. On the other side of the Court decisions reviewed here are Brennan and Marshall, who in virtually every appeal to the Court, granted certiorari to review the case and voted to overturn or stay an execution.[139]

Evidence also shows that Democrat justices were more likely to be activists (defined as declaring, with the majority, a law to be unconstitutional). For Democrat justices, the percentages of votes with the majority to declare laws unconstitutional were 97% (Brennan), 94% (Marshall), 94% (Douglas), and 78% (White). For Republican justices, the percentages were 89% (Powell), 85% (Stevens), 83% (Stewart), 76% (Blackmun), 73% (O'Connor), 69% (Burger), 69% (Scalia), and 39% (Rehnquist). Epstein and Walker define activists as justices who

> believe that the proper role of the Court is to assert independent positions in deciding cases, to review the actions of the other branches vigorously, to strike down unconstitutional acts willingly, and to impose far-reaching remedies for legal wrongs whenever necessary. Restraint-oriented justices take the opposite position. Courts should not become involved in the questions of other branches unless absolutely necessary. The benefit of the doubt should be given to actions taken by elected officials. Courts should impose remedies that are narrowly tailored to correct a specific legal wrong.[140]

There is much debate among legal scholars as to whether judicial activism is appropriate,[141] and this is a highly controversial topic among justices.[142] This debate is informed by the actions of individual conservative and liberal justices.[143] In the death penalty cases reviewed here it appears that Republican-nominated justices voted to restrain the Court's power, whereas Democrat justices voted to extend it. Yet, scholars rightly point out that conservative justices are also activists, in part by their refusal to accept changing standards of the law.[144] Of course, an activist judge does not have to be liberal, and a judge who practices restraint isn't necessarily a conservative.[145] For example, the U.S. Supreme Court's refusal to hear all but a handful of cases as witnessed by the Rehnquist Court's "shrinking docket" can be seen both as evidence of restraint and as a form of activism because Rehnquist moved the Court farther to the right of the political spectrum.[146] In fact, the shifting makeup of the Court to the right can be considered a form of activism.[147]

In the Big Four it appears that both sides were less interested in making good decisions than in ensuring the outcomes they decided. In many decisions in important cases

> narrow Court majorities transformed constitutional law on the basis of opinions the Justices knew to be wholly inadequate and unconvincing [which could explain TYPE I inconsistency]. Individual Justices sought to advance their political agendas by employing legal arguments in which they themselves did not believe or methods of interpretation they had uniformly rejected in the past [which could explain TYPE II inconsistency]. Neither side respected precedent, except when convenient; both sides tried to twist the Court's internal rules to attain narrow advantage [which could explain TYPE III inconsistency].[148]

In other words, politics intervened in a way that affected the decisions of the justices. Political party affiliation, which for Supreme Court justices roughly equates to their approach to interpreting the Constitution, best explains TYPE III inconsistency. Again, conservative and liberal justices appear to have a different approach to interpreting the Constitution, as witnessed in the analysis of the four major death penalty cases here.

Strategic Rationality and Bargaining

From the literature, it is also clear that justices bargain with one another before writing their final opinions, that they change their minds often as they bargain, and that their changing opinions sometimes are merely to please senior members of the Court.[149] Justices sometimes change votes on some issue before the Court in order to achieve their desired outcome.[150]

It appears that justices bargain with one another through verbal and written exchanges to ensure that the outcome of the law will match their own preferred positions rather than to be consistent with the principle of stare decisis.[151] In fact, abandonment of precedent is common in the Supreme Court. For example, the past three Courts (with Warren, Burger, and Rehnquist as chief justices) have overturned an average of 2.7 precedents per term, with a range of between 2.6 and 2.9 precedents per term.[152] Other studies show how little stare decisis really matters.[153] A study of 64 death penalty cases between since 1972 found that outcomes could be accurately predicted using precedents in 75% of the cases.[154] This means 25% of such cases could not be accurately predicted using stare decisis. Given the conflicting precedents from different Courts and the changing justices, this is not surprising.

Much of the bargaining that goes on behind closed doors at the U.S. Supreme Court occurs with freshman justices. The "freshman effect" suggests that veteran justices may try to sway the new justice to their side to ensure a particular outcome.[155] This effect cannot be documented absolutely in the cases reviewed here, but it may partially account for why Court opinions in death penalty cases are in some ways not consistent.

In the book *The Brethren* (1979), called the first ever inside view of the U.S. Supreme Court, two journalists examined the inner workings of the Court between 1969 and 1976.[156] Woodward and Armstrong discussed three of the key cases discussed here, *Furman*, *Woodson*, and *Gregg*. According to their account, Stewart voted in *Furman* with the majority mainly because of the horror of thinking that his one vote could send hundreds of people to their deaths through capital punishment. If true, Stewart's votes were not based on precedent or law but rather on his own rejection of capital punishment.

According to these authors, freshman Justice Powell determined to do as much research into the death penalty as he possibly could to inform his vote in *Furman*; he also thought he could sway other justices on the Court such as White and Stewart, who in conference discussions voted with the majority to outlaw capital punishment as practiced, but who had both voted in *McGautha* to uphold unguided jury discretion in capital cases (TYPE I inconsistency). These authors note: "Powell discovered an unbroken line of precedents to uphold the death penalty" and thus was determined to make sure it was upheld in line with the principle of stare decisis.[157] Of course, Powell was unsuccessful but Powell did learn that White and Stewart voted not based on the Constitution but on other grounds (their own philosophies about capital punishment). This led Lazarus to call the *Furman* decision a horrible mistake.[158]

Strangely, Woodward and Armstrong claimed that Powell privately feared that the *Furman* decision would lead to mandatory death sentencing laws—something he did not favor. As noted above, Powell voted in *Woodson* to abolish North Carolina's mandatory death sentencing laws. At the same time, during *Furman*, White told his clerks he preferred mandatory death laws to unguided discretion, at least for heinous murders, and he voted in *Woodson* to uphold North Carolina's mandatory law.

Woodward and Armstrong discussed the very strange occurrences in the Court in considering *Woodson*, *Gregg*, and the other cases announced on the same day. Chief Justice Burger, even though he was not in the majority, assigned the writing of the opinion of the Court to Justice White, supposedly to stop his wavering and ensure his vote for the justices who wanted to vote to uphold the death penalty statutes in question. Because of their agreement, a "troika" of justices emerged, consisting of Powell, Stevens, and Stewart. These justices met and worked out a rationale to strike some of the death penalty laws and to uphold others, trying their best to come up with a logical and consistent argument across cases. White, learning of the invincibility of this plurality, sent the cases back for reassignment, and the three justices would work out a way to vote together. These justices took the law into their own hands, refused to overrule the ruling in *McGautha* which held that jury guidance and bifurcated trials were not required in death penalty cases, and simply pieced together rulings that would overcome *Furman* but seem to be inconsistent with *McGautha*. These justices "were acting like a superlegislature," seemingly violating the separation of powers.[159]

In another inside look at the Court in the book *Closed Chambers* (1999), a former clerk for Justice Powell agreed with the analysis of Woodward and Armstrong.[160] Lazarus asserted that after hearing arguments in *Gregg*, Powell wrote in his conference notes that "I accept *Furman* as precedent." Lazarus thought that Powell would likely vote to reject the new death penalty statutes that provided guidance to juries.[161] During the hearing of *Woodson*, *Gregg*, and the other three cases, Powell approached Stewart and the freshman Justice Stevens to have lunch and to formulate a "centrist 'troika'" for these capital cases, meaning that these three justices controlled the Court and the direction of its decisions. Indeed, these three justices wrote with the majority in both *Woodson* and *Gregg*: "Stewart, Powell, and Stevens set a new death penalty agenda for the Court . . . the centrists had in effect appointed themselves overseers of the newly approved yet highly regulated business of capital punishment."[162] Critics of the death penalty assert that the arbitrary nature of capital punishment is a legacy that can be traced back to the agreement by these three justices to keep capital punishment legal, regardless of the evidence of arbitrariness.

Another telling example of bargaining comes from the case of *Tompkins v. Texas* (1989),[163] disposed of by the Court in 1988 by a 4–4 vote.

Phillip Tompkins was an African American male with an IQ of around 70 who abducted a young, white woman after rear-ending her car while smoking dope.[164] After abducting her he tied her to a tree and gagged her with a bed sheet while he took her ATM card and went to the bank to withdraw $1,000 from her account. Despite the fact that Tompkins confession to the crime clearly indicated that he did not intend to kill his victim, he was convicted of felony murder and sentenced to death by a Houston jury. Tompkins appealed to the Texas Court of Criminal Appeals and ultimately the U.S. Supreme Court after being convicted by an all-white jury. Of the 13 potential African American jurors at his trial, 8 were struck for cause and 5 were dismissed by the prosecutor using peremptory challenges. Tompkins alleged a *Batson* violation, suggesting that the prosecutor illegally used race to dismiss potential jurors, and a violation of the Court's ruling in *Beck v. Alabama* (1980)[165] because the trial judge did not allow the jury to consider a lesser offense of unintentional murder.

The Texas Court of Criminal Appeals, rather than following the *Batson* ruling that said a defendant would only have to raise an inference that race was used to exclude potential jurors, conducted its own inquiry into the facts of the dismissals and simply invented possible explanations that were race neutral. After the *Tompkins* oral arguments, eight of the Supreme Court justices met for a conference discussion (O'Connor excused herself because her husband worked for a law firm that had once represented Tompkins). The preliminary vote among the eight participating justices was 5–2–1 in favor of Tompkins on his *Batson* claim—Justices Rehnquist and White sided with the state of Texas, whereas Justices Brennan, Marshall, Blackmun, Stevens, and Kennedy sided with Tompkins. Justice Scalia was undecided.[166]

Justice Stevens, the senior justice in the majority, drafted an opinion and waited for responses, where the bargaining among justices could begin. Scalia quickly not only joined the two justices in the minority but also questioned the very formula for determining *Batson* violations (which was derived from plaintiff-friendly employment law that, in the view of conservatives, encouraged frivolous discrimination lawsuits). After Scalia sent out his memo, Justice Kennedy, who was in his first full term on the Court, began to express skepticism about the *Batson* claim. After sitting on his decision for more than 6 months, Justice Kennedy formally switched his vote. Lazarus claimed: "Although Kennedy still found the Texas court of appeals' *Batson* discussion 'difficult to accept,' he had done his own review of the *Batson* ruling and had concluded that the Texas district court had it right all along."[167] In other words, Kennedy accepted the invented justifications for the dismissal of potential African American jurors that were race neutral. Kennedy's revised vote, which ran counter to statements he had made to other justices about the absurdity of excuses offered by prosecutors to dismiss potential African American jurors (TYPE II inconsistency), ensured that the final vote would be 4–4 and thus the case would be dismissed by the Court:

> His revised vote guaranteed that the Court would split 4–4 on the *Batson* issue, strictly along political lines: Rehnquist, White, Scalia, and Kennedy on the one side; Brennan, Marshall, Blackmun, and Stevens on the other. . . . The Justices lined up exactly as one might have predicted before the case was briefed or argued—liberals on one side, conservatives on the other, a gorge between them and no bridge across even in an easy case.[168]

Strategic rationality and bargaining could explain any of the three types of inconsistency we have seen in the four major death penalty cases reviewed here. It could account for why an individual justice might issue an opinion that is contradictory to opinions issued in earlier cases (TYPE I inconsistency), or an opinion that appears to be contradictory to statements made in written opinions in earlier cases (TYPE II inconsistency). The bargaining that went on in the *Gregg* case, led by Justice Powell, is an example of this. Strategic rationality and bargaining could logically lead to a precedent being overturned by the Court, as well (TYPE III inconsistency). The significant point is that because justices bargain behind closed doors on issues unrelated to the facts of individual cases, it should not be surprising that inconsistencies arise in Court decisions. Strategic rationality and bargaining best accounts for TYPE I and TYPE II inconsistencies—that is, it best explains inconsistencies over time in various opinions of individual justices rather than in violations of precedent by different Courts.

Changing Justices Over Time

One obvious explanation of inconsistency in rulings over time is the change in the justices of the Court. One startling example is the case of *Maxwell v. Bishop* (1970), heard first in 1967. The justices voted secretly 6–3 to strike down the death penalty as practiced in Arkansas (with Justices Warren, Douglas, Harlan, Brennan, Fortas, and Marshall in the majority, and Justices Black, Stewart, and White in the minority).[169] Chief Justice Warren, being in the majority, assigned the writing of the majority opinion to Douglas. After reading the Douglas opinion, Harlan changed his vote, making the vote 5–4. Before the opinion was issued by the Court, Justice Fortas resigned, leaving the Court split on the case 4–4. In 1969, with Warren's vote replaced by Justice Burger, the Court now stood 5–3 to uphold the death penalty law in Arkansas. Harlan insisted that the Court not issue an opinion until the ninth justice was appointed to the Court. When Justice Blackmun arrived and voted in 1970 to uphold the death penalty without any jury guidance in *McGautha* (1971), it was clear that the Court now stood at 6–3 to uphold the Arkansas law.

Another example relevant for the cases reviewed here occurred between the ruling of *McGautha* and *Furman*. Two justices (Black and Harlan) retired and were replaced by Nixon appointees Powell and Rehnquist, both of whom had called for and/or achieved significant cutbacks in defendants' rights as attorneys prior to their arrival on the Supreme Court. *McGautha*, decided by a 5–4 majority, included Stewart and White in the majority. These two justices switched their opinions only one year later in *Furman*. Similarly, whereas Justice Douglas was ill and unavailable to hear arguments, cases would often split 4–4 until Douglas finally decided to retire in 1975. Douglas, who had ruled with the majority in *Furman*, was replaced by Stevens in 1976. Stevens ultimately ruled with the majority in *Gregg*, something Douglas may not have done.

When Justice Stewart retired in 1981, he was replaced by Reagan nominee O'Connor, who voted with the majority in *McCleskey* saying that disparities in capital sentencing were insufficient to make the sanction unconstitutional. Recall that although Stewart voted with the majority in *Gregg*, he previously voted with the majorities in *Furman* and *Woodson* to ban unguided death sentences and mandatory death sentences, respectively. In both of these opinions, Stewart expressed concern over arbitrary sentencing and thus would have likely been very distressed with the evidence presented in *McCleskey*. It is thus possible that the *McCleskey* case could have been decided 5–4 to the end of capital punishment if Stewart had stayed on the Court. Additionally Chief Justice Burger resigned and Rehnquist was elevated to chief justice and replaced by Scalia one month prior to *McCleskey*. It is possible that this affected the bargaining process and perhaps the opinions of the justices.

A final example shows how shifting justices in the Court affected outcomes. In a second appeal to the Supreme Court by McCleskey, his attorneys discovered that key evidence against him had been discovered by a prison informant eliciting incriminating information from him, a violation of *Massiah v. United States* (1964).[170] The Eleventh Circuit Court of Appeals rejected McCleskey's claim first on the basis that it was filed too late and that the error was harmless, even though the evidence was hidden by the state for years; McCleskey appealed to the Supreme Court. Four justices (Brennan, Marshall, Blackmun, and Stevens) agreed to hear the case. Upon the retirement of Brennan, Justice Souter, a Reagan appointee, joined the five justices who voted against granting certiorari to deny McCleskey's *Massiah* violation claim, meaning McCleskey lost 6–3. What is alleged by some is that the justices nominated by Republicans were motivated to reject McCleskey's *Massiah* claim, in part, by the fact that this rule was created by the more liberal Warren Court.

Changing justices on the Court could account for all three types of inconsistency. Justices sometimes change their minds when confronted with strong justices on the other side of an issue. This could produce TYPE I or TYPE II inconsistencies over time. Yet, changing justices on the Court best explains TYPE III inconsistencies, as precedents established by previous justices are more likely to be overturned by Courts with different agendas and approaches to interpreting the Constitution.

Evolving Human Standards

Another source of inconsistency is the evolution of human standards that effect how the Constitution is interpreted. In the words of Lieberman, the Supreme Court has engaged in "bending and twisting and refashioning the constitutional clauses to fit its changing circumstances."[171] This means that justices can interpret the meaning of constitutional clauses based on present-day standards. This was key to the majority justices in *Furman* and the dissenting justices in *Gregg*. That justices are free to determine the meaning of words based on modern standards does not mean they can invent meaning, but these charges have been levied against so-called activist judges.[172]

Under these conditions, it is understandable that a degree of inconsistency will emerge in Court activity and opinions of individual justices, even with a single issue such as the death penalty. In fact, as more and more opinions are written about any given issue, "the Court must engage in attempts to reconcile the unreconcilable, fitting together a pattern of cases decided at different times for different reasons by different justices with different agendas."[173]

The death penalty is an issue that is very susceptible to changing opinions over time. American society appears to be evolving away from the use of capital punishment, although remarkable slowly. At the time of this writing, there is still great debate about capital punishment in many state legislatures and Congress. Public opinion polls (e.g., Gallup) show that support for capital punishment is at its lowest levels since the early 1980s. According to numerous studies reviewed by the Death Penalty Information Center, when given alternatives such as life imprisonment without the possibility of parole plus restitution to the victim's family, roughly half of Americans now say they would not vote for capital punishment. Approximately half of Americans also now report that they would support a moratorium on capital punishment, that they believe an innocent person has been executed, and that the death penalty is not administered fairly (see Chapter 6).

Related to evolving human standards is the evolution of individual justices over time, which could easily account for either TYPE I or TYPE II inconsistency. Justice Blackmun (a supporter of capital punishment in three of the four cases reviewed here), in a dissent to deny certiorari in *Callins v. Collins* (1994),[174] second-guessed his previous opinions and wrote:

> From this day forward, I no longer shall tinker with the machinery of death. For more than 20 years, I have endeavored—indeed, I have struggled—along with a majority of this Court, to develop procedural and substantive rules that would lend more than the mere appearance of fairness to the death penalty endeavor. Rather than continue to coddle the Court's delusion that the desired level of fairness has been achieved and the need for regulation eviscerated, I feel morally and intellectually obligated simply to concede that the death penalty experiment has failed. It is virtually self-evident to me now that no combination of procedural rules or substantive regulations ever can save the death penalty from its inherent constitutional deficiencies. The basic question—does the system accurately and consistently determine which defendants "deserve" to die?—cannot be answered in the affirmative. . . . The problem is that the inevitability of factual, legal, and moral error gives us a system that we know must wrongly kill some defendants, a system that fails to deliver the fair, consistent, and reliable sentences of death required by the Constitution.[175]

Stephenson analyzed the change of heart of Justice Blackmun with regard to capital punishment and suggested that Blackmun may have been highly affected by Justices Brennan and Marshall over time, and basically worn down by the constant stream of cases that showed clearly that the administration of the death penalty was plagued by problems related to ambiguity and unfairness.[176]

Evolving human standards of society and individual justices would best account for TYPE I and TYPE II inconsistencies. That is, justices may change their minds about previous opinions and the rationale expressed within, as evidence about society's changing values mounts. Evolving human standards could also account for TYPE III inconsistency if enough justices on the Court were convinced that rulings from past Courts are inconsistent with today's understanding of the Constitution.

Public Opinion and State Legislative Activity

According to the literature, public opinion and state legislative activity also are likely to affect Court activity.[177] Both of these are seen as indicators of evolving social conditions, as noted by justices on both sides of the capital punishment cases reviewed here. It is clear from both of these indicators that a majority of Americans supported capital punishment during the 1970s and 1980s. In fact, after the *Furman* decision and subsequent speeches by President Nixon about the value of the death penalty, public support for capital punishment actually grew in public opinion polls. Justices Marshall and Brennan claimed the majority of Americans really did not support capital punishment but only said they did when asked general questions.

According to Bohm, death penalty opinion is important for five reasons.[178] First, it has effects on legislators, meaning as long as they perceive that Americans want capital punishment we will have it. Second, public opinion may influence prosecutors to seek the death penalty in cases where demand is high. Third, public opinion may pressure judges to impose death sentences even when the jury recommends life. Fourth, public opinion may dissuade governors from vetoing legislation, issuing stays, and commuting sentences. Finally, as this analysis shows, public opinion is used by the courts to justify its practice.

There are numerous surveys that assess death penalty opinion, and the findings of surveys depend on how the questions are asked. As noted earlier, people generally say they support capital punishment, but support declines to less than 50% when people are given other options such as life in prison without parole. Research shows that capital punishment is less supported by the highly educated and that support decreases with knowledge about the realities of the death penalty, especially problems with it such as racial disparities and wrongful convictions in capital cases. These results are consistent with the hypothesis stated by Justice Marshall in *Furman* and *Gregg*.

So, it is possible that Marshall and Brennan were correct when they asserted that a majority of Americans really do not support capital punishment, even though the other justices were correct when they asserted that public opinion polls at the time of these cases indicated clear support for the death penalty. Since 36 states drafted new legislation after *Furman* there was a clear message to the Court that America's legislators also perceived support for capital punishment.

Related to the issue of public opinion and state legislative activity is the "tough on crime" movement that began in the late 1960s and continues today.[179] Beginning in 1973, America began an incarceration boom that is unprecedented in world history. The tough on crime movement generated and supported by Presidents Nixon, Reagan, Bush (the first), Clinton, and Bush (the second) led to many harsh laws, including new death penalty legislation at the federal level. These presidents also nominated justices who tended to support capital punishment and principles of law that would interfere with a defendant's ability to raise appeals such as federal habeas corpus appeals. The Nixon nominees of Blackmun, Rehnquist, and

Powell would vote together in three of the four cases reviewed here, all to retain capital punishment as practiced. Reagan appointees O'Connor and Scalia had key votes in *McCleskey* and each voted to deny McCleskey's second appeal to the Court. The inference by a Supreme Court insider that politics has invaded the Court and its decision making may thus be true, although it is difficult to tell for sure given the secretive nature of Court deliberations.[180]

Changes in public opinion and state legislative activity could easily lead individual justices to change their minds about whether capital punishment is cruel and unusual punishment, for example (TYPE I inconsistency) or to back off from a rationale asserting that the public supports or does not support capital punishment (TYPE II inconsistency). It could also lead to a precedent being overturned, like we recently saw in the cases of *Atkins v. Virginia* (2002),[181] and *Roper v. Simmons*.[182] In these cases, respectively, the Court decided by a 6–3 majority that the death penalty can no longer could be used against people who are mentally retarded and by 5–4 that it is unconstitutional to execute juvenile offenders. *Atkins* overturned *Penry v. Lynaugh* (1989),[183] which decided by a 5–4 margin that states could execute people who are mentally retarded. *Roper* overturned *Stanford v. Kentucky* (1989),[184] which decided by a 5–4 margin than the execution of 16- and 17-year-old offenders was constitutionally permissible.

Why the changes? As noted earlier in the chapter, since 1989, at least 18 of the 37 death penalty states passed laws forbidding the imposition of the death penalty against people with mental retardation. Further, by 2005, at least 30 states prohibited the juvenile death penalty, including 12 that have rejected the death penalty altogether. These trends affected the decision of the Court in the *Atkins* case and the *Roper* case because the Court state legislative activity suggested that standards of decency had changed in the United States in less than two decades.

Summary

From the analysis of the Big Four significant capital punishment cases— *Furman v. Georgia* (1972), *Woodson v. North Carolina* (1976), *Gregg v. Georgia* (1976), and *McCleskey v. Kemp* (1987)—it is clear that some justices' opinions were contradictory to opinions issued in earlier cases. This is TYPE I inconsistency. It is also clear that some justices' opinions were contradictory to statements made in written opinions in earlier cases. This is TYPE II inconsistency. Finally, the Court ruled in ways that violated precedents or rules of law, which is referred to as TYPE III inconsistency.

Possible explanations for these inconsistencies include (1) the ambiguous nature of the Constitution; (2) ideology or attitudes and political party affiliation of individual justices; (3) approach to interpreting the Constitution; (4) strategic rationality and bargaining; (5) changing justices over time; (6) evolving human standards; and (7) public opinion and state legislative activity. Each of these factors leads to inconsistency in Court activity.

TYPE I inconsistency is best explained by strategic rationality and bargaining by justices and by evolving standards of decency in society. TYPE II inconsistency is also best explained by strategic rationality and bargaining by justices and by evolving standards of decency in society. TYPE III inconsistency is best explained by the ambiguous nature of the Constitution, political party affiliation of justices, the approach to interpreting the Constitution of justices, and by changing justices on the Court.

The analysis of these four cases provides some explanation for why the death penalty is still legal. The Court is not charged with reviewing the scientific evidence on a particular sanction and then deciding whether or not we should continue to impose it. Instead, it attempts to interpret the law of the Constitution in order to ascertain whether a sanction such as the death penalty as practiced is legally permissible under the Constitution. The Court is unable to give clear meaning to some sections of the Constitution, and justices disagree about the meaning.

The Court also rules on issues pertaining to capital punishment that are subject to change based on which justices sit on the Court, based on their ideology or attitudes and political party affiliation, and based on their approach to interpreting the Constitution. Evolving human standards, strategic rationality and bargaining, and public opinion and state legislative activity also seem to make consistency in Court activity impossible. Even when public opinion seems clear, or state legislative activity shows an emerging trend, some justices will disagree about the meaning of the data and/or dismiss it as invalid, irrelevant, and so forth.

It should be pointed out that social scientific evidence may not sway the Court in its rulings related to alleged problems with capital punishment, such as disparities based on extralegal factors, innocence, and similar issues. The justices already have shown both a lack of understanding of and a general disdain for studies such those offered in *McCleskey* as well as a lack of understanding of research methodology and advanced statistics. According to Lazarus, Professor Baldus, whose study was the basis for McCleskey's first appeal, was dismayed by the Court's dismissal of the findings of his study. The Court even refused to appoint an independent special master to provide a full understanding of the meaning of the Baldus study.[185]

In an analysis of 28 capital punishment cases decided in the late 1980s, it was shown that although social science evidence did figure prominently in decisions, justices were more interested in discounting the findings from studies than using them to inform their opinions.[186] Court outcomes were decided based on principles that had little or nothing to do with the scientific evidence. Other analyses of Supreme Court decision making with regard to scientific evidence on issues such as measuring "evolving standards of decency," "fitness to be executed," deterrence, and discrimination, show that the Supreme Court is inconsistent in its reasoning.[187]

In the recent *Atkins* case, discussed earlier, then Chief Justice Rehnquist dissented from the six-justice majority and wrote nearly two pages questioning the validity of public opinion polls that consistently show that Americans generally do not favor executing people who are mentally retarded.

Haney goes further, claiming: "The Court . . . has refused to consider, acknowledge, or be influenced by social research that describes a system that is too often plagued by error and tilted toward death. Many of the Justices have refused to talk candidly in their opinions about the problems that undermine the fair administration of the death penalty."[188] Further, beginning with the 1976 cases reviewed here,

> social facts of capital punishment had become too troublesome and inconvenient for the majority of Justices (who had decided to uphold the death penalty) to acknowledge. Perhaps because of the deep ambivalence about capital punishment . . . and because of the profound nature of what is at stake in any death penalty case, the Court began to deal with these troublesome and inconvenient social facts by declaring them irrelevant. . . . Because they had decided the death penalty was "really necessary," they would refuse to examine what it really was or, in the wake of the new laws they continued to approve, what it was becoming.[189]

The result is "an idealized but inaccurate account of how capital punishment actually operates in the United States" rather than "a social fact-oriented and empirically based discussion of the realities of the system of death sentencing."[190]

In essence, it is alleged that the U.S. Supreme Court has failed to do its job. On the one hand, "the Court has created an overly complex, absurdly arcane, and minutely detailed body of constitutional law that imposes an unacceptable burden on states' attempts to administer their capital punishment schemes." On the other hand, the "Court has in fact turned its back on regulating the death penalty and no longer even attempts to meet the concerns about the arbitrary and discriminatory imposition of death that animated its 'constitutionalization' of capital punishment in *Furman*."[191]

CONCLUSION

This chapter showed, based on substantive criminal law, for which crimes a person can be executed in the United States. It is generally agreed that no one will be executed for any crime other than murder, although at least one person has recently been sentenced to death for rape of a child. The constitutionality of this death sentence has not yet been determined by the U.S. Supreme Court.

This chapter also showed the numerous protections, based on procedural criminal law, that those charged with capital crimes enjoy. In spite of these protections, scholars, litigators, and activists have alleged serious problems with the application of capital punishment. Yet, as this chapter also showed, the U.S. Supreme Court has not been swayed by the results of empirical studies showing problems with the death penalty, most specifically its arbitrary nature.

Part of the reason the Court has not been swayed by the empirical realities of capital punishment in the United States is the inconsistency in its most significant death penalty decisions. This chapter illustrated three types of inconsistency in U.S. Supreme Court decisions, including opinions that are contradictory to opinions issued in earlier cases (TYPE I inconsistency), opinions that appear to be contradictory to statements made in written opinions in earlier cases (TYPE II inconsistency), and rulings in ways that appear to violate precedents or rules of law (TYPE III inconsistency). These inconsistencies are explained by various factors, including the ambiguous nature of the Constitution; ideology or attitudes and political party affiliation of individual justices; approach to interpreting the Constitution; strategic rationality and bargaining; changing justices over time; evolving human standards; and public opinion and state legislative activity.

In the next chapter, I explain the methodology of a study of death penalty experts that is aimed at capturing expert opinion on the realities of American capital punishment. The study seeks to determine if experts think capital punishment is effective and free from the serious problems that are said to plague the process.

ENDNOTES

1. *Coker v. Georgia*, 433 U.S. 584 (1977).
2. Adams, C. (2003, November). Death Watch, Louisiana jury sentences a man to death for non-murder crime; proportionality review bars prosecution seeking death in retrial; Alabama death row execution. *The Champion*

(National Association of Criminal Defense Lawyers). Retrieved from http://www.criminaljustice.org/public.nsf/941a6d5b3ad55cd485256b05008143fd/277b172862989eef85256e540074c1b1?OpenDocument

3. *State v. Wilson and Bethley*, 685 So.2d 1053 (La. 1996).
4. American Civil Liberties Union. (1997, December 31). *The case against the death penalty*. Retrieved from http://www.aclu.org/capital/general/10441pub19971231.html
5. Liptak, A. (2006, June 10). Death penalty in some cases of child sex is widening. *The New York Times*. Retrieved from http://www.nytimes.com/2006/06/10/us/10execute.html?ex=1307592000&en=75e3759eb2168dc4&ei=5088&partner=rssnyt&emc=rss
6. Bohm, B. (2003). *Deathquest II: An introduction to the theory and practice of capital punishment in the United States* (2nd ed.). Cincinnati, OH: Anderson, p. 21.
7. *Wilkerson v. Utah*, 99 U.S. 130, 134-135 (1878).
8. *In re Kemmler*, 136 U.S. 436, 447 (1890).
9. *Andres v. U.S.*, 333 U.S. 740 (1948).
10. *Weems v. United States*, 217 U.S. 349 (1910).
11. *Trop v. Dulles*, 356 U.S. 86 (1958).
12. *Coker v. Georgia*, 433 U.S. 584 (1977).
13. *Eberhart v. Georgia*, 433 U.S. 917 (1977).
14. *Enmund v. Florida*, 458 U.S. 782 (1982).
15. *Ford v. Wainright*, 477 U.S. 399 (1986).
16. *Thompson v. Oklahoma*, 487 U.S. 815 (1988).
17. *Stanford v. Kentucky*, 492 U.S. 361 (1989).
18. *Wilkins v. Missouri*, 492 U.S. 361 (1989).
19. *Roper v. Simmons*, No. 03-633 (2004).
20. *Penry v. Lynaugh*, 492 U.S. 302 (1989).
21. *Atkins v. Virginia*, 536 U.S. 304 (2002).
22. *United States v. Jackson*, 390 U.S. 570 (1968).
23. *McGautha v. California* and *Crampton v. Ohio*, 402 U.S. 183 (1971).
24. *Furman v. Georgia*, 408 U.S. 228 (1972).
25. *Gregg v. Georgia*, 428 U.S. 153 (1976).
26. *Woodson v. North Carolina*, 428 U.S. 280 (1976).
27. *Roberts v. Louisiana*, 431 U.S. 633 (1977); *Sumner v. Shuman*, 483 U.S. 66 (1987).
28. *Lockett v. Ohio*, 438 U.S. 586 (1978); *Bell v. Ohio*, 438 U.S. 637 (1978).
29. *Hitchcock v. Dugger*, 481 U.S. 393 (1987); *McKoy v. North Carolina*, 494 U.S. 433 (1990).
30. *Skipper v. South Carolina*, 476 U.S. 1 (1986).
31. *Mills v. Maryland*, 486 U.S. 367 (1988).
32. *Walton v. Arizona*, 497 U.S. 639 (1990).
33. *Godfrey v. Georgia*, 446 U.S. 420 (1980).
34. *Barefoot v. Estelle*, 463 U.S. 880 (1983).
35. *Barclay v. Florida*, 463 U.S. 939 (1983).
36. *Powell v. Alabama*, 287 U.S. 45 (1932).
37. Bohm (2003), p. 21.

38. Bohm (2003), p. 22.
39. *Murray v. Giarratano*, 492 U.S. 1 (1989).
40. *Witherspoon v. Illinois*, 391 U.S. 510 (1968).
41. *Adams v. Texas*, 448 U.S. 38 (1980).
42. *Wainwright v. Witt*, 469 U.S. 412 (1985).
43. *Lockhart v. McCree*, 476 U.S. 162 (1986).
44. *Morgan v. Illinois*, 504 U.S. 719 (1992).
45. *Strickland v. Washington*, 466 U.S. 668 (1984).
46. *Antone v. Dugger*, 465 U.S. 200 (1984).
47. *Ring v. Arizona*, 536 U.S. 584 (2002).
48. *Spaziano v. Florida*, 468 U.S. 447 (1984).
49. *Schriro v. Summerlin*, 542 U.S. 348 (2004).
50. *Beck v. Alabama*, 447 U.S. 625 (1980).
51. *Payne v. Tennessee*, 501 U.S. 808 (1991).
52. *Booth v. Maryland*, 482 U.S. 496 (1987); *South Carolina v. Gathers*, 490 U.S. 805 (1989).
53. *Simmons v. South Carolina*, 512 U.S. 154 (1994).
54. *Shafer v. South Carolina*, 532 U.S. 36 (2001).
55. *Ramdass v. Angelone*, 530 U.S. 156 (2000).
56. *Pulley v. Harris*, 465 U.S. 37 (1984).
57. *Miller-El v. Dretke*, No. 03-9659 (2004).
58. *Batson v. Kentucky*, 476 U.S. 79 (1986).
59. *Vasquez v. Hillery*, 474 U.S. 254 (1986).
60. *Turner v. Murray*, 476 U.S. 28 (1986).
61. *McCleskey v. Kemp*, 481 U.S. 279 (1987).
62. *Sawyer v. Whitley*, 505 U.S. 333 (1992).
63. *Herrera v. Collins*, 506 U.S. 390 (1993).
64. *Schlup v. Delo*, 513 U.S. 298 (1995).
65. Merriam Webster's Unabridged Dictionary. (2002). Inconsistent. Retrieved from http://www.m-w.com/dictionary/inconsistent
66. Lazarus, E. (1999). *Closed chambers: The rise, fall, and future of the modern Supreme Court*. Middlesex, England: Penguin Books; Woodward, B., & Armstrong, S. (1979). *The Brethren: Inside the Supreme Court*. New York: Simon and Schuster.
67. Epstein, L., & Walker, T. (1998). *Constitutional law for a changing America* (3rd ed.). Washington, DC: Congressional Quarterly.
68. Lazarus (1999), p. 13.
69. *Furman*, 408 U.S. at 228.
70. *Gregg*, 428 U.S. at 153.
71. *Woodson*, 428 U.S. at 280.
72. *McCleskey*, 481 U.S. at 279.
73. Robinson, M., & Simon, K. (2006). Logical and consistent? An analysis of Supreme Court opinions regarding the death penalty. *Justice Policy Journal*, 3(1), 1–59. Retrieved from http://www.cjcj.org/pdf/logical_and.pdf
74. For an excellent summary of these cases, and some others, see Haney, C. (2005). *Death by design: Capital punishment as a social psychological system*.

New York: Oxford University Press; Steiker, C., & Steiker, J. (2003). Judicial developments in capital punishment law. In J. Acker, B. Bohm, & C. Lanier (Eds.), *America's experiment with capital punishment: Reflections on the past, present, and future of the ultimate penal sanction* (2nd ed.). Durham, NC: Carolina Academic Press.

75. Bohm (2003).
76. Bohm (2003).
77. Bohm, B. (1999). *Deathquest: An introduction to the theory and practice of capital punishment in the United States.* Cincinnati, OH: Anderson, p. 23.
78. Bohm (1999), p. 24.
79. Acker, J., Bohm, B., & Lanier, C. (1998). *America's experiment with capital punishment: Reflections on the past, present, and future of the ultimate penal sanction.* Durham, NC: Carolina Academic Press.
80. *McGautha*, 402 U.S. at 183.
81. *Furman*, 408 U.S. at 257–258.
82. *Furman*, 408 U.S. at 292.
83. *Furman*, 408 U.S. at 310.
84. *Furman*, 408 U.S. at 313.
85. *Furman*, 408 U.S. at. 361.
86. *Furman*, 408 U.S. at 263–264.
87. *Furman*, 408 U.S. at 389.
88. *Furman*, 408 U.S. at 398–399.
89. *Furman*, 408 U.S. at 405.
90. *Furman*, 408 U.S. at 410.
91. *Furman*, 408 U.S. at 449.
92. *Woodson*, 428 U.S. at 280.
93. *Woodson*, 428 U.S. at 281.
94. *Woodson*, 428 U.S. at 291.
95. *Woodson*, 428 U.S. at 293.
96. *Woodson*, 428 U.S. at 295–296.
97. *Woodson*, 428 U.S. at 298.
98. *Woodson*, 428 U.S. at 302.
99. *Woodson*, 428 U.S. at 313.
100. *Roberts v. Louisiana*, 428 U.S. 325 (1976).
101. *Jurek v. Texas*, 428 U.S. 262 (1976).
102. *Proffitt v. Florida*, 428 U.S. 242 (1976).
103. *Gregg*, 428 U.S. at 155.
104. *Gregg*, 428 U.S. at 198.
105. *Gregg*, 428 U.S. at 206–207.
106. *Gregg*, 428 U.S. at 225.
107. *Gregg*, 428 U.S. at 229.
108. *Gregg*, 428 U.S. at 238.
109. Haney (2005), p. 17.
110. *McCleskey*, 481 U.S. at 281.
111. *McCleskey*, 481 U.S. at 312.

112. *McCleskey*, 481 U.S. at 313.

113. *McCleskey*, 481 U.S. at 320.

114. *McCleskey*, 481 U.S. at 336.

115. For other examples of inconsistency in these cases, see Haney (2005); Acker, J., & Lanier, C. (2003). Beyond human ability? The rise and fall of death penalty legislation. In J. Acker, B. Bohm, & C. Lanier (Eds.), *America's experiment with capital punishment: Reflections on the past, present, and future of the ultimate penal sanction* (2nd ed.). Durham, NC: Carolina Academic Press.

116. *Maxwell v. Bishop*, 398 U.S. 262 (1970).

117. *Batson v. Kentucky*, 476 U.S. 79 (1986).

118. *Gregg*, 428 U.S. at 225.

119. Lazarus (1999), p. 199.

120. *Bazemore v. Friday*, 478 U.S. 79 (1986).

121. Lazarus (1999), p. 208.

122. Lieberman, J. (1992). *The evolving Constitution: How the Supreme Court has rules on issues from abortion to zoning.* New York: Random House, p. 21.

123. Epstein & Walker (1998); Segal, J., & Spaeth, H. (1993). *The Supreme Court and the attitudinal model.* New York: Cambridge University Press.

124. Lieberman (1992), p. 12.

125. Epstein & Walker (1998).

126. Lieberman (1992), p. 149.

127. Epstein & Walker (1998); Segal, J. (1984). Predicting Supreme Courts probabilistically: The search and seizure cases, 1962–1984. *American Political Science Review, 10,* 891–900; Segal, J., & Cover, D. (1989). Ideological values and the votes of the U.S. Supreme Court justices. *American Political Science Review, 83,* 557; Segal & Spaeth (1993); Tate, C. (1981). Personal attribute models of voting behavior of U.S. Supreme Court justices: Liberalism in civil liberties and economics decisions, 1946–1978. *American Journal of Political Science, 75,* 355–367.

128. Lazarus (1999); Wagman, R. (1993). *The Supreme Court: A citizen's guide.* New York: Pharos Books.

129. Wagman (1993), p. 114.

130. Epstein, L., Segal, J., Spaeth, H., & Walker, T. (1996). *The Supreme Court compendium: Data, decisions, and developments* (2nd ed.). Washington, DC: Congressional Quarterly.

131. George, T., & Epstein, L. (1992). On the nature of Supreme Court decision making. *American Political Science Review, 86,* 323–337; Segal & Cover (1989); Tate (1981).

132. Epstein & Walker (1998), p. 7; Lieberman (1992), p. 7.

133. Peltason, J. (1997). *Corwin & Pelatson's understanding the Constitution* (14th ed.). Fort Worth, TX: Harcourt Brace.

134. Epstein & Walker (1998); Lieberman (1992); Walker, T., & Epstein, L. (1993). *The Supreme Court of the United States: An introduction.* New York: St. Martin's Press.

135. Robinson, M. (2002). *Justice blind? Ideals and realities of American criminal justice.* Upper Saddle River, NJ: Prentice Hall.

136. Epstein & Walker (1998), p. 30.

137. Epstein et al. (1996).

138. Woodward & Armstrong (1979), p. 181.

139. Lazarus (1999).

140. Epstein & Walker (1998), p. 36.

141. Cox, A. (1987). The role of the Supreme Court: Judicial activism or self-restraint? *Maryland Law Review, 47*, 118–138; Jones, G. (2001). Proper judicial activism. *Regent University Law Review, 14*, 141–179.

142. Bellacosa, J. (1992). Three little words: The nature of the judicial process revisited. *ABA Journal, 78*, 114.

143. Gates, J., & Phelps, G. (1991). The myth of jurisprudence: Interpretive theory in the constitutional opinions of Justices Rehnquist and Brennan. *Santa Clara Law Review, 31*, 567–596.

144. Shane, P. (2000). Federalism's "old deal": What's right and what's wrong with conservative judicial activism. *Villanova Law Review, 45*, 201–243; Sunstein, C. (1999). Let's not overlook activism by conservative judges. *The Los Angeles Daily Journal, 112*, 6.

145. Epstein & Walker (1998), p. 37.

146. Chemerinsky, E. (1996). The shrinking docket. *Trial, 32*, 71–72.

147. Howard, A. (1993). Pendulum swung widely in 15-year period: U.S. saw two different eras of judicial activism. *The National Law Journal, 16*, S8.

148. Lazarus (1999), p. 420.

149. Lazarus (1999).

150. Stearns, M. (1999). Should justices ever switch votes? *Miller v. Albright* in social choice perspective. *Supreme Court Economic Review, 7*, 87.

151. Epstein & Walker (1998), p. 57.

152. Segal & Spaeth (1993).

153. Segal, J., & Spaeth, H. (1996). The influence of *stare decisis* on the votes of the U.S. Supreme Court justices. *American Journal of Political Science, 40*, 971–1002.

154. George & Epstein (1992).

155. Melone, A. (1990). Revisiting the freshman effect hypothesis: The first two terms of Justice Anthony Kennedy. *Judicature, 74*, 6–13; Scheb, J., & L. Ailshie, L. (1985). Justice Sandra Day O'Connor and the "freshman effect." *Judicature, 69*, 9–12.

156. Woodward & Armstrong (1979).

157. Woodward & Armstrong (1979), p. 213.

158. Lazarus (1999).

159. Woodward & Armstrong (1979), p. 440.

160. Lazarus (1999).

161. Lazarus (1999), p. 116.

162. Lazarus (1999), p. 117.

163. *Tompkins v. Texas*, 490 U.S. 754 (1989).

164. Lazarus (1999).

165. *Beck v. Alabama*, 447 U.S. 625 (1980).

166. Lazarus (1999).

167. Lazarus (1999), p. 67.

168. Lazarus (1999), pp. 68, 72.

169. Woodward & Armstrong (1979). *Maxwell v. Bishop*, 398 U.S. 262 (1970).

170. *Massiah v. United States*, 377 U.S. 201 (1964).

171. Lieberman (1992), p. 11.

172. Cox (1987); Jones (2001).

173. Lieberman (1992), p. 19.

174. *Callins v. Collins*, 000 U.S. U10343 (1994).

175. *Callins v. Collins*, 000 U.S. at 9–10.

176. Stephenson, D. (1994). Justice Blackmun's Eighth Amendment pilgrimage. *BYU Journal of Public Law, 2*, 271–320.

177. Marshall, T. (1989). *Public opinion and the Supreme Court*. New York: Unwin Hyman; Mishler, W., & R. Sheehan, R. (1993). The Supreme Court as a counter-majoritarian institution? The impact of public opinion on Supreme Court decisions. *American Political Science Review, 87*, 89.

178. Bohm (2003).

179. Robinson, M. (2005). *Justice blind? Ideals and realities of American criminal justice* (2nd ed.). Upper Saddle River, NJ: Prentice Hall; Shelden, R. (2002). *Controlling the dangerous classes: A critical introduction to the history of criminal justice.* Boston: Allyn & Bacon; Shelden, R., & Brown, W. (2003). *Criminal justice in America: A critical view.* Boston: Allyn & Bacon.

180. Lazarus (1999).

181. *Atkins v. Virginia*, 536 U.S. 304 (2002).

182. *Roper*, No. 03-0633.

183. *Penry*, 492 U.S. at 302.

184. *Stanford*, 492 U.S. at 361.

185. Lazarus (1999).

186. Acker, J. (1993). A different agenda: The Supreme Court, empirical research evidence, and capital punishment decisions, 1986–1989. *Law & Society Review, 27*, 65–88.

187. Diamond, S., & Casper, J. (1994). Empirical evidence and the death penalty: Past and future. *Journal of Social Issues, 50*, 177–197; Haney, C., & Logan, D. (1994). Broken promise: The Supreme Court's response to social science research on capital punishment. *Journal of Social Issues, 50*, 75–101.

188. Haney (2005), p. 6.

189. Haney (2005), p. 11.

190. Haney (2005), p. 24.

191. Steiker & Steiker (2003), p. 55.

METHODOLOGY

INTRODUCTION

Although others have assessed the state of opinion with regard to the death penalty, little research to date has systematically evaluated expert opinion on capital punishment. Therefore, I surveyed American capital punishment experts in order to find out their opinions on the issues that most pertain to whether the policy succeeds or fails. The survey contained items dealing with the goals of capital punishment (i.e., whether we achieve our goals of retribution, incapacitation, and deterrence using the punishment) and items addressing the alleged problems with capital punishment (e.g., bias, innocence).

In this chapter, I explain the process of conducting a survey of death penalty experts—writing the survey, selecting a sample, and so forth—and explain in detail how I conducted the study whose findings are reported in subsequent chapters. I also discuss how I think capital punishment (and all criminal justice polices) should be evaluated by policy makers.

WHAT I DID

I created a survey addressing theoretical justifications for, and alleged problems with, capital punishment. The survey was meant to assess whether capital punishment experts thought the death penalty met its goals and whether it was plagued by significant problems. The survey also assesses whether experts support capital punishment (or alternatives such as life imprisonment without the possibility of parole), and whether they favor a temporary halt on executions (moratorium) and/or abolition of capital punishment.

I then selected a sample of death penalty experts to participate in the study. Experts consisted of capital punishment scholars—people who had recently published books and articles on the death penalty.

HOW I DID IT

I began the study by creating a survey instrument and getting it approved by my university's institutional review board (IRB). The survey was pretested on colleagues in order to identify potential problems with the way each item was worded. After minor adjustments were made to the survey instrument, I finalized the survey and began working on the sample of capital punishment experts who would be sent the survey.

Dictionary.com defines the word *expert* as "a person with a high degree of skill in or knowledge of a certain subject."[1] Wikipedia defines an expert as "someone widely recognized as a reliable source of knowledge, technique, or skill whose judgment is accorded authority and status by the public or their peers. Experts have prolonged or intense experience through practice and education in a particular field."[2]

Modifying these definitions of *expert* leads to my definition of a capital punishment expert: A capital punishment expert is a person with a high degree of knowledge of capital punishment, someone who is widely recognized as a reliable source of knowledge due to prolonged experience through practice and education related to the death penalty, whose judgment is accorded authority and status by the public or his or her peers.

An earlier study of "expert opinion" of the deterrent effect of capital punishment was based on a survey of current and former presidents of the American Society of Criminology (ASC), the Academy of Criminal Justice Sciences (ACJS), and the Law and Society Association (LSA). In the article, which focused exclusively on the issue of deterrence, the authors wrote:

> We must first answer the question of how to define "expert." One plausible definition is anyone who has published peer-reviewed research on the death penalty and deterrence. Surely those who have been active researchers in an area over many years are experts. However, such an approach has limited utility because 1) it is possible that only death penalty abolitionists, for whatever reasons, are motivated to conduct such research, 2) there would be a problem in differentially weighing the opinions of scholars who have published several acclaimed deterrence studies in major criminology journals from those whose research is less abundant or respected, and 3) surveying researchers in the field of deterrence would ask them to, in effect, evaluate their own work.[3]

For these reasons, the authors chose not to survey scholars who had published in the area of deterrence, but instead chose to survey presidents of major criminological organizations. In the current study, I chose to survey published scholarly experts, meaning the three limitations identified above apply to the study reported in this book. I address them below.

The key issue to resolve in order to successfully complete the study was how to select a sample of capital punishment experts. As an academic, my first thought was to limit the study to scholars who, because of their work, are widely thought to be and referred to as experts on the subject. These individuals would be identified by their scholarly works.

Yet, a notable capital punishment expert, in responding to a query, suggested not only surveying scholars of capital punishment (based on their published works), but also death penalty litigators (based on years of experience with capital cases and recognition by peers) and activists (based on years of experience working on the death penalty and recognition by peers).[4]

Locating a random sample of all litigators and activists was impossible due to the fact that there was no neutral, unbiased list with which to begin. I was thus uncomfortable choosing a handful of litigators and activists known to me or to any given organization, and then using a snowball sampling technique to build the sample. I wanted to ensure that any expert could have a reasonable chance of participating in my survey.

As it turns out, the sample of academic or scholarly experts was sufficiently large to warrant excluding death penalty litigators and activists. Further, there was a means to ensure a fair, objective sample of scholarly experts for the survey.

To locate academic or scholarly experts on capital punishment, I utilized two computerized databases in order to search for books and articles on the subject. To locate books, I used the WorldCat database. WorldCat contains more than 40 million records cataloged by Online Computer Library Center (OCLC) member libraries throughout the world, including primarily books, but also other manuscripts. WorldCat does not include individual articles in journals.[5] For articles, I used the Academic Search Elite and Academic Search Premier databases. They provide abstracts and indexing for almost 8,200 titles, including more than 3,600 peer-reviewed titles, as well as searchable cited references for 1,000 titles in the social sciences and other areas.[6]

Using these databases allowed me to locate every book and article indexed in these sources on the subject of "capital punishment" or "death penalty." Given the enormous numbers of books and articles published on these topics—nearly 7,000 books and articles published in English—I ultimately limited my search to books and articles published over the past 5 years (2001–2005). This resulted in 686 books and 390 articles.[7]

Another reason to limit the search to works published between 2001 and 2005 is that this ensures I would include those scholars who are currently active in death penalty scholarship. Scholars who have not written on the death penalty recently may still be considered experts. However, it is possible that they would not be familiar with the most recent developments in both death penalty practice and research. Surely some (even notable) death penalty experts were excluded from participation in this study. This is an acknowledged limitation of this study.

The next step was to review each individual library record for all capital punishment books and articles published between 2001 and 2005, in order to eliminate any that were retrieved in error (e.g., the entry was not related to the topic), that were duplicates, or that, after careful consideration, could be eliminated due to one of several reasons. First, I eliminated any article or book that dealt with the death penalty in another country. Second, I eliminated any article or book that dealt with some aspect of capital punishment that was so limited in nature that it could not be assumed from the work that the author(s) had developed expertise on the overall topic of capital punishment in the United States. Examples include topics such as the execution of juveniles, IQ and the death penalty, mental illness and capital punishment, religion (or the Bible) and the death penalty, the use of DNA in the capital punishment process, and so forth. I maintained all works that dealt with the issue of capital punishment generally.

The final population of capital punishment books and articles was made up of 240 authors. Of the 240 authors identified using these databases, 44 individuals had published at least one book and one article on capital punishment. Another 73 individuals had published a book on the topic but no articles. Finally, 123 scholars had published at least one article on the death penalty. Many of the authors of books and articles were one-time authors who might not reasonably be considered experts given their limited research on the topic. Most of these were eliminated from the population for this reason. Only 16 authors of single articles were included in the population, and they were maintained because of the particular topics of their articles. Authors of single articles on topics directly related to the book were maintained in the sample, including justifications for capital punishment (retribution, deterrence, incapacitation) and alleged problems with capital punishment (race, class, and gender bias, innocence, and so forth).

The final population of death penalty experts was made up of 133 scholars. I entered their names alphabetically into Microsoft Excel and randomly chose 90 for my sample. I wanted to keep the number below 100 experts for two reasons. First, the survey was lengthy (12 pages) and required respondents to write short answers in response to questions pertaining to their degree of support for the death penalty, their opinions about whether capital punishment achieved its goals and some alleged problems with capital punishment, as well as their views about the likely future of capital punishment in the United States. I thought it would be wise to limit the number of respondents in order to make the study manageable.

Second, I knew that each respondent would be providing me with up to 10 names of people they thought were experts (my definition of *expert* includes a person "whose judgment is accorded authority and status by the public or his or her peers"). Thus, I could potentially be sending the survey to numerous additional scholars who were identified as experts by their peers who recently published a book and/or article on the death penalty.

I attained the contact information of each of the 90 experts included in the study and first sent each expert an e-mail to let them know I would be sending the survey soon in the mail. Then, I mailed each expert a copy of the survey and followed that up with another e-mail reminding them of the deadline by which the survey should be sent back to me in the stamped, return envelopes I provided. Shortly thereafter, one expert told me he would prefer to receive an electronic copy of the survey and asked me to send it via e-mail. I did so and then decided to send an electronic copy of the survey to all of those potential respondents included in the sample, explaining to them that they could type their responses into the document and return it if they would prefer. Just before the deadline by which to participate, I contacted the experts again via e-mail and reminded them of the deadline. I also sent one final e-mail shortly after the deadline as a last call for participation.

The respondents who participated in the study identified a total of 82 different individuals whom they considered to be experts.[8] Of these, only about one quarter (21 individuals) were identified by more than 2 respondents. All but 6 of these 21 individuals were already included in the sample based on their recently published work, and the 15 individuals already in the sample were identified by an average of 8.7 respondents. Stated differently, 15 of the 21 individuals (71.4%) who were selected by more than 2 of the experts in this study were already included to receive the survey. This lends some credibility to the method I used to select experts for this study, given that only 6 individuals considered experts by more than 2 recently published scholars were not included in the original sample presumably because they had not published works recently on the death penalty.

I added these 6 additional experts to the sample. Each of these individuals was identified by an average of 6 respondents.

The total sample of death penalty experts was thus 96 individual scholars who either had written books and/or articles on the death penalty between 2001 and 2005, or were selected by more than 2 of these scholars as experts on the death penalty. This approach is not without limitations. Adding 6 new scholars to the sample means the selection process was not entirely random. Yet, this was my effort to add experts widely recognized by scholars to my sample of death penalty experts. To my knowledge, none of these 6 experts responded to the survey, so this effort likely only lowered my response rate.

After sending out surveys to each of the 96 individuals, I learned that 2 had recently passed away. Thus, my sample size was now down to 94 experts (others had moved to new jobs and may have never received the surveys). I received completed surveys from 45 respondents. Thus, 47.9% of the 94 experts chosen for the sample participated in the study. Ideally, a higher number of responses could have been potentially more useful, but a response rate of 47.9% is considered adequate for studies conducted via the mail.[9] This response rate is higher than recently published studies in the areas of police complaint mediation (18.1%),[10] men and sexual coercion (22%),[11] clergy awareness of child abuse (33%),[12] alcohol use in the United Kingdom and Germany (41%),[13] primary health professionals' perceptions of child physical abuse (44%),[14] and a study of criminal victimization among primary care medical patients (45%).[15] However, the response rate of the current study is lower than in recently published studies of violence against women seeking abortions in New Zealand (49.7%),[16] school nurses' preparedness for bioterrorism and disaster preparedness (64%),[17] physicians' opinions of prescribing medical marijuana (66%),[18] practitioners' knowledge and experience of elder abuse in Britain (68%),[19] judges' opinions of expert evidence (71%),[20] psychologists' and psychiatrists' assessment of violence risks (71%),[21] pediatric training in sexual abuse (73%),[22] services and programming for abused women (74%),[23] beliefs by Swedish legal professionals about eyewitness testimony (74%),[24] job satisfaction and level of stress among Alaskan police officers (81%),[25] alcohol use and intimate partner violence (85%),[26] and college programs for inmates (90%).[27]

After reviewing the studies above, a strongly justified conclusion about why the response rate in this study was not higher is that I did not telephone potential respondents to encourage them to participate in the survey. Most of the studies cited above preceded their mail surveys with a letter of introduction and then followed it up with telephone calls. I introduced my survey with an e-mail, informing the members of the sample that they had been selected to participate in a survey of death penalty experts due to their recent publication(s) in this area. Ten members of the sample likely never received the e-mail because it was returned to me with an error message, suggesting the e-mail addresses were either no longer valid or that they could not receive it for another reason (e.g., the accounts were over capacity). It is unlikely that I had the incorrect e-mail address for any individual because I copied them directly from the Web sites of their respective departments, schools, colleges, and/or universities.

I did not telephone potential respondents to encourage them to participate in the study for one primary reason: I did not want to bias their responses. One drawback to larger samples due to increased response rates is that error or bias is likely to be introduced with repeated appeals for participation, especially when principal investigators are asked pointed questions about the intent of their work.[28] In fact, a few individuals who did ultimately respond to the survey asked for more information about the intent of the study, as well as my plans for publishing the results. I replied with the same general e-mail to each individual, indicating that I wanted to capture the opinions of individual death penalty experts and present the overall opinions of death penalty experts in the form of a book. In response to a query, I did talk in person about the intent of the work to one expert at a national criminology conference.

Frankly, another reason I did not telephone each potential respondent was because I did not think it was necessary. Being selected to participate in a study of experts on a topic means one has reached a level of recognition in their careers through their work that, in my view, carries with it a responsibility to speak about and be heard on that topic. Naively, I expected participation in the study to be much higher, because I thought each person selected would be honored to participate.

Some possible reasons why the response rate was not higher include the length of the survey (12 pages), the controversial nature of some of the questions, and because some individuals did not want to be identified. First, at least a few people contacted me via e-mail and told me they would not be participating in the survey because they just did not have the time. These are, ironically, busy death penalty scholars. Second, some of the questions dealt with controversial topics such as whether individual scholars personally supported the death penalty, whether capital punishment deterred murder (an issue currently being hotly debated in the discipline of economics), and so forth. Third, it is likely that some individuals did not participate because they did not want their names associated with any particular response. For example, some individuals likely did not want to answer questions "off the tops of their heads" on issues about which they had already written extensively. One expert replied to my e-mail by writing, "Why would anyone answer these questions? Entire books have been written about each question." This could be due to the small possibility that their responses might contradict their own writings and/or those of other individual scholars who hold different beliefs. I did give all potential respondents the opportunity to reply anonymously and/or to identify themselves but deny me permission to attribute their responses back to them.

In spite of not having a higher rate of participation by death penalty experts, most of the highly published experts and those widely considered to be experts by my original sample did participate in this study. Because only 11 of the surveys were returned anonymously, I actually know who filled out most of the surveys (yet when data were entered into the computer, I listed only the names of those people who gave me permission to quote their responses). I decided not to reveal the identity of any respondent in the book because additional respondents who identified themselves asked me not to reveal their identities or attribute any particular quote to them. In fact, only 18 experts gave me permission to quote them directly. I felt attributing responses to only 18 experts throughout the book while presenting the responses of 27 others anonymously made little sense. In retrospect, I probably could have increased my response rate and sample size by designing the survey to be entirely anonymous.

LIMITATIONS OF DATA

The data presented in this book are limited in several ways. First, there is some question about whether all scholarly capital punishment experts had a chance to be included in the sample. When attempting to locate death penalty experts, I searched for books and articles using the search terms "capital punishment" and "death penalty" in the subject line of the databases. Conceivably, scholars who published works on capital punishment–related topics who supplied different subject terms or whose works were categorized for some reason under different terms would not show up in the searches. There is no way to know how many of these individuals were excluded.

Second, there is also some question about the representative nature of the experts. It is likely that most scholarly experts on capital punishment are opposed to the punishment. That is, it is probable that most people who write about the death penalty not only have an academic interest in the death penalty but also have recognized some problem(s) with it that motivates their writings. Similar to the suggestion of the authors of the study of presidents of major criminological organizations discussed earlier, the findings of the study presented in this book might reflect the biased opinions of the sample of experts surveyed. This assumes that scholars who support the death penalty are less active in scholarship due to the fact that they have no (or little) problem with the practice of capital punishment in the United States and/or because the sanction is legal and thus not likely to generate writings that seek to justify its use.

Third, I make no effort to distinguish between those authors who have published an enormous amount of work on the death penalty, in top journals or with university presses, from those experts who have published less work, and in lower tiered journals or with textbook publishers. Yet, as someone who teaches and reads a good bit about the death penalty, I am very confident that the individuals who participated in this study do comprise a highly qualified and respected sample of experts as a group. Perhaps follow-up research will verify or refute this claim. In this book, no single expert's voice will be given more amplification than the others.

As a result of these limitations, it is thus possible that the data presented are not representative of the opinions of all death penalty experts. There is no way to know if this is true, but again, I am confident that the sample itself is comprised of most of the top experts on the topic of capital punishment. I also believe this study is superior to the earlier study of current and past presidents of major criminological societies, introduced earlier. According to that study:

- 84% said the death penalty is not a deterrent to homicide.
- 93% said the threat of the death penalty is not a greater deterrent to murder than long prison terms.
- 0% said the death penalty significantly reduces homicide.
- 87% said abolishing the death penalty in a state would have no significant effects of murder in that state.[29]

Although the findings were interesting and useful to inform policy, not all of the presidents surveyed were death penalty experts. In fact, few likely had studied the death penalty in any detail whatsoever. The authors of the study acknowledged this, writing, "although few of these scholars have done research on capital punishment in general or deterrence in particular, they are generally well versed in central criminological issues, such as crime causation, crime prevention, and criminal justice policy."[30]

Those who participated in the current study were all capital punishment experts. Table 3.1 shows the average number of years spent teaching about, researching, and engaging in activism on the death penalty by the respondents in the study. Collectively, these experts represent at least 625 years of research on capital punishment, 345 years of teaching about the death penalty, and 273 years of activism related to the death penalty.

TABLE 3.1	Average Number of Years Spent Teaching About, Researching, and Engaging in Activism on the Death Penalty by the Respondents in the Study
Teaching	14.9 years
Research	9.1 years
Activism	8.5 years

HOW TO EVALUATE THE DEATH PENALTY

The death penalty is typically supported or rejected due to moral or emotional reasons.[31] One problem with this, like with other controversial issues such as abortion, is that people on one side of the issue have a great time talking to people on the other side of the issue. A saying on a bumper sticker on the car of a death penalty opponent provides an example: "Why do we kill people who kill people to show them that killing people is wrong?" Death penalty opponents have trouble understanding how supporters justify the taking of a human life as an acceptable lesson to teach children that killing is wrong.

Supporters also have difficulty talking to opponents of capital punishment. For example, how could a supporter of capital punishment effectively talk to an opponent about his or her view that killing a murderer actually increases the value of human life by showing all in society how much importance we place on innocent human lives? Opponents inevitably respond with a charge of hypocrisy.

Another problem with basing support or rejection of a government policy on moral or emotional reasons is that it is very difficult, if not nearly impossible, to convince someone on the other side of the issue that you are right. I have read a great many arguments on capital punishment. Typically, death penalty arguments, whether for or against, rely on *philosophical* assumptions that are controversial and debatable.

A dictionary definition of philosophy is: "Investigation of the nature, causes, or principles of reality, knowledge, or values, based on logical reasoning rather than empirical methods."[32] I believe most death penalty arguments, both for and against, and most debates about the punishment rest on logical reasoning rather than empirical evidence. One example is an excellent book written by two notable philosophers who have each carefully thought about all aspects of capital punishment.[33]

In the book, one philosopher argues passionately in favor of capital punishment, the other vehemently against. Then, the supporter responds to the argument of the opponent, and vice versa. The result is a four-chapter book debating the death penalty. Each argument is skillfully made, and each author makes a sound, logical case.

Without question, supporters of the punishment will almost universally find the argument of the death penalty supporter most convincing. Likewise, opponents of capital punishment will almost always find the argument of the death penalty opponent the better argument. When I have assigned this book to students in my death penalty classes, this is exactly what happens. The students who support capital punishment before reading the book tell me the "winner" of the debate is the supporter. The students who opposed capital punishment before reading the book tell me the "winner" of the debate is the opponent.

Although both authors rely on empirical facts to justify their arguments, neither is really arguing about evidence. Instead, they are presenting selected empirical facts to justify their own opinions about capital punishment. I believe this is backwards. Policies should be evaluated using empirical evidence, and this requires a dispassionate—not emotional or moral—lens.

The best approach to evaluate any policy, including capital punishment, is to use empirical evidence—data—to determine if the policy is effective. Assuming one evaluates a policy based upon empirical evidence, a variety of standards can be used to assess a policy. One common method of assessment is goals oriented. If data indicate that a policy is achieving its desired goals, this would lead to a positive evaluation. In contrast, under a goals-oriented perspective, if empirical evidence indicates failure to achieve policy objectives, then one should expect a negative evaluation of the policy.

Evaluating a policy based merely on whether it meets its goals is necessary, but not sufficient. The reason is that each policy has not only benefits but also costs. The death penalty, for example, which might reduce murder by executing convicted murderers (a benefit), may also lead to the conviction and execution of innocent individuals (a cost). Although the death penalty may make some family members of murder victims feel a sense of justice (a benefit), it may also cost more to execute someone than to keep him or her in prison for life and lead to the execution of innocent people (a cost).

With this in mind, another method of assessment is costs–benefits analysis. Costs–benefits analysis involves a comparison of the costs of a policy as compared to the benefits derived from the policy. Methodologically, costs and benefits should have comparable measures, thus ensuring the validity of the comparison. In practice, this can entail placing a monetary value on such benefits as saving lives through executing murderers with the death penalty. Thus, this approach is not without its problems.[34] However, mechanisms can be adopted that allow for qualitative as well as quantitative assessments of costs and benefits.[35]

Policies where benefits outweigh costs typically have a positive evaluation. Conversely, when costs outweigh benefits, policies receive a negative evaluation. Further, a positive evaluation ought to result in an agenda for continuation of the policy, whereas a negative evaluation should lead to an agenda for policy change, including the termination of the policy.

An accurate picture of the impact of the death penalty is crucial if the government and the public are to make informed decisions about whether or not to continue practicing capital punishment. In my humble opinion, we should evaluate the death penalty—like all policies based on whether (1) the policy meets its goals, and (2) the benefits outweigh the harms.

If capital punishment, as actually practiced in the United States today, achieves its goals and does not produce costs that outweigh its benefits, it should be continued. Conversely, if capital punishment, as actually practiced in the United States today, fails to achieve its goals and imposes costs that outweigh its benefits, then it should be terminated.

You'll note that I've twice specified that capital punishment should be assessed as it is actually practiced—not in theory. Debating the death penalty in the abstract is one thing, evaluating the way it exists in reality is entirely another. A person may have no problem executing murderers in theory; however, it might be harder to argue that this is worthwhile if doing so creates costs such as biases based on race, class, or gender, or if it leads to a significant risk of executing innocent individuals, or other costs that might outweigh the benefits of the punishment.

What do the experts think? In order to find out, I constructed a survey and distributed it, as explained above. The survey contained items related to justifications for capital punishment and alleged problems with capital punishment. The survey is included below.

THE SURVEY INSTRUMENT

Survey of American Capital Punishment Experts

As an expert on the death penalty, you have been selected to participate in a brief survey about capital punishment. The goals of the research are to:

1) Identify and summarize the <u>general view of death penalty experts</u> on the reality of capital punishment in the United States; and

2) Identify and present the <u>specific opinions of individual death penalty experts</u> concerning the reality of capital punishment in the United States.

Your answers may be reported anonymously if you choose. Yet, since you have been identified as an expert on the subject, I would like to use individual quotes from your responses and attribute them to you, if you agree. You can return the survey without your name on it if you do not wish to be identified and/or if you do not wish your comments to be attributed to you. In this case, your identity will not be discovered nor revealed.

If you are willing to answer the questions in this survey and are willing to give permission to the principal investigator of this research project to quote your responses and attribute them to you, simply check the box below and provide your name, signature, and mailing address.

The survey is comprised of 21 questions. I appreciate your willingness to answer any and/or all of these questions and to return them to me in a timely manner within the enclosed envelope. <u>Please return the completed survey to me by no later than April 27, 2006</u> (the sooner the better).

If you have any questions, do not hesitate to contact me.

Sincerely,

Matthew B. Robinson, PhD
Associate Professor of Criminal Justice
Appalachian State University
Boone, NC 28608
(828) 262-6560
robinsnmb@appstate.edu

❑ I grant permission for the Principal Investigator of this study to quote my responses and to attribute them to me (check box if you agree).

Printed Name and Signature _____

Complete Mailing Address _____

First, please answer the following questions about capital punishment.

(Please <u>circle your answer</u> and then <u>explain your answers by writing legibly in the space provided.</u> Feel free to use a separate sheet of paper if necessary.)

1) **Do you believe in capital punishment/the death penalty, or are you opposed to it?** (circle your answer)

   a) Believe in it   b) Opposed to it   c) Other

   Please explain why you feel this way (Attach separate paper if necessary).

   _____

   _____

   _____

   _____

   _____

   _____

   _____

   _____

2) **What is the most appropriate punishment for someone <u>convicted of first-degree murder</u>?** (circle your answer)

   a) Death penalty   b) Life imprisonment   c) Other:
                             without parole

   Please explain why you feel this way (Attach separate paper if necessary).

   _____

   _____

   _____

   _____

   _____

   _____

   _____

   _____

3) **Does capital punishment, as actually practiced in the United States, achieve <u>retribution</u> (i.e., provide justice for murder victims, their families, and society at large)?** (circle your answer)

   a) Yes   b) No   c) Unsure

Please explain why you feel this way (Attach separate paper if necessary).

_____

_____

_____

_____

_____

_____

_____

_____

_____

4) **Does capital punishment, as actually practiced in the United States, achieve deterrence (i.e., prevent future murders by causing fear in would-be murderers so that they do not commit murder)?** (circle your answer)

   a) Yes   b) No   c) Unsure

Please explain why you feel this way (Attach separate paper if necessary).

_____

_____

_____

_____

_____

_____

_____

_____

_____

5) **Does capital punishment, as actually practiced in the United States, achieve incapacitation (i.e., prevent future murders by killing murderers who would murder again)?** (circle your answer)

   a) Yes   b) No   c) Unsure

Please explain why you feel this way (Attach separate paper if necessary).

_____

_____

_____

_____

_____

_____

_____

_____

_____

_____

6)   **Is American capital punishment plagued by <u>a racial bias of any kind</u>?**
     (circle your answer)

     a) Yes   b) No   c) Unsure

Please explain why you feel this way (Attach separate paper if necessary).

_____

_____

_____

_____

_____

_____

_____

_____

_____

_____

7)   **Is American capital punishment plagued by <u>a social class bias of any kind</u>?**
     (circle your answer)

     a) Yes   b) No   c) Unsure

Please explain why you feel this way (Attach separate paper if necessary).

_____

_____

_____

_____

_____

_____

_____

_____

_____

_____

8) Is American capital punishment plagued by <u>a gender/sex bias of any kind</u>?
     (<u>circle your answer</u>)

    a) Yes   b) No   c) Unsure

Please explain why you feel this way (Attach separate paper if necessary).

_____

_____

_____

_____

_____

_____

_____

_____

_____

9) Is American capital punishment <u>ever used against the innocent</u>?
     (<u>circle your answer</u>)

    a) Yes   b) No   c) Unsure

Please explain why you feel this way (Attach separate paper if necessary).

_____

_____

_____

_____

_____
_____
_____
_____
_____

10) In your opinion, are there <u>any other problems</u> (not addressed in the questions above) with the way capital punishment is practiced in the United States? (<u>circle your answer</u>)

    a) Yes   b) No   c) Unsure

Please explain why you feel this way (Attach separate paper if necessary).

_____
_____
_____
_____
_____
_____
_____
_____
_____

11) Do you personally favor <u>a temporary halt to executions (moratorium)</u> in the United States while the practice of American capital punishment is studied? (<u>circle your answer</u>)

    a) Yes   b) No   c) Unsure

Please explain why you feel this way (Attach separate paper if necessary).

_____
_____
_____
_____
_____
_____

_____

_____

_____

12) Does capital punishment, as actually practiced in the United States, have problems that are serious enough to make it <u>unacceptable as a government-sanctioned punishment</u> (so that states should permanently stop executing convicted murderers)? (<u>circle your answer</u>)

    a) Yes   b) No   c) Unsure

Please explain why you feel this way (Attach separate paper if necessary).

_____

_____

_____

_____

_____

_____

_____

_____

_____

13) As you know, many of our allies have abolished the death penalty. In your opinion, <u>why does the death penalty persist in the United States</u>? That is, why do we still use this criminal sanction? Please list and briefly discuss the reason(s) you think the U.S. still practices capital punishment. (<u>Attach separate paper if necessary).</u>

_____

_____

_____

_____

_____

_____

_____

_____

_____

_____

_____

_____

_____

_____

_____

_____

_____

_____

_____

_____

_____

_____

_____

_____

_____

_____

_____

_____

_____

Next, please answer the following questions about you.

14) How long have you been <u>doing research</u> about the death penalty?

_____

15) How long have you been <u>teaching</u> death penalty classes?

_____

16) How long have you been involved in death penalty <u>activism</u> of any kind?

_____

17) Please list <u>UP TO 10 individuals</u> you consider to be death penalty experts.

_____

_____

_____

_____

_____

_____

_____

IMPORTANT NOTE: ONLY ANSWER QUESTIONS 18–21 IF YOU AGREED TO BE IDENTIFIED AS A RESPONDENT IN THIS SURVEY.

18) **Please list your publications concerning the death penalty (e.g., articles, books):** (Attach separate paper if necessary).

_____

_____

_____

_____

_____

_____

_____

_____

19) **Please list your other death penalty activity (e.g., activism, assisting with individual death penalty cases, etc.):** (Attach separate paper if necessary).

_____

_____

_____

_____

_____

_____

20) **Please list any affiliations you have with death penalty groups (e.g., anti-death penalty or pro-death penalty groups)** (Attach separate paper if necessary).

_____

_____

_____

_____

_____

_____

_____

_____

21) Please list any other experience or expertise you have with regard to capital punishment that you think is relevant (Attach separate paper if necessary).

_____

_____

_____

_____

_____

_____

_____

_____

THIS CONCLUDES THE SURVEY.

PLEASE INSERT THE COMPLETED SURVEY IN THE ENCLOSED RETURN ENVELOPE AND MAIL IT BACK TO THE PRINCIPAL INVESTIGATOR.

ALSO, BE SURE TO CHECK THE BOX ON THE FRONT OF THE SURVEY AND PROVIDE YOUR NAME, SIGNATURE, AND MAILING ADDRESS IF YOU GIVE ME PERMISSION TO QUOTE YOUR RESPONSES.

RESULTS WILL BE SHARED WITH ALL RESPONDENTS WHO IDENTIFY THEMSELVES AND/OR THOSE WHO REQUEST THEM FROM THE PRINCIPAL INVESTIGATOR.

THANK YOU FOR YOUR PARTICIPATION!

CONCLUSION

This chapter laid out the methodology used in a study of capital punishment experts. Capital punishment experts were defined as people with a high degree of knowledge of capital punishment, who are widely recognized as reliable sources of knowledge due to prolonged experience through practice and education related to the death penalty, and whose judgments are accorded authority and status by the public or their peers.

A sample of capital punishment experts was selected from two electronic databases containing every author of a book or article on the subject of capital punishment. The experts were sent a lengthy survey dealing with justifications or goals of capital punishment, as well as alleged problems with it. The goal of the study is to determine if the death penalty, as actually practiced in the United States, is an effective policy—i.e., does it meet its goals and do its benefits outweigh its costs?

The 45 experts who responded to the survey have conducted research on capital punishment for at least 625 years, have been teaching about capital punishment for at least 345 years, and have engaged in at least 273 years of activism on death penalty issues. These are individuals who have recently published books and articles on capital punishment and who are recognized to be experts on the topic of capital punishment.

ENDNOTES

1. Dictionary.com. Expert. Retrieved from http://dictionary.reference.com/search?q=expert
2. Wikipedia.com. Expert. Retrieved from http://en.wikipedia.org/wiki/Expert
3. Radelet, M., & Akers, R. (1996). Deterrence and the death penalty: The views of the experts. *Journal of Criminal Law & Criminology, 81*(1), 1–16. Retrieved from http://sun.soci.niu.edu/~critcrim/dp/dppapers/mike.deterrence
4. Personal e-mail communication with Richard Dieter, executive director of the Death Penalty Information Center, January 2006.
5. Appalachian State University, Carol Grotnes Belk Library & Information Commons. (2006). *About WorldCat.* Retrieved from http://www.library.appstate.edu/reference/about/worldcat.html
6. Appalachian State University, Carol Grotnes Belk Library & Information Commons. (2006). *Research guide for criminal justice.* Retrieved from http://www.library.appstate.edu/reference/subjectguides/criminaljustice.html; and *About Academic Search Premier.* Retrieved from http://www.library.appstate.edu/reference/about/academicsearch.html
7. I searched each database using the terms "capital punishment" OR "death penalty" in the "Subject" field, specifying the language of English, and for books only using the WorldCat database, and refereed articles only in scholarly (peer reviewed) journals using the Academic Search databases.
8. This was in response to the question: "Please list UP TO 10 individuals you consider to be death penalty experts."
9. Babbie, E. (2003). *The practice of social research* (10th ed.). Belmont, CA: Wadsworth.
10. Bartels, E., & Silverman, E. (2005). An exploratory study of the New York City Civilian Complaint Review Board mediation program. *Policing Bradford, 28*(4), 619–630.
11. Senn, C., Desmarais, S., Verberg, N., & Wood, E. (2000). Sampling the reluctant participant: A random-sample response-rate study of men and sexual coercion. *Journal of Applied Social Psychology, 30*(1), 96–105.

12. Grossoehme, D. (1998). Child abuse reporting: Clergy perceptions. *Child Abuse & Neglect, 22*(7), 743–747.
13. Leifman, H. (2002). The six-country survey of the European comparative alcohol study: Comparing patterns and assessing validity. *Contemporary Drug Problems, 29*(3), 477–500.
14. Russell, M., Lazenbatt, A., Freeman, R., & Marcenes, W. (2004). Child physical abuse: Health professionals' perceptions, diagnosis and responses. *British Journal of Community Nursing, 9*(8), 332–338.
15. Koss, M., Woodruff, W., & Koss, P. (1991). Criminal victimization among primary care medical patients: Prevalence, incidence, and physician usage. *Behavioral Sciences & the Law, 9*(1), 85–96.
16. Whitehead, A., & Fanslow, J. (2005). Prevalence of family violence amongst women attending an abortion clinic in New Zealand. *Australian & New Zealand Journal of Obstetrics & Gynaecology, 45*(4), 321–324.
17. Mosca, N., Sweeney, P., Hazy, J., & Brenner, P. (2005). Assessing bioterrorism and disaster preparedness training needs for school nurses. *Journal of Public Health Management & Practice, 11*, 38–44.
18. Charuvastra, A., Friedmann, P., & Stein, M. (2005). Physician attitudes regarding the prescription of medical marijuana. *Journal of Addictive Diseases, 24*(3), 87–93.
19. McCreadie, C., Bennett, G., & Tinker, A. (1998). Investigating British general practitioners' knowledge and experience of elder abuse: Report of a research study in an inner London borough. *Journal of Elder Abuse & Neglect, 9*(3), 23–39.
20. Gatowski, S., Dobbin, S., Richardson, J., Ginsburg, G., Merlino, M., & Dahir, V. (2001). Asking the gatekeepers: A national survey of judges on judging expert evidence in a post-Daubert world. *Law and Human Behavior, 25*(5), 433.
21. Heilbrun, K., O'Neill, M., Strohman, L., Bowman, W., & Philipson, J. (2000). Expert approaches to communicating violence risk. *Law and Human Behavior, 24*(1), 137–148.
22. Dubow, S., Giardino, A., Christian, C., & Johnson, C. (2005). Do pediatric chief residents recognize details of prepubertal female genital anatomy: A national survey. *Child Abuse & Neglect, 29*(2), 195–205.
23. Fisher, B., Zink, T., Pabst, S., Regan, S., & Rinto, B. (2003). Services and programming for older abused women: The Ohio experience. *Journal of Elder Abuse & Neglect, 15*(2), 67–83.
24. Granhag, P., Stromwall, L., & Hartwig, M. (2005). Eyewitness testimony: Tracing the beliefs of Swedish legal professionals. *Behavioral Sciences & the Law, 23*(5), 709–727.
25. Wood, D. (2003). A comparison of group-administered and mail-administered surveys of Alaskan village public safety officers. *Policing, 26*(2), 329–340.
26. Field, C., Caetano, R., & Nelson, S. (2004). Alcohol and violence related cognitive risk factors associated with the perpetration of intimate partner violence. *Journal of Family Violence, 19*(4), 249–253.
27. Messemer, J. (2003). College programs for inmates: The post-Pell Grant era. *Journal of Correctional Education, 54*(1), 32–39.

28. Ziegler, S. (2006). Increasing response rates in mail surveys without increasing error. *Criminal Justice Policy Review, 17*(1), 22–31.
29. Radelet & Akers (1996).
30. Radelet & Akers (1996).
31. Bohm, B. (2003). *Deathquest II: An introduction to the theory and practice of capital punishment in the United States* (2nd ed.). Cincinnati, OH: Anderson.
32. Dictionary.com. Philosophy. Retrieved from http://dictionary.reference.com/search?q=philosophy
33. Pojman, L., & Reiman, J. (1998). *The death penalty: For and against.* New York: Rowman & Littlefield.
34. See Alder, M., & Posner, E. (2001). *Cost-benefit analysis: Legal, economic, and philosophical perspectives.* Chicago: University of Chicago Press.
35. Sunstein, C. (1999). From consumer sovereignty to cost-benefit analysis: An incompletely theorized agreement? *Harvard Journal of Law & Public Policy, 23*(1), 203–211.

JUSTIFICATIONS FOR CAPITAL PUNISHMENT: IS THE DEATH PENALTY EFFECTIVE?

INTRODUCTION

In this chapter, I briefly lay out the main arguments in favor of capital punishment and introduce the main goals of and justifications for capital punishment. I briefly summarize each issue, identify the main issues of contention between supporters and opponents, and then I present the views of the experts with regard to whether capital punishment is effective. Finally, I offer my own fact check section, citing both empirical evidence and research studies to verify or refute what the experts say. This chapter is the first of two that are key to establishing the empirical realities of capital punishment, as it is actually practiced in the United States. In this chapter, we learn whether the death penalty meets its goals and provides any meaningful benefit to society. Recall that a policy that meets its goals can be considered successful, as can a policy whose benefits outweigh its costs.

ARGUMENTS IN FAVOR OF CAPITAL PUNISHMENT

The main arguments in favor of capital punishment are that it is a legal punishment, carried out under constitutional authority by the federal and state governments, and that it is simply deserved by those who receive it. In the simplest terms, advocates of capital punishment assert that death is a proper punishment for those who commit the most heinous crimes because offenders owe their lives to society as payment for the harms they inflicted on society (*retribution*). Further, the death penalty makes us safer by causing fear in would-be murderers so that they do not commit their crimes (*deterrence*) and by taking away the lives of murderers who might murder again if not executed (*incapacitation*).[1]

Some proponents of capital punishment accept it for moral reasons, arguing that it is either morally right to take the lives of murderers for taking the lives of their victims, or morally necessary. For example, death penalty proponent Lois Pojman writes that "the criminal has deliberately harmed an innocent party and so *deserves* to be punished, whether I wish it or not."[2] Further: "It is precisely because the victim's life is so sacred that the death penalty is sometimes the only fitting punishment for first-degree murder."[3]

Others accept the death penalty as it is actually applied, even after acknowledging some problems with the application of the death penalty. For example, Pojman says, with regard to mistaken convictions and executions of the innocent:

> If the basic activity or process is justified, then it is regrettable, but morally acceptable, that some mistakes are made. Fire trucks occasionally kill innocent pedestrians while racing to fires, but we accept those losses as justified by the greater good of the activity of using fire trucks. We judge the use of automobiles to be acceptable even though such use causes an average of 50,000 traffic fatalities each year. We accept the morality of a defensive war even though it will result in our troops accidentally or mistakenly killing innocent people.[4]

Similarly, when discussing alleged discrimination in the application of capital punishment, Pojman claims that "it is not true that a law that is applied in a discriminatory manner is unjust. Unequal justice is no less justice, however uneven in its application. The discriminatory application, not the law itself, is unjust."[5]

The main justifications for capital punishment include:

1) Vengeance and retribution
2) Deterrence
3) Incapacitation

Vengeance and Retribution

Brief Summary of Issue

Vengeance is a strong human emotion for revenge when a person is harmed by another. Research shows that vengeance is one of the normal emotions felt by family members of murder victims, along with grief, loss, and so forth. The five stages of grief, according to the evidence, are denial and isolation, anger, bargaining, depression, and acceptance.[6] Vengeance, which is most likely to accompany anger, is not the same as retribution—the differences are addressed below. Essentially, vengeance is a private emotion experienced by individuals rather than a collective response by society.

Retribution is a state-sponsored, rational response to criminality that is justified given that the state is the victim when a crime occurs. It is punishment given to an offender aimed at rebalancing the scales of justice that were unfairly tipped in favor of the offender when he or she committed a crime.

Although retribution and vengeance are related, they are not synonymous. First, vengeance is private but retribution is public. As noted above, vengeance is a human emotion experienced by individual people. Retribution signifies a collective response to wrongdoing from society rather than individual family members. Also, it is not rooted in emotion but instead in logic and rationality.

Second, vengeance is not justified by law but retribution is justified by law. Although it is natural to feel intense emotions when harmed and to want to get even with those who harm you, it is not appropriate in law to engage in *vigilantism*. Retribution is appropriate, legal, and justified.

Third, vengeance entails the offender being paid back by the victim, but retribution entails the offender paying back society. An example of vengeance would be a murder victim's family member taking the law into his or her own hands to settle a personal vendetta in order to (temporarily) feel better. Retribution is a rational process and outcome that instead aims to have the offender pay back society for the harm inflicted by him or her; in the case of murder, one manifestation of retribution is the offender pays society with his or her life to make amends for the harms he or she committed.

Finally, vengeance is a natural emotion rooted in our biology, but retribution is also about socialization. That is, whereas vengeance does not lead to any real (permanent) social benefit, retribution through punishment helps in the process of defining and reinforcing social norms. Capital punishment in earlier American history clearly had a better chance of achieving this function when thousands of citizens turned out to watch executions in order to state a strong moral objection to the crimes committed by offenders and to demand justice for those harmed.[7]

Issue of Contention

The main issue of contention with regard to vengeance is, should the desire to get even with murderers for the sake of emotional satisfaction on the part of murder victims' family members be used to justify a public policy such as the death penalty? Ideally, government policies—including all criminal justice policies (such as the death penalty)—will be based on reason and empirical science. Further, legally speaking, the state is the victim when a crime occurs and it is incapable of feeling any emotion, including vengeance. State actors may feel tremendous emotions when handling any aspect of murder cases; surely it would not be appropriate to utilize capital punishment for the sake of police, prosecutors, and others who experience strong emotions as a result of dealing with murder cases.

The main contention with regard to retribution is, should governments take the lives of murderers for taking the lives of victims? That is, should governments kill people who kill people to teach the lesson that killing people is wrong? Supporters of capital punishment say yes, it is not only proper but also necessary to take the lives of killers, and that doing so actually increases the value of human life. Opponents of capital punishment say no, and often contend that to take a life for a life to show that taking a life is wrong is hypocritical and lessens the value of life.

Another issue of contention with regard to retribution is whether religion justifies the use of capital punishment. Supporters often say yes, most religions either allow or even mandate capital punishment for certain crimes; they identify passages in religious texts that clearly indicate capital punishment is acceptable. Opponents typically say no, and point to passages in religious texts that appear to contradict capital punishment.

The issue I am most concerned with, however, is not whether retribution is a proper justification for the death penalty, but rather whether capital punishment actually achieves retribution. To reiterate, *the main focus of this book is on the empirical realities of capital punishment rather than on moral or philosophical arguments in favor or opposed to its practice.*

Experts' Views

> Does capital punishment, as actually practiced in the United States, achieve retribution (i.e., provide justice for murder victims, their families, and society at large)?

Experts were not asked about whether they thought capital punishment achieved vengeance, because I do not think vengeance is a legitimate goal of any punishment including the death penalty. However, some expert responses addressed the issue of vengeance.

As shown in Table 4.1, the largest portion of capital punishment experts (36%) responded that they did not think the death penalty achieves retribution, but a sizable portion of death penalty experts (31%) indicated that they thought capital punishment achieves retribution ("provide[s] justice for murder victims, their families, and society at large"). A third of the experts (33%) said they were unsure.

TABLE 4.1   Expert Opinion on Whether Capital Punishment Achieves Retribution

Does capital punishment, as actually practiced in the United States, achieve retribution (i.e., provide justice for murder victims, their families, and society at large)?

Yes	31%
No	36%
Unsure	33%

Note: N = 42.

The Death Penalty Does Not Achieve Retribution

Respondents who said that the death penalty did not achieve retribution claimed that the death penalty is not used frequently enough to achieve retribution. For example, one expert wrote that the death penalty "is imposed far too infrequently and illogically to serve as retribution." Another expert agreed, writing: "At the present time, capital punishment is utilized far too infrequently to provide justice for more than a few murder victims and their families."

One respondent wrote that capital punishment might provide retribution for families of murder victims, "but it can't for broader society. No social science evidence to suggest that it has any 'therapeutic' value for anyone." Similarly, an additional respondent reasoned: "There is no retribution possible after a murder because the scales of justice can never be balanced. No amount of punishment will redeem the value of the dead victim."

Other experts focused on what actually happens to victims' families after executions. For example, one expert explained: "Research indicates many families still feel sorrow and have no sense of closure. What is needed is counseling for the families and friends of murder victims. Additionally, retribution is not a good goal for society. The offender can be punished and society protected by using LWOP [life imprisonment without parole]." Another answered this way:

> This is a difficult question to answer because it is to some degree a matter of opinion. I expect that there are families of murder victims who do feel that the execution of the perpetrator provided justice for them. Others feel the precise opposite. In a broader sense, the failings of the criminal justice system and the inequities of society at large make it unlikely that any punishment could be imposed in a way that provided retribution. In an ideal society in which burdens and benefits were distributed solely on the basis of merit, the situation might be different. Given the system we have and the propensity of humans to error, it is impossible that we can impose

death sentences in a just way, making it impossible that we can achieve justice through this punishment.

One expert who answered that the death penalty does not achieve retribution focused on philosophical issues related to retribution and the issue of wrongful convictions and execution of the innocent, writing:

> Retributivism, at least as Kant and other deontological philosophers have postulated it, requires equal respect for the individual autonomy of all persons. Thus, the consistent retributivist must show equal concern for innocent people who are executed. Moreover . . . our present capital punishment system increases the probability of convicting and executing the innocent.[8] While the retributivist might argue that in an ideal world there would be a one-to-one correlation between guilt and execution, in the real world and any we can hypothesize, it is inevitable that we will execute the innocent. And the true retributivist is not concerned with instrumental justifications—it should not matter whether the death penalty deters, is racist, or has excessive costs associated with it. The retributivist is not concerned with justifying moral outcomes by appealing to consequences; the only thing that matters is whether each individual gets his or her just deserts. So the true retributivist must be concerned by a system that systematically gets it wrong as much as ours does. Those who are innocent are plainly getting unjust punishment, not just deserts. The problem of innocence is the Achilles heel for retributive justifications of capital punishment. A mixed retributivist fares no better on this analysis. What is this claimed benefit of "respect for the majesty of the law" that they gain as against the loss of innocent persons lives. These kinds of arguments strike me as bootstrapped and bordering on incoherence.

Another expert who also answered that the death penalty does not achieve retribution focused on not only philosophical issues related to retribution but also on harms caused by the death penalty process:

> I don't think retribution is an appropriate motivation for punishment. How can you make things right for someone who is dead? You cannot. That is nonsense. It is also highly variable as to how well the families are served. Many think that it will bring closure, but it usually does not. Others are more victimized by the death penalty than served. Many families of victims oppose capital punishment. None benefit from going through the repeated cycles of the appeals process and concurrent media attention. As for society, I think it feeds into a very negative part of our psyche, feeds our aggression. Furthermore, it creates a new class of victims—friends and families of the accused as well as those working within the system.

Similarly, one expert who indicated that the death penalty does not achieve retribution focused on his belief that the death penalty is destructive:

> Of course, I can't speak for any particular murder victims or their families, so this is a tough question to answer. In the broader sense, I don't think the death penalty serves these populations well at all. It may indeed achieve some sense of revenge or retribution for some co-victims or some members of society at large, but it certainly does not for others. The bigger question is: Is serving this form of revenge constructive or destructive for these individuals (or society at large)? My answer to this would be that it is destructive.

One capital punishment expert who answered that the death penalty does not achieve retribution addressed the wording of the question, suggesting that capital punishment is destructive and also nontransparent.

> The wording of your question implies that retribution (i.e., "a paying of tribute," "something given or exacted in recompense," as my Webster's has it) is justice: a life for a life. I'm sure you're aware that this model of justice is only one of several proposed by criminologists and sociologists. I don't think the retributive model is the most constructive one. It throws away a human life and makes killers of every citizen of the polity—man, woman, and child. At the same time, the way execution is handled distances us from what our political and enforcement representatives are doing in our name. Last, retribution encourages us to believe that meting out punishment is a transparent process, potentially a simple one. Our retributive system hides the realities, including but not limited to the prevalence of plea bargaining, the inequalities of legal representation, and the numerical tokenism of the death penalty.
>
> "A life for a life" will always attract a following if only because it's a story—someone is killed, the killer is pursued while we look on in breathless suspense, then the killer is killed in turn. That's hard to beat for closure. And recent research into the human brain suggests that we're wired to look for closure with almost as much urgency as for food, shelter, and sex. Story trumps argument. That's why we need our justice system—so that argument, reason, and making the case can sometimes win.

The Death Penalty Achieves Retribution

Respondents who said that the death penalty achieves retribution explained that capital punishment "provides justice for murder victims, their families, and society at large" in at least some cases. For example, one expert wrote that "in some cases it clearly does." Another respondent said: "Sporadically so, for some." And another expert wrote: "It does in some cases but fails to do so in many cases."

One respondent was adamant about the retributive effect of capital punishment, writing: "Of the various historical, economical, political, ideological, and practical arguments made by those who favor capital punishment, retribution is the ONLY issue supported by empirical evidence; that is, when analyzed by the [totality] of events, circumstances, and experiences of the offender, victim, legal system, and society." Another expert who answered that capital punishment achieves retribution wrote: "It is an emotional response to the horrific crime of murder."

One expert, who answered that the death penalty achieves retribution, explained:

> By "retribution," I mean taking from the criminal the advantage he has unfairly taken by committing the crime in question. Any penalty assigned according the principles of reasonably just legal system . . . will do that (the death penalty as much as any human penalty). Justice for the victims or families is a civil matter for which a tort claim is the appropriate remedy; it is a matter of compensation rather than retribution. Criminal justice is retribution (with or without clemency).

Although a large portion of experts acknowledged that the death penalty achieves retribution, they did so reluctantly and with major caveats. For example, one expert wrote: "I would think the [death penalty] does provide for retribution, but the delay in actually carrying out the execution may serve to lessen any retributive effect." Another expert agreed, writing: "To a limited extent. Because of its uncertainties and delays, it is often uncertain as to if [and] when families of victims will receive the sense of completion that an execution sometimes brings."

Others pointed out that alternatives to capital punishment would also provide for retribution. For example, one expert wrote: "It can reasonably be argued that death for murder is a morally just punishment. It is not the only morally just punishment, but it is one." Another said: "Yes—it may achieve retribution for murder victims & some families but LWOP would also [serve] retribution (I feel)."

One expert who indicated that capital punishment achieves retribution focused on the issue of fairness. He wrote: "It is administered in a manner that is as fair as humanly possible. The crime categories narrow the types of murder that are death-eligible & prosecutors further narrow the pool to those that are most culpable."[9]

Unsure

Those many death penalty experts who were unsure whether the death penalty achieved retribution provided numerous justifications for their answers. One simply said: "Retribution is a philosophical notion with no unambiguous empirical referent." Another respondent who answered unsure wrote that it is "hard to pinpoint what is 'deserved' and what punishment is 'equal in value' to any crime based largely on moral considerations. I would generally think this impossible to determine." Another who answered unsure wrote: "The definition of 'retribution' as encompassing 'justice' remains a contested concept. I would say it allows for 'an eye for an eye,' but whether that is just is difficult to say." Another answered: "Unsure. . . . As a philosophical matter, one can be a retributivist while at the same time rejecting death as a legitimate form of punishment."

One respondent wrote that it

> depends on whether you consider retribution to be a subjective experience or an objectively identifiable phenomenon. We know that many victims' families are not satisfied with [capital punishment] while others are satisfied by a life sentence. I am not sure what people (i.e., politicians) mean when they say a punishment must be consistent with the wishes of the community. Who is this "community"? How does a prosecutor or judge or politician know what the will of the people is other than a survey/poll that shows a majority opinion? I am not sure that making justice decisions upon the majority opinion is always the best policy.

Another pointed out: "You can argue this point both ways: in some cases it has brought 'closure.' Many people maintain that retribution requires the death penalty. I would argue that a life sentence achieves retribution without risking the execution of an innocent person. Besides, and to my point about victims' families, that most people 'feel' a sense of retribution does not justify the use of the death penalty." Another expert who answered unsure wrote: "I suppose it achieves retribution for some victims' families, but other victims' families don't necessarily want retribution—it won't bring their loved ones back and, once the offender is dead, closure may not necessarily follow. It is a desire to see someone pay for their actions, and all of us feel this way at one time or another. However, I am not sure the [death penalty] is the way to do it." Similarly, another respondent wrote: "Probably some murder victims' families and some members of society think so, but non-death penalty jurisdictions (both inside & outside the U.S.) are apparently able to achieve justice without capital punishment."

Some experts who answered unsure to the question of retribution also focused on harms produced by the death penalty process. For example, one expert said: "It seems that victims are re-victimized by having to re-live the nightmare—as the justice wheels slowly turn." Another expert said: "There are no studies that establish one way or the other what, if anything, the death penalty does for victims' families. It is my suspicion that the death penalty actually harms family members and victims' families would be better off without it. So even if victims' families were to say that the death penalty provided them with retribution, I think it may come at a high cost to them." And one expert pointed out that although the death penalty "may be expressive of moral condemnation (retribution) it may also be, instead, an expression of moral outrage (vengeance)."

Finally, two respondents who answered unsure to retribution questioned the way the definition of retribution was defined in the survey and whether retribution was even an appropriate goal of capital punishment. The first wrote: "Justice for murder victims is not an element of retribution. Retribution is about giving the offender what he deserves." The second said: "I'm not sure that retribution is or should be a goal of capital punishment."

Fact Check

As for vengeance, research shows that some family members of murder victims do express satisfaction and relief upon learning that the murderer of their loved one has been executed.[10] For example, scholars Robert Lifton and Greg Mitchell write: "Many of the family members elect to attend the execution ceremony, to which they often respond with public expressions of relief."[11] Other family members of murder victims express completely different emotions, including a desire for forgiveness and closure.[12] For example, some merely "balance their anger with sad resignation."[13] Stated plainly, with every execution, there are family members of murder victims that speak in support of the execution, those that speak against it, and those who say nothing.[14]

According to the Capital Punishment Research Initiative:

> The survivors of murder victims have mixed views about capital punishment, and uniquely formulate those views only after the issue becomes a stark reality in their lives. Little is known about how survivors' psychological orientations and personal values, as well as their relationships with the murder victim, shape their thinking about the appropriate punishment. Nor do we understand the effects of the lengthy delays and frequent case reversals on the wishes for "closure" that often are attributed to murder victims' family members. Precious little is known about the short- and long-term effects of executions on survivors.[15]

We do know that some families of murder victims have formed groups in favor of capital punishment. For example, Justice For All stands for the death penalty and victims' rights.[16] Some families of murder victims have formed groups opposing capital punishment. Murder Victims' Families for Reconciliation, Inc. stands against capital punishment as a form of violence that does not heal their loss.[17]

One very interesting analysis focused on the experiences of both families of murder victims and those condemned to die for the murders they committed.[18] As part of addressing the issue of the tremendous losses and emotions faced by murder victims' families, criminologist Margaret Vandiver examines experiences with the criminal justice system. She writes:

> The end of the trial and sentencing may mark an end to the involvement of the victim's family with the legal system. If the defendant is sentenced to life without parole or to a very long term of imprisonment, the sentence will begin immediately, and there should be no reason for the family to have to deal with the defendant again. If the defendant is sentenced to a short term of years, or will be eligible for parole after a short time, or above all, if he is sentenced to death, then the victims' family is likely to face a prolonged engagement with the criminal justice system. . . . If the sentence is death, the family's involvement will continue beyond the trial for three or four years at a minimum, and may go on for as many as 20 or more years.[19]

Returning to four recent cases of lethal injection described in Chapter 1 in the section dealing with inmate challenges to the method of execution, each case dealt with a murder committed in the early 1980s! First, there is Willie Brown Jr. who was put to death by lethal injection in North Carolina in 2006 for the 1983 killing of Vallerie Ann Roberson Dixon.[20] Second, there is Marvin Bieghler, who was executed in 2006 in Indiana for the 1981 killing of Tommy Miller and his pregnant wife, Kimberly Jane Miller. Recall that when about to be executed, Bieghler said: "Let's get it over with." The brother of the slain woman said afterward, "Each time something came out, you [were] wondering, 'Is it going to be another 25 years?' It was just a strange situation."[21] Third, there is the case of Joseph Clark who was executed in 2006 in Ohio for the 1984 murder of David Manning as part of a drug-induced robbery.[22] Clark is the man who had to tell prison officials that his execution was not working!

Finally, there is the case of Clarence Hill, who killed police officer Larry Bailly in Pensacola, Florida, in 1982. Already strapped to a gurney and awaiting his execution in April 2006, 24 years after his crime, the U.S. Supreme Court granted Hill a stay of execution, effectively putting an indefinite end to death sentences in the state of Florida and the halting of at least four other executions, one in Florida and three in other states. According to interviews with the media, "Taylor's family is growing weary after 24 years of delays. . . . They want Hill dead, and they were angry when his execution was halted." Taylor's brother, now 61 years old, said: "If they want me to, I'd put a bullet in his brain." Taylor's sister said: "It needs to be done, and it needs to be over with."[23]

These cases show all too well one significant problem with the reality of capital punishment in the United States—it simply takes too long (the average length of the cases mentioned is 23 years from the time of the crimes to the executions, and one of the four men still has not been executed). If victims' families are waiting for executions to make them feel better and reach closure, they will be forced to wait because of the many procedural barriers to a swift system of capital punishment that have been put into place since the *Furman* and *Gregg* decisions of the 1970s.

Given that the families of the executed also lose a loved one in the death penalty process, they share the same pattern of grief and loss as families of crime victims. Yet, the differences are as follows:

- The families of condemned prisoners know for years that the state intends to kill their relatives and the method that will be used. They experience a prolonged period of anticipatory grieving, complicated by the hope that some court or governor will grant relief.
- Their relatives' deaths will come about as the result of actions of dozens of respected and powerful persons. Their deaths are caused not by a breakdown in social order but by a highly orchestrated and cooperative effort of authority.
- Their relatives are publicly disgraced and shamed; they have been formally cast out by society and judged to be unworthy to live.
- The deaths of their relatives are not mourned and regretted as other violent deaths are; rather, the death is condoned, supported and desired by many people, and actively celebrated by some.[24]

Perhaps these are the reasons many families of murder victims choose not to seek or support the death penalty for the killers of their loved ones. It is possible that because they have experienced losing a close loved one, they do not want other families to experience it as well.

There are many reasons that family members of murder victims do not want the killers of their loved ones executed, including:

- They do not support capital punishment.
- An execution would diminish the memory of their relative.
- They do not want to be forced to have prolonged contact with criminal justice agencies.
- They do not want the condemned killer to have any added public attention for his or her wrongdoing.

- They prefer the finality of a sentence of life imprisonment without the possibility of parole and the obscurity of prisoners over the continued uncertainty and publicity of the death penalty.
- They want the offender to reflect on his or her wrongdoing for life and to feel remorse.
- They may hope to develop, from the offender, a sense of understanding of why he or she committed the act.[25]

Clearly, the death penalty cuts both ways for families of murder victims. Some feel better because of it; some don't. Keep in mind, however, that the state never truly gets even with murderers—even when it does (rarely) kill them—for it does not do to them what they do to their victims. That is, when we put killers to death, we do so with a concerted effort to minimize their pain and discomfort as much as possible (to avoid cruel and unusual punishment), which is clearly different than the methods murderers use when they kill their victims (e.g., fists, knives, guns, strangulation, torture, etc.).

Finally, because capital punishment is a state-sanctioned and state-administered policy, the important issue is not whether it achieves vengeance but instead if the death penalty actually achieves retribution for society. That is, does it provide just deserts for violent criminals?

As for retribution, it is illogical to argue that the death penalty effectively achieves retribution because it is so rarely applied to murderers. That is, if retribution means getting even with offenders for the sake of murder victims and society (as the question asked), then surely we fail to achieve retribution by executing so few murderers.

As pointed out in the preface to this book, between 1977 and 2004, there were 558,745 murder and nonnegligent manslaughters in the United States, or an average of 19,955 murders and nonnegligent manslaughters per year.[26] During this time, 6,806 people were sentenced to death, or an average of 243 death sentences per year. Further, 944 people were executed, or an average of 33.7 executions per year. This means only 1.3% of killings from 1977 to 2004 led to death sentences, and only 0.17% of killings led to an execution. The odds of receiving a death sentence and ending up on death row or being executed for such a killing between 1977 and 2004 were only 0.8%.[27]

Is such a low rate of death sentencing and executions consistent with retribution? That is, does killing so few murderers achieve retribution? According to the largest portion of the experts, the answer is no. Most of those experts who said the death penalty achieves retribution acknowledged that it is only achieved in those cases where it is used, and even then, in only some of those cases.

It may be fair to say that with each murderer that is executed, we gain that much more retribution, so that some retribution is better than none. However, as pointed out earlier in the book, when evaluating any policy—including the death penalty—one must weigh the benefits of the policy with its costs. In the case of retribution, it is clear that there is very little benefit gained by executing such a small number of murderers. And the experts in this study thought that retribution could be achieved through alternatives to the death penalty such as life imprisonment without the possibility of parole. For the sake of argument, if we accept that justice is achieved when we execute any murderer who is deserving of death, the conclusion remains that we rarely achieve justice given that most murderers who deserve death do not receive it. That is, overall, the death penalty is failed policy when it comes to retribution.

Summary of Vengeance and Retribution

The experts indicated their strong belief that capital punishment, as actually practiced by states in the United States, does not achieve the goal of retribution. This is largely due to the rare nature of the punishment—nearly all murder victims' families do not see the killer of their loved one sentenced to death and ultimately executed. The facts show that capital punishment is extremely rare and that when executions do happen, the process takes a very long time to complete; even after the process is over and the execution is carried out, victims' families do not always achieve closure and a sense of retribution.

Deterrence

Brief Summary of Issue

Deterrence is the notion that by administering punishment to offenders, the state can cause fear in both the offender (*special deterrence* or *specific deterrence*) and in others (*general deterrence*) so that they will not want to commit crimes in the future. Obviously, capital punishment cannot achieve special or specific deterrence because once the offender is dead, he or she cannot be afraid of future punishment. When people speak of the death penalty as a special deterrent or specific deterrent, they actually mean it prevents the murderer from killing again (which is actually a form of *incapacitation* rather than deterrence).

There are at least two meanings of deterrence. First, special (or specific) deterrence is aimed at creating fear in the offender by punishment so that he or she will not commit another crime. Second, general deterrence is aimed at creating fear in all members of society by sending a message through punishment of an offender so that we will not commit crimes.

Issue of Contention

Although it is obvious that the death penalty is not a specific deterrent (because once the punishment is administered, the offender is dead and thus cannot fear future punishment for future criminality), does capital punishment serve as a general deterrent by deterring would-be murderers, thereby saving lives?

Supporters of the death penalty assert that the death penalty has to be a general deterrent, that it is a general deterrent, and that even if it cannot be proven statistically, it is better to assume that there is a deterrent effect even if there is not. Opponents of capital punishment say that the death penalty does not deter murder and may even increase murder by devaluing human life or brutalizing the population.

Both supporters and opponents of capital punishment generally agree that general deterrence is a proper justification for punishment. So the real issue is whether the death penalty actually achieves deterrence, according to the evidence. This is perhaps the most important empirical question related to the reality of capital punishment in the United States: Does the death penalty save lives?

Experts' Views

> Does capital punishment, as actually practiced in the United States, achieve deterrence (i.e., prevent future murders by causing fear in would-be murderers so that they do not commit murder)?

TABLE 4.2   Expert Opinion on Whether Capital Punishment Achieves Deterrence

Does capital punishment, as actually practiced in the United States, achieve deterrence (i.e., prevent future murders by causing fear in would-be murderers so that they do not commit murder)?

Yes	9%
No	79%
Unsure	12%

Note: N = 43.

As shown in Table 4.2 on the previous page, only a small fraction of death penalty experts (9%) indicated that they thought capital punishment achieves deterrence ("prevent[s] future murders by causing fear in would-be murderers so that they do not commit murder"). The largest portion of capital punishment experts (79%) responded that they did not think the death penalty achieves deterrence, and 12% said they were unsure.

The Death Penalty Does Not Achieve Deterrence

Many experts were insistent that the death penalty does not deter. For example, one expert answered: "It clearly does not. I am in the midst of a meta-analysis of studies examining the deterrent effects of capital punishment. So far only poorly executed studies produce evidence of any deterrent effect. Upon correction the data used for many of these studies fails to support deterrence." Another said: "The empirical evidence I know does not convince me that death is any better a deterrent than life in prison."

Another expert, citing the empirical evidence, wrote: "The research strongly suggests that capital punishment has little deterrence value. Most murderers are not rational people who think out their actions. Moreover, many murderers give little care about living or dying. In fact, the research suggests that the death penalty may actually increase violent crime." Another expert agreed: "No debate here for me. Never has deterred; never will deter. [Cesare] Beccaria is on target here: life imprisonment carries as much, if not more, deterrent value (of course, Beccaria argues for life imprisonment at hard labor, which I cannot support)." And so did another: "Studies show that the death penalty is not a superior deterrent than LWOP—no I don't feel that [capital punishment] achieves deterrence."

One expert suggested that the "evidence is clear: it doesn't deter [and] probably increases murder rates." Another respondent agreed, writing:

> A detailed, careful, and honest investigation of capital punishment in the United States does not support the deterrence thesis. Likewise, a sound examination of the existing empirical literature on capital punishments reveals that deterrence is minimally achieved, if at all. To the contrary, there is some evidence showing the *increase* of homicide, following an execution—better known as the "brutalization effect." Hence, the concept of "deterrence" has little to do with practicality . . . it's simply a powerful political weapon used by policymakers during elections . . . and to silence a feared society.

One expert answered that the "weight of evidence suggests little if any deterrent effect." Another wrote that capital punishment "does not deter others from committing similar crimes in the future." An additional expert answered no and wrote: "I assume you mean by comparison to a system of sentencing murderers to life in prison." Similarly, another respondent answered: "In this question . . . it is not a matter of how I feel; it's a matter of what the evidence shows. My study of the history of capital punishment and my reading of the research evidence leads me to conclude that the death penalty has no marginal deterrent effect greater than that of alternate punishments."

One respondent answered that the death penalty does not deter, and referenced an example from England in the 16th through 18th centuries: "The research clearly demonstrates that it does not. I always tell my students about hangings at Tyburn, which were public outings, almost festivals. As the pickpockets swung from the gallows, guess who worked the crowds? Yep, you've got it—the pickpockets. Not much deterrence, was there?"

Other answers from experts who said the death penalty does not deter murder include:

- "Not the way it is currently carried out in the U.S."
- "No. I'm not persuaded by the recent studies finding a deterrent effect."
- "I know of no credible studies that suggest capital punishment is an effective deterrent."
- "Deterrence is a scientifically weak claim, no evidence to support it that meets social science standards for causal inference."
- "Lots of evidence on this."
- "To the best of my knowledge, there is not meaningful evidence that [capital punishment] deters murder or any other crime. The earlier studies that reported deterrent effects have been seriously challenged on methodological & substantive grounds. It simply defies common sense, logic, and human experience to think that [capital punishment] will prevent a murder, but a life sentence will not. Individuals contemplating death eligible crimes are simply not evaluating potential punishment in a manner necessary of [capital punishment] to be a deterrent. On the other hand, I do not think that [capital punishment] has a significant 'brutalization' impact either. I do not think that we conduct enough executions to affect public/individual psyches in the manner suggested by such hypotheses."
- "If deterrence is achieved, then states that use the [death penalty] extensively—[Texas, Virginia], etc.—should have the lowest murder rates in the nation. Deterrence assumes that offenders are thinking about the consequences of their actions [and] the [death penalty] is largely the result of prosecutorial discretion—these cases are so selectively chosen to move forward, how could it possibly be a deterrent?"

- "Except for specific deterrence [incapacitation], the death penalty does not deter. States with the death penalty often have higher murder rates than neighboring states without the death penalty."

Perhaps the most forceful answer about the deterrence issue was this one: "No one, not even the most vehement prosecutor, makes this argument today. With only one in a hundred killers getting a death sentence, and only one in three or four of these eventually being executed, the odds are pretty slim—if murderers were calculating odds, which most are not at the time of the crime."

Another forceful answer addressed the issue of the irrational nature of murder:

> Please—I can't believe anyone is still wasting time on this one. Playing the game of finding that one 0.001th of a statistical advantage point and getting a journal article/consulting career out of it. What does actual observation say about how a killing takes place? "Let's see (mmm, this rock is some good sh*t, must put the dealer on my dialer!)—does this state have the death penalty, or should I go to Michigan to rob a convenience store/kill my ex-wife's boyfriend/cover up my other illegal activities with a little murder? Screw it, my beater of [a] car won't take me that far. Anyway, they'll never catch me . . ." Someone under a compulsion—be it addiction, rage, sexual desire, jealousy, or deviance, fear, greed—making up the scenario as s/he goes along, and dumb, egotistical, or unimaginative enough to believe in not getting caught.

Some respondents who said that the death penalty did not achieve deterrence were less adamant about their responses. For example, one expert wrote: "Probably not." Another responded:

> The empirical evidence is mixed. Sociologists say no. Economists say yes. My research . . . shows that what first appears to support the relationship is but an illusory correlation upon closer examination. Given that [Texas] actually accounts for the overall relationship found by economists examining U.S. data . . . it is unlikely that a properly specified model will find evidence of deterrence. However, this is not to say that it may not exist, but that it is simply impossible to measure empirically (you know, an event that does not occur).

Other experts who answered that capital punishment is not a deterrent speculated that it might actually deter some murderers but that the effect would be cancelled out by the opposite effects of executions on crime. For example, one expert wrote: "It may deter some individuals, but that effect is probably canceled out by its counter deterrent or brutalizing effect. It does not appear to have a marginal deterrent effect." Other respondents answered: "I do not believe that the death penalty provides any additional deterrent value beyond LWOP. I also think that some of the research indicating that the death penalty may actually increase crime is very persuasive"; and: "The evidence suggests that deterrence of any consequence does not occur due to the death penalty. Of course, this is still debated by many, but my own personal feeling on it is that any marginal amount of deterrent effect is overridden by a brutalization effect."

The Death Penalty Achieves Deterrence

The few respondents who said that the death penalty achieves deterrence cited some research. For example, one expert answered that the "latest studies support this." Another answered: "At the present time, capital punishment is utilized far too infrequently to provide a strong deterrent to homicide. But on the basis of my own research on capital punishment, I believe there is a statistically perceivable deterrent effect, although it is a numerically quite weak effect owing to the infrequency of application."

Finally, one respondent answered this way:

> To say otherwise would be to admit that potential murderers are not rational (and thus admit that they should not be subject to criminal justice at all). I have no doubt that the death penalty, like most lesser penalties, has some deterrent effect. I also have no doubt that is the wrong question to ask. The right question is whether the death penalty has significantly more deterrent effect than lesser penalties (even, say, ten years imprisonment). After two centuries of trying to establish that it does, I think we are entitled to conclude that whatever added deterrent effect the death penalty has (and I believe it must have some), it is not large—not large enough to measure.

Unsure

Two respondents said they were unsure about the deterrent value of capital punishment. One said the death penalty "probably has a slight effect." Another answered: "There [are] data on both sides of the deterrence argument. I don't believe it has (or can be) adequately studied in order to assess—certainty and timeliness have never been part of the research equation." Finally, one respondent who did not provide a yes or no answer to the question nevertheless noted that the question I asked about deterrence was "poorly framed." He added: "I believe that [capital punishment] probably does deter some crimes but so does imprisonment. I think there is no evidence that [capital punishment] deters better than prison."

Fact Check

Deterrence is logical and underlies most forms of criminal punishment. When we punish pets for peeing on the floor and scratching up the furniture, we do it so the animals will not do it again (prevention). We assume pets learn through punishment, as do people. This is why there is a huge market in the name of child discipline—there are literally hundreds of approaches to disciplining children, the majority of which likely rest on the deterrence hypothesis.

When it comes to humans, we assume that people are *hedonistic* (pleasure-seeking), *rational* (can think in advance of behavior), that they want to avoid pain such as punishment, and thus the thought of punishment should deter wrongful behavior. Further, seeing punishment administered to others should also deter. Of course, all of this assumes people who murder are rational and that murder is a rational act.

The vast majority of the available scientific evidence with regard to general deterrence suggests that the death penalty is not a deterrent to murder and cannot be for the simple reason that the most important element of punishment is missing—*certainty*.[28] Punishment must be certain in order to deter. As explained by deterrence experts William Bailey and Ruth Peterson, the death penalty "cannot be expected to be an effective deterrent to murder if its level of certainty is zero or very slight." They continue: "Similarly, even if administered with a high level of certainty, capital punishment will not be effective in discouraging crime if it is administered secretly. Rather, deterrence is a communication theory, and it is the *perceived* severity, certainty, and celerity of punishment that result from sanctioning practices that are predicted to influence offense rates."[29]

In the United States, the administration of the death penalty is so rarely applied and so unlikely to be applied to any individual that the likelihood that it is a general deterrent is extremely small. As noted earlier, less than 5% of aggravated murderers and less than 1% of all killers are actually executed, and even when executions occur, they are carried out secretly in the middle of the night.

Deterrence studies tend to compare states with the death penalty and without, nations with the death penalty and without, changes in crime rates in jurisdictions before and after having death penalty, the effects of highly publicized executions, and relationships between executions and the murder rate, controlling for other factors.[30] All of these studies lead to conclusions inconsistent with the deterrence hypothesis.

One example of this kind of research is a group of studies by the late capital punishment scholar Thorsten Sellin examining murder rates in "five groups of three contiguous states: three groups in the Mid-West, and two in

New England." The states were similar across many important variables but differed in that some had the death penalty and some did not. The results showed no evidence that the presence of the death penalty had any effect on murder rate differentials during the years 1940 to 1955, and "a later review of such comparisons carried out between 1919 and 1969 showed that, in the majority of cases, abolitionist states had lower rates of homicide than their retentionist neighbors and that states that abolished the death penalty generally tended to have a smaller increase in homicides than did retentionist neighboring states."[31] More recent replications, correcting for some of the original studies' weaknesses, found the same results through 1995, that generally there is little to no evidence of deterrence.[32]

According to the evidence, murder rates are lower in states without the death penalty than those with it and lower in nations without the death penalty than with it.[33] Additionally, when states and nations abolish capital punishment or simply stop carrying out executions, the murder rate generally falls.[34] Highly publicized executions tend not to have any effect on murder rates.[35] And empirical studies, properly conducted, rarely find a deterrent effect of executions on murder rates, as I will show below. This includes in studies of the effects of executions on murder within states and across states, and regardless of the type of murder examined.[36]

The largest, most sophisticated study of murder rates from 1935 to 1969 that did find evidence of deterrence concluded that for each execution, eight murders would be prevented.[37] However, this study was replicated numerous times and no effect was found.[38] The study was plagued by numerous flaws, including the fact that when the years 1963 to 1969 were removed from the analysis, no deterrent effect was found.[39] Bailey and Peterson thus ask: "Why was the death penalty *not* a significant deterrent to murder from 1933 through the mid 1960s although capital punishment *was* a significant deterrent from the period 1933–69? What could have happened during the latter half of the 1960s to so radically change the truth of the matter?"[40] The National Academy of Sciences did not accept Ehrlich's findings. Its 1978 report concluded that "the real contribution to the strength of Ehrlich's statistical findings lies in the simple graph of the upsurge of the homicide rate after 1962, coupled with the fall in the execution rate in the same period."[41]

Although there have not been many, most studies from the modern execution period have found no evidence consistent with the deterrence hypothesis.[42] After a review of 60 deterrence studies, Bailey and Peterson note: "The available evidence remains 'clear and abundant' that, as practiced in the United States, capital punishment is not more effective than imprisonment in deterring murder."[43]

In spite of this, some death penalty defenders maintain that the evidence does not disprove deterrence either. For example, philosopher Lois Pojman notes, "we must conclude that we lack strong statistical evidence that capital punishment deters. . . . There is no such evidence for nondeterrence either. The statistics available are simply inconclusive."[44] Similarly, the late legal scholar Ernest van den Haag wrote: "Statistics have not proved conclusively that the death penalty does or does not deter murder more than other penalties."[45] Interestingly, in another work, Pojman concludes that "while we cannot prove conclusively that the death penalty deters, the weight of evidence supports its deterrence. Furthermore, I think there are too many variables to hold constant for us to prove via statistics the deterrence hypothesis, and even if the requisite statistics were available, we could question whether they were cases of mere correlation versus causation."[46]

Supporters also point to the "best bet hypothesis," which says that if we do not know if the death penalty is a deterrent, we should bet that it is.[47] It asserts that it would be better to assume there is a deterrent (*when there is not*) and use the death penalty (because this unnecessarily kills only guilty murderers), than to assume there is not a deterrent (*when there is*) and not use the death penalty (because this allows innocent people to die). Following this logic, executions become a moral imperative.[48]

Supporters also put forth anecdotal evidence of individuals who say they were deterred because of the death penalty. Stories do exist of those who claim to have been deterred by fear of capital punishment.[49]

Some of the most recent studies do support a general deterrent effect of executions.[50] These studies, using various methodologies and data sets, find each execution results in 3 fewer murders,[51] 5 fewer homicides,[52] between 3 and 25 fewer murders with an average of 14,[53] between 8 and 28 murders with an average of 18,[54] and even 150 fewer murders.[55]

The author of one of the studies finding a deterrent effect of capital punishment testified to Congress that the research has led to a "strong consensus among economists that capital punishment deters crime," and concluded that "studies are unanimous." When questioned about research that ran counter to her conclusion, she replied: "There may be people on the other side that rely on older papers and studies that use outdated statistical techniques or older data, but all of the modern economic studies in the past decade have found a deterrent effect. So I am not sure what the other people are relying on."[56]

This research, some of which has not been published in peer-reviewed journals or replicated, offers findings that are inconsistent with the great breadth and depth of knowledge on this topic. The studies are thus viewed with great skepticism by capital punishment experts, including those in this study and those in the previous study of presidents of major criminological organizations, discussed in Chapter 3.

A few authors claim the findings of the recent studies that support deterrence are flawed.[57] For example, Richard Berk claims that statistical problems with data analyses reported in the prodeterrence studies explain the findings.[58] One example is that state-specific measures of executions are extremely skewed; Texas executed 336 people from 1977 to 2004, versus 94 executions in the next highest state of Virginia. Only 10 other states executed more than 20 people since 1977, whereas 20 states executed none.[59] This means that some findings of deterrence may rest on effects from 1 or 2 states.[60]

More important, professors John Donohue and Justin Wolfers, who examined recent studies finding deterrent effects of the death penalty, point out several significant problems with the studies. Among the many problems with the prodeterrence studies include failing to control key (and also unknown) variables leading to spurious findings, confounding the effects of capital punishment with broader trends in society, failing to use rates of executions to control for population size in states, failing to consider the effects of imprisonment on crime rates, presenting results that are inconsistent with the regression models actually run, relying on measures of key variables generated by scholars with clear ideological biases, using invalid instruments,[61] reporting faulty confidence intervals,[62] and reporting biases caused by inappropriate treatment of standard errors. When Donohue and Wolfers changed a single key variable dealing with citizen partisanship, it actually changed the direction of the findings from the original study, meaning that executions not only failed to deter homicides but actually increased them.[63] They thus conclude that "one has little reason to prefer the conclusion that the death penalty will save lives to the conclusion that scores will die as a result of each execution."[64]

Further, "the existing evidence for deterrence is surprisingly fragile" and "extremely sensitive to very small changes in econometric specifications."[65] Their own "reanalysis shows that small changes in specifications, samples, or functional form can dramatically change the results. Indeed, several of the more expansive specifications point to an antideterrent effect of the death penalty."[66] Donohue and Wolfers write:

> We are led to conclude that there exists profound uncertainty about the deterrent (or antideterrent) effect of the death penalty; the data tell us that capital punishment is not a major influence on homicide rates, but beyond this, they do not speak clearly. Further, we suspect that our conclusion that econometric studies are highly uncertain about the effects of the death penalty will persist for the foreseeable future. . . . Aggregating over all of our estimates, it is entirely unclear even

whether the preponderance of evidence suggests that the death penalty causes more or less murder.[67]

Rather than relying on flawed methodological approaches to studying deterrence, Donohue and Wolfers assert that scholars should first determine if the real-world evidence is consistent with deterrence. Thus, they examine fluctuations in homicide rates and executions over decades. This leads to the following conclusion:

> No clear correlation between homicides and executions emerges from this long time series. In the first decade of the twentieth century, execution and homicide rates seemed roughly uncorrelated, followed by a decade of divergence as executions fell sharply and homicides trended up. Then for the next forty years, execution and homicides rates again tended to move together—first rising together during the 1920s and 1930s, and then falling together in the 1940s and 1950s. As the death penalty fell into disuse in the 1960s, the homicide rate rose sharply. The death penalty moratorium that began with *Furman* in 1972 and ended with *Gregg* in 1976 appears to have been a period in which the homicide rate rose. The homicide rate then remained high and variable through the 1980s while the rate of executions rose. Finally, homicides dropped dramatically during the 1990s. By any measure the resumption of the death penalty in recent decades has been fairly minor, and both the level of the execution rate and its year-to-year changes are tiny: since 1960 the proportion of homicides resulting in execution ranged from 0% to 3%. By contrast, there was much greater variation in execution rates over the previous sixty years, when the execution rate ranged from 2.5% to 18%. This immediately hints that—even with modern econometric models—it is unlikely that the last few decades generated enough variation in execution rates to overturn earlier conclusions about the deterrent effect of capital punishment.[68]

Donohue and Wolfers also examine murder rates in the United States and Canada across decades. This leads to the conclusion that "the homicide rate in Canada has moved in virtual lockstep with the rate in the United States, while approaches to the death penalty have diverged sharply."[69]

Finally, Donohue and Wolfers compare murder rates in states that have the death penalty with states that do not have the death penalty. Based on a comparison of six states that did not execute anyone from 1960 to 2000 and all other states, they conclude:

> Both sets of states experienced higher homicide rates during the death penalty moratorium than over the subsequent decade; the gap widened for the subsequent decade and narrowed only in the late 1990s. It is very difficult to find evidence of deterrence . . . most of the

> action in homicide rates in the United States is unrelated to capital punishment . . . most of the variation in homicide rates in driven by factors that are common to both death penalty and non-death penalty states.[70]

This explains why states that did not change their capital punishment laws had similar changes in murder rates over time to those that abolished or reinstated capital punishment.

After reexamining the data from the various prodeterrence articles, Donohue and Wolfers explain:

> We find considerable variation in the estimated relationship between execution and murder rates. Our reading of these results suggests (weakly) that the preponderance of the evidence supports the view that increases in executions are associated with *increases* in lives lost, although further permutations of the full array of plausible models would be needed before strong conclusions could be reached.[71]

That is, there is more evidence of a *brutalization effect* of executions than a deterrent effect. Whatever the case, the bottom line, according to Donohue and Wolfers, is that

> the view that the death penalty deters is still the product of belief, not evidence. The reason for this is simple: over the past half century the U.S. has not experimented enough with capital punishment policy to permit strong conclusions. . . . On balance, the evidence suggests that the death penalty may increase the murder rate although it remains possible that the death penalty may decrease it. If capital punishment does decrease the murder rate, any decrease is likely small. In light of this evidence, is it wise to spend millions on a process with no demonstrated value that creates at least some risk of executing innocents when other proven crime-fighting measures exist? Even consequentialists ought to balk.[72]

In response to this article, Paul Rubin, author of one of the prodeterrence articles, claims that "they simply found different models and data yielded different results. Moreover, in my Congressional testimony, I cited not only my own article but a total of 12 studies by 15 different authors that find a deterrent effect."[73] In a reply to this reply, it is claimed that, in the original study claiming to find that capital punishment *prevents* 18 homicides, "Rubin and coauthors described their key instrument for executions as 'the Republican presidential candidate's percentage of the statewide vote in the most recent election.' But, we found that using that precise instrument leads to the exact opposite finding that they reached: each execution *causes* 18 *more* homicides."[74]

Another capital punishment expert, Jeffrey Fagan, in testimony to the Massachusetts Joint Committee on the Judiciary (which was considering legislation to initiate a "foolproof" death penalty), commented: "A close reading of the new deterrence studies shows quite clearly that they fail to touch this scientific bar, let alone cross it." He was referring to standards of social science research.[75] Among his specific concerns were "technical and conceptual errors, including inappropriate methods of statistical analysis, failures to consider all relevant factors that drive murder rates, missing data on key variables in key states, weak to non-existent tests of concurrent effects of incarceration, and other deficiencies."[76]

Finally, an article by sociologist Ted Goertzel about the main methodology used by economists in studies such as the recent prodeterrence studies, leads to this conclusion:

> It would be handy for social scientists if we lived in a Flatland (where everything moves along straight lines, flat plains, or rectangular boxes and) . . . where everything else was equal and questions could be answered with a few calculations. But multivariate statistical analysis does not answer real-world questions such as, "does Texas, with a high execution rate, have a lower homicide rate than similar states?" or "did the homicide rate go down when Texas began executing people, compared to trends in other states that did not?" Instead, it answers the question, "If we use the latest, most sophisticated statistical methods to control for extraneous variables, can we say that the death penalty deters homicide rates other things being equal?" After decades of effort by many diligent researchers, we now know the answer to this question: There are many ways to adjust things statistically, and the answer will depend on which one is chosen. We also know that of the many possible ways to specify a regression model, each researcher is likely to prefer one that will give results consistent with his or her predispositions.
>
> It is time to abandon the illusion that mathematics can convert the real world into the mythical land of Ceteris Paribus (a place where everything is constant except the variables they choose to write about). . . . Social science can provide valid and reliable results with methods that present the data with as little statistical manipulation as possible and interpret it in light of the best qualitative information available. The value of this research is shown by its success in demonstrating that capital punishment has not deterred homicide.[77]

The research finding a deterrent effect of executions is also inconsistent with views of law enforcement chiefs[78] and the views of the many major organizations that have taken a stand against capital punishment, including the American Society of Criminology (ASC). ASC's National Policy Committee (NPC) states:

> The NPC's review of the scientific literature has observed little evidence that the death penalty has a deterrent effect on violent crimes.

A comparison of homicide rates both pre- and post-death penalty eras have not shown a deterrent effect, either within a single state or between states. More troubling are studies showing that the application of the death penalty is not carried out in an equitable manner and is often based on non-legal factors such as the defendant's or victim's race and socio-economic status. Finally, a number of well-publicized cases within the U.S. have shown wrongful convictions for persons sentences to death due to improper prosecutorial and sentencing practices as well as inadequate defense counsel.[79]

Further, the survey of presidents of the American Society of Criminology (ASC), the Academy of Criminal Justice Sciences (ACJS), and the Law and Society Association (LSA), introduced in Chapter 3, found the following:

- 84% say the death penalty is not a deterrent to homicide.
- 93% say the threat of the death penalty is not a greater deterrent to murder than long prison terms.
- 87% say abolishing the death penalty in a state would have no significant effects of murder in that state.
- 0% say the death penalty significantly reduces homicide.
- 100% say politicians support death penalty to appear tough on crime.
- 87% say debates about the death penalty distract law makers from focusing on real solutions to crime problems.[80]

Although the surveys of law enforcement chiefs and the presidents of the ASC, ACJS, and LSA, and the conclusion of the ASC's National Policy Committee preceded the studies finding a deterrent effect of executions, it is doubtful given the problems with the prodeterrence studies that the minds of these individuals would be changed.

Stated plainly, the facts refute the findings of econometric studies claiming to find a deterrent effect of modern executions. Executions have become rarer and thus less certain, and the capital punishment process has become slower and thus less swift. If anything, one should not even expect to find a deterrent effect—any deterrent effect present in periods when executions were more common and the process occurred more quickly should now be absent. The evidence simply flies in the face of deterrence.

Summary of Deterrence

The experts indicated their strong belief that capital punishment, as actually practiced by states in the United States, does not achieve the goal of deterrence. This is largely due to the rare nature of the punishment; the death penalty is too rarely used for it to be a certain enough punishment to cause fear in world-be murderers. The facts show that capital punishment is extremely rare and that it does not reduce murder through deterrence.

Incapacitation

Brief Summary of Issue

Incapacitation means taking away a person's freedom so that he or she cannot commit another crime. Whereas the typical form of incapacitation is incarceration (in a jail, prison, etc.), and the most common form is relatively mild (probation), the ultimate form of incapacitation is death.

As with retribution, this is a legitimate justification for the administration of punishment because the primary responsibility of government is to protect its citizens from harm, and one of the goals of America's systems of criminal justice is to reduce criminality.

Issue of Contention

The main issue of contention with regard to incapacitation is: Is the death penalty needed to achieve incapacitation? That is, could incapacitation be better achieved using another form of punishment, such as life imprisonment without the possibility of parole? Supporters say that the death penalty is needed to ensure incapacitation for the worst of criminal offenders because it would be possible for offenders in prison to escape and/or commit more crimes while in prison. Opponents often say the death penalty is not needed to achieve incapacitation because it can be achieved through other forms of (typically less expensive) punishment, such as incarceration.

Experts' Views

> Does capital punishment, as actually practiced in the United States, achieve incapacitation (i.e., prevent future murders by killing murderers who would murder again)?

As shown in Table 4.3, most death penalty experts (64%) indicated that they thought capital punishment achieves incapacitation ("prevent[s] future murders by killing murderers who would murder again"). Yet, a portion of capital punishment experts (24%) responded that they did not think the death penalty achieves incapacitation, and 12% said they were unsure.

TABLE 4.3 Expert Opinion on Whether Capital Punishment Achieves Incapacitation

---

Does capital punishment, as actually practiced in the United States, achieve incapacitation (i.e., prevent future murders by killing murderers who would murder again)?

Yes	64%
No	24%
Unsure	12%

Note: N = 41.

The Death Penalty Achieves Incapacitation

Respondents who said that the death penalty achieves incapacitation explained that evidence of incapacitation was obvious with each execution. One expert, speaking about incapacitation, wrote that the death penalty "has a specific deterrent effect—those who are executed are unable to commit more crimes. While death row and life sentence murderers do (very rarely) escape, generally, life sentences serve a similar function." Another replied similarly, saying only that capital punishment provided "specific deterrence." Another responded: "Presumably, once the delays in execution have passed and the defendant is put to death, he or she is incapacitated."

Yet, experts did offer caveats to their responses. For example, one expert wrote: "The incapacitative effect is self-evident, however, murderers do not have high rates of recidivism." Another expert answered: "No doubt there is some downward pressure on the homicide rate owing to an incapacitation effect, but owing to the infrequency of application, it would have to be a very minor effect, probably statistically unmeasurable." Similarly, another expert answered that the "incapacitation effect is probably very modest."

Another expert asked,

> Incapacitation compared to what? The logic of incapacitation is simple and convincing. Yet, the fact is that states or countries that let their murderers out of prison after twenty years do not have higher murder rates than those that keep them for life or execute them. Hence, whatever effect incapacitation has cannot be large. And, of course, incapacitation presupposes that each murder is an independent event, that executing (or imprisoning for life) one murder does not, for example, open a position for another to enter (as may well be the case with hired killers or gang members). Like deterrence, incapacitation is a utilitarian argument lacking actual evidence of utility.

Another expert agreed, writing:

If the person is actually executed right after s/he commits the murder, capital punishment achieves incapacitation, by definition. Why? The defendant will not be released back into society, and his/her stay in prison will be short—reducing incarceration time and thus possibility of killing while incarcerated. However, reality differs. First, the typical murderer tends to be young—meaning that if s/he is going to kill again, it will be shortly after—indicating a quick execution. If the person is not executed right after committing the murder, the "aging" process begins—eventually diminishing incapacitation and the rationale behind the incapacitation. And indeed, it takes several years (about 11) before a person is actually executed in the United States. This means, then, that in regards to achieving incapacitation (i.e., preventing murderers from killing again), the death penalty in the United States has little utility. The other reality is even more important: the concept of incapacitation, as practiced in the US, hides the reality of death row. First, young or old, the possibility of killing while on death row is next to nothing. Hence, if a person commits an additional murder, it will be after s/he is removed from death row or leased back into the community. However, in both situations, the chances are very low. Why? Because even if a person commits a homicide while s/he is fairly young, s/he will serve many years in prison before s/he is released back into society.

Other experts who said that capital punishment produces incapacitation mentioned that alternative punishments also achieve the same goal. Many experts discussed how life imprisonment without parole (LWOP) would also provide incapacitation of offenders:

- "Yes, it does guarantee that an executed murderer will not kill again. LWOP does almost as good a job at incapacitation but it cannot guarantee it."
- "While capital punishment incapacitates a person, LWOP does the same at a lower cost and at no risk of killing an innocent person."
- "Certainly, in some cases; cannot argue this point. . . . However, life imprisonment also achieves incapacitation (yes, some could kill in prison but policies can be implemented which limit that concern or threat)."
- "LWOP would also serve incapacitation."
- "In some cases. Some executed people are unlikely to murder again. For those that are, life imprisonment without parole would be equally effective."

- "If LWOP is to work, it has to be utilized and enforced. The [death penalty] itself does not achieve incapacitation, but alternatives like LWOP can achieve it, if utilized properly."

Other experts who said that capital punishment achieved incapacitation pointed out other issues that need to be resolved. For example, one wrote: "Definitely—though the question should be whether it incapacitates an especially dangerous population." Another said: "The problem, of course, is that we cannot accurately predict which convicted murderers would kill again. Thus, we would have to execute all of them to prevent any one of them from killing again. We don't do that [and] I don't think we ever would. Only about 1–2% of convicted murderers are ever executed, and some of them will turn out to be innocent of the murder charge."

Other experts provided similar answers, including:

- "But with lots of false positives who would never kill again."
- "But only to the extent that those executed would murder again."
- "Murderers are unlikely to murder again."
- "Most murderers do not murder again. Most are not sentenced to death. This question is tied to a misperception by the public about murder and murderers. Most first-degree murders are actually robberies or other felonies that go awry—someone panics."

One expert was more definitive, saying: "Yes. If the question is do we eliminate any possibility that a person who is executed could cause future harm, then the answer is obvious." Another expert agreed, but also raised additional issues:

I think that it obviously does . . . killing someone is the most effective way to incapacitate them. But, my response to this is a bit more complex. I think the death penalty system fails to incapacitate when it convicts innocent people of the crime. In this case, the murderer is allowed to remain in society due to the fact that the wrong person has been tried, convicted, incarcerated, and potentially killed in his or her place. Of course, this is not a problem unique to the death penalty system, but I do believe that the death penalty system contributes to a higher rate of wrongful convictions for numerous reasons. One final thought on this is that the question works on the assumption that the executed murderers would have murdered again had they not been killed. Although this may be true in some of the cases, I believe that most murderers would not murder again regardless of whether or not they received the death penalty (and we have plenty of evidence to support this).

The Death Penalty Does Not Achieve Incapacitation

Respondents who said that the death penalty does not achieve incapacitation justified their answers on the grounds that the death penalty is too rarely used to provide an incapacitative effect and that most murderers would not kill again. For example, one expert answered: "Obviously, for those executed, it serves an incapacitative function. However, my own research shows that the probability of a future homicide being committed by a first-degree murderer while incarcerated for a life term is less than 1%." Another said: "Evidence shows murderers almost never have a second victim." Another respondent raised an additional issue about the failure of capital punishment to incapacitate, saying: "The answer is no, simply because of replacement or substitution."

One expert provided a more detailed answer. He wrote:

> James Marquart and Jon Sorensen's classic study of post-*Furman* death row inmates whose sentences were commuted demonstrates that we would have to execute massive numbers of persons to prevent even a few murders.[81] They followed 558 of these inmates (out of 613 total) for 15 years and found only seven killed again. They reported that four of the 558 had been exonerated and later figures by Radelet and Bedau upped that to five exonerated persons. While the recidivism number is no doubt quite solid, I view the number of persons exonerated as quite conservative. This is because murders tend to get reported and solved, while exoneration is a matter of luck. So we likely would execute more lives than we would save, thus making it a poor trade-off for society.

Another expert echoed this answer, writing: "Those condemned prisoners whose death sentences were commuted to life after *Furman* did not commit additional murders at a rate any higher than non-condemned convicted murderers."

Finally, another expert who answered no to the incapacitation question, wrote: "In the simplest sense, of course the death penalty incapacitates the offender. But in the modern US, offenders serve such long sentences before their executions that many of them have aged out of their dangerous years before they are executed. While it is possible that some convicted murderers may kill again in prison, with reasonably good supervision this is likely to be exceptionally rare."

Unsure

Those who were unsure about the incapacitative effects of capital punishment said:

- "Unsure how to answer this one. One might say that [capital punishment] is ineffective [regarding] incapacitation as so few are executed.

On the other hand, having inmates under tight security effectively incapacitates them. Is this really LWOP or 'capital punishment as practiced in the US?'"

- "Undoubtedly those persons executed cannot harm society again—absolute incapacitation. This is true of even the innocents who have been executed. The question is 'does the death penalty provide a marginally superior incapacitation effect above that provided by alternative punishments?' While the research on this question is sparse, it appears that there is no marginal incapacitation effect of the death penalty relative to LWOP or life sentences."

- "I do not think there are studies on this one way or the other but my concern is that people who have been sentenced to death may actually be more dangerous to other people in the prison environment than those who were not sentenced to death. For example, if I hated my cell mate or a particular guard I might decide to murder him or her because I didn't have anything to lose since I was going to be executed anyway."

- "Can't answer. By comparison to what? Not by comparison to a system of sentencing murder defendants to prison for their natural lives."

- "We <u>know</u> that [capital punishment] incapacitates—but we do <u>not</u> know whether it prevents future murders."

- "There are two questions. Obviously it incapacitates the murderer. Whether this person would kill again is another matter."

Fact Check

Unless you believe in reincarnation, you will agree that the death penalty achieves the objective of incapacitation for those it is used against. For each murderer we execute, we get that much closer to a meaningful incapacitative effect. This is probably why a majority of experts in this study indicated they thought that capital punishment achieved incapacitation. Yet, it is also fair to conclude that we largely fail to meet this objective simply for the fact that the death penalty is so rarely applied. According to the experts and the evidence, we do not use the punishment often enough to claim we actually achieve the goal of incapacitation.

As for whether murderers need to be executed in order to protect society (and other prison inmates) from future killing behaviors, the question is open for debate. One issue that is unresolved is that of *future dangerousness*. As noted in Chapter 1, jurors in some states are permitted to consider future dangerousness (the likelihood that an offender will commit another act of violence) as an aggravating factor to justify a death sentence.

Yet, "the process of determining who may pose a future threat renders the ideal of incapacitation meaningless unless those who will kill or commit serious assaultive acts in the future can be adequately predicted."[82] Unfortunately, we lack the ability to predict future acts of criminality.

Supporters of capital punishment point to the fact that some murderers released after the *Furman* decision did in fact commit additional murders and thus we need capital punishment at least to protect us from future violence of those who have already committed it.[83] Probably the most dramatic example is the case of Kenneth Allen McDuff, who "raped, tortured, and murdered nine women in Texas in the early 1990s, and probably many more."[84] McDuff had been incarcerated under a death sentence in the late 1960s for killing two teenage boys and sexually assaulting and killing their teenage female friend, and came close to being executed three times before having his death sentence overturned by the U.S. Supreme Court in the *Furman* decision. He was ultimately released by the state of Texas in 1989.

Yet, the fact remains that the vast majority of inmates released after *Furman* did not commit another murder. According to the evidence, the majority of murderers who are released due to having their sentences commuted are no more dangerous nor any more of a risk to society than other offenders.[85] They also tend to commit very low levels of violent behavior in prison![86]

One major study found that

> the released *Furman*-commuted offenders have lived a combined total of 1,282 years in the community while committing twelve violent offenses—approximately two violent offenses per year for the released inmates or nine violent offenses per 1,000 releases per year. Recidivism occurred an average of 3.4 years after release for murderers. . . . Of the 238 paroled offenders, one killed again . . . overall, only a small percentage (less than 1%) of released murderers were returned to prison for committing a subsequent homicide. For example, of 11,532 murderers released between 1971 and 1975, twenty-six committed new homicides in the first year after release from prison . . . after five years on parole, only one murderer committed a second murder while in the larger society. . . . Seven (1.3%) *Furman*-commuted prisoners were responsible for seven additional murders.[87]

The typical releasee, according to the study, was "a southern male black murderer without a lengthy history of serious violence or repeated trips to prison."[88] In fact, only 3% of offenders released after *Furman* had previous murder convictions. Statistics from the 1980s also showed that of the approximately 52,000 inmates incarcerated for murder in state prisons, more than 800 of them had already committed another murder, meaning that had they been executed the first time, more than 800 lives would have been saved.[89]

Of course, the debate over this particular issue—whether those who have murdered once in free society will murder again if released back into free society—is moot if we decide to incarcerate all aggravated murderers for terms of life imprisonment without the possibility of parole. For example, one could obviously argue that LWOP in the 1980s would have achieved the outcome of saving more than 800 lives. After all, it is literally impossible for incarcerated murderers to commit future killings of people outside prisons. The key would be building and maintaining prisons to ensure that inmates cannot escape. Given that we can put a human on the moon, photograph footprints on earth from outer space, communicate instantly with others across the globe, it is certain we can build an escape-proof prison.

After reviewing the studies dealing with incapacitation and capital punishment, death penalty scholar Hugo Adam Bedau concluded: "Some offenders, returned to the general public after years served in prison for murder, do murder again. Perhaps it is more surprising that the great majority do not."[90] If we release murderers in the future, there is a question to be considered: Is the risk that a small number will kill again worth it? One way to satisfy the question without it being posed would be to replace capital punishment (and prison terms of less than life) with LWOP. The experts in this study generally agreed that LWOP would achieve incapacitation as well as the death penalty (if not better).

The argument could be made that LWOP is a harsher sentence than death. For this reason, many capital punishment opponents also oppose life sentences. The point here is not what sentences should be imposed on murderers, but whether it would be possible to incapacitate murderers without executing them. The answer is clearly yes.

Summary of Incapacitation

A majority of experts indicated that capital punishment does achieve incapacitation when it is used. However, they commonly noted its rare nature, calling into question its incapacitative value. Further, they noted that predicting future dangerousness is impossible and that incapacitation can be achieved through other means such as life imprisonment without the possibility of parole. The facts show that capital punishment is extremely rare and that it does not reduce murder through incapacitation above and beyond that reduced by other mechanisms such as long-term imprisonment.

CONCLUSION

From the comments of the respondents who participated in this study, it is safe to conclude that capital punishment experts generally feel that the death penalty, as actually practiced in the United States, does not meet its goals. First, most experts did not indicate that they thought the death penalty achieves retribution—defined as providing justice for murder victims, their families, and society at large. Second, a very large majority indicated that they thought the death penalty does not achieve deterrence of murder or other crimes. Third, although most capital punishment experts indicated that they thought capital punishment achieves incapacitation, many concluded that the size of the effect was small (because of the infrequency with which executions actually occur in America), that the incapacitative effect was not without significant costs, and that incapacitation could be achieved through other means, such as life imprisonment without the possibility of parole. Empirical evidence supports each of these conclusions. Thus, from the perspective of whether the death penalty meets its goals, a review of the empirical evidence leads to the conclusion that it does not, and by this standard, capital punishment is thus a failed policy. The inefficiency of capital punishment largely owes itself to its extremely rare implementation, as shown earlier in the book.

Another way to evaluate a policy is whether its benefits outweigh its costs. Policies whose benefits outweigh the costs can be considered successful. Conversely, policies whose costs outweigh the benefits can be considered failing. Given that capital punishment does not achieve its goals, what are its benefits? As this chapter showed, there are retributive benefits to some family members of murdered victims and there is an incapacitative effect of executions. Some experts suggested these benefits were real, although very small.

I did not specifically ask the experts in this study what the benefits of capital punishment are, but their answers to other questions on the survey might provide some reasonable degree of understanding with regard to how they feel about this issue. For example, in Chapter 6, the issue of why capital punishment persists in the United States is addressed. In their responses to the question on the survey that addressed this issue, the experts suggested that the death penalty is beneficial to politicians who use the issue to get elected and stay in power, as well as to citizens who want vengeance and retribution and believe in deterrence. These can be considered additional ideological benefits of capital punishment.

The benefits offered by capital punishment must be weighed against the costs of capital punishment in order to determine if the policy succeeds or fails by the costs–benefits standard. In the next chapter, I examine the evidence in regard to alleged problems with capital punishment. Specifically, I present expert opinion with regard to alleged biases in capital punishment practice (race, class, gender), whether innocent people have been executed in the United States, as well as other alleged problems.

ENDNOTES

1. Cassell, P. (2004). In defense of the death penalty. In H. Bedau & P. Cassell (Eds.), *Debating the death penalty: Should America have capital punishment? The experts on both sides make their case.* New York: Oxford University Press; Pojman, L., & Reiman, J. (1998). *The death penalty: For and against.* Lanham, MD: Rowman & Littlefield; Pojman, L. (2004). Why the death penalty is morally permissible. In H. Bedau & P. Cassell (Eds.), *Debating the death penalty: Should America have capital punishment? The experts from both sides make their case.* New York: Oxford University Press; van den Haag, E. (1997). The death penalty once more. In H. Bedau (Ed.). *The death penalty in America: Current controversies.* New York: Oxford University Press.

2. Pojman, L. (1998). For the death penalty. In L. Pojman & J. Reiman (Eds.), *The death penalty: For and against.* Lanham, MD: Rowman & Littlefield, p. 52.

3. Pojman (1998), p. 61.

4. Pojman (1998), p. 54.

5. Pojman (1998), p. 56.

6. Kubler-Ross, E., & Kessler, D. (2005). *On grief and grieving: Finding the meaning of grief through the five stages of loss.* UK: Scribner.

7. Banner, S. (2003). *The death penalty: An american history.* Cambridge, MA: Harvard University Press.

8. This respondent cited the work of Samuel Gross.

9. This expert continued: "The AVC for a recent study I performed in [Texas] showed that death sentences were predictable 91% of the time among a cohort of death eligible case[s]."

10. Lifton, R., & Mitchell, G. (2000). *Who owns death? Capital punishment, the American conscience, and the end of executions.* New York: William Morrow.

11. Lifton & Mitchell (2000), p. 197.

12. King, R. (2005). *Capital consequences: Families of the condemned tell their stories.* Rutgers, NJ: Rutgers University Press; King, R. (2003). *Don't kill in our names: Families of murder victims speak out against the death penalty.* Rutgers, NJ: Rutgers University Press; Vandiver, M. (1989). Coping with death: Families of the terminally ill, homicide victims, and condemned prisoners. In M. Radelet (Ed.), *Facing the death penalty: Essays on cruel and unusual punishment.* Philadelphia: Temple University Press.

13. Lifton & Mitchell (2000), p. 202.

14. For stories of individual families who tell how they felt after the execution of the murderers of their loved ones, see Lifton & Mitchell (2000), pp. 197–212; King (2003, 2005).

15. State University of New York, University at Albany, School of Criminal Justice. (n.d.) *Capital punishment research initiative*. Retrieved from http://www.albany.edu/scj/cpri.htm

16. Justice For All Web site, http://www.jfa.net/index.html

17. Murder Victims' Families for Reconciliation, Inc. Web site, http://www.mvfr.org/AboutMVFR.htm

18. Vandiver, M. (2003). The impact of the death penalty on the families of homicide victims and of condemned prisoners. In J. Acker, B. Bohm, & C. Lanier (Eds.), *America's experiment with capital punishment: Reflections on the past, present, and future of the ultimate penal sanction* (2nd ed.). Durham, NC: Carolina Academic Press.

19. Vandiver (2003), p. 621.

20. Weigl, A. (2006, April 21). North Carolina first to monitor consciousness of inmate during lethal injection. *The News & Observer*. Retrieved from http://www.constitutioncenter.org/education/TeachingwithCurrentEvents/ConstitutionNewswire/16062.shtml

21. Wilson, C. (2006, January 30). Indiana inmate executed amid federal court drama. Law.com. Retrieved from http://www.law.com/jsp/article.jsp?id=1138356402268

22. Cable News Network. (2006, May 2). Killer executed the hard way. Retrieved from http://www.cnn.com/2006/LAW/05/02/lethal.injection.reut/index.html

23. Word, R. (2006, April 25). High court to consider appeal on last-minute challenges to injection executions. Law.com. Retrieved from http://www.law.com/jsp/article.jsp?id=1145885163985

24. Vandiver (2003), pp. 624–625.

25. Vandiver, M. (1998). The impact of the death penalty on the families of homicide victims and of condemned prisoners. In J. Acker, B. Bohm, & C. Lanier (Eds.), *America's experiment with capital punishment: Reflections on the past, present, and future of the ultimate penal sanction*. Durham, NC: Carolina Academic Press.

26. Murder and nonnegligent manslaughter is defined as "the willful (nonnegligent) killing of one human being by another." See Federal Bureau of Investigation. (2005). *Crime in the United States 2004*. Retrieved from http://www.fbi.gov/ucr/cius_04/offenses_reported/violent_crime/murder.html

27. This was calculated by adding the total number of people on death row at the end of 2004 (3,503) and the total number of people executed from 1977 to 2004 (944), and then dividing by the number of murders and nonnegligent manslaughters from 1977 to 2004 (558,745).

28. Bailey, W., & Peterson, R. (1997). Murder, capital punishment, and deterrence: A review of the literature. In H. Bedau (Ed.). *The death penalty in America: Current controversies*. New York: Oxford University Press.

29. Bailey & Peterson (1997), p. 137.

30. Bohm, B. (2003). *Deathquest II: An Introduction to the Theory and practice of Capital Punishment in the United States* (2nd ed.). Cincinnati, OH: Anderson; Bailey & Peterson (1997), p. 138.

31. Hood, R. (2002). *The death penalty: A worldwide perspective.* New York: Oxford University Press, p. 217, summarizing Sellin, T. (1959). *The death penalty* (1959). Philadelphia: American Law Institute; Bowers, W., Pierce, G., & McDeavitt, J. (1984). *Legal homicide: Death as punishment in America, 1864–1982.* Boston: Northeastern University Press.

32. See Lempert, R. (1983). The effect of executions on homicides: A new look in an old light. *Crime and Delinquency, 29,* 88–115; Peterson, R., & Bailey, W. (1998). Is capital punishment an effective deterrent for murder? An examination of social science research. In J. Acker, B. Bohm, & C. Lanier (Eds.), *America's experiment with capital punishment: Reflections on the past, present, and future of the ultimate penal sanction.* Durham, NC: Carolina Academic Press.

33. According to two deterrence experts, this is consistent with a lack of deterrence, "but it does not prove that capital punishment is not a deterrent to murder. Nor does it prove that capital punishment produces higher homicide rates (brutalization). It is possible that death penalty and abolitionist jurisdictions in the U.S. differ in other significant respects which influence lethal violence." Peterson, R., & Bailey, W. (2003). Is capital punishment an effective deterrent for murder? An examination of social science research. In J. Acker, B. Bohm, & C. Lanier (Eds.), *America's experiment with capital punishment: Reflections on the past, present, and future of the ultimate penal sanction* (2nd ed.). Durham, NC: Carolina Academic Press, p. 254.

34. The opposite happened in the United States: When executions slowed in the 1960s and stopped in the 1970s, homicides rose. See Carrington, F. (1978). *Neither cruel nor unusual.* New Rochelle, NY: Arlington. However, the simple correlation between falling executions and rising homicide rates was spurious, since it did not control for "the lower costs and greater availability of weapons, increased racial tension, a general reduction in the severity of prison sentences, . . . an increased gap between people's economic expectations and their actual economic status . . . [and] the effect of the postwar baby boom, which resulted in a great increase in the size of the most violent group within society, males between eighteen and twenty-five years old." Further, "While the homicide rate did increase, it increased at a much slower rate than other crimes, which really did skyrocket during this period. Since the death penalty had never been a factor in these other crimes, its absence could not have accounted for their increase." Finally, in comparative studies of homicide increases in abolitionist and retentionist counties, "there was no evidence that death penalty states experienced greater increases as a result of the moratorium and their inability to execute murderers." Nathanson, S. (2001). *An eye for an eye: The immorality of punishing by death.* Lanham, MD: Rowman & Littlefield, pp. 27–28.

35. Bohm (2003); Peterson & Bailey (2003).

36. For specific studies and their findings, see Peterson & Bailey (2003), pp. 261–273.

37. Ehrlich, I. (1975). The deterrent effect of capital punishment: A question of life and death. *American Economic Review, 65,* 397–417.

38. Beyleveld, D. (1982). Ehrlich's analysis of deterrence. *British Journal of Criminology, 22*, 101–123; Forst, B. (1977). The deterrent effects of capital punishment: A cross-state analysis. *Minnesota Law Review, 61*, 743–767. For a discussion of other replications, see Bailey & Peterson (1997).

39. Cassell, P., & Taylor, J. (1977). The deterrent effect of capital punishment: Another view. *American Economic Review, 67*, 445.

40. Bailey & Peterson (1997), p. 142.

41. Blumstein, A., Cohen, J., & Nagrin, D. (Eds.). (1978). *Deterrence and incapacitation: Estimating the effects of criminal sanctions on crime rates.* Washington, DC: National Academy of Sciences.

42. Bailey, W. (1998). Deterrence, brutalization, and the death penalty: Another examination of Oklahoma's return to capital punishment. *Criminology, 36*(4), 711; Cochran, J., & Chamlin, M. (2000). Deterrence and brutalization: The dual effects of executions. *Justice Quarterly, 17*(4), 685; Cochran, J., Chamlin, M., & Seth, M. (1994). Deterrence or brutalization? An impact assessment of Oklahoma's return to capital punishment. *Criminology, 32*(1), 107; Peterson, R., & Bailey, W. (1991). Felony murder and capital punishment: An examination of the deterrence question. *Criminology, 29*(3), 367; Sorensen, J., Wrinkle, R., Brewer, V., & Marquart, J. (1999). Capital punishment and deterrence: Examining the effect of executions on murder in Texas. *Crime and Delinquency, 45*(4), 481–493. Stack, S. (1993). Execution publicity and homicide in Georgia. *American Journal of Criminal Justice, 18*(1), 25–39; Thomson, E. (1997). Deterrence versus brutalization: The case of Arizona. *Homicide Studies, 1*(2), 110–128; Yunker, J. (2001). A new statistical analysis of capital punishment incorporating U.S. postmoratorium data. *Social Science Quarterly, 82*(2), 297–311.

43. Bailey & Peterson (1997), p. 155.

44. Pojman & Reiman (1998).

45. Van den Haag, E. (1997). The death penalty once more. In H. Bedau (Ed.), *The death penalty in America: Current controversies.* New York: Oxford University Press, p. 449.

46. Pojman & Reiman (1998); Pojman (2004).

47. Van den Haag, E. (1968, July). On deterrence and the death penalty. *Ethics, 78*(4), 280–288.

48. Pojman & Reiman (1998).

49. Cassell (2004); Pojman (2004); Pojman & Reiman (1998).

50. Brumm, H., & Cloninger, D. (1996). Perceived risk of punishment and the commission of homicides: A covariance structure analysis. *Journal of Economic Behavior and Organization, 31*(1), 1–11; Cloninger, D., & Marchesini, R. (2001). Execution and deterrence: A quasicontrolled group experiment. *Applied Economics, 33*(5), 569–576; Cloninger, D., & Marchesini, R. (2005). *Execution moratoriums, commutations and deterrence: The case of Illinois.* Retrieved from http://www.cjlf.org/deathpenalty/IIIStudyRevised.pdf; Dezhbakhsh, H., Rubin, P., & Shepherd, J. (2003). Does capital punishment have a deterrent effect? New evidence from postmoratorium panel data. *American Law &*

Economics Review, 5(2), 344–376; Dezhbakhsh, H., & Shepherd, J. (2003). *The deterrent effect of capital punishment: Evidence from a "judicial experiment."* Department of Economics, Emory University (Working Paper No. 03-14). Retrieved from http://people.clemson.edu/~jshephe/CaPuJLE_submit.pdf; Ehrlich, I., & Liu, Z. (1999). Sensitivity analysis of the deterrence hypothesis: Let's keep the econ in econometrics. *Journal of Law and Economics, 42*(1), 455–487; Mocan, H., & Gittings, R. (2003). Getting off death row: Commuted sentences and the deterrent effect of capital punishment. *Journal of Law and Economics, 46*(2), 453–478; Shepherd, J. (2004). Murders of passion, execution delays, and the deterrence of capital punishment. *Journal of Legal Studies, 33*(2), 283–322; Zimmerman, P. (2004). State executions, deterrence and the incidence of murder. *Journal of Applied Economics, 7*(1), 163–193.

51. Shepherd (2004).

52. Mocan & Gittings (2003).

53. Zimmerman (2004).

54. Dezhbakhsh et al. (2003).

55. Dezhbakhsh & Shepherd (2005).

56. *Terrorist Penalties Enhancement Act of 2003: Hearing on H.R. 2934 Before the Subcommittee on Crime, Terrorism, and Homeland Security of the House Committee on the Judiciary.* (2004). 108th Congress, 10–11. Retrieved from http://judiciary.house.gov/media/pdfs/printers/108th/93224.pdf

57. For a good discussion of methodological issues related to deterrence research generally, see Hood (2002).

58. Berk, R. (2005). New claims about executions and general deterrence: Déjà vu all over again? *Journal of Empirical Legal Studies, 2*(2). Retrieved from http://www.blackwell-synergy.com/doi/abs/10.1111/j.1740-1461.2005.00052.x

59. Donohue, J., & Wolfers, J. (2005). Uses and abuses of empirical evidence in the death penalty debate. *Stanford Law Review, 58,* 791–846.

60. Shepherd (2005).

61. Some of the invalid instruments include "1) the statewide aggregate number of prison admissions; 2) total statewide aggregate police payrolls; 3) judicial expenditures (albeit not adjusted for inflation or state size); and 4) the statewide percent Republican vote in the most recent Presidential election". Donohue, J., & Wolfers, J. (2006, April 3). The death penalty: No evidence for deterrence. *The Economists' Voice, 3*(5). The authors explain: "To be valid, they would have to influence executions *and there would have to be no other link between these variables and the homicide rate.* This is not the case."

62. An example of a valid confidence interval from one of the studies ranges "from 429 lives saved per execution to 86 lives lost" which is "outside the bounds of credibility" (Donohue & Wolfers [2006], p. 3).

63. Donohue & Wolfers (2005), pp. 825–826.

64. Donohue & Wolfers (2005), p. 827.

65. Donohue & Wolfers (2005), p. 794.

66. Donohue & Wolfers (2005), p. 836.

67. Donohue & Wolfers (2005), pp. 841, 843.

68. Donohue & Wolfers (2005), pp. 796–797.
69. Donohue & Wolfers (2005), p. 799.
70. Donohue & Wolfers (2005), p. 801.
71. Donohue & Wolfers (2006), p. 5.
72. Donohue & Wolfers (2006), pp. 5–6.
73. Rubin, P. (2006, April). The death penalty once more. *The Economists' Voice, 3*(6).
74. Donohue, J., & Wolfers, J. (2006, April). A reply to Rubin on the death penalty. *The Economists' Voice, 3*(6).
75. Fagan, J. (2005, July 14). *Public policy choices on deterrence and the death penalty: A critical review of new evidence.* Testimony before the Joint Committee on the Judiciary of the Massachusetts Legislature on House Bill 3934. Retrieved from http://www.deathpenaltyinfo.org/MassTestimonyFagan.pdf
76. Death Penalty Information Center. (2006). *Deterrence news and developments— previous years.* Retrieved from http://www.deathpenaltyinfo.org/article.php?did=1705
77. Goertzel, T. (2004, July). Capital punishment and homicide: Sociological realities and econometric illusions. *Skeptical Enquirer* magazine. Retrieved from http://www.deathpenaltyinfo.org/article.php?scid=12&did=1176
78. Dieter, R. (1995). *On the front line: Law enforcement views on the death penalty.* Washington, DC: Death Penalty Information Center.
79. American Society of Criminology, National Policy Committee. (2001). *The use of the death penalty.* Retrieved from http://www.asc41.com/policypaper2.html
80. Radelet, M., & Akers, R. (1996). Deterrence and the death penalty: The views of the experts. *Journal of Criminal Law & Criminology, 81*(1), 1–16.
81. Marquart, J., & Sorensen, J. (1989). A national study of the *Furman*-commuted inmates: Assessing the threat to society from capital offenders. *Loyola University of Los Angeles Law Review, 23*(1), 5–28.
82. Sorensen, J., & Marquart, J. (2003). Future dangerousness and incapacitation. In J. Acker, B. Bohm, & C. Lanier (Eds.), *America's experiment with capital punishment: Reflections on the past, present, and future of the ultimate penal sanction* (2nd ed.). Durham, NC: Carolina Academic Press, p. 287.
83. Cassell (2004).
84. Cassell (2004), p. 183.
85. Marquart, J., & Sorensen, J. (1997). A national study of the *Furman*-commuted inmates: Assessing the threat to society from capital offenders. In H. Bedau (Ed.), *The death penalty in America: Current controversies.* New York: Oxford University Press.
86. For a summary of studies examining the issue of dangerousness of capital offenders, see Marquart & Sorensen (1997), p. 289.
87. Marquart & Sorensen (1997), pp. 171–172, 174.
88. Marquart & Sorensen (1997), p. 166.
89. Cassell (2004), p. 188.
90. Bedau, H. (1997). Prison homicides, recidivist murder, and life imprisonment. In H. Bedau (Ed.), *The death penalty in America: Current controversies.* New York: Oxford University Press, p. 166.

ALLEGED PROBLEMS WITH CAPITAL PUNISHMENT: IS THE APPLICATION OF THE DEATH PENALTY PLAGUED BY BIAS, ERROR, AND OTHER PROBLEMS?

INTRODUCTION

In this chapter, I briefly lay out the main arguments against capital punishment and introduce the most significant problems that critics claim characterize the American death penalty practice. I briefly summarize each issue, identify the main issues of contention between supporters and opponents, and then I present the views of the experts with regard to whether capital punishment is biased (by race, class, and gender or sex), used against the innocent, and characterized by other problems. Finally, I offer my own fact check section, citing both empirical evidence and research studies to verify or refute what the experts say. This chapter is the second of two that are key to establishing the empirical realities of capital punishment, as it is actually practiced in the United States. In this chapter, we learn the costs of capital punishment. Recall that a policy can be considered successful if its benefits outweigh its costs. Conversely, a policy whose costs outweigh its benefits can be considered a failing policy.

ARGUMENTS AGAINST CAPITAL PUNISHMENT

The main arguments against capital punishment are that it is morally wrong, it is cruel and unusual, it constitutes a human rights violation, and that its practice is plagued by numerous problems.[1]

Some opponents of capital punishment reject it for moral reasons. For example, death penalty abolitionist Hugo Adam Bedau says that humanity cannot be "forfeitable and cannot be waived"; that a person "cannot do anything that...nullifies his or her 'moral worth' or standing as a person."[2] Others reject the death penalty for the way it is applied. For example, the National Coalition to Abolish the Death Penalty (NCADP) says that the death penalty is plagued by racial disparities, is used against innocent people, is used against people who are mentally retarded, is used against juveniles, and costs more than life imprisonment (the U.S. Supreme Court now prohibits capital punishment for mentally retarded offenders and juveniles, as discussed in Chapter 2).[3]

Others accept the morality of retributivist arguments in favor of the death penalty but still reject the actual punishment. For example, one scholar writes that although governments have the right to impose death legally on convicted murderers, they are not compelled to do so. That is, citizens of a government must not stoop to the level of criminals to achieve justice, simply to get even with them. As noted by philosopher Jeffrey Reiman: "Surely it is counterintuitive (and irrational to boot) to set the demands of justice so high that a society would have to choose between being barbaric and being unjust. That would effectively price justice out of the moral market."[4] Thus, we ought not beat, rape, and torture those who commit assault, rape, and torture, *even if it was their just deserts.*"[5]

The main problems that allegedly plague the application of capital punishment in the United States are:

1) It is political in nature.
2) It is excessively costly.
3) It is applied in an arbitrary and discriminatory manner.
4) It is occasionally used against the innocent.
5) Capital juries are confused about their job and often make mistakes.

The survey on which this study is founded addressed the issues of bias (arbitrariness and/or discrimination) by race, class, and gender/sex, and this issue of innocence. Capital punishment experts were also given the opportunity to list and discuss other aspects of the death penalty that they felt were problematic (including politics, problems with capital juries, costs, as well as others).

Arbitrariness and Discrimination

Brief Summary of Issue

The death penalty in America, because it is not mandatory and because it is guided by prosecutorial and jury *discretion*, is possibly arbitrary. Arbitrary means "determined by chance, whim, or impulse, and not by necessity, reason, or principle."[6] Arbitrariness would be seen in disparities in capital punishment based on *extralegal factors* (race, class, gender/sex) that are not explained away by legal factors such as statutorily prescribed aggravating factors.

Issue of Contention

The main issues of contention in terms of arbitrariness include: Are death sentences and executions arbitrary? If so, does the presence of arbitrariness mean capital punishment is discriminatory?

Opponents of capital punishment assert that disparities in criminal punishments including capital punishment cannot be explained by legal factors and thus clearly are indicative of some form of discrimination in criminal justice. Further, opponents declare that disparities and discrimination in America's capital punishment system violate protections granted defendants by the U.S. Constitution and thus make the punishment illegal under American law. For example, opponents show that whereas African Americans make up only 12% of the U.S. population, they make up roughly one third of people executed since 1976.[7] Supporters of capital punishment explain away disparities in death penalty sentencing, death row, and executions by comparing these statistics not with demographic characteristics of American citizens but instead with criminal populations. For example, they claim that African Americans commit about half of all murders in the United States and are thus underrepresented among those executed at one third.[8] Further, supporters say what determines death sentences and executions are not extralegal factors but instead legal factors such as the level of aggravation across homicides.[9]

Experts' Views

The experts were asked about possible race, class, and gender/sex biases in capital punishment, and were given the opportunity to raise these issues in the open-ended questions about whether there were any problems with capital punishment and whether any of those problems are serious enough to make the punishment unacceptable as a government punishment.

TABLE 5.1   Expert Opinion on Whether Capital Punishment Is Racially Biased

Is American capital punishment plagued by a racial bias of any kind?

Yes	84%
No	7%
Unsure	9%

Note: N = 43.

Is American capital punishment plagued by a racial bias of any kind?

Racial Bias

As shown in Table 5.1, a very large majority of capital punishment experts (84%) believes that the death penalty is "plagued by a racial bias" of some kind. Some respondents (7%) do not think that the death penalty is "plagued by a racial bias" of some kind, and a few respondents (9%) suggested that they were unsure.

The Death Penalty Is Racially Biased

Respondents who said that the death penalty is racially biased cited empirical evidence, anecdotal evidence, and historical evidence in support of their answers. And they tended to mention the race-of-victim effect that seems to drive most death sentences. For example, respondents said:

- The death penalty "appears to discriminate on basis of race of victim."
- "Studies show that racial bias (especially race of victim) persists with the administration of [capital punishment] in this country."
- Empirical evidence "indicates that race of victim has strong effect of execution risk."

One respondent simply cited the "race-of-victim bias."
Other experts who discussed race-of-victim bias wrote:

- There is "very little evidence of race of [defendant] discrimination, but a lot of evidence of race-of-victim discrimination—killers of whites more likely to get [death sentences] even after adjudicated for case severity."
- "Race of victim still controls how bad the defendants' moral merit is seen to be. The killers of the most valuable victims receive the worst punishments."

- "Although race of [defendant] literature is waning, race of victim literature points to a reverence for white victims. Also, even though [black on black] homicides are perhaps the most common, they are the least likely to get a [death sentence]—even when controlling for legally relevant factors. Disparity exists, but whether it is due to racism/discrimination is hard to prove, especially given the high standard of proof required by courts."
- "There is not doubt. All one needs to do is look at the statistics on race of offender and race of victim across all executions which have occurred in the United States. I think that the primary racial bias comes in when we look at the race of the victim. An offender is much more likely to be executed for killing a white person than a racial minority."

One expert wrote: "Just look at the data. Not only is race of the offender an issue, but the race/gender/age intersection of the victim is perhaps the biggest predictor that a death sentence will be sought." Similarly, another respondent answered: "A quarter century of research documents racial bias in the administration of the modern death penalty. The evidence on this point is overwhelming." One expert wrote: "Selection of cases eligible for [capital] punishment is racially skewed." And another expert blamed "systemic racism in the criminal justice system."

Another expert cited evidence indicating "both race of offender and race of victim bias." The opinion of another expert supported this view: "There are numerous studies from around the country establishing that race plays a role in the death penalty—either due to the race of the defendant or the victim. In my own experience, I believe race plays a role, too. One way that racism manifests itself that is often not discussed is that the police are less likely to solve crimes where black people are the victims."

An additional respondent answered:

Yes. During the pre-*Furman* era, there was clear and convincing evidence of a race-of-defendant effect. In the post-*Gregg* or present era, there is now clear and convincing evidence of a strong race-of-victim effect and less clear evidence of a race-of-defendant effect. Also there is emergent evidence that legally relevant factors are not racially invariant. Aggravating circumstances are more aggravating for black defendants and mitigating circumstances are stronger mitigators for white defendants.

Another expert agreed, writing: "The evidence I am aware of convinces me that the race of the victim does play a role in the capital punishment process not of legally relevant factors."

One expert was more specific, pointing out that

those of color who kill a white female are the most likely to be put to death. In addition, those who are poor are more likely to receive the death penalty. In the U.S., race and SES [socioeconomic status] are highly correlated. The least likely to receive the death penalty are poor minorities who kill a poor minority person. This sends a message that some lives are worth more/more important than others.

Another respondent similarly answered:

Generally. I think the post-*Furman* reforms have reduced the amount and changed the type of racial disparity in [capital punishment]. "Bias" implies intentional discrimination and I think it is more subtle than this. Great improvements have been made, especially in the South. Most of the research suggests that little race of defendant disparity is found, but race-of-victim disparity continues. Generally, those who kill whites are treated more severely than those who kill blacks. The research that I and my colleagues have conducted, however, suggests this may be a function of how severely the criminal justice system responds to the murder of white females, though this has only been recently examined.

One expert asserted that racial bias is a more significant problem than thought by most:

Historically, capital punishment has been plagued by racial and ethnic bias, prejudice, and discrimination....[10] For years, researchers have been documenting the differential treatment, particularly against African Americans. More recently, scholars are showing vis-à-vis empirical investigations that the situation of discrimination in capital punishment is worse than we thought... when we take two additional factors into consideration: 1) the inclusion of ethnic variation...[11] and 2) the investigation of capital punishment by the totality of final outcomes.

One respondent compared the question to that of deterrence, writing: "Another dead horse we can go on beating, or not. As a [capital punishment] opponent, I do think racial bias might be a more worthwhile topic to keep pursuing than deterrence, simply because racial bias seems to carry some weight in courts."

Another expert argued that the real problem is not so much race but instead is social class:

I think that justice serves those with more resources better than those with limited or no resources. This has more to do with social class than race.

> Race affects the [death penalty] because blacks are disproportionately poor. With ample resources, not only can we afford more justice, we have an advantage in all of society's institutions. We live in better and safer homes, attend better and safer schools, drive better and safer vehicles, and work in better and safer environments, etc.

Two experts discussed the issue of racial bias in all criminal justice operations. The first said: "I regard this question as irrelevant to capital punishment since it is true of the entire criminal justice system. Racial stereotypes change over time, but at any time a society will have some and the criminal justice system will show it." Another wrote: "Racial bias is deeply embedded in most aspects of the criminal justice system, including [the] death penalty."

Four experts noted studies by David Baldus in justifying their belief that capital punishment is racially biased:

- "Yes. See the Baldus studies."
- "See the Baldus research, for openers."
- "The Baldus studies, and others, are quite convincing on this point. The effect is too strong and too pervasive, both in the North and South, for this to be a statistical artifact. As others have pointed out, the correlation between race and capital punishment is stronger than the correlation between smoking and heart disease."
- "Obviously. The statistics tell the story. See the Baldus study and all other racial analyses since then."[12]

The Death Penalty Is Not Racially Biased

A few respondents said that the death penalty is not racially biased. One reasoned:

> No, the only recent evidence supporting this argues for a white victim effect at the prosecutorial stage of processing. Recent evidence from [Texas] does not support this relationship. Regardless, these studies do not adequately control for victim SES, enough circumstances of the crime, wishes of the victims' families, and failure of the defendants (in cases of [blacks killing whites] to accept a plea negotiation).

Another expert agreed that the "race-of-victim effect is not proven to be caused by race discrimination." Finally, one expert acknowledged the possibility of discrimination "very rarely, mostly in smaller towns and I think most often in sex crimes."

Unsure

Three respondents said they were unsure about racial bias in capital punishment. One answered:

> Clearly in the past there was disproportionate application of capital punishment to blacks and other non-whites. I'm quite confident that this problem has been considerably reduced, but I would not go so far as to say it has been eliminated. The OJ [Simpson] case suggested strongly that under some circumstances, black-dominated juries will set impossibly high standards of proof where the accused is black and the victim white. But cases like this are exceptionally rare and are not necessarily indicative of a statistically meaningful phenomenon. Another factor in the OJ case was that the accused was sufficiently wealthy to afford an exceptionally competent defense. Conceivably in that case it was the high-powered defense even more than the racial aspect that resulted in the acquittal.

Another responded:

> This is a difficult question to answer. Studies are very divided on this point. There does seem to be some correlation between race and capital punishment, but other variables, especially class and wealth, also affect the imposition of a death sentence. I suspect that even if these variables are controlled for, racial bias exists; however, the nature and strength of the relationship remains muddled.

Finally, one respondent took issue with the wording of the question and provided what sounds like support for his belief that there are biases in the death penalty based on race: "I resent the use of the value-laden word 'plagued.'[13] Is there a racial bias of any kind? There are several: more whites are executed than any other race (historically); more executions of those with white victims; etc."

Is American capital punishment plagued by a social class bias of any kind?

Social Class Bias

As shown in Table 5.2, a very large majority of capital punishment experts (80%) believe that the death penalty is "plagued by a social class bias" of some kind. Some respondents (4%) do not think that the death penalty is "plagued by a social class bias" of some kind, and more (16%) suggested that they were unsure.

The Death Penalty Is Class Biased

Some respondents related class bias in the death penalty to class bias in the criminal justice system. For example:

TABLE 5.2   Expert Opinion on Whether Capital Punishment Is Class Biased

Is American capital punishment plagued by a social class bias of any kind?

Yes	80%
No	4%
Unsure	16%

Note: N = 45.

- "Of course. The entire justice system is plagued by a social class bias."
- "It is unrealistic to think that a class bias which permeates the decision making of the criminal justice system, would not exist in [capital punishment]. However, it is likely that the class bias is least prominent in capital cases. There is significant research (and from my own experience) to indicate that there is some validity to the liberation hypothesis. Thus, in the most serious cases (i.e., death eligible homicides) we are likely to see the least amount of disparity, though the fact that some disparity remains, even in the most restricted & public decision areas, is disturbing."

Others pointed to data and studies. For example, one expert answered: "Absolutely. I think that this is a great source of bias in regard to the offenders who are likely to be charged with a capital crime and ultimately convicted and sentenced to death. Look at any death row and this becomes immediately apparent. Even when taking into account the class distribution of murder, the bias persists." Another answered: "Most of all death row inmates are from the lower class." And another expert said: "The studies ... convincingly demonstrate class bias."

One respondent who concluded that capital punishment was class biased wrote: "There is much less research on this than on racial bias and it is likely to be harder to measure. The effects of social class permeate society, from prenatal care to schooling to access to mental health services to the ability to hire top notch legal representation. Many of the effects of social class occur before engagement with the criminal justice system." Another respondent answered: "Retribution is a class-based system. It promises justice by lowering another human; it is classist to assume that justice involves wielding coercive power to subjugate another."

Respondents who said that the death penalty is biased by social class focused on the quality of defense attorneys of those accused and convicted of capital crimes. One expert, for example, characterized such defense attorneys as "incompetent." Others wrote:

- "The poor cannot afford good legal representation, and a good lawyer makes a great deal of difference."
- "The poor cannot afford defense attorneys that are competent [and] thus are more likely to be falsely convicted & executed."
- "With very few exceptions, only the poor are executed. One of the biggest problems are class differences in legal representation."
- "Poor people, with or without bad lawyers, are the prime pool for the death penalty."
- "How many of those on death row would be considered middle-upper class? Also, how many were represented by appointed attorneys/public defenders?"
- "To state the obvious: A relevant aspect of social class, maybe the main one, is whether or not the individual has the money to mount an effective defense. It's also the case that people with more money profit more than the poor from long-range planning and can more often get what they want without resorting to murder."
- "With a few notable exceptions, middle class or upper class people do not end up on death row. The aphorism, 'Capital Punishment—them that don't have the capital, get the punishment,' is true."
- "Those without the capital get the punishment."
- "To paraphrase a wise observation: The criminal justice system knows who pays for it—and no place in the world are they the poor."

One expert who also focused on the quality of defense attorneys wrote:

> Unquestionably, capital punishment in the United States is plagued with social class bias, even more than race and ethnic bias. As point[ed] out in several recent investigations, "the American legal system is divided into four distinct systems: one for the poor and defenseless, one for the rich and powerful, one for Euro-Americans, and one for African Americans and Latinas/os, particularly Mexicans." Here too, legal theory and reality clash, in that due process and justice are more a matter of money than a matter of guilt or innocence. Those who have money can buy "justice," but those who live from pay check to pay check (which constitutes a large segment of society) cannot afford justice . . . and so they are further victimized by the state—legally![14]

The issue for many experts was clearly access to resources. For example, one expert explained: "I believe that social class is more relevant than race when it comes to the [death penalty]. I believe that blacks with ample resources will be just as likely to avoid the [death penalty] as whites with similar resources." Another said that only the "poor and disadvantaged get the death penalty."

Other answers that revolved around the issue of resources included:

- "It mainly is a SES or victim effect—higher SES victims, risk of [death sentence] is higher."
- "Name one wealthy murderer on death row. See OJ Simpson: death not even sought for a wealthy man accused of a brutal double murder."

The Death Penalty Is Not Class Biased

Two respondents who said that the death penalty is not biased by social class explained that the poor are more likely to get death sentences and be executed simply because they commit more capital crimes. One claimed that the "death penalty is applied fairly, overall, to those sorts of crime statutorily determined to be capital. Wealthy persons do not (rarely) commit robbery, murders, or killings of police officers. Those that kill for insurance money appear to be as likely (in [Texas]) to receive a death sentence, regardless of their SES." Another expert agreed, saying "upper class persons rarely engage in violent crime such as capital murder."

Unsure

At least two of the four experts who answered that they were unsure about class biases in the death penalty seemed to suggest through their answers that the death penalty is biased against the poor. For example, one expert claimed: "Systematic data on the SES of defendants and/or victims are not available. But proxy or surrogate data suggest such a bias, especially as reflected in attorney type & quality." Another expert who said he was unsure also wrote: "I can't recall what the studies find, but I think they do detect class bias."

One expert did challenge the wording of the question, and then offered his own interpretation of the issue:

It would depend on how you define "plagued."[15] Certainly wealthy defendants who can afford top quality lawyers are less likely to suffer capital punishment than defendants of more modest means. Wealthy people can afford more of everything, including legal defense when they commit murder or are accused of committing murder. But I would not go so far as to say this is a "plague" on the enforcement system. It is an imperfection, like the various adverse side effects of "wonder drugs." I can't imagine America becoming so egalitarian that all accused murderers would receive the same state-sponsored defense, no more and no less. The vast majority of people today believe that someone accused of a serious crime has a "natural right" to buy as competent a defense as he or she can afford.

Another respondent noted his trouble with the term "plagued," but then he wrote: "Obviously more lower class than upper class."

Finally, one respondent who answered unsure wrote: "Race & class are inextricably linked."

Is American capital punishment plagued by a gender/sex bias of any kind?

Gender/Sex Bias

As shown in Table 5.3, half of capital punishment experts (50%) indicated that they thought the death penalty is "plagued by a gender/sex bias" and only 12% answered no. A sizable portion of the experts said they were not sure (38%).

The Death Penalty Is Gender/Sex Biased

Respondents who said that the death penalty is biased by gender or sex explained that killers of females would be most likely to get death sentences. For example, one expert wrote: "Defendants are more likely to be executed if they killed female victims. Females convicted of capital murder are less likely to be executed than males." Another wrote: "Killers of female victims are more likely to receive the death penalty, ceteris peribus, males are more likely to receive the death penalty than females." He added that this disparity, along with those dealing with race and social class, are "the result of prosecutorial discretion."

TABLE 5.3   Expert Opinion on Whether Capital Punishment Is Gender/Sex Biased

Is American capital punishment plagued by a gender/sex bias of any kind?

Yes	50%
No	12%
Unsure	38%

Note: N = 42.

Others suggested the following:

- "American capital punishment is reserved, almost exclusively, for males."
- "Clearly females are less likely to receive the [death penalty] and are less likely to be executed."
- "Women escape death sentences under circumstances which would result in death for male defendants."
- "Women are disproportionately treated with mercy."
- "Females, though the gender discriminated against generally, generally are less likely to receive a capital sentence than males otherwise similar."
- "Men are disproportionately violentized & locked into using violence. Women still are not perceived as violent as men."

One even seemed to justify the disparity by gender by rhetorically asking, "Who wants to kill a woman?" Similarly, one expert pointed out: "We seem to be remarkably squeamish when it comes to executing women." And another wrote: "We seem to have difficulty bringing ourselves to execute mothers. And I think that agency, or autonomy of intention and action, is in general attributed less to women than to men. But these remarks are completely impressionistic. I would love to see psychologists devote themselves to controlled experiments about 'executability.'"

One expert offered a different line of thought, writing: "Capital punishment in the United States is plagued with gender prejudice and discrimination. Even though women are not given the sentence of death at the same rate that men do, women are treated as second and third class citizens ... suffering oppression, manipulation, exploitation, and brutality."

One expert wrote about his own research, which concludes a gender bias in capital punishment that often hurts women:

> I wrote a report about women on death row, which involved studying all of the cases of women on death row since 1976. Although I cannot establish conclusively that there is sexual bias, I observed much bias anecdotally. For example, most women who are on death row are there for killing family members or close intimates, whereas this does not appear to be the case with men who are more likely to be sentenced to death for killing a stranger. I observed that women received a more severe sentence for crimes than men did in cases with male co-defendants. Also, women on death row were frequently the victims of abuse from their spouses or their families of origin and many did not have this abuse adequately raised at trial in either the guilt or the punishment phases.

Perhaps the clearest evidence of a gender/sex bias offered by a death penalty expert was this response: "We just don't execute many women (they represent 1.5% of those on death row and about 1% of those executed since 1977), even though they account for a significant proportion of murderers." The underrepresentation of women, according to one expert, made it difficult for him to answer the question: "There are so few female defendants in death eligible homicides that it is difficult to confidently assess this aspect with any confidence. However, it appears (and certainly historically in the South especially) that those who kill females, especially white females, may be treated more severely." Another expert agreed with this last point, writing: "White and female victims are singled out, according to recent research that killers of females are considered more offensive points to bias. However, black females don't necessarily have the same status as white females, so the combo. Of the revered white female victim is where potential gender bias comes in."

The Death Penalty Is Not Gender/Sex Biased

Respondents who said that the death penalty is not biased by gender or sex explained that either they were unaware of any evidence showing a bias or that there were other explanations for disparities by gender or sex. For example, one expert wrote: "There may be an exception, sort of a chivalry, given to mothers who kill their children. Under the law, however, there is typically a means of lessening their mens rea, so I am not sure about this. Similarly, fathers & live-in boyfriends are not likely to get death for killing their children." Another expert said, simply: "Women tend not to commit 1st degree murder; thus, they are not likely to be sentenced to death."

Unsure

Those who were unsure said that the death penalty "probably discriminates against male defendants by affording more leniency to female killers"; and "Possibly women convicted of homicide are less likely to suffer capital punishment than equivalent males owing to the persistence of traditional sexual stereotypes. . . . I would not describe this situation, even if it exists, as serious enough to be described as a 'plague.'" Another who questioned the use of the term "plague" wrote: "Certainly more males than females have been executed."

Another expert's answer was more complex, stating:

> This has many different answers. At first glance, one could argue that capital punishment is chivalrous, that it is directed towards men. However, that would tend to ignore the very different nature of homicides (on average) perpetrated by men and by women. There is certainly a bias in terms of the type of victims that we think should be avenged through death sentencing. If the victim is a young (or elderly)

white female, the crime is seen as more horrendous than if the victim is a black male in his early 20s. This is about more than gender, though. It is about age, race, sex and social class.

Another respondent who indicated he was unsure about the issue of a gender bias in capital punishment wrote: "Not too many studies [exist] on gender bias to make an informed decision." Similarly, an additional expert answered: "Since so few women are convicted of crimes for which capital punishment might be imposed, at least compared to men, this is a difficult question to answer. Perhaps there is a bias in conviction rates in the first place. In any case, I am unaware of data showing gender bias, although there may be."

Another expert wrote that the evidence is "mixed. Most female murder [is] less aggravated than male murder." Another expert who answered unsure wrote: "Women commit so few of the sorts of murders that usually are prosecuted as capital cases it is difficult to draw firm conclusions. There is some evidence that women may be condemned in cases involving prior abuse by the victim. These are cases that present strong mitigating circumstances and perhaps should not even have been charged as capital crimes." Finally, one expert who answered unsure wrote: "Murder rates for [women] are too low to detect bias."

Fact Check

There are at least two mechanisms to evaluate whether the process of capital punishment is biased against particular groups of people. The first is to examine basic demographic information about who is subjected to it. The second is to examine empirical studies about race, class, and gender or sex biases. Both of these mechanisms are utilized below.

Race

Table 5.4 compares known demographic information of American citizens, with those arrested for murder and nonnegligent manslaughter, convicted murderers, death row inmates, and those executed from 1976 through early 2006.

According to the U.S. Census, in 2000, whites made up 75% of the U.S. population, Hispanics made up 12.5%, and blacks made up 12.3%.[16]

According to the *Sourcebook of Criminal Justice Statistics*, blacks made up 56.6% of those arrested for murder and nonnegligent manslaughter in 2002, versus 41.2% whites, and 2.3% members of another race ("other").[17] Further, blacks made up 51% of those convicted for murder and nonnegligent manslaughter in 2002, versus 45% whites, and 4% other.[18]

TABLE 5.4   Comparing Demographic Characteristics of the U.S. Population
with Murderers, Death Row Inmates, and Executions

	White	Hispanic	Black	Other
U.S. population (2000)	75%	12.5%	12.3%	0.2%
Murder arrests (2002)	41.2%	n/a	56.6%	2.3%
Murder convictions (2002)	45%	n/a	51%	4%
Death row (2006)	45.5%	10.4%	41.7%	2.3%
Executions (1976–2005)	58%	6%	34%	2.3%

Note: Percentages do not add up to 100%, as reported in the tables.

Sources: From *Overview of Race and Hispanic Origin*, by the U.S. Census Bureau, 2001. Retrieved from http://www.census.gov/prod/2001pubs/c2kbr01-1.pdf; Table 4.12, "Arrests in Cities, by Offense Charge, Age Group, and Race, 2002," in *Sourcebook of Criminal Justice Statistics*, 2006. Retrieved from http://www.albany.edu/sourcebook/pdf/t412.pdf; Table 5.45, "Characteristics of Felony Offenders Convicted in State Courts, by Offense, United States, 2002," in *Sourcebook of Criminal Justice Statistics*, 2006. Retrieved from http://www.albany.edu/sourcebook/pdf/t5452002.pdf; "Death Row USA," by the NAACP Legal Defense and Educational Fund Inc., 2006. Retrieved from http://www.naacpldf.org/content/pdf/pubs/drusa/DRUSA_Fall_2005.pdf

Whites make up the largest share of death row inmates in the United States at 45.5%, blacks make up 41.7%, Hispanics 10.4%, and members of other races only 2.3%.[19]

As for executions, the majority (58%) of those executed from 1976 through March 2006 were white. Yet, blacks are overrepresented among those executed (34%, followed by 6% Hispanics and 2.3% other).[20]

If one looked at only these numbers, one might conclude that capital punishment is biased against white people. Although they are underrepresented among death row populations and executions relative to their share of the U.S. population, whites are overrepresented based on their share of arrests and convictions for murder. The opposite is true with regard to blacks. At first glance, the death penalty appears least likely to be used against them. Although they are overrepresented among death row populations and executions relative to their share of the U.S. population, blacks are underrepresented based on their share of arrests and convictions for murder.

There are at least two possible explanations for this. First, it is possible that the ways in which whites and blacks commit murder are different. Perhaps white offenders are more likely than black offenders to commit murders that are aggravated in nature and thus eligible for the death penalty.[21] Another possibility, related to the first, is that what matters is whom you kill.[22]

Evidence suggests that about 90% of murders are intraracial (committed by a person of one race against a person of the same race).[23] Because whites tend to kill whites and blacks tend to kill blacks, one possible explanation as to why whites are more often sentenced to death and executed than blacks is the race of the victims killed.

According to the data, between 1976 and March 2006, 80% of all people executed in the United States killed white victims. Only 14% of people executed during these years killed blacks, 4% killed Hispanics, and 1.9% killed someone from another race.[24]

More telling is an examination of interracial murders (murders between members of different races) since 1976. After excluding cases involving multiple victims of several different races, the remaining 221 cases (5%) involved a white defendant and black victim in only 12 cases, versus 209 (95%) cases of black defendants and white victims. Looking even further back, a study of 15,978 executions since 1739 found only 30 cases in which a white was put to death for a crime against a black.[25]

State-specific examinations allow disparities to be witnessed more clearly. For example, in Georgia between 1976 and 2002, 80% of murder victims of those executed were white and 12% were black. Yet, 56% of defendants executed were white and 35% were black. When breaking it down by race of defendants and victims, whites who killed whites made up more than half of the cases (52.6%), followed by blacks who killed whites (22.5%), blacks who killed blacks (10.2%), and whites who killed blacks (1.4%).[26]

Similar results were found in Texas, Virginia, North Carolina, Maryland, New Jersey, Indiana, Ohio, Kansas, California, and Washington, where killers of whites were between 2.5 and 5.0 times more likely to be executed over various time periods.[27]

A recent study in Maryland analyzed 1,311 murders between 1978 and 1999 held to be punishable by the death penalty. It found significant racial and geographic bias in the state's capital sentencing. Blacks who kill whites were 2.5 times more likely to be sentenced to death than whites who kill whites, and 3.5 times more likely than are blacks who kill blacks. Authors Raymond Paternoster and Robert Brame concluded:

> In sum, offenders who kill white victims, especially if the offender is black, are significantly and substantially more likely to be charged with a capital crime. Those who kill white victims are also significantly more likely to have their death notification "stick" than those who kill non-whites. . . . Moreover, while these effects do not appear at other, later decision-making points in the capital sentencing process, they are generally not corrected.[28]

In New Jersey, a study by the New Jersey Supreme Court reported that the death penalty is used more against killers of whites. It concluded: "There is unsettling statistical evidence indicating that cases involving killers of white victims are more likely to progress to a penalty phase than cases involving killers of African-American victims."[29] In Pennsylvania, a Pennsylvania Supreme Court Committee study reported that the death penalty is affected by race: "Empirical studies conducted in Pennsylvania to date demonstrate that, *at least in some counties*, race plays a major, if not overwhelming, role in the imposition of the death penalty."[30]

In California, a study found that white-victim murder cases are most likely cases to end in a death sentence. The study found that killers of whites were more than three times more likely to be sentenced to death as killers of blacks and that individuals convicted of the same crimes were more than three times more likely to be sentenced to death due to the location of the crime (homicides in predominantly white rural communities were more likely to lead to death sentences than homicides in diverse, urban areas).[31]

A study in Ohio by the Associated Press found similar results, showing that killers of whites were twice as likely to be sentenced to death as killers of blacks.[32] Interestingly, it mattered little who the killer was, as 18.3% of white killers of whites got death sentences, versus 17.6% of black killers of whites, versus only 8.4% of blacks who killed blacks and 8.7% of whites who killed blacks.

In North Carolina, a study examined all homicide cases that occurred in the state over a 5-year period, from January 1, 1993, through December 31, 1997, during which there were 3,990 homicides. Among these 3,990 murders, 99 first-degree-murder cases eventually received death sentences, and 303 first-degree cases received life sentences. The study looked at every one of those cases and examined a scientific sample of the remainder of the second-degree-murder cases in which life sentences were imposed, and then sampled from among those cases in which sentences less than life were imposed.[33]

The study employed a 33-page data collection instrument (DCI) that included over 113 questions about each case, as well as a narrative summary that captured the special features of each case. Data collectors obtained their data from the public records of the state of North Carolina—judicial records from superior courts statewide, from the North Carolina Court of Appeals, and from the North Carolina Supreme Court, as well as from the files of the Office of the State Medical Examiner, the Department of Corrections, and the Administrative Office of the Courts. They also spoke with prosecutors and defense attorneys where necessary to complete their investigation of each case. DCIs were completed on over 502 defendants, including every defendant convicted of first-degree murder anywhere in the state who received either a life sentence or a death sentence during this period.

As such, the study was the most comprehensive study of North Carolina's system of capital sentencing, and the first substantial study of death sentencing conducted anywhere in the South since 1984. The study concluded that racial factors—specifically the race of the homicide victim— played a real, substantial, and statistically significant role in determining who received death sentences in North Carolina during the 1993–1997 period. The odds of receiving a death sentence rose by 3.5 times or more among those defendants (of whatever race) who murdered white persons.

An earlier review by the U.S. General Accounting Office (GAO) of 28 studies by 21 sets of researchers with 23 data sets found "a pattern of evidence indicating racial disparities in the charging, sentencing, and imposition of the death penalty" since 1976. It concluded the following:

> In 82 percent of the studies, race-of-victim was found to influence likelihood of being charged with capital murder or receiving the death penalty, i.e., those who murdered whites were found to be more likely to be sentenced to death than those who murdered blacks. This finding was remarkably consistent across data sets, states, data collection methods, and analytic techniques. The finding held for high, medium, and low quality studies. The race-of-victim influence was found at all stages of the criminal justice system process, although there were variations among studies as to whether there was a race-of-victim influence at specific stages. The evidence for the race-of-victim influence was stronger for the earlier stages of the judicial process (e.g., prosecutorial decision to charge defendants with a capital offense, decision to proceed to trial rather than plea bargain).[34]

This GAO study found that

> the evidence for the influence of the race-of-defendant on death penalty outcomes was equivocal. Although more than half of the studies found that race-of-defendant influenced the likelihood of being charged with a capital crime or receiving the death penalty, the relationship between race-of-defendant and outcome varied across studies . . . the extent to which the finding was influenced by race-of-victim rather than race-of-defendant was unclear.[35]

A review of 18 more recent studies found results that "are consistent with those summarized in the GAO report."[36] Twelve of these 18 studies found race-of-victim effects but not race-of-defendant effects.[37]

Although it is difficult to explain data indicating disparities based on race-of-victim, one possible explanation is "innocent bias" created by stereotypes of the "typical criminal" that emerge from the criminal law and media coverage of crime and criminal justice.[38] This would be most consistent with studies of capital jurors, who "first construct a sense of themselves as a small group, and through this sense they respond to the accused and to the characteristics of the accused." Then, the "small-group identity they construct is one of insiders, and through it they cast the accused as an outsider. Racial and other characteristics of the accused figure in as related to outsider identity."[39] Another possible explanation is that African Americans are underrepresented among criminal justice employees, particularly members of the "courtroom workgroup" (e.g., prosecutors and judges), and that American juries are disproportionately white.[40] For example, attorney and author Stephen Bright points out that in those states where the death penalty is legal, "97.5 percent of the chief prosecutors are white.... In 18 of the states, all of the chief prosecutors are white." Further, "the rest of the criminal justice system is almost as unrepresentative of America's racial diversity as prosecutors' offices ... people of color are seldom involved as judges, jurors, prosecutors, and lawyers in the courts" in the South.[41]

At the federal level, evidence of race-of-defendant bias has been found. Two studies showed evidence of racial bias at the federal level. First, a study by the Subcommittee on Civil and Constitutional Rights of the Committee of the Judiciary found:

> Racial minorities are being prosecuted under federal death penalty law far beyond their proportion in the general population or the population of criminal offenders. Analysis of prosecutions under the federal death penalty provisions of the Anti-Drug Abuse Act of 1988 reveals that 89% of the defendants selected for capital prosecution have been either African-American or Mexican-American. Moreover, the number of prosecutions under this Act has been increasing over the past two years with no decline in the racial disparities. All ten of the recently approved federal capital prosecutions have been against black defendants. This pattern of inequality adds to the mounting evidence that race continues to play an unacceptable part in the application of capital punishment in America today.[42]

A second study reported that 80% of the cases submitted by federal prosecutors for consideration of the death penalty in the previous 5 years involved racial minorities as defendants, and in more than half of the cases the defendant was African American.[43] A subsequent report by the Justice Department attempted to explain these results away, saying:

> First, in cases submitted by the United States Attorneys for departmental review, the proportions of Black and Hispanic defendants were greater than the proportions of Blacks and Hispanics in the general

population. Of the 682 defendants reviewed under the Department's death penalty decision-making procedures in the period 1995 to 2000, 134 (20%) were White, 324 (48%) were Black, and 195 (29%) were Hispanic.

Second, recommendations and decisions to seek the death penalty were less likely at each stage of the process for Black and Hispanic defendants than for White defendants. In other words, United States Attorneys recommended the death penalty in smaller proportions of the submitted cases involving Black or Hispanic defendants than in those involving White defendants; the Attorney General's capital case review committee likewise recommended the death penalty in smaller proportions of the submitted cases involving Black or Hispanic defendants than in those involving White defendants; and the Attorney General made a decision to seek the death penalty in smaller proportions of the submitted cases involving Black or Hispanic defendants than in those involving White defendants.

In the cases considered by the Attorney General, the Attorney General decided to seek the death penalty for 38% of the White defendants, 25% of the Black defendants, and 20% of the Hispanic defendants.... The finding that the death penalty was sought at lower rates for Black and Hispanic defendants than for White defendants held true both in "intraracial" cases, involving defendants and victims of the same race and ethnicity, and in "interracial" cases, involving defendants and victims of different races or ethnicities.[44]

Later in the report, the Justice Department concludes that the issue to be determined is "whether there is empirical evidence which ... demonstrates that the system is subverted by [racial or ethnic] bias. The findings of the ... report and the further study conducted thereafter do not support such a conclusion."

In fact, the findings do justify a conclusion of racial bias. The Justice Department's own evidence suggests that the attorney general sought authorization for capital prosecutions in 37% of cases with white victims, versus only 21% in minority-victim cases. This alone could explain why there is a higher likelihood that prosecutors were more likely to seek death in cases with white defendants. Finally, there are race-of-victim disparities in the federal capital punishment system.[45]

A more recent study of the federal death penalty system from 1995 to 2000 found no evidence of racial bias in the stage where cases are recommended for death penalty prosecution.[46] The study, conducted by the Rand Corporation, illustrated that the death penalty was more sought after when defendants killed white victims than when defendants killed black victims. Yet, the factors that explained the disparity were the characteristics of the crime (e.g., the heinousness of the murder, such as when a person was brutally murdered and when there was more than one victim). The authors of the study assert that the findings should not be generalized to earlier or later time periods, and they admit that bias could still be present at other points in the criminal justice process at the federal level.

Statistics and studies like those described have led some scholars to state clearly and unequivocally that the practice of capital punishment is generally biased against minorities. For example, one writes that the "death penalty is a system plagued by racism."[47] Author Pam McAllister says that racism is "inherent in our criminal justice system" and that racism manifests itself in the more serious treatment of people of color generally and the more serious punishment given to those who harm whites.[48]

Not all scholars agree with this assessment, but most do. Capital punishment supporters generally acknowledge that racial disparities exist in American capital punishment systems, but simultaneously deny that they are relevant for whether the death penalty is fundamentally flawed and should be abandoned. For example, John McAdams writes that "there is indeed a huge disparity in the way the death penalty is meted out, but the disparity is radically different from what more people suppose."[49] Later, he writes: "All of the best studies of racial disparity show strong race-of-victim effects."[50] He offers several studies that found race-of-victim bias in the capital punishment process from several states,[51] and concludes that the capital punishment "system is not tougher on black suspects, other things being equal. Indeed, it is more lenient with black suspects—but only because they likely killed other blacks."[52]

McAdams blames racial disparities in capital punishment on us and our expectations of African Americans. He writes:

> Perhaps we deal leniently with black defendants because we expect large numbers of blacks to be criminals. Perhaps we have come to expect black neighborhoods to be unsafe and therefore consider crime in those neighborhoods to be pretty much a routine matter. Perhaps we view murders as "heinous" when the circumstances are rare and shocking, and we have ceased to view murders of black people as rare and shocking.[53]

After acknowledging that American punishment generally "consistently undervalues the lives of black victims," McAdams rejects abolition of capital punishment as a ploy that would not address the root problem of racism in our systems of criminal justice.

What McAdams is aware of but does not consider relevant is that it is an abuse of *discretion* throughout the capital punishment process that leads to these disparities based on the race of the victim. At least three actors in our systems of criminal justice exercise discretion in processing death penalty cases—prosecutors (who seek death sentences or not), juries (who impose death sentences or not), and governors or boards of pardons and paroles "who generally have complete discretion to commute a death sentence to life without possibility of parole or a term of years."[54] In addition, there is evidence that law enforcement can play a significant role in whether a murder case is processed as a capital case.[55]

The key decisions in death penalty cases are made by prosecutors, making them the most powerful member of the courtroom workgroup.[56] Stephen Bright explains: "The two most important decisions in every death penalty case are made not by juries or judges, but by prosecutors to seek the death penalty or take a capital case to trial. A prosecutor has complete discretion in deciding whether to seek the death penalty and, even if death is sought, whether to offer a sentence less than death in exchange for the defendant's guilty plea."[57] The result is that "whether the death sentence is imposed may depend more on the personal predilections and politics of local prosecutors than the heinousness of the crime or the incorrigibility of the defendant."[58]

Further, blacks are far less likely than whites to serve on capital juries.

> [The] exclusion is the product of discrimination at either or both of two stages of the jury selection process. At the very beginning of the process, when a pool of potential venirepersons is assembled, the pool frequently underrepresents eligible African Americans. . . . At the later stage of selection of the jury for trial, racial discrimination resurfaces in the form of prosecutors' use of peremptory challenges to remove African Americans from the jury. Although the Supreme Court outlawed this practice in *Batson v. Kentucky*, prosecutors continue to use a variety of tactics to attempt to evade the protections established by *Batson*.[59]

In fact, the U.S. Supreme Court recently decided the case of *Miller-El v. Dretke* (2005). The Court held that Texas death row inmate Thomas Miller-El should receive a new trial because of "strong evidence of racial bias during jury selection at his original trial." During the jury selection process in Miller-El's trial (Miller-El is African American), prosecutors struck 10 of the 11 potential black jurors. "The Supreme Court said the prosecutors chosen race-neutral reasons for the strikes do not hold up and are so far at odds with the evidence that pretext is the fair conclusion. The selection process was replete with evidence that prosecutors were selecting and rejecting potential jurors because of race. And the prosecutors took their cues from a manual on jury selection with an emphasis on race." Evidence cited by the Court included "disparate questioning of white and black jurors, jury shuffling, a culture of bias within the prosecutor's office, and the fact that the prosecutor's race-neutral explanations for the strikes were so far at odds with the evidence that the explanations themselves indicate discriminatory intent."[60]

It is the misuse of discretion—being more likely to seek death sentences and impose them when the victim is white (and especially when the offender is black and the victim is white)—that makes the racial disparities intolerable. As noted by scholars David Baldus and George Woodworth, "the principal concern about race discrimination in the administration of the death penalty relates to the differential treatment of similarly situated defendants who are in fact guilty of capital murder. The core ethical concern is fairness—treating like cases alike, especially when the consequences of the decision are so severe."[61] It might not be a relevant legal issue, like it would be if it constituted purposeful discrimination (consider the U.S. Supreme Court's ruling in the *McCleskey* (1987) case, for example), but it may constitute a relevant moral issue for legislatures and policy makers.[62]

The reason that capital punishment opponents claim that abuse of discretion is relevant for the morality of the practice of capital punishment is because it leads to *systemic discrimination*, which is present when race impacts "a substantial proportion of prosecutorial decisions to seek and/or jury decisions to impose the death sentence." It is evidenced when "black defendants or defendants with white victims are treated more punitively than similarly situated white defendants and defendants with black victims."[63] Given that there is clearly statistical evidence of disparities based on the race of the victim, and that this disparity is present even after controlling for legally relevant factors such as the aggravated nature of the killing,[64] the evidence suggests "that when the disparities in the death-sentencing rates are adjusted for legitimate case characteristics, the unadjusted disparities often, but not always, decline. The most reliable evidence of discrimination, therefore, consists of racial disparities that are adjusted to reflect the different levels of culpability of the cases in the different racial groups."

According to the evidence, even after controlling for legally relevant variables, in "83% (25/30) of the jurisdictions with relevant data, there is some evidence of race-of-victim disparities (adversely affecting defendants whose victims are white), and in 33% (10/30) of these jurisdictions, there is some evidence of race-of-defendant disparities (adversely affecting black defendants)." In other words, the race-of-victim bias is present in virtually every death penalty jurisdiction, making it a systemic flaw with the way in which capital punishment is carried out in the United States. It is the "overall pattern across so many jurisdictions and the implausibility of non-racial factors as a casual explanation, especially with respect of race-of-victim discrimination" that makes the case so clear.[65] Given that it is in the borderline cases—where prosecutors could seek death or not—where the race-of-victim effect is most pronounced, this further strengthens the conclusion that the death penalty is racially biased.[66]

Finally, it should be pointed out that many death penalty opponents frame this in the context of other biases that plagued criminal justice (and extracriminal justice) processes in our nation's history. Thus, to some "the death penalty is a direct descendant of lynching and other forms of racial violence and racial oppression in America"[67] (the link between lynching and capital punishment is reexamined in Chapter 6). That is, the bias is "long-standing, pervasive, systemic deficiencies in the criminal justice system. . . . ".[68] One only needs to look inside the nation's courtrooms to see proof of this allegation:

> In many courthouses, everything looks the same as it did during the period of Jim Crow justice. The judges are white, the prosecutors are white, the lawyers are white and, even in communities with substantial African American populations, the jury may be all white. In many cases, the only person of color who sits in front of the bar in the courtroom is the person on trial. The legal system remains the institution that has been least affected by the civil rights movement.[69]

Class

In terms of social class, the vast majority of inmates currently on death row were represented by public defenders or court-appointed attorneys. Because one must be *indigent* to be granted public assistance, this implies that most people processed through the capital punishment process in the United States are poor. But this does not answer the question of whether poor people are more likely to receive the death penalty and wealthy murderers are less likely to receive it. Capital punishment expert Franklin Zimring presents evidence that what often decides whether a defendant charged with capital crimes receives a death sentence and is eventually executed is the quality of representation, which is clearly a function of social class.[70]

Unfortunately, data are not available on the social class of arrested and convicted murderers, nor are data available on the social class of those sentenced to death and executed. Yet, it is generally agreed by scholars that the "death penalty disproportionately affects the poor" and "those with mediocre legal representation."[71] Supreme Court Justice Ruth Ginsburg stated: "People who are well represented at trial do not get the death penalty. I have yet to see a death penalty case among the dozens coming to the Supreme Court on the eve-of-execution stay applications in which the defendant was well represented at trial."[72] Thus, individuals have been sentenced to death and executed in spite of being defended by attorneys who slept through parts of their trials, showed up for court drunk, offered no mitigating evidence for the jury to consider, offered little more than one sentence as a closing argument, failed to investigate the prosecution's case or challenge eyewitness and scientific evidence, and failed to attempt to corroborate alibi evidence.[73]

Author Burk Foster, who has studied capital punishment carefully and gotten personally involved in the lives of death row inmates, wrote a "neutral" book about what he considers to be the realities of capital punishment. In it, he explains how a murder case goes to a death penalty case.[74] He discusses systemic variables and variables that pertain to the offender and the victim that explain why some cases lead to death sentences and most do not. One of the factors is the *availability of competent defense counsel with supporting resources, including investigators, expert witnesses, and supporting staff.* Foster continues: "A defense attorney with skills and resources equal to those of the prosecutor can make it very difficult to get a death penalty case to trial and can reduce at least a portion of the prosecutor's built-in advantage." Another factor he describes is the *"victim's race (and class)."* He explains: "The defendant is much more likely to get a death sentence if the victim was white and middle-class."[75]

The one area related to social class that has received the most attention, in terms of scholarship and litigation, is quality of defense for those accused and convicted of capital crimes.[76] It was not until 1932, in the case of *Powell v. Alabama*, that the U.S. Supreme Court held that those charged with capital crimes in state courts have the right to court-appointed attorneys.[77] In this case, nine African American boys and young men (ages 13 to 21 years) were convicted and sentenced to death for the rape of two young white women (a rape that did not actually occur). The boys were falsely accused after getting into a fight with some white youths on a train.

Since then, capital defendants have enjoyed the right to defense counsel, as have some of those convicted of capital crimes. Yet, many allege that the quality of defense counsel afforded the indigent amounts to a bias against the poor in the capital punishment process. Author David Dow claims that

> close to 100 percent of capital murder defendants are indigent. At some level, everyone in America already knows this.... If you were accused of capital murder, would you rather be rich or poor?... Rich people generally have advantages that poor people do not and that is especially true in the criminal justice system.... The population of death

row in America is close to 100 percent poor.... Rich people often do not even get convicted to begin with; when they do, they never get sentenced to death.[78]

Money matters in the capital punishment process, as one expert explains:

> The single most important factor that determines whether a defendant will be sentenced to death is the quality of the defendant's lawyer. In jurisdictions without public defender systems, indigent defendants get lawyers who cannot afford—and who are at times simply unqualified—to put on effective and vigorous defenses.... In contrast, where defendants have the resources to hire their own lawyers, or where there is a public defender system for capital defendants, the defendants fare much better.[79]

Michael Mello and Paul Perkins assert that "part of the problem here is resources—the legal system in capital trials gets what it pays for. And what it pays for is often the equivalent of sub-minimum wage. You could make more money flipping burgers at McDonald's than you'd make trying capital cases in many southern States enthusiastic about enforcing capital punishment." This problem is further exacerbated by the fact that it is very difficult to prove to the U.S. Supreme Court that a defendant had ineffective assistance of counsel and that one must have a lawyer to even file a *habeas* petition. That is, "for a condemned person to prove his trial lawyer was constitutionally lousy, that person must have a good lawyer at the *habeas* stage. But there is no constitutional 'right' to counsel in *habeas* at all."[80]

Habeas corpus relief works this way: First, an individual must present an issue to a state court before a federal court can even consider the merits of the issue (the "exhaustion requirement"). Second, both the courts and the U.S. Congress have restricted the issues that federal courts can even consider in habeas cases.[81] Here are two examples. First, in 1995 "Congress made it more difficult for those under death sentence to obtain competent lawyers to represent them in state post-conviction proceedings by eliminating federal funding for the programs that provided lawyers to the condemned."[82]

Second, the Antiterrorism and Effective Death Penalty Act of 1996 "further forecloses federal review of state court proceedings" by barring "habeas corpus review of issues that were not developed factually in state proceedings" and "federal habeas review of claims adjudicated in state court unless the state decision is contrary to clearly established law as determined by the Supreme Court."[83] It also places a "one-year time limit for the filing of any habeas corpus actions and even provides for a six-month deadline for capital cases in states where certain conditions have been met. This is the first time in the nation's history that Congress has imposed a statute of limitations on habeas corpus actions."[84]

In order to show ineffective assistance of counsel, the U.S. Supreme Court held, in the case of *Strickland v. Washington* (1984), that defendants must make a two-pronged showing, demonstrating that

1) defense counsel's performance was deficient (e.g., falling below "prevailing professional norms")
2) this deficiency caused some prejudice (e.g., the outcome of the trial would likely have been different)[85]

The result of this standard is that "claims of ineffective assistance can be brushed away by the federal courts. In fact, they have been. One recent decision by the U.S. Supreme Court shows how bad the situation has gotten for people with lousy attorneys. In the case of *Florida v. Nixon* (2004), the Court held that "counsel's failure to obtain the defendant's express consent to a strategy of conceding guilt in a capital trial does not automatically render counsel's performance deficient."[86] In this case, Joe Nixon's attorney told the jury that Nixon was guilty even though he had not gotten permission to do so, and the Florida Supreme Court overturned his conviction on the basis of incompetent defense counsel. The U.S. Supreme Court overturned the decision 8–0 (with Rehnquist not participating).

This would be less troubling if the quality of legal air were high. It is not."[87] Given the lack of "knowledge, skill, resources—and sometimes even the inclination—to handle a serious criminal case" by many capital defense attorneys, it should not be surprising that the poor are disadvantaged in capital cases.[88]

So, a fair conclusion is that

> poor people accused of capital crimes are often defended by lawyers who lack the skills, resources, and commitment to handle such serious matters. This fact is confirmed in case after case. It is not the facts of the crime, but the quality of legal representation, that distinguishes this case, where the death penalty was imposed, from many similar cases, where it was not.[89]

Thus, the arbitrary nature of capital punishment in the United States often stems from ineffectiveness of counsel. This has been confirmed by the American Bar Association (ABA)[90] and the *National Law Journal*.[91]

In fact, inadequate legal representation for the poor may be "the core problem surrounding capital punishment."[92] In addition to helping explain the arbitrary nature of capital punishment, poor-quality defense attorneys helps us understand why allegedly innocent people have been put to death in the United States, an issue addressed later in this chapter. For example, in the case of Gary Graham—who was convicted and sentenced to death (and ultimately executed) based on the eyewitness testimony of one witness who saw him from 40 feet away and saw his face for only a second or two—his defense attorney was Ron Mock. Mock "had so many clients sentenced to death that some refer to the 'Mock Wing' of death row. Mock failed to seriously contest the state's case, conduct an independent investigation, and present witnesses at the scene who would have testified that Graham was not the person who committed the crime and that the perpetrator was much shorter than Graham."[93] Oftentimes, the problem is a systemic one "because many states do not provide the structure, resources, independence, and accountability that is required to ensure competent representation in an area of such specialization."[94]

In spite of all this, it is generally understood that poor people commit a disproportionate share of what is called "murder" every year in the United States.[95] Aside from the real disadvantages of being poor and involved in the criminal justice system, the main source of bias in criminal justice (including capital punishment practice) is bias in the criminal law itself. The criminal law is written almost universally by wealthy, older, white males.[96] Thus, the forms of culpable killings (intentional, reckless, negligent) that are called "murder" are predominantly what nonwealthy, younger (but still male) nonwhites do. The result is a built-in bias against people whose main opportunities to kill are on the streets of America and in favor of those who kill in ways that are either legal or illegal but not widely pursued by agencies of criminal justice in the United States.

Murder, for example, killed about 16,000 Americans in 2004.[97] Some examples show how much more deadly some "nonmurders" are:

- Unsafe and defective merchandise kills about 20,000 people per year.
- Occupational diseases and hazards kill about 35,000 people per year.
- "Hospital error" kills about 100,000 people per year.
- Poor diets and inactivity kill about 300,000 people per year.
- Tobacco use kills about 430,000 people per year.[98]

Although there are clearly differences between murder and the nonmurder deaths listed, the point is that other things are committed with culpability by people with resources, and these acts are far more deadly than the one crime for which a person becomes eligible for a death sentence—aggravated homicide. Further, any of these acts could be legislated as criminal at any time, as long as an interest group with enough clout and power made it a priority. Until the criminal law actually is used to define those acts that are the most dangerous to us, the criminal justice system will continue to arrest, convict, and occasionally sentence to death only murderers who, because of the definition of "murder" in the United States, are rarely wealthy.

Gender/Sex

Although about 98% of people executed in the United States have been men, most women who were put to death in this country were executed prior to 1866 by local governments.[99] Since then, women rarely have been executed in the United States. In fact, only 11 women were executed between 1977 and 2005, or 0.4 per year! Women were executed in North Carolina in 1984, Texas and Florida in 1998, Texas and Arkansas in 2000, Oklahoma in 2001 (3 women in 1 year), Alabama and Florida in 2002, and Texas in 2005.[100]

As shown in Table 5.5, women make up about 10% of murder arrests in any given year. Yet, they make up only about 2% of death sentences imposed, less than 2% (1.4%) of people on death row, and just over 1% (1.1%) of people executed since 1976.[101] This is a form of criminal justice "filtering" that has various potential explanations.

It is unclear if the gender disparity in capital punishment suggests a bias against men or in favor of women. It is quite possible that the death penalty is less applied to women than men due to the fact that murder committed by men is more likely to be aggravated in nature and thus eligible for death sentences. Death penalty scholar Robert Bohm suggests that the percentage of death-eligible homicides committed by women is unknown, but he cites research that women should receive somewhere between 4% and 6% of death sentences "if women and men were treated equally" and if "no other factor other than offense was considered."[102]

TABLE 5.5   Women and the Death Penalty

Murder arrests	10%
Death sentences	2%
Death row inmates	1.4%
Executions (1976–)	1.1%

Source: Death Penalty for Female Offenders, January 1, 1973, through December 31, 2005, by V. Streib, 2004. Retrieved from http://www.deathpenaltyinfo.org/FemDeathDec2005.pdf.

Of course, it is extremely unlikely that no other factor is considered. It is possible, and is likely in a large number of cases, that prosecutors are less likely to seek death sentences against women, and that juries are less likely to impose them against women. This can be considered a chivalry effect that benefits women.[103]

Anecdotal evidence strongly suggests the chivalry effect is real. For example, when Karla Faye Tucker was to be executed in Texas for a brutal double murder committed with a pickax (one of her victims had parked his motorbike in her living room), even death penalty supporters such as Christian Coalition leader Pat Robertson, and founder of the Moral Majority Jerry Falwell, spoke out against her execution. Although each claimed his stance against her death was because Tucker had become a born-again Christian in prison, comments by them and others suggest otherwise. For example, Robertson called Tucker a "sweet woman of God." Death penalty proponent Oliver North, who also opposed her execution, acknowledged on a TV news show: "I don't think chivalry can ever be misplaced." And TV news personality Geraldo Rivera went a step further, pleading to then governor George W. Bush: "Please, don't let this happen. This is—it's very unseemly. Texas, manhood, macho swagger .... What are ya' going to kill a lady? Oh jeez. Why?"[104] Much earlier, Tucker admitted that she had an orgasm with each swing of the pickax!

In South Carolina, Susan Smith was also spared from the death penalty after killing her two young sons by strapping them in the back seat of her car and letting the car ride down a boat ramp into a cold lake. Her car took more than 20 minutes to sink below the surface, meaning Smith had plenty of chances to save her children. Instead, she watched them drown and then blamed their "disappearance" on a fictional black man who supposedly took her car with the children still in the back seat, after she stopped at a red light.

This chivalry effect has its limits, however.[105] For example, professor Victor Streib suggests that those women who have been executed in the United States have tended to be "very poor, uneducated, and of the lowest social class in the community," whereas their "victims tended to be white and of particularly protected classes, either children or social prominent adults." Further:

> Most of the executed females manifested an attitude of violence, either from past behavior or present acts, that countered any presumption of nonviolence. Finally ... they committed shockingly "unladylike" behavior, allowing the sentencing judges and juries to put aside any image of them as "the gentler sex" and to treat them as "crazed monsters" deserving of nothing more than extermination.[106]

If true, these findings suggest that in some cases of female murders, other biases in capital punishment related to race (e.g., race of the victim) and social class overtake the chivalry effect. That is, when women act "evil," which is typically out of their "prescribed gender roles," capital punishment is more likely to be utilized against women.[107] This might explain media and prosecutorial representation of some lesbian murderers as "manly" and "man-hating."[108] This line of reasoning should not be considered definitive but rather speculative.

Another possibility, also based on research, is that part of the racial and gender disparities in capital punishment might have roots in a chivalry effect of a different type. Some research suggests that murders against white females are those that are most likely to lead to death sentences.[109] Prosecutors may be more likely to seek death sentences, and juries more likely to impose them, when murder is committed against society's most "valued" members—white women. Because white females tend to be murdered by white males, this phenomenon (if widespread) could account for some of the racial and gender disparities in capital punishment.

The biases pertaining to biases of capital punishment and gender are likely mostly unconscious or unintended. According to Bohm, "judges (who are predominately male) admit that, in general, they tend to be more lenient toward female offenders. They also tend to believe that women are better candidates for rehabilitation than are men. Jurors also tend to be more lenient toward female offenders, particularly in cases of serious crimes."[110] This is likely a function of the divergent views of men and women in society.

One interesting argument suggests that death penalty laws themselves are biased as both aggravating and mitigating factors favor women. For example, women are less likely to have criminal records and to commit felonies (and thus felony murders). Men, being more violent generally, and far more involved in every type of violent crime than women, are likely more involved with the death penalty process due to the fact that they commit far more capital crimes.[111] Women are also less likely to commit premeditated murders. Roughly one quarter of women currently on death row killed their husbands, often in unplanned acts, and this is crime that has historically not led to death sentences due to factors such as spousal abuse.[112] Because it is the criminal law that determines aggravating and mitigating circumstances pertaining to these circumstances, this can be considered a built-in bias against men in capital punishment laws.

Summary of Arbitrariness and Discrimination

The experts overwhelmingly indicated their belief that capital punishment, as actually practiced by states in the United States, is arbitrary and discriminatory. They overwhelmingly agreed that the death penalty is plagued by race and social class biases, and to a lesser degree, by a gender/sex bias. Generally, the experts surveyed in this study felt that race of victim, class of defendant, and even gender/sex of defendant play significant roles in who gets sentenced to death and executed and who does not. The facts show that capital punishment is plagued by significant biases against people of color and the poor. These are significant costs associated with capital punishment as it is actually administered in the United States that threaten the fundamental values of fairness and justice on which this country was supposedly founded.

Innocence

Brief Summary of Issue

The most troubling allegation against the administration of capital punishment in the United States is that occasionally innocent people are wrongly convicted, sentenced to death, and executed. One might think that if this criticism could be proven empirically, every state would either halt using capital punishment or develop such severe restrictions on it to ensure that innocent people could not be wrongly convicted and that the punishment would virtually never be used. Conversely, it is possible that the execution of the innocent might be seen as a necessary evil in the pursuit of justice.

Issue of Contention

The main issues of contention with regard to innocence are whether any innocent persons have been executed, how many, and if it matters.

Opponents of capital punishment typically see the innocence issue as the most severe problem with capital punishment. They point out that more than 100 people have been released from death row since 1976, after being wrongly convicted of capital crimes, and an unknown number have been wrongly executed.[113] Supporters of capital punishment typically deny that innocent people have been wrongly executed, at least during the era of super due process since 1976. They also contend that the discovery of wrongful convictions is proof that the system works rather than is faulty (because the innocent people were not executed). Further, death penalty supporters claim that wrongful executions are extremely rare, inevitable, and just a small cost to pay in pursuit of retribution and justice for murder victims and greater society.[114]

Experts' Views

> Is American capital punishment ever used against the innocent?

The experts were asked about the issue of innocence in capital punishment, as well as given the opportunity to raise the issue in the open-ended questions about whether there are any problems with capital punishment and whether any of those problems are serious enough to make the punishment unacceptable as a government punishment.

As shown in Table 5.6, a clear majority of capital punishment experts (76%) indicated that they thought the death penalty had been "ever used against the innocent," but many were also unsure (22%). Only a small number of respondents (2%) indicated that they thought the death penalty had never been used against the innocent.

The Death Penalty Is Used Against the Innocent

Respondents who said that the death penalty has been used against the innocent often spoke confidently. For example, experts said:

- "For years, researchers have been documenting case after case of innocent people being executed by the state. More recently, comprehensive investigations have revealed that capital punishment in the United States is contaminated with gross error."
- "The evidence is quite clear on this count. Irrevocable errors of this type occur on a rate of about 5% annually. While most are not executed, some have been and some more likely will be."
- "The literature is replete with innocent persons released from death row. Over 100 innocent people have been set free from death row. Every year Project Innocence proves that many innocent people receive a death sentence."[115]

TABLE 5.6   Expert Opinion on Whether Capital Punishment Is Used Against the Innocent

Is American capital punishment ever used against the innocent?

Yes	76%
No	2%
Unsure	22%

Note: N = 42.

- "Certainly regarding the <u>sentence</u> of death, facts to this effect are readily available. Studies of executions of the innocent are now in progress."
- "A number of studies attempt to illustrate this point. The Innocence Project is attempting to highlight this point."
- "Absolutely—there is irrefutable proof of this. It also is common sense that mistakes are made."
- "Absolutely."
- "The evidence indicates it has. Innocent people were certainly executed pre-*Furman*."
- "Sure, though I think we catch most of them before they are executed."
- "This has been documented with reasonable certainty."

One expert who indicated he thought innocent people were subjected to capital punishment wrote: "There is no doubt that innocent people are accused, prosecuted, and convicted in death penalty cases. While there is no absolutely proven case of an innocent person being executed post-*Furman*, the likelihood that this has happened is high." Yet, another expert noted a specific case—the "Griffin case out of Missouri"—that he said

> seems the most likely candidate at present, but it is almost inevitable that we will discover that we have in fact executed innocent people. There have been 122 exonerations and most of those occurred not because the system worked but because a ragged band of volunteers persisted after prosecutors and police had given up. Indeed, career oriented police and prosecutors have little incentive to admit errors of this magnitude. That was certainly the case for my friend Gary Gauger— despite overwhelming evidence to the contrary, Gary's prosecutors continue to insist that they prosecuted the right person. We discover cases of innocence only through blind luck, and it would be amazing if there were no additional error rate over and beyond that which we can, under the current circumstances, discover. Even a small error rate calculated over the thousand plus executions (say 1%) yields a probability of less than 3 in 10,000 that we have only executed the guilty.

Another expert, citing information provided by the Death Penalty Information Center (DPIC), wrote: "A good proportion of the people on the DPIC's list of innocents released from prison are factually innocent." Another referred to the DPIC's list, saying: "This has been shown over 122 times."[116]

Others answered that they believe the death penalty is sometimes used against the innocent, but expanded with far less certainty. For example, one expert answered: "I would think so. I doubt that any system of justice is completely flawless." Another respondent wrote: "Yes. I have to believe that we've made at least one mistake somewhere along the line."

One expert who said he thought the death penalty is used against the innocent found it nonproblematic, saying:

> I am pretty sure that there have been at least a few cases in which people who were executed were later absolutely proven to have been innocent. It happens in the movies. ... It seems reasonable that it has also happened in reality, even excluding cases of lynching. Since I personally believe that capital punishment could be a strong deterrent to homicide, I don't have a major problem with erroneous application of capital punishment. That happens far too infrequently—although clearly if capital punishment were used more frequently than it is now, there would be more cases of erroneous application. I would describe this possibility as no more than an "imperfection." Excepting those who commit homicide, people would be safer against premature death if capital punishment were being applied frequently.

Another expert answered:

> I am sure that historically (pre-*Furman*) there were numerous cases of factually innocent persons having been executed—especially against minorities. Today, it is more likely that defendants who could have been legally adjudicated as either not guilty or guilty on less than capital charges would occur due to attorney error. Recently, there have been several cases . . . that appear to identify post-*Gregg* factually innocent executions. But, I am not sure this is generally accepted yet. I do believe it is just a matter of time before this happens or we find out about it.[117]

Another expert spoke of a personal experience that indicates to him that innocent people do in fact end up on death row. He wrote:

> I have a close friend who spent several years on death row for a crime he did not commit. In his case, the prosecution ignored evidence pointing to someone else. In fact, 20 years after the murder, the police have only recently decided to reopen the case to see if they can find a match to a bloody fingerprint found at the scene. This is just one of many cases. Our criminal justice system is composed of humans, and humans make mistakes.

Similarly, another said that innocent people are subjected to capital punishment "all too frequently, including my former client."

Another expert expounded on ways in which the death penalty has been used against the innocent. He wrote:

> It's used against the innocent in a couple of ways. First, it is used against the innocent when an innocent person is apprehended, tried, convicted, and/or sentenced to death for a capital crime they did not commit. At every step along this path it is being "used" against an innocent person. Second, it is used against the innocent when the threat of the death penalty is used to coerce an innocent defendant to plea bargain for a lesser sentence by "admitting" to a lesser offense (usually non-capital murder). We know of numerous examples of both of these situations. It is a little more difficult to determine if innocent people have been executed, although I think we have pretty good evidence that it has happened at least several times (see, for example, the case of Ruben Cantu in Texas) [this case is discussed later in the chapter]. Capital punishment is "used" against the innocent in all of these cases and I say "used" because I believe that capital punishment makes the conviction of innocent people inherently more likely in the criminal justice system. Emotions, public outrage, pressure on public officials and law enforcement & prosecutorial zealousness run high in such cases of brutal and disturbing murder, death qualification biases juries toward conviction, and defense attorneys are ill-equipped to defend capital clients. These are just some of the documented problems contributing to capital punishment being used against the innocent.

Finally, at least two experts explicitly wrote about the use of DNA testing as it relates to the issue of innocence. These responses included:

- "Yes, of course, anyone who would deny that would in effect deny that humans administer criminal justice. But I think the question is more serious. Thanks to DNA tests, Illinois was able to check the accuracy of its process in ... 22 capital cases. These were all cases where DNA bearing material happened to service as part of the evidence kit. Half of the 22 were exonerated. Philosophers will debate whether ten guilty men should go free rather than one innocent be convicted or whether it should be one hundred guilty men should go free to prevent one innocent conviction. But no one would argue that the standard of judicial safety should be so low as one to one. The evidence so far is that this low safety rate was a characteristic of death penalty cases in particular, not of criminal justice in general. Apparently, prosecutors tried harder than they should have to get convictions. Death penalty cases are "sexy" in a way other cases are not. They are good for one's career, etc. Illinois has not abolished the death penalty, but it has now adopted procedures to protect the accused making it likely that very few will receive a death sentence in the years to come."

- "There seems to be mounting evidence that innocent defendants are given capital punishment sentences, as recent DNA analysis and other new evidentiary techniques have demonstrated. As to whether innocent defendants have been executed, I do not know of any modern examples—setting aside Ethel Rosenberg or Sacco and Venzetti, for example—but there probably are instances when these things have occurred."[118]

One expert seemed to question whether the issue of innocence even mattered. He answered: "At sentencing they are considered guilty."[119]

The Death Penalty Is Not Used Against the Innocent

The one expert who said that the death penalty has never been used against the innocent answered: "There is no evidence that convinces me that during the modern period of capital punishment that an innocent was executed. Maybe ... but not convincing proof."

Unsure

Those who were unsure as to whether capital punishment was used against the innocent provided answers such as: "Perhaps? I'm not sure if it has happened since *Gregg*, but we have come close—too close." Another answered: "Probably not. No evidence that any innocent was executed since 1976." Similarly, another expert wrote that "innocent people are surely sentenced to die; whether an innocent has been executed post-*Gregg* is yet unproven." Still another expert said: "It probably has, but we'll never know for a vast majority of those executed (because tests can't be done, etc.). It is best to hope that the system can catch those individuals before execution, but with legislation in place to curb appeals, etc. it is going to be harder to prove. I guess we'll have to rely on groups such as The Innocence Project to do the job of the government."

Finally, one respondent questioned the wording of the question and wrote:

> This question should result in 100% responding yes [and] as written is unfair.[120] So, I will pick unsure. I can tell you that the likelihood of this happening is extremely small. The List of Innocent published by DPIC confuses legal with factual innocence. In [my book] I found that the seven [Texas] cases included on the list were almost certainly guilty, but were released due to problems with particular evidence, or witnesses (co-offenders) who now were unhappy with their "deal,"

refusing to cooperate. DNA evidence applies to only a few commuted offenders [and] none completely excludes the offenders' involvement.

A similar answer was: "Ever is a big word. Obviously there have been innocent men and women executed. The question is 'How many innocent executions are acceptable in a system that is not perfect and [is] run by human beings subject to their own imperfections?'"

Fact Check

Let there be no doubt that innocent people are wrongly convicted of capital crimes every year in the United States. Some are unquestionably sentenced to death, as well. There is also no doubt that innocent people have been executed at many points in America's history. Yet, the most relevant question is whether an innocent person has been executed in the modern death penalty era of super due process. Recent evidence proves it has happened.

Before turning to the issue of wrongful execution, it is useful to first examine the issue of wrongful conviction and sentencing to death. The largest study, from 30 years of research, found 496 wrongly convicted individuals.[121] The study showed 23 individuals were executed and another 22 were freed within 72 hours of execution. In the study, 84% of wrongful death sentences occurred prior to 1976, meaning only 16% occurred in the modern era of super due process. Almost 60 wrongful convictions (59) occurred per decade.

The famous (or infamous, depending on one's perspective) list compiled by the DPIC includes 117 individuals wrongly convicted and freed from death row between 1976 and February 2006. The DPIC notes that it "uses the traditional objective criteria that have determined innocence since the founding of this country. In order to be included on the list, defendants must have been convicted and sentenced to death, and subsequently either: a) their conviction was overturned and they were acquitted at a re-trial, or all charges were dismissed; or b) they were given an absolute pardon by the governor based on new evidence of innocence."[122] A description of each case is presented on the DPIC's Web site.[123]

Approximately five wrongful convictions are discovered every year. More specifically: "In the 25 years from 1973 to 1998, there were an average of 2.96 exonerations per year. In the five years since 1998, thru 2003, that average has risen to 7.60 exonerations."[124]

An alarming study, *A Broken System: Error Rates in Capital Cases, 1973–1995*, is "the first statistical study ever undertaken of modern American capital appeals."[125] The study was of 4,578 appeals in state capital cases between 1973 and 1995. It found that capital trials end up placing people on death row who do not belong there (either because serious errors were made during their cases or because they were innocent of the crimes of which they were charged), and that it takes a long time to carry out sentences of death in the United States because of the numerous errors in the process. According to the findings of this report, "American capital sentences are so persistently and systematically fraught with error" that their reliability is seriously undermined. Authors James Liebman, Jeffrey Fagan, and Valerie West claim that capital punishment in the United States is "collapsing under its own mistakes . . . a system that is wasteful and broken and needs to be addressed."

Some of the key findings of this report include:

- Nationally, the overall rate of prejudicial error was 68%—that is, "courts found serious, reversible error in nearly 7 of every 10 of the thousands of capital sentences that were fully reviewed during the period."
- "Serious error was error substantially undermining the reliability of capital verdicts."
- "Capital trials produce so many mistakes that it takes three judicial inspections to catch them, leaving grave doubt whether we do catch them at all."
- State courts dismissed 47% of death sentences because of errors, and a later federal review dismissed 40% of the remaining cases.
- The most common errors found in the cases were (1) egregiously incompetent defense attorneys who missed evidence of the defendant's innocence or evidence that he or she did not deserve a death sentence, and (2) suppression of evidence by police and prosecutors.
- Eighty-two percent of those whose death sentences were overturned by state courts were found to be deserving of less than a death sentence, and 7% were found to be innocent of the crimes for which they were convicted.
- Serious errors have been made in every year since the death penalty was reinstated, and more than half of all cases were found to be seriously flawed in 20 of the 23 study years.
- Serious errors are made in virtually every state that still executes people, and over 90% of these states make errors more than half of the time.
- "In most cases, death row inmates wait for years for the lengthy review procedures needed to uncover all this error. Then, their death sentences are reversed."
- This much error, and the time needed to cure it, imposes terrible costs on taxpayers, victims' families, the judicial system, and the wrongly condemned. And it renders unattainable the finality, retribution, and deterrence that are the reasons usually given for having a death penalty.

- The death penalty ranges from 2.5 to 5.0 times as expensive as life imprisonment without parole. When you add the costs of posttrial reviews, executions become about 24 times as expensive as life imprisonment without parole. The death penalty is so much more expensive than life imprisonment because of the high rates of error that occur at each stage and the persistence of high error rates over time and across the nation, which mandate multiple expensive judicial inspections.
- The death penalty is rarely applied. Of the 5,760 state death sentences handed down between 1973 and 1995, only 313 (5.4%) led to an execution during this time.
- Additionally, since 1984 when post-*Furman* executions began in earnest, we have executed only about 1.3% of our nation's death row inmates each year. This makes "the retributive and deterrent credibility of the death penalty" very low.
- Homicide rates were slightly higher in death sentencing states than in non-death-sentencing states during the study years.

From their findings, Liebman and colleagues conclude that the administration of capital punishment in America is irrational. They note: "Death penalty states sentenced 22 times more defendants per 1,000 homicides than they executed. And they sentenced 26 times more defendants per 100,000 population than they executed."[126] Further, there is no relationship between death-sentencing and execution rates.[127]

The study also found a relationship between politics and the death penalty—that political pressure plays a role in capital punishment. Liebman et al. explain:

> In general, the more electoral pressure a state's judges are under, the higher the state's death-sentencing rate, but the lower the rate at which it carries out its death sentences. [This] suggests that political pressure tends to impel judges—or to create an environment in which prosecutors and jurors are impelled—to impose death sentences, but then tends to interfere with the state's capacity to carry out the death sentences that are imposed. . . . A desire to curry favor with voters may lead elected prosecutors and judges to cut corners in an effort to secure that premium—simultaneously causing death-sentencing rates, and error rates, to increase.[128]

In Part II of the study, titled *Broken System II: Why There Is So Much Error in Capital Cases*, attempted to assess the causes of the errors in America's capital punishment processes. According to the study's authors:

> This study uncovered a number of conditions related to error in capital cases, including politics, race, crime control and the courts. But

running through all the data was a simple finding—the more a state or county sentences people to death, the more often they make mistakes....Everything else being equal, when death sentencing increases from the lowest to the highest rate in the study, the reversal rate increases six-fold, to about 80%. The more often states and counties use the death penalty for every, say 10 or 100 homicides, the more likely it is that any death verdict they impose will later be found to be seriously flawed, and the more likely it is that the defendant who was found guilty and sentenced to die will turn out to be not guilty.[129]

Additionally, the authors found that there are four key factors that lead to errors:

homicide risk to whites and blacks; the size of the black population; the rate at which police catch and punish criminals; and politically motivated judges.... Everything else being equal, when the risk of a white person getting murdered is high relative to the risk of an African-American getting murdered, twice as many appeals are reversed than where that risk is low... when whites and other influential citizens feel threatened by homicide, they put pressure on officials to punish as many criminals as severely as possible—with the result that mistakes are made, and a lot of people are initially sentenced to death who are later found to have committed a lesser crime, or no crime at all.[130]

The more African Americans there are in a state, the more likely it is that serious mistakes will be made in death penalty trials. This could be because of fears of crime driven by racial stereotypes and economic factors. Whichever the case, race plays a role in the outcome of death penalty cases.

The limitations of the study call into question some of its conclusions. Some have claimed that James Liebman, the lead author of the study, who is a capital punishment opponent, may have let his own biases consciously or unconsciously influence the results. Possible limitations of the study include its methodology (failing "to distinguish between conviction rates and sentence reversal rates");[131] its confusing of a true reversal rate ("an error rate is computed by dividing the number of innocent persons executed by the total number executed");[132] its overstatement of the reversal error ("a more accurate reversal rate before retrials and rehearings, assuming a significant undercount of the number of death sentences undergoing judicial inspection, was an effective reversal rate that was closer to 43 percent, not 68 percent" and "error rate was based on cases actually reviewed at each of three stages rather than on all cases available for review at each stage... if the Columbia researchers had used this approach, the error rate would have been 52 percent");[133] its failure to include data on some states ("limits its scope by not including death penalty reversals in three key eastern states: New York, New Jersey, and Connecticut. Had the study included these states, the error rate probably would have been lower");[134] its failure to find evidence of wrongful execution (They "failed to find a single case in twenty-three years in which an innocent person had been executed. This failure undercuts virtually everything else they conclude about the error rate in death penalty cases.").[135]

Liebman's responses to these limitations show effectively that they do not change the meaning of the results.[136] Further, other scholars point to similar statistics and draw similar conclusions. For example, Elizabeth Smith writes: "Of the 6,139 persons sentenced to death from 1973 to 1997, 33.1 percent have had sentences or convictions subsequently overturned.... Of cases that reach appeals courts, about 40 percent have either the conviction or the sentence overturned."[137]

Other studies have identified problems in capital cases that lead to false convictions: false confessions; eyewitness identification mistakes; inappropriate use of forensic evidence; false statements by jailhouse informants; shoddy investigative policies (police work); sloppy lab work; dishonest prosecutors (misconduct); political pressure on judges; defense counsel inadequacies; death-qualified jury bias; and flawed jury instructions.[138]

As noted in Chapter 1, the governor of Illinois ordered a moratorium on all executions in 2000 after serious problems were discovered with the state's capital punishment system. One inmate—Anthony Porter—had come within 48 hours of his execution date prior to being released after an investigation by a group of journalism students identified the real killer.[139]

The state of Illinois discovered that since 1977, the state had executed 12 people but released 13 people from death row. Believing there to be a serious problem with the state's capital punishment system, the governor established the Commission on Capital Punishment to study the state's death penalty system. The commission put forth 85 specific recommendations that it said should improve the accuracy and fairness of Illinois's death penalty system, and a narrow majority of the commission members said they believed the death penalty should be abolished in the state. Some said so due to moral objections, others because no system could reasonably guarantee total fairness and a lack of error, and others because the resources spent on the death penalty outweighed the benefits.[140] In 2003, the Illinois legislature took action on some of the recommendations but not others. The net effect of these proposed changes would be to decrease the use of capital punishment even more, making it rarer and more random.

Proponents of capital punishment often suggest these "mistakes" are really "successes" because wrongful convictions that do not lead to an execution are proof the system works.[141] Most notably, Ari Fleischer, who would later go on to be spokesperson for President George W. Bush, said: "It is proof that there is an extra level of vigilance and caution in death penalty cases ... people who have their cases overturned are still guilty of something ... 93 percent of inmates who are retried are convicted later, albeit of a lesser offense."[142]

Yet, one significant issue is, are all the mistakes discovered? Opponents of capital punishment point out that most errors were discovered due to luck and the hard work by media reporters and college students, meaning that many cases are probably not caught.[143] That is, not every individual is lucky. In fact, there are cases that clearly suggest innocent people have been executed.[144]

Capital punishment scholars Michael Radelet and Hugo Adam Bedau review the evidence and conclude that three things prove that innocent people have been executed: close calls (where inmates are released from death row just prior to their scheduled executions), calculation of the odds (based on figures from studies of wrongful conviction), and the role of lady luck (where the innocence of individuals was discovered due to luck and/or the hard work of individuals outside the criminal justice system).[145]

The availability of DNA evidence has saved at least 15 individuals from death row. Reliable and admissible DNA testing was not available or utilized to reexamine cases until recently, suggesting the very real possibility that we executed innocent people in the past who did not have access to DNA testing. Franklin Zimring makes this very point, referring to wrongful executions in the past:

> The increasing rate of exonerations and the sudden impact of the new technology on 24 percent of recent exonerations suggest that some were put to death who would have been exonerated with the newer technology were put to death under the older system. No conviction in the United States prior to 1979 generated any DNA exclusion, while the number of 1980s convictions reversed by DNA totaled seven. Did the chances of convicting the innocent suddenly increase in the 1980s, or did misidentifications slip through the cracks before then?[146]

In spite of DNA tests in the modern execution era, case studies suggest that several "innocent" people have been executed since 1976.[147] Two of the following cases were mentioned by death penalty experts in this study:

- Ruben Cantu—executed in Texas in 1993. He was 17 years old when he was charged with capital murder for shooting a man during an attempted robbery. Both the prosecutor and the jury forewoman have expressed doubts about Cantu's guilt, and "a key eyewitness in the state's case against Cantu and Cantu's co-defendant have come forward to say that Texas executed an innocent man." Juan Moreno, an eyewitness in the case, "says that it was not Cantu who shot him and that he only identified Cantu as the shooter because he felt pressured and was afraid of the authorities. Moreno said that he twice told police that Cantu was not his assailant, but that the authorities continued to pressure him to identify Cantu as the shooter after Cantu was involved in an unrelated wounding of a police officer." David Garza, Cantu's codefendant, "signed a sworn affidavit saying that he allowed Cantu to be accused and executed even though he wasn't with him on the night of the killing. Garza stated, 'Part of me died when he died. You've got a 17-year-old who went to his grave for something he did not do. Texas murdered an innocent person.'... Miriam Ward, forewoman of the jury... said 'With a little extra work, a little extra effort, maybe we'd have gotten the right information. The bottom line is, an innocent person was put to death for it. We all have our finger in that.'"
- Larry Griffin—executed in Missouri in 1995. A "man injured in the same drive-by shooting that claimed the life of Quintin Moss says Griffin was not involved in the crime, and the first police officer on the scene has given a new account that undermines the trial testimony of the only witness who identified Griffin as the murderer. Based on its findings, the NAACP has supplied the prosecution with the names of three men it suspects committed the crime, and all three of the suspects are currently in jail for other murders."
- Joseph O'Dell—executed in Virginia in 1997. "New DNA blood evidence has thrown considerable doubt on the murder and rape conviction of O'Dell. In reviewing his case in 1991, three Supreme Court Justices, said they had doubts about O'Dell's guilt and whether he should have been allowed to represent himself. Without the blood evidence, there is little linking O'Dell to the crime.... O'Dell asked the state to conduct DNA tests on other pieces of evidence to demonstrate his innocence but was refused."
- David Spence—executed in Texas in 1997. Spence was alleged to have been hired by a convenience store owner to kill a girl, but killed three others by mistake. "The convenience store owner, Muneer Deeb, was originally convicted and sentenced to death, but then was acquitted at a re-trial. The police lieutenant who supervised the investigation of

Spence, Marvin Horton, later concluded: 'I do not think David Spence committed this crime.' Ramon Salinas, the homicide detective who actually conducted the investigation, said: 'My opinion is that David Spence was innocent. Nothing from the investigation ever led us to any evidence that he was involved.' No physical evidence connected Spence to the crime. The case against Spence was pursued by a zealous narcotics cop who relied on testimony of prison inmates who were granted favors in return for testimony."

- Leo Jones—executed in Florida in 1998 for murdering a police officer. He had "signed a confession after several hours of police interrogation, but he later claimed the confession was coerced. In the mid-1980s, the policeman who arrested Jones and the detective who took his confession were forced out of uniform for ethical violations. The policeman was later identified by a fellow officer as an 'enforcer' who had used torture. Many witnesses came forward pointing to another suspect in the case."

- Gary Graham—executed in Texas in 2000. He was 17 when he was charged with robbery and a shooting outside a grocery store and "was convicted primarily on the testimony of one witness, Bernadine Skillern, who said she saw the killer's face for a few seconds through her car windshield, from a distance of 30–40 feet away. Two other witnesses, both who worked at the grocery store and said they got a good look at the assailant, said Graham was not the killer but were never interviewed by Graham's court appointed attorney, Ronald Mock, and were not called to testify at trial. Three of the jurors who voted to convict Graham signed affidavits saying they would have voted differently had all of the evidence been available."[148]

- Cameron Willingham—executed in Texas in 2004 for starting a fire in his own home that killed his three children. Now, "four national arson experts have concluded that the original investigation of Willingham's case was flawed and it is possible the fire was accidental," finding that "prosecutors and arson investigators used arson theories that have since been repudiated by scientific advances....Arson expert Gerald Hurst said, 'There's nothing to suggest to any reasonable arson investigator that this was an arson fire. It was just a fire.' Former Louisiana State University fire instructor Kendall Ryland added, 'It made me sick to think this guy was executed based on this investigation.... They executed this guy and they've just got no idea—at least not scientifically—if he set the fire, or if the fire was even intentionally set.' ... Among the only other evidence presented by prosecutors during the trial was testimony from jailhouse snitch Johnny E. Webb, a drug addict on psychiatric medication, who claimed Willingham had confessed to him in the county jail. . . . Coincidentally, less than a year after Willingham's execution, arson evidence presented by some of the same experts who had appealed for relief in Willingham's case helped free Ernest Willis from Texas's death row. The experts noted that the evidence in the Willingham case was nearly identical to the evidence used to exonerate Willis."[149]

Estimates about the number of innocent executions vary. Wyatt Espy Jr. suggests we have killed 950 innocent people out of 19,000 executions.[150] Death penalty expert Robert Bohm estimates we have executed 16 people since 1976.[151] Franklin Zimring suggests about seven.[152] Of course, there is no way to know for sure, but these cases at least point to the fact that some innocent people likely have been executed in the United States very recently.

The bottom line is that in the United States, the application of the death penalty is plagued by a significant threat of executing the innocent. We definitely continue to wrongly convict and sentence people to death, and it is made more likely the more we carry it out, when appeals are limited, and when the punishment is politicized. If there is any good news, it is that the risk of executing innocent people decreased with super due process (1976) and with a lessening of death-eligible crimes and less use of the penalty. However, the risk still exists.

In spite of this, the U.S. Supreme Court has refused to take action. When confronted with the issue of innocence in capital punishment in 1993, the Court decided *Herrera v. Collins*. In this case, the Court addressed the issue of whether a habeas petition could be used to argue "actual innocence." In holding that it could not, the Court wrote that a "claim of actual innocence does not entitle [one] to federal habeas relief." Claims for relief

> based upon . . . newly discovered evidence of innocence must be evaluated in light of the previous . . . proceedings in [each] case. In criminal cases, the trial is the paramount event for determining the defendant's guilt or innocence. Where . . . a defendant has been afforded a fair trial and convicted of the offense for which he was charged, the constitutional presumption of innocence disappears. Federal habeas courts do not sit to correct errors of fact, but to ensure that individuals are not imprisoned in violation of the Constitution.[153]

Elizabeth Smith notes that "according to Rehnquist's majority opinion, innocence is not a bar to execution so long as the trial was fair and the inmate had the opportunity to invoke executive clemency. Once a defendant has had a fair trial, the presumption of innocence is erased.... In cases in which innocence was manifest, Supreme Court review is unnecessary because the prisoner can request commutation of the death sentence."[154]

Summary of Innocence

The experts overwhelmingly indicated their belief that capital punishment has been used against the innocent. That is, innocent people have been and continue to be convicted and sentenced to death, and it is a virtual certainty that we have (even recently) executed people factually innocent of the crimes for which they were sentenced to die. The empirical evidence shows that capital punishment is plagued by a significant risk of being used against innocent people. This is another cost of capital punishment, as actually practiced in the United States, that calls into question our ability to punish the guilty through the most severe punishments while simultaneously protecting the innocent.

> In your opinion, are there any other problems (not addressed in the questions above) with the way capital punishment is practiced in the United States?

Other Problems

In response to the open-ended question as to whether there were any other problems with the way capital punishment was administered, most death penalty experts (80%) said yes. In fact, only 10% said no. An additional 10% responded with unsure. Table 5.7 illustrates these values.

The Death Penalty Has Other Problems

Respondents who indicated yes, discussed many other problems with capital punishment, including its excessive costs; the length of time it takes to complete the appeals process; problems with jury selection, jury instructions, interpreting how to weigh aggravating and mitigating circum-

---

TABLE 5.7   Expert Opinion on Whether Capital Punishment Has Other Problems

In your opinion, are there any other problems (not addressed in the questions above) with the way capital punishment is practiced in the United States?

Yes	80%
No	10%
Unsure	10%

Note: N = 39.

stances; the problematic nature of victim impact statements; ineffectiveness of counsel; politics; geographic disparities; its arbitrary nature; a lack of proportionality, judicial, and appeals review; inadequate resources and representation for the poor; the unwillingness of parole boards or governors to grant clemency in deserving cases; improperly being applied when the victim is culpable; conditions of death row and the length of confinement; the effects of the death penalty on families of defendants; the potential for a brutalizing effect; and executing defendants who are mentally ill. Others reiterated that they felt the punishment is immoral, that methods of execution are inhumane (e.g., with botched executions), and that the reputation of the United States is suffering as a result of continuing to utilize capital punishment. Another expert wrote that the death penalty "is expensive and polarizes communities." Finally, one expert noted that "the Illinois Commission that was created by Gov. Ryan identified many other issues of unfairness & unreliability in the way [capital punishment] is administered."

Respondents indicated these legal and judicial aspects of capital punishment as being problematic:

- "I feel that it is applied too often in cases where the victim is clearly culpable. I don't think that it should be involved when someone robs & kills a drug dealer or kills a rival gang member."
- "Jury selection is highly problematic, especially the death-qualification process. Also problematic are jury understanding of penalty phase instructions, effectiveness of counsel, opportunity for judicial override of a jury recommendation of life."
- "A) instructions to juries remain vague or problematic. B) how are aggravating and mitigating circumstances (factors) to be weighed? C) problematic nature of victim impact statements. D) confusion between mental retardation and mental illness."
- "The variable nature of the selection process resulting from prosecutorial discretion in local jurisdictions."
- "Lack of proportionality review. Lack of judicial review—procedures limit courts. Lack of clemency review."
- "There is a general complaint about the complexities of legal procedures in death penalty cases. This complexity is itself a product of using the death penalty when so many people are uncomfortable with it. Legal systems that have the death penalty tend to carry over these complex procedures into cases involving less serious crimes, making the who system more cumbersome than necessary. "
- "Lots. 1) death qualified juries predispose a jury to be pro death penalty, pro victim, and more punitive. 2) quality of representation—although there is some evidence this is improving, for much of

post-*Gregg*, there were few requirements for defense [attorneys] to represent capital defendants—Texas in particular had a bad reputation for capital defense. 3) lack of willingness among parole boards or governors to exercise clemency in deserving cases. Politically, it is suicide to commute a death sentence—that is why nearly all death sentence commutations occur at the end of a governor's last term in office."

- "Inadequate legal representation at and before trial. Inordinately complex rules for collateral challenges."
- "prosecutorial discretion is largely ignored in [death penalty] cases—how many homicides that are truly death-eligible get downgraded to 2nd degree, etc. by prosecutors? Also, how many 'iffy' cases get upgraded to 1st degree by prosecutors? What factors play a role in prosecutorial discretion? We consider juries and judges, but why not prosecutors? Also, use of victim impact statements at sentencing—research has shown that some victims are more 'worthy' than others."
- "Arbitrary—depends unduly on the local prosecutor's agenda and budget as well as nonrelevant characteristics of the accused and of the crime. Numerically insufficient in application to be treated as a legitimate punishment."
- "Appeals take too long."
- "The methods of execution are inhumane (botched executions), proportionality issue (2 Co-d[efendant]s)."
- "There are enormous problems with representation at trial and on appeal. . . . The doctrine of procedural default limits access to appellate courts. . . . Capriciousness of decisions by prosecutors, jurors, trial and appellate judges, and governors. . . . The cruelty of methods of execution."

Comments related to costs included:

- "It is expensive and polarizes communities."
- "It costs far more to execute a person than to keep her/him behind bars."
- The penalty is "too costly."
- "Cost is disproportionately high relative to any of its putative benefits."

Two experts discussed issues related to the political nature of capital punishment and failures of law enforcement and prosecutors to adequately investigate cases. For example, one expert noted that the death penalty is "too political at the local level." He also described the death penalty as "disproportionate" and noted the "geographic disparity within a state," implying differential use of capital punishment across counties. Another expert wrote:

> There are so many, I would not know where to begin. It bothers me when police and prosecutors get a theory of the crime and fail to explore other avenues. It bothers me even more when they do underhanded things to promote that theory or suppress alternate ones. In Oklahoma City, the prosecution used a police chemist who was woefully inadequate for the job, had her testify in ways that they knew were not defensible. People have been executed as a result, countless cases overturned and retried, at a huge expense to the state.

Other experts responded:

- "I don't think there can ever be [a] fair way of administering the [death penalty] when those with ample resources will almost always be able to avoid this punishment, while those who are poor will be the most likely candidates for execution."
- "The only other one that springs to mind is the concern about the lapse of time between conviction and execution. Critics of capital punishment say the time is cruel because it makes defendants wait with a death sentence hanging over his head. Proponents of capital punishment say the time lapse hurts deterrence because defendants know they have a long time to wait and it may make them secure in the possibility that they will die naturally before they can be executed."
- "The ideology or story that supports it plagues the way we approach all wrongdoers & undermines just retaliation based on need, not merit."

Three experts specifically mentioned how the "use of [capital punishment is diminishing [the] reputation of the U.S." One expert gave an expansive explanation of this idea:

> Our international isolation on this issue is presenting problems with extradition, the Vienna Convention on Consular Relations and the International Criminal Court. I am amazed at how isolated we are. There are 122 abolitionist nations, many of which will not extradite without assurances that the death penalty will not be imposed. Of the 74 retentionist nations, 4 provide 97% of all executions and even if the outlier China were to be excluded, the 5 remaining "leader" nations

would still conduct the vast majority of all executions. We are truly isolated on this, and the costs to the U.S. legal system are immense. Capital punishment imposes significant diplomatic costs and the consequences reach beyond time-consuming diplomatic protests. It adversely affects substantive cooperation as well. As recently as January 26, 2006, Felix G. Rohatyn, former ambassador to France, wrote in the *New York Times*: "No single issue was viewed with as much hostility as our support for the death penalty. Outlawed by every member of the European Union, the death penalty was, and is, viewed in Europe as a throwback to the Middle Ages. When we require European support on security issues—Iran's nuclear program; the war in Iraq; North Korea's bomb; relations with China and Russia; the Middle East peace process—our job is made more difficult by the intensity of popular opposition in Europe to our policy." Moreover, sentiment against the death penalty is getting stronger in those nations that have abolished capital punishment. I have recently acquired the data from the Gallup Millennium Survey and have looked at several other recent surveys and have found that: 1. Public opinion in abolitionist countries is resoundingly hostile to the U.S. position. According to the Gallup Millennium Survey from 2000 ... only 34% of European respondents supported capital punishment while 60% opposed. In some parts of Europe, such as Scandinavia, support approaches single digits (13% support in Iceland with the greatest support coming from Denmark at 20% for and 74% against), while in Spain only 19% support the death penalty. Even in the former communist countries of Eastern Europe, support for capital punishment is noticeably weak, with majorities or pluralities opposing it in six of the Eastern European countries surveyed. Similarly, in Latin America 55% oppose capital punishment and in Africa death penalty only a majority of 56% support the death penalty and opposition runs strongly in some regions. 2. Support has dropped even among our closest allies with similar criminal justice systems. The United Kingdom provides a prime example. In 1960, 70% of all British supported capital punishment. According to Roger Hood, by 1965 the possible capital conviction of a possibly innocent (and later exonerated) man, 'produced a healthy majority for abolishing the death penalty for murder' leading to suspension in 1965 and outright abolition in 1969. Support for capital punishment has waxed and waned since then and currently (January 2006) support has again dropped below 50% even for the murder of police officers. 3. Similarly, by 2001 Canadian support for capital punishment had dropped to 52%. Support dropped even further to 37.6% when respondents are given the option of life imprisonment without the possibility of parole. A more recent poll in 2004 showed a plurality of 49% opposed to the death penalty.

Another expert offered two reasons related to mental illness and two related to human rights and international law:

> There are many other problems facing the capital punishment process in the United States. The list is too long to even begin dialogue, but here are a few: the US has a tradition of executing mentally ill criminals; it is common to execute in violation of human rights; it is common to execute foreign nationals in violation of international treaties; and it is common to execute criminals suffering from severe illness, like depression.

And another expert pointed out the deleterious effects of capital punishment when it comes to America's "consistent violations of the Geneva Convention on Consular Relations when prosecuting foreign nationals" and cooperation from foreign allies "on extradition and evidence gathering on terrorism suspects."

Finally, two experts specifically pointed out that it "is morally wrong to take a life" and "there is a moral issue of asking jurors to decide death. There are problems turning prison staff into executioners."

The Death Penalty Does Not Have Other Problems

Of the four respondents who answered that the death penalty does not have other problems, only one wrote anything to explain his answer. He wrote: "No other problems that come readily to my mind."

Unsure

One expert who said he was unsure about other problems with capital punishment wrote: "The criminal justice system, in general, has extensive inherent problems. The reality is that these cannot and will not be remedied. Capital punishment (or any other punishment) is surely a reflection of these inherent problems."

REFLECTIONS ON THESE OTHER PROBLEMS: POLITICS, CAPITAL JURIES, AND COSTS

At least three of the alleged problems raised by these capital punishment experts deserve some commentary and explanation through fact-checking. The section that follows examines the issues of politics and death, capital juries, and costs. Most of the other problems with capital punishment identified by the experts have already been addressed.

Politics

Brief Summary of Issue

Like all criminal justice policies and forms of punishment, capital punishment is significantly affected by politics. Politics is about who gets what economic benefits in society, when they get them, and how they get them.[155] Whereas it is generally concerned with deciding who gets to keep most of the income generated in the United States and how that income will be used,[156] politics is also about how society's values will be allocated.[157] As resources are allocated for purposes of legitimating values through government authority, one mechanism to achieve this is criminal justice and all forms of punishment, including capital punishment.

Death penalty murders and non-death-penalty murders should be distinguishable based on legal factors (aggravating and mitigating factors). Yet, many claim it is actually based on extralegal factors like those discussed earlier (race, class, and gender or sex). For example, whether a murder case results in a death sentence is affected by the region of the country where the crime occurred, the state where the crime occurred, the county within a state where the crime occurred, and the nature of politics within each, among many other important factors.

Issue of Contention

The main issue of contention with regard to politics and the death penalty is not whether politics plays a role in the death penalty, but instead, whether it matters. Opponents of capital punishment have asserted that geography should not play a role in whether a murderer is executed—that is, where a person commits a murder should not determine if he or she lives or dies.[158] Supporters of capital punishment have responded by pointing out that all government and criminal justice policies are affected by politics, that this is an unchangeable reality, and that geographic disparities are normal and nonproblematic in a system of government rooted in federalism.[159]

Experts' Views

As noted earlier in this chapter, some experts were troubled by the political nature of the death penalty process in the United States. The implication is that the death penalty is not used for those who most deserve it, but rather for those who happen to commit murders in certain places in the country and within certain counties of certain states.

Fact Check

First, with regard to geographic disparities in capital punishment, it is inherently up to the *discretion* of a prosecutor to pursue a death sentence. Because the states in the South, and especially Texas, are "tougher on crime," most executions have been in the South. There is, without any debate, a geographic disparity in American capital punishment. Further, capital punishment is used as a political issue for advancement of personal careers and particular ideologies.

Nationally, from 1976 until March 2006, 830 of the 1,016 executions (82%) occurred in the southern United States. This was followed by 118 (12%) in the Midwest, 64 (6%) in the West, and only 4 (0.4%) in the Northeast. Further, Texas and Virginia combined for 456 (45%) executions, and Texas alone was responsible for 362 (36%) executions.[160]

The fact that the vast majority of executions occur in the South has several potential explanations. One potential explanation is that some prosecutors are simply more willing and able to seek and obtain capital convictions and sentences based on available resources and juries that are more supportive of the punishment.[161]

Another explanation is provided by the Death Penalty Information Center:

> Regional variation in death sentences suggests arbitrariness in application. While one expects to see some variation from state to state, given differences in population, crime rates and laws, one also expects that in a just system, the law of a particular state would be applied uniformly in that state. A just system ought not to have death sentences concentrated in only one region. However, whether a person receives the death penalty depends heavily on where the crime was committed.[162]

The regional nature of capital punishment also is partly due to the "federalization" or "nationalization" of the death penalty that occurred with the U.S. Supreme Court's decision in *Gregg*, which not only failed to eradicate arbitrariness in death sentences and especially executions, but has in some ways made it worse. For example, after federal standards for capital punishment were imposed by the Court, executions became *more* concentrated in the South: "At the extremes in state policy, the range in execution risk given a death sentence varies by about 50 to 1 when Northern industrial states such as Ohio, Pennsylvania, and California are compared with the highest-risk Southern jurisdictions such as Virginia, Texas, and Oklahoma."[163] Thus, even if one knew "the proportion of the U.S. population in a region, the number of states with a death penalty, and the homicide rate in the region will tell the observer *less* about the rate of execution in that region after the federal standards are in place than before."[164] Currently, a death sentence in the South is about 24 times more likely than a death sentence in the East to produce an execution.[165] This is evidence of "troublesome differences in standards of justice."[166]

Another outcome of the federalization of the death penalty is increased delay in the death penalty process. Requiring states to exhaust potential remedies before giving access to federal courts means the appellate review process takes a long time. Delay is an issue identified by death penalty experts when asked about other problems with capital punishment, which are addressed later in the chapter.

The Death Penalty Information Center provides evidence of geographical disparities not only by state and region of the country, but also within states, including Maryland (where a disproportionate number of death sentences come from suburban Baltimore County), Ohio (where a disproportionate number come from Hamilton County [Cincinnati]), as well as New York, Indiana, and Texas.

The federal system is also significantly affected by geographical disparities: "The country is divided into federal districts, and local U.S. Attorneys are required to submit all potential death penalty cases to the Attorney General for review and may make a recommendation about seeking the death penalty. [There are] large disparities in the geographical distribution of federal death penalty recommendations." For example, between 1995 and 2000, "42% of the federal cases submitted to the Attorney General for review came from just 5 of the 94 federal districts."[167]

With regard to the use of capital punishment as a political issue, perhaps the clearest proof of the political nature of capital punishment is statements by national politicians about the punishment. Only perhaps twice in the past 20 years has the issue of capital punishment been specifically addressed at the presidential level. First, when capital punishment supporter and Republican nominee George Bush (the first) and capital punishment opponent and Democratic nominee Michael Dukakis met in a debate in 1988, CNN's Bernard Shaw asked Governor Dukakis: "Governor, if Kitty Dukakis were raped and murdered, would you favor an irrevocable death penalty for the killer?" Dukakis's response was: "No, I don't, Bernard. And I think you know that I've opposed the death penalty during all of my life. I don't see any evidence that it's a deterrent, and I think there are better and more effective ways to deal with violent crime. We've done so in my own state."[168]

Of course, Governor Dukakis lost to George Bush, and this was due in part to his refusal to support capital punishment. It most likely affected voters in the Deep South, who have not voted for a capital punishment opponent for president in modern American history.

Then, in the 2000 presidential debates between George W. Bush (the second) and Al Gore, Americans saw that each candidate supported capital punishment. When asked about his support for capital punishment, Governor Bush said: "I believe it saves lives ... I'm proud that violent crime is down in the state of Texas." Gore replied: "I think it is a deterrence [*sic*] ... I know that's a controversial view but I do think it's a deterrence [*sic*]." With follow-up about whether they think capital punishment is a deterrent, Bush replied: "I do, it's the only reason to be for it.... I don't think you should support the death penalty to seek revenge. I don't think that's right." Gore agreed: "Yes. If it was not, there would be no reason to support it."[169]

That both candidates supported capital punishment and agreed the punishment was a deterrent simply reinforced the conception among most voters that there was little detectable difference between the two candidates and served as further evidence to viewers that to be president of the United States, one must support the punishment. Strangely, given the evidence presented in the last chapter with regard to deterrence, neither candidate was faulted or even questioned about his belief that capital punishment deterred murder.

Summary of Politics

The experts indicated that capital punishment is a system less of justice and more of politics. That is, geography (state and county) largely determines one's risk of being tried and sentenced for capital crimes. Further, politicians use the death penalty issue to appear "tough on crime" in spite of the evidence pointing to the conclusion that capital punishment is an ineffective system of crime control. The facts show that capital punishment is a political issue plagued by significant geographic bias and manipulation by elected officials. Whether these are relevant to the debate about capital punishment is debatable.

Capital Juries

Brief Summary of Issue

Juries are at the heart of America's criminal justice process. Their main purpose is to protect citizens from overzealous and arbitrary prosecution. After the case of *Ring v. Arizona* (2002),[170] the U.S. Supreme Court now requires that death sentences be recommended by a jury.

Issue of Contention

The main issue of contention with regard to capital juries is, do capital juries do their jobs effectively, or are they plagued by serious problems that cast doubt on the efficacy capital sentencing? Opponents of capital punishment point out that juries often are confused about their basic responsibilities, including what is required to justify criminal convictions and sentences of death, as well as how to weigh aggravating and mitigating factors.[171] Supporters of capital punishment respond that juries are given guidance by the criminal law, which specifies both aggravating and mitigating factors, as well as numerous protections including checks on prosecutorial power, competent defense attorneys, and postconviction review and opportunity to appeal their sentences.[172]

Experts' Views

As discussed earlier in this chapter, many experts noted that the death penalty process is flawed because of problems with capital juries. Experts specifically mentioned issues such as problems with jury selection, jury instructions, and interpreting how to weigh aggravating and mitigating circumstances.

Fact Check

Studies show that capital juries are conviction prone. This is because of the process of *death qualification*, where potential jurors are asked about their views of capital punishment prior to being seated on a capital jury.[173] The purpose of bifurcated capital trials—which determine legal guilt in the first phase and then determine appropriate sentence in the second phase—is to reduce the possibility of arbitrary sentences.

The U.S. Supreme Court has decided several cases with regard to the death qualification process. First, in the case of *Witherspoon v. Illinois* (1968),[174] the Court found that it was constitutional for

> the State to execute a defendant sentenced to death by a jury from which the only veniremen excluded for cause were those who made unmistakenly clear 1) that they would *automatically* vote against the imposition of capital punishment without regard to any evidence that might be developed at the trial before them, or 2) that their attitude toward the death penalty would prevent them from making an impartial decision as to the defendant's guilt.[175]

Thus, jurors who were generally opposed to capital punishment but were willing to consider it could still serve on a capital jury.

Then, in the case of *Wainwright v. Witt* (1985),[176] the U.S. Supreme Court concluded that

> the proper standard for determining when a prospective juror may be excluded for cause because of his views on capital punishment is

whether the juror's view would "prevent or substantially impair the performance of his duties as a juror in accordance with his instruction and his oath."[177]

As a result of this decision, "prospective jurors no longer have to make it 'unmistakably clear' that they would 'automatically' vote against the death penalty before they can be successfully challenged for cause." Further, jurors who would automatically vote for death sentences in every case can also be challenged for cause. Thus, attorneys under *Witt* had greater latitude to challenge potential jurors, generally, and judges had greater latitude to decide which jurors should be eliminated for cause.

Then, in *Lockhart v. McCree* (1986),[178] the Court ruled that jurors who are strongly opposed to capital punishment can be removed for cause. The ruling was that the Constitution did not prohibit excusing "prospective jurors whose opposition to the death penalty is so strong that it would prevent or substantially impair the performance of their duties as jurors at the sentencing phase of the trial."[179]

Jurors who would automatically impose death may also be removed for cause based on the U.S. Supreme Court case *Morgan v. Illinois* (1992).[180] In this case, the Court held that "a capital defendant may challenge for cause any prospective juror" who would vote automatically for the death penalty because this person "will fail in good faith to consider the evidence of aggravating and mitigating circumstances as the instructions require."[181] Although defense attorneys can and do ask this question and occasionally use it to excuse jurors, "death qualified" juries still seem to be stacked against the defendant.

The main problem with the death qualification process is that death-qualified juries are more likely to convict defendants. The Capital Jury Project, which studied 1,198 jurors from 353 capital trials in 14 states, has identified significant problems with capital juries.[182] These problems include:[183]

- *Bias in jury selection*—jury selection methods produce guilt-prone and death-prone juries.[184]
- *Premature decision making*—about half of capital jurors decided on a penalty prior to the sentencing phase of the trial.[185]
- *Failure to understand jury instructions*—almost half of capital jurors do not understand they are allowed to consider any mitigating evidence during sentencing, and about two thirds of capital jurors do not understand that unanimity is not required for findings of mitigation.[186]
- *Erroneous beliefs that death is required*—almost half of capital jurors believe the death penalty is required if a murderer's conduct

is heinous, vile, or depraved, and more than one third of capital jurors believe the death penalty is required based on future dangerousness.[187]

- *Underestimating the death penalty alternative*—most capital jurors underestimate the period of imprisonment a convicted murderer will serve in prison if not sentenced to death.[188]
- *Influence of race*—the odds of death sentences for black defendants and white victims are highest when there are five or more white males on the jury and lowest when there is at least one black male on the jury.[189]

The issues of race and gender on capital jury outcomes—with African Americans and women less likely to vote for death—show the importance of the death qualification process. As noted by death penalty scholar Craig Haney:

> a process that selects eligible jurors on the basis of death penalty support will exclude disproportionately greater numbers of women and blacks. And, because blacks are already underrepresented on the jury lists in many parts of the country, death qualification may act to compound a preexisting problem … the process insures that actual capital juries will be selected from a group of prospective jurors who are, by definition, unrepresentative of the community at large.[190]

These homogenized juries are more likely to find defendants guilty, as discussed previously. Haney notes: "The fact that the legal system does not trust death penalty decision making to a group that reflects a broad and unbiased cross-section of the community says something unsettling yet important about the nature of the process in which it asks citizens to participate."[191]

Similar problems likely exist across all trials in America's criminal justice system, including noncapital murder trials that lead to sentences other than death, but the difference with capital trials is the finality of death. That is, such problems are less tolerable because "death is different." Sentences to life imprisonment or other sanctions would be no more just if plagued by these problems. Yet, at least American governments would not be killing people as a result.

Strangely, 15 published studies were presented to the Court in the *McCree* case, all of which found that death-qualified jurors were more conviction prone than other jurors. The Court rejected the studies for various reasons, in spite of the unanimity of the findings and thus its

> opinion reflects a fundamental misunderstanding of one of the basic concepts taught in every introductory research methods class: convergent

validity. There is no such thing as a perfect study. Rather, knowledge is accumulated, and confidence in a finding established, when numerous different researchers, employing different methods and materials, produce a similar pattern of findings. That was clearly the case with the research presented to the Court in *McCree*. However, the Court took the easy way out, avoiding the possibility of having to reverse convictions returned by death-qualified juries, and ignored the evidence.[192]

In fact, the Court deemed the evidence irrelevant, stating

> we will assume for the purposes of this opinion that the studies are both methodologically valid and adequate to establish that "death qualification" in fact produces juries somewhat more "conviction prone" than "non death-qualified" juries. We hold, nonetheless, that the Constitution does not prohibit the States from "death qualifying" juries in capital cases.[193]

The Court's ignorance of evidence in this case is reminiscent of its treatment of the evidence of racial disparities in Georgia's death penalty system in the *McCleskey* case, which was discussed in Chapter 2.

In conclusion, bifurcated capital trials and the death qualification process do not ensure impartial jurors who will follow the law and carefully weigh the evidence against a defendant, nor aggravating and mitigating evidence. Instead, capital jurors "are more conviction prone, less concerned with due process, and they are more inclined to believe the prosecution than are excludable jurors." That is, the process "does little to reduce arbitrariness in capital sentencing if the current practice simply physically separates, but does not keep psychologically separate, these difficult and distinct decisions to be made by the jury."[194]

Summary of Capital Juries

The experts indicated that the capital punishment jury selection process is flawed and that capital juries are largely incompetent. That is, death-qualified capital juries are conviction prone and are significantly incapable of doing the job expected of them. The facts show that capital punishment juries are conviction prone, that they engage in premature decision making with regard to sentencing, that they do not understand jury instructions, that they misunderstand alternative sanctions, and that race and gender or sex of juries play a meaningful role in the likelihood of a death sentence. This is another cost of capital punishment, as actually practiced in the United States, which calls into question our allegiance to "innocent until proven guilty," which ideally underlies all criminal justice processes.

Costs

Brief Summary of Issue

The financial costs of capital punishment are enormous. Generally, capital punishment, because of the way we do it in the United States, allegedly costs between two to five times more than life prison sentences.[195] Given the finality and irreversibility of death, as well as the requirements of super due process in death penalty cases, every part of the capital punishment process is purported to be more expensive than noncapital cases. This includes all phases of pretrial, trial, and posttrial activity.

Issue of Contention

The major issues of contention in terms of costs of capital punishment are 1) does capital punishment cost more than other punishments, such as life imprisonment? And 2) does it matter when the government is seeking justice for crimes committed against it?

Opponents of capital punishment assert that capital punishment costs more than alternative punishments such as life imprisonment without the possibility of parole and that costs are relevant for consideration.[196] Supporters of capital punishment say that costs are irrelevant when it comes to justice and that capital trials need not be more expensive than noncapital trials if done efficiently, and with the understanding that appeals should be restricted to expedite the death penalty process for each convicted offender.[197]

Experts' Views

As noted earlier in this chapter, some experts noted that the death penalty costs more than alternative punishments including life imprisonment without the possibility of parole.

Fact Check

Some surely say that the cost of capital punishment is not relevant to whether justice is achieved; however, it is true that the death penalty is generally more expensive than life imprisonment.

Some examples bear this out. A study in Texas in the 1990s, for example, found that the death penalty costs about three times as much as a 40-year maximum security prison term.[198] In Florida, each capital punishment case from 1976 to 1999 cost $24 million. From 1973 to 1988, each execution cost $3.2 million. One study showed that ending executions would save the state $51 million per year if life sentences without parole were used for all first-degree murderers.[199]

In 2003, California spent $90 million more on capital cases than it would have without capital punishment. The most significant share of this ($78 million) was on trials. A study from 2000 found that abolishing the death penalty would save the state tens of millions of dollars. Further, California spent $1 billion on 10 executions from 1977 to 1988.[200] Additionally, the average cost of 11 executions over 27 years in California was $250 million.[201]

In New York, where the death penalty was reinstated in 1995 (but later struck down as unconstitutional), the total cost per death sentence was $23 million through 2003, and the state carried out no executions during this time. A single death penalty trial was 3.5 times more expensive than a non-death-penalty trial.[202]

In Indiana, the total costs of the death penalty are 38% more expensive than total costs of life without parole. In Kansas, death penalty cases are 70% more expensive than comparable non-death-penalty cases. The costs of death penalty cases in that state were made up of pretrial and trial costs (49%), appeals (29%), and incarceration and execution (22%). Investigation costs were 3 times greater in death cases, trial costs were 16 times greater, appeals costs were 21 times greater, but incarceration and execution costs were only half as much.[203] In Idaho, the state spends as much as $5 million for a death penalty case versus $1 million for a life imprisonment case (2003).[204]

In New Jersey, a study found that taxpayers paid more than a quarter billion dollars in 23 years on a capital punishment system that led to no actual executions (but 197 capital trials and 60 death sentences, of which 50 were reversed).[205]

In North Carolina, where the "most comprehensive death penalty study in the country" was conducted, the cost of a death penalty case all the way to execution above adjudication and a 20-year sentence was $163,000. The extra cost per death penalty sentence was $216,000, and the total costs per execution were $2.16 million more than life imprisonment.[206]

The Death Penalty Information Center has documented other costs attributed to a death penalty system in states, including:

- A shortage of money for defense attorneys (Nebraska, Ohio, 2003; Illinois, 2002; Mississippi, 1999).
- Less money for highways and police (U.S. counties, 2001).
- Tax increases (U.S. counties, 2001).
- Cuts to indigent care, libraries, freeze on employee raises (Florida, 2003).
- Less money for police, cuts to officers (Oregon, California, New York, 2003).

- Cuts to crime fighting, prison guards (Oregon, 2003).
- Delays of up to 6 weeks in other prosecutions (Texas, 2003).
- Delays in pay raises, small pay raises, layoffs, cuts to equipment (Washington, 1999).
- Cuts to higher education, health care (California, New York, 1995).[207]

Summary of Costs

The experts indicated that capital punishment is more costly than alternatives, including life imprisonment without the possibility of parole. The facts show that capital punishment is not only generally more expensive than alternative sentences, but also that maintaining a capital punishment system is costly to states and counties such that cuts to other areas of services commonly must be made to pursue death sentences. These are additional costs of capital punishment, as actually practiced in the United States.

CONCLUSION

From the comments of the respondents who participated in this study, it is safe to conclude that capital punishment experts feel as if the application of the death penalty is plagued by significant problems. That is, the experts feel that the death penalty is racially biased, class biased, and to a lesser degree, biased based on gender or sex. Additionally, a clear majority of capital punishment experts also indicated that they thought the death penalty had been used against the innocent. Furthermore, a large majority of capital punishment experts in the study listed other problems with the reality of capital punishment in America, including excessive costs; the length of time it takes to complete the appeals process; problems with jury selection, jury instructions, and interpreting how to weigh aggravating and mitigating circumstances; the problematic nature of victim impact statements; ineffectiveness of counsel; politics; geographic disparities; a lack of proportionality, judicial, and appeals review; inadequate resources and representation for the poor; the unwillingness of parole boards or governors to grant clemency in deserving cases; improperly being applied when the victim is culpable; the immoral nature of the punishment; inhumane methods of execution; that the reputation of the U.S. is suffering as a result of continuing to utilize capital punishment; and the polarizing nature of the punishment.

If these experts on capital punishment are correct, the lesson is that not only does the death penalty generally fail to meet its goals and thus provides little benefit to society, it is also characterized by significant costs such as biases based on race, class, and gender or sex and a significant risk of convicting and/or executing innocent people, among many other problems. Empirical evidence supports the conclusion of the death penalty experts whose opinions are heard in this book.

Given this, one might wonder what are our options. Two possibilities come to mind. First, we could use capital punishment more. This would increase the likelihood of achieving our goals of retribution, deterrence, and incapacitation. It would also probably lessen the likelihood of arbitrary and discriminatory application, especially if we executed all murderers. Second, we could stop using capital punishment at all.

Given the ruling by the U.S. Supreme Court in *Woodson v. North Carolina* (1976)[208] that mandatory death for all murderers in not permissible, we cannot kill them all. Further, given the unwillingness of prosecutors to seek the death penalty, of juries to impose it, and the inability of counties to pay for it, it is unlikely that we could kill more murderers in order to achieve our objectives. As shown earlier in the book, the death penalty is becoming less common rather than more. Thus, it appears the better option is to stop using capital punishment.

In the next chapter, I discuss the future of capital punishment, including the issues of temporarily halting executions (moratorium) to study capital punishment to determine if problems like those illustrated in this book plague its practice in individual states, and complete abolition of the death penalty. I also examine the issue of public opinion of the death penalty and provide the opinions of the experts with regard to capital punishment generally, how they feel about a moratorium on executions and abolition, as well as why capital punishment persists in the United States in spite of its many problems. Finally, I lay out policies justified by the findings of this book.

ENDNOTES

1. Bedau, H. (2004). An abolitionist's survey of the death penalty in America today. In H. Bedau & P. Cassell (Eds.), *Debating the death penalty: Should America have capital punishment? The experts on both sides make their case.* New York: Oxford University Press; Pojman, L., & Reiman, J. (1998). *The death penalty: For and against.* Lanham, MD: Rowman & Littlefield; Bright, S. (2004). Why the United States will join the rest of the world in abandoning capital punishment. In H. Bedau & P. Cassell (Eds.), *Debating the death penalty: Should America have capital punishment? The experts from both sides make their case.* New York: Oxford University Press; Zimring, F. (2003). *The contradictions of American capital punishment.* New York: Oxford University Press.

2. Bedau, H. (1997). *The death penalty in America: Current controversies.* New York: Oxford University Press.

3. See the National Coalition to Abolish the Death Penalty Web site, http://www.ncadp.org/

4. Reiman, J. (1998). Why the death penalty should be abolished. In L. Pojman & J. Reiman (Eds.), *The death penalty: For and against*. Lanham, MD: Rowman & Littlefield.

5. Reiman (1998), p. 107.

6. Dictionary.com. (2006). Arbitrary. Retrieved from http://dictionary. reference.com/search?q=arbitrary

7. Robinson, M. (2005). *Justice blind? Ideals and realities of American criminal justice*. Upper Saddle River, NJ: Prentice Hall.

8. Robinson (2005).

9. Cassell, P. (2004). In defense of the death penalty. In H. Bedau & P. Cassell (Eds.), *Debating the death penalty: Should America have capital punishment? The experts from both sides make their case*. New York: Oxford University Press; Pojman & Reiman (1998); Pojman, L. (2004). Why the death penalty is morally permissible. In H. Bedau & P. Cassell (Eds.), *Debating the death penalty: Should America have capital punishment? The experts from both sides make their case*. New York: Oxford University Press; van den Haag, E. (1997). The death penalty once more. In H. Bedau (Ed.), *The death penalty in America: Current controversies*. New York: Oxford University Press.

10. This respondent noted Martin Urbina's book: Urbina, M. (2003). *Capital punishment and Latino offenders: Racial and ethnic differences in death sentences*. New York: LFB Scholarly Publishing.

11. This respondent noted the work of Adalberto Aguirre and Martin Urbina.

12. Some of David Baldus's studies include Baldus, D., Woodworth, G., & Pulaski, C., Jr. (1990). *Equal justice and the death penalty: A legal and empirical analysis*. Boston: Northeastern University Press; Baldus, D. C., Woodworth, G., Zuckerman, D., Weiner, N. A., Broffitt, B. (1998). Racial discrimination and the death penalty in the post-*Furman* era: An empirical and legal overview, with recent findings from Philadelphia. *Cornell Law Review, 83,* 1638. For more, see http://www.law.uiowa.edu/documents/faculty_bib/baldus-bib.pdf

13. The verb *plague* is defined as "to smite, infest, or afflict with or as if with disease, calamity, or natural evil"; "to cause worry or distress to" (as in to hamper or burden); "to disturb or annoy persistently"; "To pester or annoy persistently or incessantly" (as in harass); "To afflict with or as if with a disease or calamity." The question I was asking was, is the death penalty as actually practiced in the United States infested with, afflicted with, hampered by, or burdened by a bias? See Merriam-Webster Online Dictionary. (2006). Plague. Retrieved from http://m-w.com/cgi-bin/dictionary;Dictionary.com. (2006). Plague. Retrieved from http://dictionary.reference.com/search?q=plague

14. This respondent quoted the work of Martin Urbina.

15. Again, the meaning of the question was whether the death penalty as actually practiced in the United States is infested with, afflicted with, hampered by, or burdened by a bias. See Merriam-Webster (2006); Dictionary.com (2006).

16. U.S. Census Bureau. (2001). *Overview of race and Hispanic origin.* Retrieved from http://www.census.gov/prod/2001pubs/c2kbr01-1.pdf

17. *Sourcebook of Criminal Justice Statistics.* (2006). Table 4.12, Arrests in cities, by offense charged, age group, and race, 2002. Retrieved from http://www.albany.edu/sourcebook/pdf/t412.pdf

18. *Sourcebook of Criminal Justice Statistics.* (2006). Table 5.45, Characteristics of felony offenders convicted in state courts, by offense, United States, 2002. Retrieved from http://www.albany.edu/sourcebook/pdf/t5452002.pdf

19. NAACP Legal Defense and Educational Fund, Inc. (2006). *Death row U.S.A.* Retrieved from http://www.naacpldf.org/content/pdf/pubs/drusa/DRUSA_Fall_2005.pdf

20. Death Penalty Information Center. (2006a). *Race and the death penalty.* Retrieved from http://www.deathpenaltyinfo.org/article.php?did=105& scid=5

21. Scheidegger, K. (2003). *Maryland study, when properly analyzed, supports death penalty.* Criminal Justice Legal Foundation. Retrieved from http://www.cjlf.org/deathpenalty/MdMoratorium.htm

22. Death Penalty Information Center (2006a).

23. Robinson (2005).

24. Death Penalty Information Center (2006a).

25. Radelet, M. (1989). Executions of whites for crimes against blacks: Exceptions to the rule? *Sociological Quarterly, 30*(4), 529–544.

26. Bohm, B. (2003). *Deathquest II: An introduction to the theory and practice of capital punishment in the United States* (2nd ed.). Cincinnati, OH: Anderson.

27. Death Penalty Information Center (2006a).

28. Paternoster, R., & Brame, R. (2003). *An empirical analysis of Maryland's death sentencing system with respect to the influence of race and legal jurisdiction.* Retrieved from http://www.newsdesk.umd.edu/pdf/finalrep.pdf

29. Baime, D. (2001). *Report to the Supreme Court systemic proportionality review project, 2000–2001 term.* Retrieved from http://www.judiciary.state.nj.us/baime/baimereport.pdf

30. Pennsylvania Supreme Court Committee on Racial and Gender Bias in the Justice System. (2000). *Final report of the Pennsylvania Supreme Court Committee on Racial and Gender Bias in the Justice System.* Retrieved from http://www.courts.state.pa.us/Index/supreme/BiasCmte/FinalReport.pdf

31. Pierce, G., & Radelet, M. (2005). The impact of legally inappropriate factors on death sentencing for California homicides, 1990–1999. *Santa Clara Law Review, 46,* 1–47.

32. Welsh-Huggins, A. (2005, May 7). Death penalty unequal. Associated Press; Roberts, K. (2005, May 8). Capital cases hard for smaller counties. Associated Press; Seewer, J. (2005, May 9). Two killers; one spared. Associated Press. Retrieved from http://www.otse.org/Design/Assets/News%20and%20reports/AP%20study%202005.pdf

33. Unah, I., & Boger, J. (2001). *Race and the death penalty in North Carolina: An empirical analysis: 1993–1997.* Retrieved from http://www.deathpenalty info.org/article.php?scid=19&did=246

34. U.S. General Accounting Office. (1990). Death penalty sentencing: Research indicates pattern of racial disparities. In H. Bedau (Ed.), *The death penalty in America: Current controversies*. New York: Oxford University Press, p. 271; Baldus, D., & Woodworth, G. (2003). Race discrimination and the death penalty: An empirical and legal overview. In J. Acker, B. Bohm, & C. Lanier (Eds.), *America's experiment with capital punishment: Reflections on the past, present, and future of the ultimate penal sanction* (2nd ed.). Durham, NC: Carolina Academic Press, pp. 517–518.

35. U.S. General Accounting Office (1990), p. 4.

36. Baldus & Woodworth (2003), p. 518.

37. These studies include: Baldus, D., & Woodworth, G. (2001). *Race-of-victim and race-of-defendant disparities in the administration of Maryland's capital charging and sentencing system (1978–1999): Preliminary findings*. Unpublished manuscript; Bortner, P., & Hall, A. (2002). *Arizona first-degree murder cases summary of 1995–1999 indictments: Death Set II Research Report to Arizona Capital Case Commission*. Phoenix: Arizona Capital Case Commission; Brock, D., Cohen, N., & Sorensen, J. (2000). Arbitrariness in the imposition of death sentences in Texas: An analysis of four counties by offense seriousness, race of victim, and race of offender. *American Journal of Criminal Law, 28*, 43–71; Joint Legislative Audit and Review Commission of the Virginia General Assembly. (2002). *Review of Virginia's system of capital punishment*. Retrieved from http://jlarc.state.va.us/reports/rpt247.pdf; Klein, S., & Rolph, J. (1991). Relationship of offender and victim race to death penalty sentences in California. *Jurimetrics, 32*, 33–48; Lenza, M., Keys, D., & Guess, T. (2003). *The prevailing injustices in the application of the death penalty in Missouri (1978–1996)*. Retrieved from http://www.umsl.edu/division/artscience/forlanglit/mpb/Lenza1.html; McCord, D. (2002). A year in the life of death: Murders and capital sentences in South Carolina. *South Carolina Law Review, 53*, 250–359; Paternoster & Brame (2003); Unah & Boger (2001); Ziemba-Davis, M., & Myers, B. (2002). *The Application of Indiana's Capital Sentencing Law: A Report to Governor Frank O'Bannon and the Indiana General Assembly*. Indiana Criminal Justice Institute. Retrieved from http://www.in.gov/cji/home.html

38. Robinson (2005).

39. Fleury-Steiner, B. (2004). *Jurors' stories of death*. Ann Arbor: University of Michigan Press, p. 8.

40. Bright, S. (2002a). Discrimination, death, and denial: Race and the death penalty. In Dow, D., & Dow, M. (Eds.), *Machinery of death: The reality of America's death penalty regime*. New York: Routledge.

41. Bright (2004), p. 165.

42. Subcommittee on Civil and Constitutional Rights, Committee on the Judiciary. (1994). Racial disparities in federal death penalty prosecutions 1988–1994. Retrieved from http://www.deathpenaltyinfo.org/article.php?scid=45&did=528

43. U.S. Department of Justice (2001a). *The federal death penalty system: A statistical survey (1988–2000).* Retrieved from http://www.usdoj.gov/dag/pubdoc/dpsurvey.html

44. U.S. Department of Justice. (2001b). *The federal death penalty system: Supplementary data, analysis and revised protocols for capital case review.* Retrieved from http://www.usdoj.gov/dag/pubdoc/deathpenaltystudy.htm

45. Statement of David C. Baldus to the Committee on the Judiciary, U.S. Senate, June 6, 2001, Retrieved from http://www.deathpenaltyinfo.org/article.php?scid=18&did=252

46. Klein, S., Berk, R., & Hickman, L. (2006). *Race and the decision to seek the death penalty in federal cases.* Rand Corporation. Retrieved from http://rand.org/pubs/technical_reports/TR389/

47. McAllister, P. (2003). *Death defying: Dismantling the execution machinery in 21st century U.S.A.* New York: Continuum International Publishing Group, p. 67.

48. McAllister (2003), p. 68.

49. McAdams, J. (2002). Race and the death penalty. In J. Martinez, R. Richardson, & B. Hornsby (Eds.), *The Leviathan's choice: Capital punishment in the twenty-first century.* Lanham, MD: Rowman & Littlefield, p. 175.

50. McAdams (2002), p. 185.

51. The studies include: Bowers, W. (1983). The pervasiveness of arbitrariness and discrimination under post-*Furman* capital statutes. *Journal of Criminal Law and Criminology, 74*(3), 1067; Ekland-Olson, S. (1988). Structured discretion, racial bias, and the death penalty: The first decade after *Furman* in Texas. *Social Science Quarterly, 69*(3), 851–873; Paternoster, R. (1983). Race of victim and location of crime: The decision to seek the death penalty in South Carolina. *Journal of Criminal Law and Criminology, 74*(3), 754–785; Radelet, M. (1981). Racial characteristics and the imposition of the death penalty. *American Sociological Review, 46*(3), 918–927; Sorensen, J., & Wallace, D. (1995). Capital punishment in Missouri: Examining the issue of racial disparity. *Behavioral Sciences and the Law, 13*(1), 61–80; Vito, G., & Keil, T. (1988). Capital sentencing in Kentucky: An analysis of the factors influencing decision making in the post-*Gregg* period. *Journal of Criminal Law and Criminology, 79*(2), 483–503.

52. McAdams (2002), p. 187.

53. McAdams (2002), p. 189.

54. Baldus & Woodworth (2003), pp. 502–503.

55. For examples, see Bright (2002a).

56. Robinson (2005).

57. Bright (2004), p. 163.

58. Bright (2004), p. 165.

59. Stevenson, B. (2003). Close to death: Reflections on race and capital punishment in America. In H. Bedau & P. Cassell (Eds.), *Debating the death penalty: Should America have capital punishment? The experts from both sides make their case.* New York: Oxford University Press, p. 90.

60. Death Penalty Information Center. (2006b). *News from the U.S. Supreme Court.* Retrieved from http://deathpenaltyinfo.org/article.php?did=248&scid=38#0607; *Miller-Elv. Dretke,* No. 03-9659 (2005).

61. Baldus & Woodworth (2003), p. 508.

62. There is the theory of "adverse legal impact" which holds that "when the evidence indicates that an adverse disparate impact is produced by the even-handed administration of the law, it is certainly appropriate for the legislature to address the issue with standards deigned to bring geographic uniformity to the administration of the law." Baldus & Woodworth (2003), p. 511.

63. Baldus & Woodworth (2003), p. 512.

64. For discussion and examples of studies showing that racial disparities persist even after controlling for aggravation and other relevant legal factors, see Baldus & Woodworth (2003), pp. 513–516.

65. Baldus & Woodworth (2003), p. 519.

66. Spohn, C., & Cederblom, J. (1991). Race and disparities in sentencing: A test of the liberation hypothesis. *Justice Quarterly, 8,* 305–327.

67. Bright (2002a), p. 45.

68. Bright (2004), p. 158.

69. Bright (2004), p. 166.

70. Zimring (2003), p. 148.

71. McAllister (2003), pp. 70, 73.

72. Quoted in McAllister (2003), p. 74.

73. For examples, see Bohm (2003); Bright (1997); McAllister (2003).

74. Foster, B. (2001). How the death penalty really works: Selecting death penalty offenders in America. In Nelson, L., & Foster, B. (Eds.), *Death watch: A death penalty anthology.* Upper Saddle River, NJ: Prentice Hall.

75. Foster (2001), p. 19.

76. For example, see Bright, S. (1997). Counsel for the poor: The death sentence not for the worst crime but for the worst lawyer. In H. Bedau (Ed.), *The death penalty in America: Current controversies.* New York: Oxford University Press; Bright (2004); McAllister (2003); Mello, M., & Perkins, P. (2003). Closing the circle: The illusion of lawyers for people litigating for their lives at the *fin de siècle.* In J. Acker, B. Bohm, & C. Lanier (Eds.), *America's experiment with capital punishment: Reflections on the past, present, and future of the ultimate penal sanction* (2nd ed.). Durham, NC: Carolina Academic Press; Stevenson (2003).

77. For an excellent summary of this case and its implications, see Mello & Perkins (2003).

78. Dow, D. (2002). How the death penalty really works. In Dow, D., & Dow, M. (Eds.), *Machinery of death: The reality of America's death penalty regime.* New York: Routledge, p. 21.

79. Dow (2002), p. 21.

80. Mello & Perkins (2003), pp. 362–363.

81. For more on this, see Dow (2002), pp. 16–19.

82. Bright, S. (2002b). The politics of capital punishment: The sacrifice of fairness for executions. In J. Acker, B. Bohm, & C. Lanier (Eds.), *America's experiment*

with capital punishment: Reflections on the past, present, and future of the ultimate penal sanction (2nd ed.). Durham, NC: Carolina Academic Press, p. 138.

83. Smith, E. (2002). The implementation of the death penalty in the states. In J. Martinez, R. Richardson, & B. Hornsby (Eds.), *The Leviathan's choice: Capital punishment in the twenty-first century.* Lanham, MD: Rowman & Littlefield, p. 169.

84. Bright (2002b), p. 139.

85. Mello & Perkins (2003), p. 366; *Strickland v. Washington,* 466 U.S. 668 (1984).

86. *Florida v. Nixon,* No. 03-931 (2004).

87. Mello & Perkins (2003), p. 367.

88. Bright (2004), pp. 157–158.

89. Bright (1997), p. 275.

90. American Bar Association. (1990). Toward a more just and effective system of review in state death penalty cases. *American University Law Review,* 40(1), 79–92.

91. Coyle, M., Strasser, F., & Lavelle, M. (1990, June 11). Fatal defense: Trial and error in the nation's death belt. *National Law Journal,* 12(40), 29–44.

92. Stevenson (2003), p. 85.

93. Bright (2004), p. 160.

94. Bright (2004), pp. 167–168.

95. Robinson (2005).

96. Reiman, J. (2004). *The rich get richer and the poor get prison: Ideology, class, and criminal justice* (7th ed.). Boston: Allyn & Bacon; Robinson (2005); Shelden, R. (2002). *Controlling the dangerous classes: A critical introduction to the history of criminal justice.* Boston: Allyn & Bacon.

97. U.S. Department of Justice, Federal Bureau of Investigation. (2005). *Crime in the United States, 2004.* Retrieved from http://www.fbi.gov/ucr/cius_04/

98. Robinson (2005).

99. Schneider & Smykla (1991).

100. Death Penalty Information Center. (2006c). *Women and the death penalty.* Retrieved from http://www.deathpenaltyinfo.org/article.php?did=230&scid=24

101. Streib, V. (2004). *Death penalty for female offenders, January 1973 through December 31, 2005.* Retrieved from http://www.deathpenaltyinfo.org/FemDeathDec2005.pdf

102. Bohm (2003), p. 211.

103. Robinson (2005).

104. Young, C. (2000, May 4). Sexism and the death chamber: Chivalry lives when a woman must die. *Salon.* Retrieved from http://archive.salon.com/mwt/feature/2000/05/04/death/print.html

105. Goethals, J., Maes, E., & Klinckhamers, P. (1997). Sex/gender-based decision-making in the criminal justice system as a possible (additional) explanation for the underrepresentation of women in official criminal statistics—a review of international literature. *International Journal of Comparative and Applied Criminal Justice,* 21(1), 207–240; Laster, K. (1994). Arbitrary chivalry: Women and capital punishment in Victoria, Australia. *Women & Criminal Justice,* 6(1), 67.

106. Streib, V. (1993). Death penalty for female offenders. In V. Streib (Ed.), *A capital punishment anthology*. Cincinnati, OH: Anderson, p. 144.

107. Belknap, J. (1996). *The invisible woman*. Belmont, CA: Wadsworth; Morgan-Sharp, E. (1999). The administration of justice based on gender and race. In. R. Muraskin & A. Roberts (Eds.), *Visions for change: Crime and justice in the 21st century*. Upper Saddle River, NJ: Prentice Hall.

108. Fan, K. (2000). Defeminizing and dehumanizing female murderers: Depictions of lesbians on death row. *Women & Criminal Justice, 11*(2), 49.

109. Holcomb, J., Williams, M., & Demuth, S. (2004). White female victims and death penalty disparity research. *Justice Quarterly, 21*(4), 877–902.

110. Bohm (2003), p. 212.

111. Robinson, M. (2004). *Why crime? An integrated systems theory of antisocial behavior*. Upper Saddle River, NJ: Prentice Hall.

112. Streib (2004).

113. Bedau (2004); Reiman (1998); Bright (2004); Zimring (2003).

114. Cassell (2004); Pojman & Reiman (1998); Pojman (2004); van den Haag (1997).

115. This respondent was referring to the Innocent Project, which also goes by the name Project Innocence. For more information, see http://www.innocenceproject.org/

116. See Death Penalty Information Center. (2006d). *Innocence and the death penalty*. Retrieved from http://www.deathpenaltyinfo.org/article.php?did=412&scid=6

117. This respondent mentioned the Web site of Samuel Gross at the University of Michigan Law School. See Social Science Research Network. (2006). *Social science electronic publishing presents papers by Samuel R. Gross*. University of Michigan Law School. Retrieved from http://papers.ssrn.com/sol3/cf_dev/AbsByAuth.cfm?per_id=46767

118. For more on these cases, see Bohm (2003).

119. The question referred to "factual innocence" rather than "legal innocence."

120. The respondent was referring to the word "ever" in the question, "Is American capital punishment ever used against the innocent?" Actually, I chose this word specifically because some capital punishment supporters claim that the death penalty has "never" been used against the innocent. Further, the question is written in the present tense, not referring to whether capital punishment ever *has* been used against the innocent, but rather, whether capital punishment ever *is* used against the innocent.

121. Radelet, M., Bedau, H., & Putnam, C. (1994). *In spite of innocence: Erroneous convictions in capital cases*. Boston: Northeastern University Press.

122. Death Penalty Information Center. (2006e). *Innocence: Those freed from death row*. Retrieved from http://www.deathpenaltyinfo.org/article.php?scid=6&did=110

123. Death Penalty Information Center. (2006f). *Cases of innocence—1973 to present*. Retrieved from http://www.deathpenaltyinfo.org/article.php?scid=6&did=109

124. Death Penalty Information Center (2006d).

125. Liebman, J., Fagan, J., & West, V. (2000). *A broken system: Error rates in capital cases, 1973–1995.* Retrieved from http://www2.law.columbia.edu/instructionalservices/liebman/

126. Liebman et al. (2000), p. 45.

127. Liebman et al. (2000), p. 92.

128. Liebman et al. (2000), p. 103.

129. Death Penalty Information Center. (2006g). *A broken system II: Why there is so much error in capital cases, questions and answers.* Retrieved from http://www.deathpenaltyinfo.org/article.php?scid=19&did=244

130. Death Penalty Information Center (2006g).

131. Cagle & Martinez (2002), pp. 149–150, citing Latzer, B., & Cauthen, J. (2001). Another recount: Appeals in capital cases. *The Prosecutor, 35*(1), 26.

132. Cagle & Martinez (2002), p. 151, citing Sneider, J. (2001, February 6). The rationality syndrome: Statistics fail activists. *Columbia Daily Spectator.* Retrieved from http://www.columbiaspectator.com/Opinion/article.asp?articleID=1649

133. Cagle & Martinez (2002), pp. 149–150, citing Latzer & Cauthen (2001).

134. Cagle & Martinez (2002), p. 156, citing Barylan, B. (2000, November 3–4). A response to Professor Liebman's "A Broken System." *Criminal Justice Legal Foundation.* Retrieved from http://www.prodeathpenalty.com/Liebman/LIEBMAN2.htm

135. Cagle & Martinez (2002), p. 151, citing Sneider (2001).

136. Liebman, J., Fagan. J., & West, V. (2000). Death matters: A reply to Latzer and Cauthen. *Judicature, 84*(2), 6. Retrieved from http://www.lib.jjay.cuny.edu/docs/liebman.htm

137. Smith (2002), pp. 160–161.

138. American Bar Association. (2006). *Achieving justice: Freeing the innocent, convicting the guilty.* Retrieved from http://www.abanet.org/abastore/index.cfm?section=main&fm=Product.AddToCart&pid=5090103; Smith (2002).

139. For a detailed account of the Anthony Porter case from a journalism student who helped free him from death row, see Armhurst, S. (2002). Chance and the exoneration of Anthony Porter. In D. Dow & M. Dow (Eds.), *Machinery of death: The reality of America's death penalty regime.* New York: Routledge. Armhurst describes his experience on the case and writes that "the investigation of the Porter case required investigation and strategic skills . . . and it required my fellow students and me not to screw anything up. But the bottom line is that we only interviewed four people in our entire investigation, and all of those people had been interviewed before. . . . And that's why the story of Anthony Porter, rather than making me feel ecstatic about a life saved, scares me" (pp. 164–165).

140. State of Illinois. (2002, April). *Report on the Commission on Capital Punishment.* Retrieved from http://www.idoc.state.il.us/ccp/ccp/reports/commission_report/

141. Cassell (2004); Pojman & Reiman (1998); Pojman (2004); van den Haag (1997).

142. Cagle, M., & Martinez, J. (2002). Social science data and the death penalty: Understanding the debate over "A Broken System." In J. Martinez, R. Richardson, & B. Hornsby (Eds.), *The Leviathan's choice: Capital punishment in the twenty-first century*. Lanham, MD: Rowman & Littlefield, p. 149.

143. For example, Amhurst (2002) writes, based on his work with wrongly convicted death row inmates, that "the death penalty system in America is irreparably broken. Proponents of the death penalty will argue that there is no proof that an innocent person has ever been executed in the United States, and that the exoneration of 100 men proves that our current safeguards save the lives of the innocent. Some will even say that there are so many safeguards in place that executions don't happen fast enough. But those proponents are just plain wrong. My experiences with the Porter case, as well as the [Gary] Graham case, have proved to me that there are not enough safeguards in the system, and that it requires actors outside the system and some lucky breaks to prove your innocence once you have been sentenced to death. Regardless of how one feels about the death penalty, I don't think anyone but the most ardent supporter of the practice could be comfortable with a system in which chance—not order or fairness—rules the day. The death penalty—intended to result in the deaths of horrible murderers—could, and probably has, resulted in the deaths of other innocent victims. I don't think the life of Anthony Porter or any other innocent person sentenced to death is worth that risk" (pp. 165–166).

144. Prejean, H. (2004). *The death of innocents: An eyewitness account of wrongful executions*. New York: Random House.

145. Radelet, M., & Bedau, H. (2003). The execution of the innocent. In J. Acker, B. Bohm, & C. Lanier (Eds.), *America's experiment with capital punishment: Reflections on the past, present, and future of the ultimate penal sanction* (2nd ed.). Durham, NC: Carolina Academic Press.

146. Zimring (2003), p. 167.

147. Death Penalty Information Center. (2006h). *News and developments, innocence*. Retrieved from http://www.deathpenaltyinfo.org/newsanddev.php?scid=6; Death Penalty Information Center. (2006i). *Executed but possibly innocent*. Retrieved from http://www.deathpenaltyinfo.org/article.php?scid= 6&did=111#executed

148. For more on the specifics of the Gary Graham case, including clear evidence of his innocence, see Welch, M., & Burr, R. (2002). The politics of finality and the execution of the innocent: The case of Gary Graham. In D. Dow & M. Dow (Eds.), *Machinery of death: The reality of America's death penalty regime*. New York: Routledge. This author writes: "Graham was convicted of capital murder and sentenced to death in 1981 for a crime that, by 1993, newly discovered evidence showed he did not commit. For seven years following 1993, Graham tried to get a hearing in the state and federal courts—a proceeding in which the newly discovered evidence of innocence could be presented through the testimony of witnesses, and the fairness of his trial, in which his court-appointed lawyer had failed to find and present the

evidence of his innocence, could be examined. No hearing was held for Graham, and on June 22, 2000, he was executed" (p. 128). Part of the reason Graham could not gain a hearing is because he could not show that "his original lawyers could not have discovered [new] evidence of his innocence" through due diligence, as required by the Anti-Terrorism and Effective Death Penalty Act of 1996 (pp. 140–141).

149. Death Penalty Information Center. (2006j). *Additional innocence information, executed but possibly innocent.* Retrieved from http://www.deathpenalty info.org/article.php?scid=6&did=111#executed

150. Personal communication between M. Watt Espy, Jr. and B. Bohm. Reported in Bohm (2003), p. 156.

151. Bohm (2003).

152. Zimring (2003).

153. *Herrera v. Collins,* 506 U.S. 390 (1993).

154. Smith (2002), p. 170, citing Newton, B. (1994). A case study in system unfairness: The Texas death penalty, 1973–1994. *Texas Forum on Civil Rights and Civil Liberties, 1*(1), 11; Palacios, V. (1996). Faith in fantasy: The Supreme Court's reliance on commutation to ensure justice in death penalty cases. *Vanderbilt University Law Review, 49*(1), 347–348.

155. Lasswell, H. (1936). *Politics: Who gets what, when, how.* New York: McGraw-Hill.

156. Harrigan, J. (2000). *Empty dreams, empty pockets: Class and bias in American politics.* New York: Addison-Wesley/Longman.

157. Easton, D. (1953). *The political system.* New York: Knopf.

158. Bedau (2004); Reiman (1998); Bright (2004); Zimring (2003).

159. Cassell (2004); Pojman & Reiman (1998); Pojman (2004); van den Haag (1997).

160. Death Penalty Information Center. (2006k). *Number of executions by state and region since 1976.* Retrieved from http://www.deathpenaltyinfo.org/article.php?scid=8&did=186

161. Scheidegger (2003).

162. Death Penalty Information Center. (2006l). *Arbitrariness.* Retrieved from http://deathpenaltyinfo.org/article.php?did=1328#Geography

163. Zimring (2003), pp. 77, 189.

164. Zimring (2003), p. 77.

165. Zimring (2003), p. 87.

166. Zimring (2003), p. 189.

167. Death Penalty Information Center. (2006l); also see U.S. Department of Justice. (2001). *The federal death penalty system: A statistical survey (1988–2000).* Retrieved from http://www.usdoj.gov/dag/pubdoc/dpsurvey.html

168. PBS. (2000). *Debating our destiny* [1988 election interviews]. Retrieved from http://www.pbs.org/newshour/debatingourdestiny/1988.html

169. CNN. (2000). *Vice President Al Gore and Governor George W. Bush participate in third debate sponsored by the commission on presidential debates.* Retrieved from http://www.cnn.com/ELECTION/2000/debates/transcripts/u221017.html

170. *Ring v. Arizona,* 536 U.S. 584 (20002).

171. Bedau (2004); Reiman (1998); Bright (2004); Zimring (2003).

172. Cassell (2004); Pojman & Reiman (1998); Pojman (2004); van den Haag (1997).

173. See Northeastern University. (n.d.). *Capital Jury Project: What is the CJP?* Retrieved from http://www.cjp.neu.edu/. Also, see Sandys, M., & McClelland, S. (2002). Stacking the deck for guilt and death: The failure of death qualification to ensure impartiality. In J. Acker, B. Bohm, & C. Lanier (Eds.), *America's experiment with capital punishment: Reflections on the past, present, and future of the ultimate penal sanction* (2nd ed.). Durham, NC: Carolina Academic Press; Bowers, W. J., Steiner, B. D., & Antonio, M. E. (2003). The capital sentencing decision: Guided discretion, reasoned moral judgment, or legal fiction. In J. Acker, B. Bohm, & C. Lanier (Eds.), *America's experiment with capital punishment: Reflections on the past, present, and future of the ultimate penal sanction* (2nd ed.). Durham, NC: Carolina Academic Press.

174. *Witherspoon v. Illinois*, 391 U.S. 510 (1968).

175. Quoted in Sandys & McClelland (2002), p. 388.

176. *Wainwright v. Witt*, 496 U.S. 412 (1985).

177. Quoted in Sandys & McClelland (2002), p. 389.

178. *Lockhart v. McCree*, 476 U.S. 162 (1986).

179. Quoted in Sandys & McClelland (2002), p. 395.

180. *Morgan v. Illinois*, 504 U.S. 719 (1992).

181. Quoted in Sandys & McClelland (2002), p. 400.

182. Northeastern University (n.d.).

183. Death Penalty Information Center. (2006l). *Arbitrariness*. Retrieved from http://deathpenaltyinfo.org/article.php?did=1328#Juror_Misperceptions, citing the article by Bowers, W., & Foglia, W. (2003). Still singularly agonizing: Law's failure to purge arbitrariness from capital sentencing. *Criminal Law Bulletin, 39*, 51.

184. Bowers, W. (1995). The Capital Jury Project: Rationale, design, and a preview of early findings. *Indiana Law Journal, 70*, 1043; Bowers, W. (1996). The capital jury: Is it tilted toward death? *Judicature, 79*, 220; Blume, J., Eisenberg, T., & Garvey, S. (2003). Lessons from the Capital Jury Project. In S. Garvey (Ed.), *Beyond repair? America's death penalty*. Durham, NC: Duke University Press; Bowers et al. (2003); Sandys & McClelland (1998).

185. Bowers, W., Sandys, M., & Steiner, B. (1998). Foreclosed impartiality capital sentencing: Jurors' predispositions, guilt trial experience, and premature decision making. *Cornell Law Review, 83*, 1474.

186. Bentele, U., & Bowers, W. (2002). How jurors decide on death: Guilt is overwhelming; aggravation requires death; and mitigation is no excuse. *Brooklyn Law Review, 66*, 1013; Bowers, W., & Steiner, B. (1999). Death by default: An empirical demonstration of false and forced choices in capital sentencing. *Texas Law Review, 77*, 605; Eisenberg, T., & Wells, M. (1993). Deadly confusion: Juror instructions in capital cases. *Cornell Law Review, 79*, 1; Foglia, W. (2003). They know not what they do: Unguided and misguided decision-making in Pennsylvania capital cases. *Justice Quarterly, 20*(1), 187–211; Garvey, S., Johnson, S., & Marcus, P. (2000). Correcting deadly

confusion: Responding to jury inquiries in capital cases. *Cornell Law Review,* *85,* 627; Luginbuhl, J., & Howe, J. (1995). Discretion in capital sentencing instructions: Guided or misguided? *Indiana Law Journal, 70,* 1161.

187. Blume, J., Garvey, S., & Johnson, S. (2001). Future dangerousness in capital cases: Always "at issue." *Cornell Law Review, 86,* 397; Eisenberg, T., Garvey, S., & Wells, M. (1996). Jury responsibility in capital sentencing: An empirical study. *Buffalo Law Review, 44,* 339; Garvey, S. (1998). Aggravation and mitigation in capital cases: What do jurors think? *Columbia Law Review, 98,* 1538.

188. Hoffman, J. (1997). How American juries decide death penalty cases: The Capital Jury Project. In H. Bedau (Ed.), *The death penalty in America: Current controversies.* New York: Oxford University Press; Hoffman, J. (1995). Where's the buck? Juror misperception of sentencing responsibility in death penalty cases. *Indiana Law Journal, 70,* 1137; Sarat, A. (1995). Violence, representation, and responsibility in capital trials: The view from the jury. *Indiana Law Journal, 70,* 1103; Steiner, B., Bowers, W., & Sarat, A. (1999). Folk knowledge as legal action: Death penalty judgments and the tenet of early release in a culture of mistrust and punitiveness. *Law and Society Review, 33,* 461.

189. Bowers, W., Sandys, M., & Brewer, T. (2004). Crossing racial boundaries: A closer look at the roots of racial bias in capital sentencing when the defendant is black and the victim is white. *DePaul Law Review, 53,* 1497; Bowers, W., Steiner, B., & Sandys, M. (2001). Death sentencing in black and white: An empirical analysis of the role of jurors' race and jury racial composition. *University of Pennsylvania Journal of Constitutional Law, 3,* 171; Eisenberg, T., Garvey, S., & Wells, M. (2001). Forecasting life and death: Juror race, religion, and attitude toward the death penalty. *Journal of Legal Studies, 30,* 277; Foglia, W., & Schenker, N. (2001). Arbitrary and capricious after all these years: Constitutional problems with capital jurors' decision making. *The Champion, 25*(6), 26–31.

190. Haney, C. (2005). *Death by design: Capital punishment as a social psychological system.* New York: Oxford University Press, pp. 107–108.

191. Haney (2005), p. 139.

192. Sandys & McClelland (2002), p. 397.

193. Quoted in Sandys & McClelland (2002), p. 398.

194. Sandys & McClelland (2002), p. 408. For more on the psychology of capital punishment, see Haney (2005).

195. Bohm (2003).

196. Bedau (2004); Reiman (1998); Bright (2004); Zimring (2003).

197. Cassell (2004); Pojman & Reiman (1998); Pojman (2004); van den Haag (1997).

198. Death Penalty Information Center. (2006m). *Costs of the death penalty.* Retrieved from http://deathpenaltyinfo.org/article.php?did=108&scid=7

199. Death Penalty Information Center (2006m).

200. Death Penalty Information Center (2006m).

201. Death Penalty Information Center (2006n).

202. Death Penalty Information Center (2006m).

203. Death Penalty Information Center (2006m).

204. Death Penalty Information Center (2006m).

205. Death Penalty Information Center (2006m).

206. Death Penalty Information Center (2006m).

207. Death Penalty Information Center (2006n). *Archive of cost news and developments*. Retrieved from http://deathpenaltyinfo.org/article.php?scid=7&did=851

208. *Woodson v. North Carolina*, 428 U.S. 280 (1976).

DEATH PENALTY OPINION
AND THE FUTURE OF AMERICAN
CAPITAL PUNISHMENT

INTRODUCTION

In this chapter, I discuss the issue of public opinion of capital punishment, identifying those groups that most support it and those that least support it. As part of this discussion, I examine the Marshall hypothesis, which predicts that as people gain more information about the realities of capital punishment they are less likely to support it. Also in this chapter, I present the opinion of the experts with regard to their degree of support of capital punishment, and which punishment they think is most appropriate for first-degree murderers. I also present the opinions of the experts on why capital punishment persists in America in spite of its ineffectiveness and the many problems with its application. Further, I examine whether the experts support a temporary halt to executions (moratorium) and/or the complete abolition of capital punishment. Finally, I discuss the issue of the future of the death penalty in the United States and lay out the policies that I think are justified by the findings of the study reported in this book.

AMERICAN OPINION ABOUT CAPITAL PUNISHMENT

Why Opinion Matters

Public opinion on capital punishment is important for at least five reasons.[1] First, what American citizens think about the death penalty is likely to have effects on legislators at the local, state, and federal levels of government. If people support capital punishment, it is likely that legislators will also support the punishment. In fact, in modern America, it is nearly impossible for politicians to take a stand against the death penalty and get elected or reelected to office.

It is also certainly true that politicians who speak in support of capital punishment—usually through sound bites in the media—increase support of the masses for the death penalty. This would be consistent with the literature on politics and ideology and law making.[2]

Second, to the degree Americans support capital punishment, it will influence the decision of prosecutors to seek the death penalty or not. Prosecutors, as elected officials, must answer to the people. For example, in a county that supports capital punishment, logic would suggest that prosecutors would be more likely to seek death sentences for potentially capital crimes. Conversely, when citizens do not support capital punishment, prosecutors would be less likely to support the death penalty.

Third, a supportive public may pressure judges to impose the death penalty when it is recommended by a jury. Conversely, as with prosecutors, a less supportive public may encourage judges to impose sentences other than death.

Fourth, a supportive public may dissuade governors from vetoing legislation, issuing pardons, or commuting death sentences. Governors are often the last hope for those sitting on death row. It is extremely rare for governors to veto death penalty legislation, issue pardons, or even commute death sentences to lesser punishments, notwithstanding the recent case of Governor Ryan of Illinois. Given the political nature of capital punishment and the presumed pressure on politicians to support the death penalty, a highly supportive public would serve to discourage governors to take any action against the death penalty that might upset the masses.

Fifth, public opinion is often used by courts to justify the continuation of capital punishment. As shown in Chapter 2, the U.S. Supreme Court often cited measures of public opinion—including polls and legislative activity at the state level—to indicate evolving standards of decency with regard to specific issues of capital punishment (e.g., executing juveniles and those who are mentally retarded). Thus, if Americans turn against capital punishment, this will likely affect decisions by courts in the United States.

Findings From Public Opinion Polls

There are numerous surveys that have assessed American public opinion with regard to capital punishment. For almost all of American history, a majority of citizens have answered that they support capital punishment. Yet, an important caveat should be noted at the outset: The findings of surveys depend on how questions are asked.

With this in mind, it is still true that generally, people say they support capital punishment. Figure 6–1 shows one measure of support for capital punishment as determined by a Gallup poll, in response to the question, "Are you in favor of the death penalty for a person convicted of murder?"[3]

As you can see in the figure, there is only 1 year for which opposition to capital punishment exceeded support: 1966. In this year, only 42% favored capital punishment. In March 2006, 65% of Americans said they support the death penalty for persons convicted of first-degree murder.[4]

Support for capital punishment declines when people are given other options such as life imprisonment without parole (LWOP). For example, a 2004 Gallup poll showed support for LWOP at 46% and support for the death penalty at 50%. In 2005, the numbers changed to 39% and 56%, respectively. When Americans are given the alternative of life imprisonment without the possibility of parole plus restitution to the family of the victim (LWOP+R), support for the death penalty drops to 50% and less, near to the same percentage as was found in 1966, when support

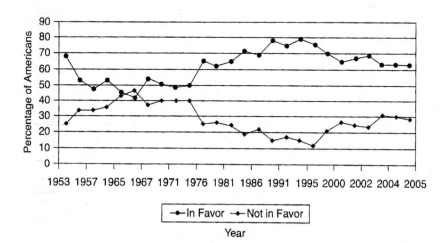

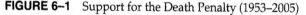

FIGURE 6–1 Support for the Death Penalty (1953–2005)

Source: Bureau of Justice Statistics (2006). Sourcebook of Criminal Justice Statistics (2006). Table 2.51.2006. Attitudes toward the death penalty for persons convicted of murder. Retrieved from http://albany.edu/sourcebook/pdf/t2512006.pdf

for the death penalty was its lowest level ever measured. The Death Penalty Information Center notes: "Over the past 20 years, support for the death penalty instead of life imprisonment has fluctuated between a low of 49% and a high of 61%."[5] This means current support for the death penalty over life is *very similar* to its lowest levels ever recorded (when respondents were given alternatives such as LWOP+R).

Figure 6–2 shows support for the death penalty and LWOP, in response to the question, "If you could choose between the following two approaches, which do you think is the better penalty for murder—the death penalty or life imprisonment, with absolutely no possibility of parole?"[6]

The DPIC also reports that polls of citizens in several states show that a majority of people there offer greater support for LWOP than capital punishment. These states include New York, New Jersey, California, Maryland, and at least some cities in Texas.[7]

So, a key question that has different answers is whether Americans *really* support capital punishment or do they just *say* they do when asked by researchers, as a matter of mere acceptance. A 2005 Gallup poll found that 64% of Americans find capital punishment morally acceptable. Support is higher in the United States than in other countries, including Great Britain (where about 49% say they support it) and Canada (where 44% say they support it). Neither Great Britain nor Canada has the death penalty.[8]

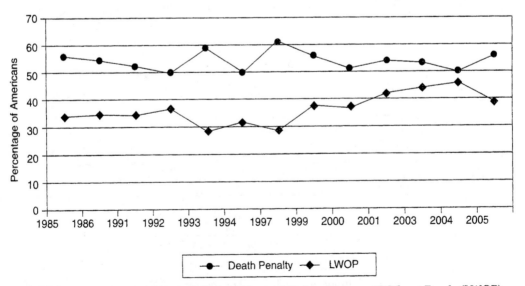

FIGURE 6–2 Support for the Death Penalty Versus Life Imprisonment Without Parole (LWOP) (1985–2005)

Source: Bureau of Justice Statistics (2006). Sourcebook of Criminal Justice Statistics (2006). Table 2.49.2006. Attitudes toward the penalty for murder. Retrieved from http://albany.edu/sourcebook/pdf/t2512006.pdf

Most would probably say that yes, Americans really do support capital punishment. In fact, it is possible that support for capital punishment may be higher than indicated in public opinion polls, given that most people never are directly influenced by murder. That is, with a greater exposure to murder (or a poll that asked about support for capital punishment after first graphically describing a real murder), people may be more likely to support capital punishment.

Yet, studies call this assumption into question. Support for the death penalty may very well be a better indicator of support for "tough on crime" approaches and a "law and order" orientation than actual support for the death penalty.[9] This might explain why surveys find that although a majority of Americans say they support capital punishment, less than half of Americans answer that they could pull the trigger or flip the switch that would lead to the inmate's death, or even sentence a murderer to death.[10]

This could explain why a majority of citizens in some states say they support a moratorium on executions, including North Carolina (65% of citizens), Texas (64% of citizens), and Alabama (57% of citizens).[11] In fact, some national polls conducted in 2000 and 2001 found that a majority of Americans (between 51% and 64%) said they support a national moratorium on executions.[12]

Another possible reason why some Americans support a moratorium in their state is an increased awareness of problems with the application of the death penalty. Studies show that as people think the death penalty is applied unfairly or has been used against the innocent, support for capital punishment declines.[13] A December 2003 Harris poll, for example, found that only 37% of people say they would continue to support capital punishment if they thought that "quite a substantial number of innocent people are convicted of murder."[14]

Table 6.1 shows the main reasons Americans say they support capital punishment. As you can see, 61% of Americans say they support the death penalty for reasons related to retribution, versus only 11% for deterrence and 10% for incapacitation.

Table 6.2 shows the main reasons Americans say they are against capital punishment. As you can see, 46% of people who oppose capital punishment do so because they think the punishment is wrong, versus 25% of people who think it may be used against the innocent.

Deterrence is not widely accepted by Americans. For example, a 2004 Gallup poll showed that 62% of Americans believed that the death penalty did not deter crime, versus 35% who said it was a deterrent. This can be explained by the infrequency with which executions occur in the United States. The Gallup poll showed that 48% of Americans believe

---

TABLE 6.1   Top Reasons People Support Capital Punishment,
                 2003 Gallup Poll

Retribution (61%)

An eye for an eye/they took a life/fits the crime	37%
They deserve it	13%
Biblical reasons	5%
Serve justice	4%
Would help/benefit families of victims	2%

Deterrence (11%)

Deterrent for potential crimes/set an example	11%

Incapacitation (10%)

They will repeat their crime/keep them from repeating it	7%
Don't believe they can be rehabilitated	2%
Life sentences don't always mean life in prison	1%

Other (28%)

Save taxpayers money/cost associated with prison	11%
Depends on the type of crime they commit	4%
Fair punishment	3%
If there's no doubt the person committed the crime	3%
Support/believe in the death penalty	2%
Relieves prison overcrowding	1%
Other	4%
No opinion	2%

Note: Percentages do not add up to 100% because respondents could offer more than one answer.
Source: Table 2.56, "Reported Reasons for Favoring the Death Penalty for Persons Convicted of Murder, United States, 1991, 2000, 2001, and 2003," in *Sourcebook of Criminal Justice Studies,* 2006. Retrieved from http://www.albany.edu/sourcebook/pdf/t255.pdf

capital punishment is not used with enough frequency. Interestingly, among those who say they think the death penalty is a deterrent, 69% say they would continue to support it even if executions did not lower the murder rate.

What has been well established is that support for capital punishment is highest for whites, males, older citizens, the wealthy, Republicans, people who consider themselves to be "conservatives," people living in the South and the West, Protestants (among religious denominations), and people who do not attend religious services regularly. In terms of religion,

TABLE 6.2 Top Reasons People Oppose Capital Punishment, 2003 Gallup Poll

Wrong to take a life	46%
Person may be wrongly convicted	25%
Punishment should be left to God/religious belief	13%
Possibility of rehabilitation	5%
Need to pay/suffer longer/think about their crime	5%
Does not deter people from committing murder	4%
Unfair application of death penalty	4%
Depends on the circumstances	4%
Other	3%
No opinion	4%

Note: Percentages do not add up to 100% because respondents could offer more than one answer.
Source: Table 2.56, "Reported Reasons for Opposing the Death Penalty for Persons Convicted of Murder, United States, 1991 and 2003," in *Sourcebook of Criminal Justice Statistics,* 2006. Retrieved from http://www.albany.edu/sourcebook/pdf/t256.pdf

some research shows that fundamentalists (who believe strongly in free will and personal responsibility and who take the Bible literally) are more likely to support the death penalty, whereas evangelicals (who believe in compassion for others) are less likely to support it.[15]

The death penalty is also more supported by people who fear crime, who think courts treat people leniently, and who do not know actual sentences imposed by courts. Support for capital punishment is also directly related to racial animosity.[16] Support is highest among people who (wrongly) believe the death penalty meets its goals and is cheaper than alternatives such as life imprisonment.[17] Table 6.3 shows some diversity in death penalty support by different groups of Americans.

Finally, support for capital punishment is inversely related to level of education, so that the most educated people are the least supportive of the punishment. For example, a May 2003 Gallup poll found that support for life imprisonment without parole was highest (at 62%) for those who did work in college beyond graduation.[18] This might explain the fact that support for capital punishment is found to decrease with knowledge about realities of death penalty, especially problems with it such as racial bias and innocence. I return to this issue below.

From all this information, a fair characterization of public opinion of the death penalty in the United States is that it is wide but not deep.[19] Death penalty scholar Franklin Zimring claims Americans are quite

TABLE 6.3   Support for the Death Penalty by Demographic Group, 2005 Gallup Poll

	In favor	Not in favor	Don't know/refused
Sex			
Male	70%	24%	6%
Female	59%	34%	7%
Race			
White	69%	26%	5%
Black	35%	56%	9%
Age			
18–29 years	60%	36%	4%
30–49 years	64%	29%	7%
50–64 years	69%	25%	6%
65+ years	61%	31%	8%
Education			
College post graduate	54%	41%	5%
College graduate	62%	34%	4%
Some college	69%	24%	7%
High school graduate or less	66%	27%	7%
Income			
$75,000+	64%	29%	7%
$50,000–74,999	68%	26%	6%
$30,000–49,999	68%	29%	3%
$20,000–29,999	67%	26%	7%
Under $20,000	57%	33%	10%
Community			
Urban area	59%	33%	8%
Suburban area	66%	29%	5%
Rural area	67%	25%	8%
Region			
East	59%	35%	6%
Midwest	64%	30%	6%
South	68%	25%	7%
West	65%	29%	6%

(*continued*)

TABLE 6.3 (Continued)

Politics			
Republican	77%	18%	5%
Democrat	56%	37%	7%
Independent	63%	31%	6%

Source: Table 2.52, "Attitudes Toward the Death Penalty for Persons Convicted of Murder, by Demographic Characteristics, United States, 2005, in *Sourcebook of Criminal Justice Statistics*, 2006. Retrieved from http://www.albany.edu/sourcebook/pdf/t2522005.pdf

ambivalent about the death penalty, because we claim to support it but we are also deeply troubled by its very real problems.[20] Robert Lifton and Greg Mitchell write that "ambiguity around this issue abounds. Nearly everyone feels that there is *something* wrong about capital punishment, perhaps it violates our fundamental commitment to life without claiming to uphold it."[21]

Jeffrey Reiman agrees, writing:

> When Americans are asked in polls whether they favor the death penalty for convicted murderers, they answer overwhelmingly in the affirmative. Asked a more complicated question, such as whether they would favor life in prison without [chance] of parole over the death penalty, large numbers defect from the death penalty camp in favor of genuine lifetime incarceration—especially if it includes work by convicted murderers aimed at making some restitution to victims' loved ones. Likewise, since the Supreme Court gave the green light to death penalty legislation in 1976, almost every state in the union has passed laws providing capital punishment for specially grave murders. And yet, for all that, few convicted murderers get executed. Prosecutors ask for the death penalty in only a fraction of the cases in which they could, juries approve it in only a fraction of the cases in which it is asked, and a substantial number of death sentences are overturned on appeal. It seems in short that Americans are deeply ambivalent about the death penalty—they believe it's right but they're reluctant to impose it.[22]

So it would seem the rarity of capital punishment in the United States is a sign of the weak nature of support among Americans.

Finally, it is possible that Americans, who are largely ignorant of the realities of capital punishment practice, may not be highly in favor of executions but instead may only support the death penalty in the abstract. The Marshall hypothesis,[23] discussed below, suggests that if Americans knew more about how capital punishment was actually administered in the United States, they would be less supportive of it.

The Marshall Hypothesis

As noted in Chapter 2, the U.S. Supreme Court temporarily suspended capital punishment by invalidating arbitrary death penalty statutes in *Furman v. Georgia* (1972). In his opinion as part of the five-justice plurality, Justice Thurgood Marshall examined the issue of what is cruel and unusual punishment and related it to the evolving standards of decency in a maturing society. He suggested that a punishment would be cruel and unusual if it met any of four conditions: 1) it causes too much physical pain or is excessive; 2) it has not been practiced prior; 3) it serves no valid purpose or it is unnecessary; and 4) popular sentiment is against it or it is immoral.

In Marshall's *Furman* opinion—which to this day remains one of the most significant antideath penalty arguments—he dismissed all justifications for capital punishment by suggesting that the death penalty as practiced does not actually serve retribution, deterrence, or incapacitation, and that it is more expensive than life imprisonment (in agreement with the opinions of the experts surveyed for this book).

The most significant part of the Marshall opinion is what became known as the Marshall hypothesis. Marshall wrote that "the question with which we must deal is not whether a substantial proportion of American citizens would today, if polled, opine that capital punishment is barbarously cruel, but whether they would find it so in the light of all information presently available."[24] Marshall put forth what he viewed as the reality of capital punishment and suggested that people would not support it if they knew this reality.

Marshall wrote: "I believe the following facts would serve to convince even the most hesitant of citizens to condemn death as a sanction: capital punishment is imposed discriminatorily against certain identifiable classes of people; there is evidence that innocent people have been executed before their innocence can be proved; and the death penalty wreaks havoc with our entire criminal justice system."[25] Although Marshall believed that support for capital punishment would vary inversely with knowledge about the punishment and that greater attainment of knowledge about the realities of capital punishment would lead to lessened support, he also stated that support for capital punishment would not be reduced among those who favor the punishment due to retributive reasons.[26]

Perhaps the strongest evidence that the Marshall hypothesis is correct comes from anecdotal evidence. Justice Harry Blackmun wrote in his dissent to deny certiorari in *Callins v. James* (1994):[27]

From this day forward, I no longer shall tinker with the machinery of death. For more than 20 years, I have endeavored—indeed, I have struggled—along with a majority of this Court, to develop procedural and substantive rules that would lend more than the mere appearance of fairness to the death penalty endeavor. Rather than continue to coddle the Court's delusion that the desired level of fairness has been achieved and the need for regulation eviscerated, I feel morally and intellectually obligated simply to concede that the death penalty experiment has failed. It is virtually self-evident to me now that no combination of procedural rules or substantive regulations ever can save the death penalty from its inherent constitutional deficiencies. The basic question—does the system accurately and consistently determine which defendants "deserve" to die?—cannot be answered in the affirmative. It is not simply that this Court has allowed vague aggravating circumstances to be employed . . . relevant mitigating evidence to be disregarded . . . and vital judicial review to be blocked. . . . The problem is that the inevitability of factual, legal, and moral error gives us a system that we know must wrongly kill some defendants, a system that fails to deliver the fair, consistent, and reliable sentences of death required by the Constitution.

Blackmun had voted to uphold capital punishment in *Furman* and *Gregg* and was considered a capital punishment supporter on the Court. His firsthand experience with the realities of capital punishment apparently led him to change his mind.

As for empirical evidence, studies of the Marshall hypothesis show mixed results. Since the *Gregg* decision, the Marshall hypothesis has been tested in published articles at least 19 times.[28] Some tests of the Marshall hypothesis and death penalty opinion find little support for Marshall's main idea and/or have offered different conclusions. For example, some studies find that gaining increased information about the death penalty can polarize opinions, so that those who supported it before, support it more afterward and those who opposed it before, oppose it more afterward.[29] Other studies suggest that when people become emotional about capital punishment—for example, because of reading or learning about heinous murders—they may be more likely to indicate support for capital punishment in such cases even though they may not generally support the death penalty.[30]

In spite of such findings, most studies of the Marshall hypothesis offer at least qualified support—regardless of the nature of the testing—but significant caveats exist.[31] Studies testing the Marshall hypothesis tend to ask subjects about their opinions on the death penalty before and after reading scripts or short essays containing facts about the administration of capital punishment in the United States.[32,33] Other studies were based on first-day and last-day surveys of students who were taking death penalty classes.[34]

Death penalty expert Robert Bohm conducted many of the latter types of studies. He summarizes the findings of his tests by saying:

> In sum, results of this research provided at least qualified support for all three of Marshall's hypotheses. Subjects generally lacked knowledge about the death penalty and its administration prior to exposure to the experimental stimulus but were more informed following it. To the degree that retribution provided the basis for support of the death penalty, knowledge had little effect on opinions. The hypothesis that an informed public would generally oppose the death penalty was supported in one test but not in others.[35]

Even though more students reported being against capital punishment after taking death penalty classes than before, a follow-up with the students 2, 3, and 10 years later found that their support for capital punishment had rebounded to about its original levels. Bohm suggests that the changed opinions "do not appear to be a function of a loss of knowledge, the irrelevancy of the death penalty class, or the influence of the instructor." It may be because "death penalty opinions are based primarily on emotion rather than on cognition and that, in the long run, cognitive influences on death penalty opinions give way to emotional factors."[36]

The most recent published study of the Marshall hypothesis at the time of this writing is a study of 70 undergraduate students at a large, urban Florida university.[37] It found that death penalty supporters were somewhat less informed than death penalty opponents, and that increased knowledge of realities of capital punishment were associated with increased opposition of the punishment. However, those who based their support on retribution were no less likely to change their minds than those who based their support on other justifications. The study found that half of the students in the class either stopped supporting the punishment, supported it less, or opposed it more. Students were also more likely to support life imprisonment without the possibility of parole at the end of the course than before it.

Although it is not clear what an effective strategy for spreading information about the realities of American capital punishment is, I speculate that if Americans knew and truly understood the problems with the death penalty identified by the experts in this book, they would be far less likely to support it than they currently do.

In fact, a reasonable conclusion reached by death penalty scholar Craig Haney is that public support for capital punishment . . . has depended on a *lack* of understanding about . . . how the death penalty actually operates in our society. The more people know about what really happens in the overall administration of capital punishment, the less inclined they are to support it. Thus, preserving our system of death sentencing depends in some ways on preserving the public's lack of accurate knowledge about how it actually functions.[38]

Conversely, reforming (or abolishing) capital punishment will likely require informing people about the realities of capital punishment in the United States.

Some may wonder whether the American way of execution—hiding executions from the public and conducting them at night—is intended to keep the death penalty invisible. If so, why? Two possible explanations are that Americans don't support capital punishment strongly enough to actually see it, and the invisibility of America's death penalty practice maintains our ignorance.[39] I don't know if either (or both) of these explanations is true, but each is logical enough given what we know about capital punishment.

THE OPINION OF THE EXPERTS

Support of Capital Punishment

> Do you believe in capital punishment/the death penalty, or are you opposed to it?

As shown in Table 6.4, a very large majority of death penalty experts in this study (80%) indicated that they are opposed to capital punishment. Only 9% of experts who responded to the survey expressed support for capital punishment, and 11% said they were not sure.

TABLE 6.4   Degree of Support by Experts for Capital Punishment

Do you believe in capital punishment/the death penalty, or are you opposed to it?	
Believe in	9%
Opposed	80%
Unsure	11%

Note: N = 44.

I Am Opposed to the Death Penalty

The experts indicated a variety of reasons why they oppose the death penalty, including that they felt it is immoral, politically motivated, ineffective at meeting its goals and providing closure to families, discriminatory by race and social class, arbitrary and capricious, highly costly, and that it produces wrongful convictions and executions of the innocent.

Most experts did not explicitly mention the morality issue, but some did. For example, one expert explained that he is "ethically/morally opposed to [the] deliberate taking of life except when necessary and unavoidable." Another expert rejected the utility of the "facts" and provided a response dealing only with ethics, writing that

> supporting/opposing the [death penalty] is finally a value judgment or ethical statement—that is, the factual content of the situation doesn't support either the pro or the anti position. So I'll use this space to state my own ethical position (a pretty utopian one, I admit). My ideal is a participatory democracy in which citizens are active in information-seeking and debate, and can apply reason and interpret facts, especially statistical findings. I also have a concern for every person's ethical integrity (what I think some would call the soul). The integrity of one who murders is already compromised, but the rest of us can retain that part of our integrity by not taking yet another life. I also have concern for those whose loved one has been murdered. I'm writing a book on this subject now, and I find that survivors are, understandably, vulnerable to the appeal of vengeance. But those who do best emotionally are those who resist that appeal.

However, most experts addressed the issue of ineffectiveness. For example:

- "It does not deter others from committing similar crimes in the future."
- "Capital punishment fails on every empirical criterion. It does not provide any benefits that can be demonstrated to outweigh its many failures."
- "Although I understand family and community's need for closure & 'vengeance,' I do not think capital punishment (CP) provides the benefits that are often attributed to it. Furthermore, there are significant costs and problems associated with CP. It is operationally insignificant (in terms of overall criminal justice system functioning) yet it demands considerable attention & concern. In general, I just do not think the state should be in the business of killing its citizens. While some extreme cases, such as Timothy McVeigh, occasionally

reduce my outrage factor about CP, I generally just do not think it is necessary, fool proof, or appropriate."

Other experts expounded on the issue of ineffectiveness and also pointed out issues with the death penalty that they felt were problematic. For example, one expert explained: "There is no need for it, and there are many problems with it." Another expert added: "Studies do not indicate that capital punishment resolves criminal justice issues apart from retribution. Given the high possibility of mistakes and/or biases in its application, I cannot in good conscience condone capital punishment." Still another expert wrote: "I oppose capital punishment not for religious beliefs, but on practical and ethical [grounds]. In particular, the death penalty is the most barbaric criminal sanction in the world, serving no fundamental purpose other than retribution. In addition, executions end an additional life and the possibility of correcting error, striking at one of the most fundamental elements of democracy: 'no innocent person should be executed.'"

Still another expert wrote:

> It fails to serve as an effective deterrent; it fails to provide an effective marginal incapacitative effect; it expresses vengeance not retribution; it fails to provide or delays closure; it is administered in an arbitrary and capricious manner; it is discriminatory; it leads to irrevocable errors (innocents sentenced to death <u>and</u> executed); it is costly; and most Americans would prefer an alterative to it. In short, it meets none of its designed purpose[s] and is dysfunctional and harmful.

Another expert discussed the issue of effectiveness and offered his own assessment of the problems with capital punishment:

> There are so many reasons, but the overriding one is that I just simply believe that it makes no sense to kill people in response to them killing people. Beyond this, I believe that the death penalty is deeply and inherently flawed as social policy. It has very little utility (i.e., it does not deter, save money, etc.) and, I believe, does only more harm to co-victims, death workers, family of the condemned, and to society more generally.

Another expert wrote: "In the abstract I don't believe that the state has the right to take a life. [Capital punishment] is barbaric and uncivilized. In application, there are too many problems with the [death penalty]—racial disparity, innocence, etc." Similarly, another expert noted: "I believe that there are many problems with the administration of capital punishment in this country. My main reasons include the following—innocence, racial discrimination [and] cost."

Problematic aspects of the way in which capital punishment is administered were commonly noted by respondents. One expert explained: "Historically, the death penalty has been plagued by problems—racial, gender, class bias—and it is too easy to believe that these problems have been eliminated. Also, it is a retributive punishment that goes against what many civilized nations stand for. In some cases, supporters of the death penalty are just as fierce as the offenders they want to execute." Another said: "My experience is that achieving fairness in capital cases is an unattainable goal. Racism, poverty, incompetence of counsel and prosecutorial misconduct infect capital prosecutions. Mortals are not equipped—whether judges, jurors or prosecutors to play God." Another agreed, noting "errors in judgment" in capital punishment, and saying the punishment "communicates [the] message of [the] appropriateness of killing."

Still another expert identified four problems with the death penalty that explain his opposition to the punishment: "1) Costs—it is very costly to put a person to death. 2) Innocent people are sentence[d] to death. 3) It is wrong to take life. 4) It is unfairly administered—the poor and people of color [are] most likely to be sentenced to death."

An additional expert listed his own reasons for opposing the punishment: "1) Ineffective, as a crime control policy. 2) Immoral, in using the state's power to kill. 3) Expensive, with the costly appellate process. 4) Haphazard, in failing to select those who deserve death. 5) Uncertain, in sometimes convicting the innocent. 6) Traumatic, to family and friends on both sides."

And another respondent explained:

> I oppose the death penalty for a number of different reasons. First and foremost, though, my opposition is based on the fact that there is little sense in how it is applied. You may have two crimes, essentially the same. One person gets death and one gets a lesser sentence. I saw that here in Oklahoma, six weeks before a woman was executed for hiring someone to kill her husband, another woman was sentenced to ten years for an almost identical murder. It also does not make sense to me to sentence someone to death for the crime of murder—how have we solved anything? Often, we have instead created a whole new class of victims—the family of the offender. Additionally, it is costly, it does not serve as a general deterrent, it is racially biased, and it is really often a political tool to advance the career of a prosecutor.

One expert offered his own reasons for opposing capital punishment, citing both philosophical and empirical realities:

> First, I agree with Beccaria and disagree with Mill in that the death penalty does not necessarily demonstrate respect for life; rather, it

demonstrates quite the opposite. Second, the penalty cannot be administered fairly (as Justice Stewart noted in *Furman v. Georgia*, there is no way to distinguish between those who get it and those who do not). Third, the punishment is given to the poor and disadvantaged. Granted, the injustices apply across the system of punishment in America, but as the Court has noted on numerous occasions, "death is different."

Another expert explained his opposition to capital punishment, saying the issue is "not always a question of belief or disbelief: If necessary to keep a society together, then I favor it. Some states can't afford proper trials. Justice isn't free and often [is] imperfect in poorer states. Wealthy states don't need it to continue into the future. They can easily afford—[and] do afford—life imprisonment. I oppose capital punishment in the US, UK & elsewhere on these grounds."

Two respondents (one a Quaker and the other a Catholic) explicitly explained their opposition to capital punishment on religious grounds. One added that he opposed it "also for policy reasons. I do not think the death penalty does anything to reduce crime and I believe it increases crime."

The most complete answer to the question regarding belief in or opposition to the death penalty was this:

> The death penalty has not been shown to deter crime; if there is any deterrent effect it is beyond our ability to measure. Recent econometric studies purporting to find a deterrent effect do not change that conclusion because they suffer from a variety of defects, including failure to utilize appropriate comparisons, inappropriate methods of statistical analysis, missing or erroneous data, inappropriate selection of time frames, inappropriate lag times, failure to test for alternative factors, failure to appropriately consider the effect of a few strong outliers, and the like.[40]

This expert added:

> As James Marquart and Jon Sorensen's research shows, the death penalty also fails to incapacitate effectively. We would have to execute nearly 600 people to prevent seven murders, and would likely execute as many or more innocent people than we could save by incapacitation. There have been 122 persons exonerated since the reinstitution of capital punishment since Gary Gilmore was executed in 1977. Moreover, it is almost certain that we have executed one or more innocent persons. The Griffin case from Missouri comes to mind. Execution of the innocent undercuts both utilitarian (consequentialist) and deontological (retributive or non-consequentialist) bases for capital punishment.

. . . Studies . . . convince me that we are unable to administer capital punishment in a racially neutral fashion.[41] Moreover, socioeconomic disparities in administration give us a punishment that is almost exclusively for the poor irrespective of desert. The weight of scholarship on this issue is quite persuasive and is about as conclusive as things can get in a social science that is by its nature provisional.

Executions cost far more than imprisonment. The tax dollars saved would provide more police, jails, prisons, courts, treatment programs, schools, universities and the like, thus making us safer in the long run. Speeding executions up, by reducing the protections afforded by the judicial system, would not likely reduce costs to the point of making capital punishment cost less than life imprisonment and, we would exacerbate the already difficult issue of executing the innocent.

Moreover, the present system is unnecessarily cruel—inmates (some of whom are innocent) stay on death row for many years thus subjecting them to the psychologically and emotionally debilitating "death row syndrome" first noted by their Lordships of the Privy Counsel, in *Pratt v. Jamaica*. The innocence problem thus cuts directly against the cost problem. We cannot reduce costs by speeding things up because we will then execute more innocent people. At the same time, we cannot provide more judicial protections (thus slowing things down further) without making the emotional and psychological strain of death row even worse. Thomas Hobson could not have devised a more difficult conundrum.

Finally, our international isolation on this issue, which manifests itself in more difficult extradition practices, lack of compliance with the Vienna Convention on Consular Relations, diplomatic friction, and lessened cooperation internationally on a host of other issues, make us pay an increasingly steep price for keeping this ultimate punishment.

One respondent did offer less harsh opposition, based on his experience with the death penalty in the Northeast: "I am opposed to the death penalty as practiced in the South, but I am ambivalent to a more careful statute such as that proposed by the Hoffman Commission in Massachusetts."[42]

Another offered what might be considered qualified support:

As I have said in print, I do not think the death [penalty] is in itself inhumane or out of proportion to some crimes. I have, however, lived in a state without the death penalty as well as in two states with it. My impression is that the death penalty badly muddles criminal justice, leading judges, prosecutors, and defense attorneys to thing[s] they ought not (and would not were a life not at stake). Those convicted do not go quietly to their punishment but themselves become objects of sympathy and notoriety. All this without any obvious effect on the murder rate.

I Believe in the Death Penalty

Of the supporters, two expressed unqualified support for the punishment. One wrote: "I believe that if capital punishment is used with sufficient frequency, it would be a strong deterrent to homicide. I also believe that it could be applied with adequate fairness to obviate any reasonable equity objection." Another said: "Retribution: some crimes are so horrible that the perpetrators deserve to die."

Two others offered reserved support for death as a punishment. For example, one expert wrote: "I am not morally opposed to capital punishment. I regard it as a reasonable policy option, the adoption of which is the province of the electorate. I wouldn't go as far as to say 'I believe in it.'" Finally, one expert noted: "I'm not sure I believe in it, but I can see myself supporting it in some rare but especially atrocious cases."

Unsure

The two experts who answered "unsure" wrote: "I believe a society has a right to impose whatever sanction it wishes on those who violate its norms and laws. However, I do not trust the capricious justice system to do so fairly and equitably"; and: "Instrumental questions & moral questions are inseparable."

Appropriate Punishment for First-Degree Murderers

> What is the most appropriate punishment for someone convicted of first-degree murder?

When asked what the most appropriate punishment is for someone convicted of first-degree murder, all capital punishment experts who participated in this study answered "life imprisonment without parole" (37%) or "other" (63%). As shown in Table 6.5, no experts (0%) indicated capital punishment. Other punishments specified by respondents included life imprisonment with the opportunity for parole, 25 years imprisonment to life, and other terms of imprisonment (e.g., a long term of imprisonment with parole consideration after 10 years, life with the possibility of parole after 20 years, life imprisonment with the possibility of parole after 25 years, 50 years with the possibility of parole after 25 years).

TABLE 6.5   Expert Opinion on the Appropriate Sentence for Convicted
Murderers

What is the most appropriate punishment for someone convicted of first-degree murder?

Death sentence	0%
Life imprisonment without the possibility of parole	37%
Other	63%

Note: N = 43.

The Appropriate Punishment Depends

Many experts noted that the appropriate sentence "depends." Answers included:

- "Depends on [the] circumstances. I can imagine some circumstances where capital punishment would be an excessive penalty even for first-degree murder. Possibly the 'victim' had been terrorizing the 'perp' and the police were unable to intervene. To deal with these cases, however, there should possibly be added to the criminal code a new justification for homicide in the nature of 'preemptive self-defense' or some such thing. I'm thinking of potentially violent stalkers."
- "Depends on the circumstances of the murder."
- "It would depend on the circumstances of the crime and culpability of the defendants. Someone who rapes and kills a child, absent strong mitigating circumstances, should be executed. I would not recommend the death penalty for someone who robs & kills a criminally involved acquaintance (i.e., drug dealer)."
- "I could not support the [death penalty] in all first-degree murder cases. I could support it in exceptional cases, such as for serial murderers."
- "Depends on [the] reprehensibility of [the] offense."
- "It depends on the circumstances of the case. First-degree murder can cover a wide range of situations and levels of culpability. I support LWOP for the most aggravated cases; less aggravated cases might more appropriately receive life with a chance of parole after some term of year[s]."
- The sentence "needs to be flexibly assessed in each case."

Another expert (who suggested both life imprisonment with a minimum term with the possibility of parole for some offenders and life imprisonment without parole for others) wrote: "I think it depends on the offender of the crime. I think some states, such as Ohio, have good options of life without parole and life with parole eligibility after 20, 25, or 30 years. Retributively, I think there is some minimum incarceration, but I also recognize that some offenders may never be ready to rejoin society or it may require a very long sentence."

Another respondent also agreed, suggesting a term of imprisonment

varying on factors of the offense and offender: I don't think we should simply lock up all people who commit certain crimes and "throw away the key." I think it denies the humanity of individuals to use either the death penalty or LWOP across the board (I do believe that there may be rare cases in which someone should perhaps never be released, but to make either of these the default punishment for all first-degree murder is not acceptable to me). Finally, I believe in the ability for transformation and change in human beings, including first-degree murderers.

An additional expert provided a similar response, writing:

Whatever is the maximum penalty in the state: My view is that there is no absolutely right penalty for any crime, only a relatively right penalty given the scale. The end points of that scale may be set, without injustice or waste, within a wide range. The lowest penalty should not be so low as to be a matter of indifference to a rational person; the highest penalty should be no higher than necessary to keep crime within reasonable bounds. My personal judgment is that a state like Illinois might do about as well as it does now with a maximum penalty of twenty, perhaps even ten, years imprisonment. If so, then that is the maximum penalty I'd assign even for multiple or serial murder—even with all the aggravating circumstances the press so loves.

Another respondent asked:

How can you assume that all first-degree murders are the same and that there is just one appropriate response? Circumstances vary, offenders vary, crimes vary. If you asked what I considered to be the most appropriate response for "the worst of the worst" (perhaps someone who repeatedly took lives for the pleasure of it), I would say most likely life without parole. But, even this would depend. That person might belong in a psychiatric hospital with locked wards.

A final expert suggested that "either or both [death sentence or life imprisonment without parole] are appropriate depending on the nature of the crime and the disposition of the offender."

Respondents justified selecting these alternatives to the death penalty with several different rationales. One expert explained that "life with parole maintains <u>hope</u>, provides a deterrent effect (both general and specific), is an effective incapacitant, is retributive, is correctable (not irrevocable), is supported by the public, and is less expensive." Another respondent who specified the punishment of life imprisonment with the possibility of parole after 25 years and 50 years with the possibility of parole after 25 years said:

> I cannot suggest "life without hope," which is what life w/o parole constitutes; that, to my mind, constitutes cruel and unusual punishment. Of course, I believe that some people can never be granted parole (Charles Manson comes to mind). But while in prison some people do change [and] can return to society and make a meaningful contribution perhaps. I also believe that family members of murder victims should be heard, if they want, when it comes time to consider parole; their voices, however, should not be a deciding factor one way or the other; their opinions need to be considered as part of the process.

Another respondent agreed about the importance of having the opportunity to correct errors: "In general, I believe that if someone is convicted of 1st [degree] murder, they are dangerous [and] should be locked up for life. If it turns out that the person did not commit the crime, they could be released from prison."

An additional expert indicated he supported alternatives to death because of "systemic racism in the criminal justice system." Presumably, this expert was not comfortable taking life given the irrevocability of the punishment. Another expert wrote:

> Considering the nature of homicide in the United States, life imprisonment with the possibility of parole would be the most logical, practical, and just sanction for first-degree murder—allowing time to uncover possible error and preventing the state from warehousing elderly inmates who no longer pose a threat to society, at a high expense due to issues like medical care. Given the increase in elderly population, it is probable that law suits will increase for age discrimination in prison, including people on death row.

One expert wrote that LWOP "will provide a severe enough penalty not to trivialize murder (meets the goal of retribution)." Another respondent agreed: "Life imprisonment without parole (LWOP) is an appropriate sentence. . . . A tough sentence like LWOP is needed. Without LWOP, some people would feel the need to impose the death penalty on offenders." Similarly, a different expert suggested: "Without capital punishment as an option, LWOP becomes the next available option." Another expert agreed, writing that LWOP "provides just deserts, provided executive clemency is a real option." Still another expert added: "I think judges should have discretion to determine sentence. I think LWOP should be available as an option because some people need to be permanently incapacitated, but I think that is in the minority of cases. Otherwise, long-term imprisonment should be available and in most cases 20 years is a sufficient sentence."

One expert answered that she did not "know the answer, and I haven't found much creative thinking out there in the literature." She continued by suggesting LWOP may be too harsh of an alternative:

> Our focus on this subject seems one-dimensional—lock them up and throw away the key. I don't think every criminal can be rehabilitated; a percentage are probably permanently dangerous. But, as wardens have pointed out to me, there are problems with even "effective" life sentences of 40–50 years, let alone life without parole. How do you manage (=control) a large population of individuals who have no hope of release? I would like to see an in-prison environment where the convicted have the obligation and opportunity to make some degree of restitution. Equally important, an environment that might be a constructive society-within-a-society, where incarceration is the given, but education and meaningful work are available. If life without parole is served in a super-max, where conditions are almost those of solitary confinement, I think LWOP may eventually be challenged legally as inhumane. Michigan's legislature, when discarding the [death penalty] in 1846, first mandated solitary confinement as part of the life sentence, but removed that stipulation after finding that long-term solitary confinement caused prisoners to lose their sanity. Unfortunately, there are very few cases in human history where the tax-paying public has been willing to spend money on a rational system of incarceration.

Another expert proposed the opportunity for parole "recognizing that many convicted first-degree murderers would never get paroled." He offered the following as his rationale: "Follow-ups of the *Furman*-commuted inmates show that some of them, following parole, have lived exemplary lives. Also, an inmate in his 70s or 80s probably poses little risk to the community, if paroled. It would probably be much cheaper to support him outside of prison than inside of prison."

Another rationale for alternatives to the death penalty included this: "Executing persons often has a brutalization effect where murder rates rise slightly after executions. We can never be absolutely certain a person has committed a first-degree offense [and] there is always the possibility of new evidence or scientific techniques that might support innocence. We must leave open the window for such a state of affairs, if we can."

Here is another rationale offered by an expert for alternatives to the death penalty:

> Most, but not all, murderers will either be rehabilitated or will grow out of the point at which they are likely to commit further crimes. Parole should be an option for most murderers. Serial killers, stickup artists, and perhaps some others, are the exception. Indeed, in many democracies, life without the possibility of parole is not an available sentencing option, and, indeed, an increasing number of countries not only refuse to extradite without assurances as to the death penalty but also limit the number of years that a person may serve, thus eliminating true life sentences.

Finally, two experts noted their belief that LWOP may actually be a worse punishment than death. One wrote: "For some offenders, LWOP is a far worse punishment than death, especially if the offender must serve a term that is decades long. LWOP should mean just that––what is the harm in keeping an offender in prison for life if he/she cannot kill again?" Another suggested: "I consider LWOP to be a worse, more severe punishment than death."

Moratorium or Abolition?

> Do you personally favor a temporary halt to executions (moratorium) in the United States while the practice of American capital punishment is studied?

As shown in Table 6.6, the vast majority of death penalty experts (79%) answered in the affirmative to the question, "Do you personally favor a temporary halt to executions (moratorium) in the United States while the practice of American capital punishment is studied?" Another 14% of experts answered no and 7% said they were not sure.

TABLE 6.6   Degree of Support by Death Penalty Experts for a Moratorium of Executions

Do you personally favor a temporary halt to executions (moratorium) in the United States while the practice of American capital punishment is studied?

Yes	79%
No	14%
Unsure	7%

Note: N = 44.

I Favor a Moratorium

The reasons given by experts in support of moratoria were diverse. One expert said that the death penalty, under the precedent of *Furman*, should "be ruled per se unconstitutional. That is, the extant research since *Gregg* has well established that all of the infirmities found under *Furman* are still present under *Gregg*." Another wrote: "I think we must look at the system. There are so many flaws. The ones that the *Gregg* ruling was designed to overcome are more prevalent than ever. It is a 'broken system,' to quote so many others such as Liebman."[43]

Some experts were adamant about a moratorium. One simply replied: "Executions are pointless." Another said: "If we as a society want to show the world that we are civilized then we need to." Another wrote: "Until unanswered questions are answered, yes, a moratorium is appropriate." And another expert suggested: "A moratorium would delay if not prevent some executions. Repeated application and withdrawal of a moratorium might help expose [capital punishment] as the political football it is."

One expert gave an affirmative response, saying:

> As former Governor of Illinois, George Ryan, did recently, a moratorium should be implemented nationwide to fix the logistics of capital punishment and fix the mechanics of the execution process. In regards to investigation, there is plenty of information documenting some of the most pressing issues . . . what's needed is the will, energy, honesty, and resources to begin the rehabilitation process of capital punishment in America. . . . We need to rehabilitate the system before we rehabilitate criminals.

One expert was more cautious, saying he supports moratoria on "a state-by-state basis." Another said: "The death penalty is perhaps THE most studied aspect of the criminal justice system. I am not sure what more research is going to say or whether it would change policy. Perhaps the publicized reports of factually innocent executions could swing public opinion, but perhaps not—and that is a scary thought." One respondent simply answered: "Sure. Good luck with this one."

Other experts actually said that they wanted to see abolition of capital punishment instead of a moratorium on executions. These responses included:

- "I wish capital punishment to be ended. I will accept a moratorium at this time. I hope a moratorium will show people that murderers can be punished without death, and the death penalty does not deter people from committing murder."

- "Frankly, I don't believe it needs to be studied any longer to abolish it. Thirty years after *Gregg*, the system is still flawed and probably can never be made acceptable (to those who want a fair system)."
- "I prefer abolition of the death penalty, but since that is not politically feasible in many jurisdictions a moratorium is a way to stop the killings temporarily."
- "I favor a permanent halt, but I'm not going to reject a temporary one."
- "It's better than nothing."
- "But I would go further and abolish the [death penalty] altogether. It is hypocritical of the U.S. to champion human rights while at the same time stand on the same level as China, North Korea, and other countries in utilizing capital punishment."

Another expert noted how abolition would be superior to a moratorium on executions:

> This is a difficult subject and the answer is too complex for a short survey answer. . . . An experimental moratorium to fix the system may result in fewer innocent people being executed, but it cannot solve the problem. Thus, there are good retributive arguments for abolishing capital punishment. But most nations have experimented with moratoria before abolishing capital punishment entirely. So as a practical matter a moratorium is probably a necessary first step but I am not in favor [of] trying to fix an inherently unfixable system.

Two other experts said they support a moratorium due to "too many examples of innocents sentenced to death" and "errors in judgment."

I Do Not Favor a Moratorium

Of those few experts who did not support a moratorium, they replied:

- "Absolutely not. The death penalty has been studied to death. This is a ploy by abolitionists to save the lives of condemned murderers."
- "I think it has been studied enough. We all know the issues. However, I believe that there are some defendants that are deserving of the [death penalty]."
- "I doubt study would produce any new information one way or the other. And it would certainly put off the state-by-state abolition that seems to be occurring—mostly by the indefinite postponement of executions. It would also put off the federal government's rethinking of capital punishment. Every time the feds try to extradite

someone from Europe, South America, Canada, or almost anywhere else, they must promise not to use the death penalty. Globalization is making the death penalty ever more inconvenient. Let the process work itself out."

- "We had a moratorium from the mid-sixties to the mid-seventies. The homicide rate skyrocketed. Capital punishment opponents either ignored the rise or shrugged it off. If an experiment is desired, I'd rather see an experiment in more liberal application of capital punishment. For example, prior to 1950, approximately 50 percent of those convicted of first-degree homicide in the United Kingdom were executed by hanging. If in the United States over a period of 10 years, we executed 50 percent of those convicted of first-degree homicide, and there was no perceptible downward movement in the homicide rate, then I would be more likely to believe the claims of capital punishment opponents that capital punishment has little if any deterrent effect. I would certainly be far more receptive to abolition than I am now."

Unsure

Those experts unsure about a moratorium offered similar answers. One simply said that "the question must be state specific." Another wrote:

The moratorium strategy is based on the assumption that if executing jurisdictions pause to assess their post-*Furman* system, they will conclude that the system is too flawed to be allowed to continue. Then, presumably, they will abolish the death penalty. This strategy ignores several points: 1) We had a de facto moratorium from 1967 till 1977 and that did not result in abolition; 2) Correcting the most egregious flaws in the current death sentencing systems may very well simply give new life to those systems and continue executions for a longer period than would otherwise have been the case; 3) Correcting obvious flaws (such as sleeping lawyers) may increase public confidence in the system without making any difference in other more deeply embedded flaws (such as racial bias in charging). The strength of the moratorium strategy is that it allows alliances with people who are not concerned about the use of the death penalty as such, but who are concerned that the system not commit blatant injustices.

Does capital punishment, as actually practiced in the United States, have problems that are serious enough to make it unacceptable as a government-sanctioned punishment (so that states should permanently stop executing convicted murderers)?

TABLE 6.7   Degree of Support by Death Penalty Experts for Abolition of Capital Punishment

Does capital punishment, as actually practiced in the United States, have problems that are serious enough to make it unacceptable as a government-sanctioned punishment (so that states should permanently stop executing convicted murderers)?

Yes	84%
No	14%
Unsure	2%

Note: N = 44.

As shown in Table 6.7, the vast majority of death penalty experts (84%) also answered in the affirmative to the question, "Does capital punishment, as actually practiced in the United States, have problems that are serious enough to make it unacceptable as a government-sanctioned punishment (so that states should permanently stop executing convicted murderers)?" Another 14% of experts answered no, and only one respondent (2%) indicated he was unsure.

Capital Punishment Is Unacceptable as a Government-Sanctioned Punishment

The reasons given by experts in support of indicating that capital punishment is an unacceptable punishment included racial and geographic disparities, cost, innocence, unfair administration, and immorality. Many of the experts merely referred to answers given on previous questions about racial bias, class bias, gender bias, and a moratorium on executions. For example, one expert wrote: "The points above indicate the scope of problems with the current administration of the death penalty and make abolition a matter of justice. In addition, our use of the death penalty isolates us from our allies abroad and contributes to the terrible reputation of the US around the world."

Some experts justified their opinions about abolishing capital punishment with lists of problems with the penalty. For example, one wrote: "There are substantial assistance of counsel issues, prosecutorial & police misconduct, jury problems, procedural problems, arbitrary & discriminatory application, & miscarriages of justices (wrongful convictions & probably wrongful executions)—to name a few." Another expert answered: "Absolutely—the justice systems in the United States at both the federal and state levels have been trying for decades to improve their systems to ensure fairness and accuracy. This has not happened and I do not believe it is an attainable goal." Yet another expert agreed, writing: "With so many problems of implementation, capital punishment cannot be applied with sufficient provisions to make it an acceptable punishment, even assuming one does not object to it on philosophical grounds." Another expert wrote: "Cost, errors, innocence, bias all combine to make it a poor public policy choice."

Other respondents referred to the issue of mistakes and innocence:

- "Yes. For every innocent person freed, you have to wonder how many were executed."
- "I do not think it is possible to create governmental actions that will be error free. Given the consequences of capital punishment, that is particularly problematic. I always find it interesting that people who do not trust the government to collect taxes, educate children, fix potholes, provide health care, etc., because they believe [government] is corrupt, inefficient, and incompetent are often the same people who strongly support the state's ability to execute its citizens."
- "Human error has fatal consequences."
- "Given that there are no good instrumental reasons to retain the death penalty, given the problem of executing the innocent, and given our international isolation on this with their attendant legal and diplomatic costs, we will have no choice in the long run but to abolish capital punishment. If abolition is inevitable, then. . . 'Is it right to kill death row inmates during this period of experimentation'?"[44]

Another expert did refer to philosophical grounds to justify his answer, saying: "The state should never send out the message that killing is ok." An additional expert concluded: "It is mainly a symbolic punishment, in which states pick and choose who will be executed. This simply is not fair." And another said capital punishment should be abolished because there are "few benefits and high costs." He concluded that capital punishment is a "bad, unnecessary policy." Similarly, another offered this rationale:

> If we stop for a second, analyze the data by the totality of events, issues, circumstances, and experiences, we will realize that the ramifications (which are many) of capital punishment outweigh the benefits (which are few) substantially. In fact, if we take a serious and honest venture into capital punishment, we will have great difficulty finding a "benefit," beyond retribution. Yet, we will quickly find a substantial number of consequences—e.g., executing innocent people, executing mentally ill people, executing people in violation of human rights,

executing foreign nationals in violation of international treaties, executing people in violation of constitutional rights, executing people with limited due process. For example: constitutional rights are conveyed in words. Yet, foreign nationals who cannot read or write have been forced to sign homicide confessions in English they cannot understand. In court, it is common not to provide quality court interpretation (and, at times, no interpretation at all) to non-English defendants. In which case, the legal system is making a mockery out of the Constitution.

Capital Punishment Is Not Unacceptable as a Government-Sanctioned Punishment

Of those handful of experts who answered no to the question regarding abolition of capital punishment, their reasons included:

- "The death penalty, as currently administered in most jurisdictions and with oversight of the courts, is being implemented in a manner that is as safe and fair as humanly possible."
- "I don't think it needs to be abandoned, but it should be limited to the most serious cases."
- "The key is deterrence. If you believe in deterrence, as I do, then the adverse side-effects of capital punishment can be accepted without concluding that capital punishment, on the whole, is a dysfunctional social institution."
- "I don't think there is any knock-down argument against the death penalty—as there is, say, against torture. There are, however, a good many arguments that ought to incline a reasonable person to favor prohibition—and very few good arguments on the other side."

Unsure

Only one expert was unsure about whether capital punishment was unacceptable, but he did not give a reason for his response.

Summary of Expert Opinion of Capital Punishment

In summary, the death penalty experts who participated in this study were generally opposed to capital punishment and unanimously favored alternatives to capital punishment for convicted first-degree murderers, such as life imprisonment without parole, life imprisonment with the opportunity for parole, and very long prison sentences depending on the nature of the offender and the offense. The rationales offered in defense of alternatives to capital punishment were varied, but tended to revolve around the inability of capital punishment to meet its goals of retribution, deterrence, and incapacitation, as well as the numerous problems with the application of the death penalty in the United States. Although 78% of capital punishment experts who responded to this survey stated their opposition to capital punishment, not a single expert (0%) answered that the most appropriate sentence for convicted murderers was death. Instead, the experts recommended life imprisonment without the possibility of parole (37.5%) or some other term of imprisonment (62.5%). This is perhaps the clearest indication in this study that capital punishment experts do not support the death penalty.

Additionally, the vast majority of death penalty experts said they supported a temporary halt to executions (moratorium) in the United States so that the death penalty can be studied, and that they would support a permanent end to capital punishment due to problems that were serious enough to make capital punishment "unacceptable as a government-sanctioned punishment." Their stated rationales were varied, but again tended to focus on the ineffectiveness of capital punishment and the very real problems with its application in the United States.

POLICIES JUSTIFIED BY THE FINDINGS OF THIS BOOK

The research presented in this book found that capital punishment experts think the death penalty does not achieve its goals of retribution, deterrence, and incapacitation, that the administration of capital punishment is biased against people of color and the poor (and to a lesser degree women), that the death penalty has been used against the innocent, and that it is plagued by many other significant problems. Not surprisingly, death penalty experts are overwhelmingly against the punishment, unanimously do not recommend death sentences as the most appropriate punishment for convicted first-degree murderers, and overwhelmingly support a moratorium on executions, as well as abolition of capital punishment.

By both standards of policy evaluation laid out in Chapter 3—goals analysis and costs–benefits analysis—the death penalty, as actually practiced in the United States, is a failed policy. Thus, it is reasonable to suggest that states in the United States abandon capital punishment and replace it with alternative sanctions that would more effectively meet the goals of punishment and achieve benefits that might outweigh the costs (e.g., life imprisonment without the possibility of parole, or LWOP).

Although it is true that LWOP would still be plagued by the same problems as capital punishment—biased against people of color, the poor (and to a lesser degree women), used against the innocent, and so forth—it is generally cheaper to administer than capital punishment, and it is correctable. Given the finality of death, we cannot afford to continue to utilize a policy that has clearly failed, not when (sometimes innocent) lives are on the line.

As noted by abolitionist Hugo Adam Bedau, the *Minimal Invasion* principle asserts the following:

1) Punishment is justified only if it is necessary as a means to some socially valid end.
2) The death penalty is more severe—more invasive—than long-term imprisonment.
3) Long-term imprisonment is sufficient as an invasion of individual liberty, privacy, and autonomy (and other fundamental values) to achieve valid social goals.
4) Society ought to abolish any lawful practice that imposes more violation of individual liberty, privacy, or autonomy (or other fundamental value) when it is known that a less invasive practice is available and is sufficient.[45]

Bedau concludes: "Killing killers is not minimally invasive."[46]

Notice that by citing this line of reasoning, I am not making, nor have I made anywhere in this book, a moral, ethical, or philosophical argument against capital punishment. Instead, I have used empirical evidence—data—to reach the conclusion that capital punishment is a failed policy. This is consistent with what scholar Herbert Haines calls "pragmatic abolitionism"—attacking the punishment not "as an immoral and inhuman practice" but instead as "an unwise, counterproductive criminal justice policy."[47] This approach focuses on three claims: "1) the crippling expense of maintaining a criminal justice apparatus that includes capital punishment, 2) the demonstrable failure of the death penalty to enhance the safety of law-abiding citizens, and 3) the availability of numerous alternative measures for addressing violent crime that are both just and cost-effective."[48]

Haines concludes that the death penalty makes little sense "in *instrumental* terms": "Its fatal flaw is not its immorality, about which there is vast space for disagreement, but rather its enormous lack of cost-effectiveness," as well as inefficiency.[49] The findings of this book support this conclusion.

Toward Pragmatic Abolition

What line of action should be taken to bring about the end to capital punishment in the United States? At the outset, it should be acknowledged that those who will be involved in efforts to abolish capital punishment should be prepared for a struggle that will take time. For example, abolition in the United Kingdom and Canada went through stages, beginning with the restriction of capital punishment to only certain forms of killings.[50] This may provide further evidence that the process of abolition has already begun in the United States, as death-eligible crimes have shrunk over the years.

There are those who offer specific reforms to "tinker" with the death penalty;[51] however, I prefer to recognize the fallibility of *any* capital punishment system, remove from the table the death penalty option, and set forth strategies aimed at abolition. Many ideas have been presented about how to organize for abolition and what activities to engage in to bring about an end to capital punishment. They generally exist in the areas of "protest and persuasion" (actions to educate people about the realities of American capital punishment), "noncooperation" (refusing to participate in the death penalty process), and "intervention" (efforts to interfere with the death penalty process).[52] The first includes actions such as banner projects, bells and drapes, street theater, protests, mock executions, leafleting, marches, speaking tours, public hearings, classroom teaching, letter writing, petition drives, and vigils. The second includes actions such as economic boycotts. The third involves actions such as fasting, hunger strikes, physical obstruction, and sit-ins. Such efforts should be state specific—organized to address the specific conditions within each state that allow capital punishment to persist.

The most important of these efforts are those that inform Americans and policy makers of the realities of American capital punishment—ones that shine light on the truths of how the death penalty is actually practiced within our country and help overcome the "limited, narrow, and even inaccurate base of knowledge from which to reason and decide about whether and when the ultimate punishment may be justified."[53] Those who believe the findings of this book reflect those truths should write, speak, testify, and engage in other activities that heighten awareness of the realities of capital punishment to policy makers and to citizens. Citizens should be told (and shown) that the death penalty does not achieve its goals of retribution, deterrence, or incapacitation, and that it is plagued by problems of significant extralegal bias and is used against the innocent. They should also be educated about all the other problems of capital punishment identified by experts in this book. Conservatives (who tend to favor capital punishment) should be informed of the economic costs of maintaining and utilizing executions.

Further, the mass media should be challenged to more frequently and diligently cover the realities of America's death penalty practices and stop sensationalizing stories of crime and criminal justice (which has the effect of reinforcing ignorance and strengthening support for crime control policies such as the death penalty).

Finally, citizens in the United States must dedicate themselves to being represented by a government that respects international law and the human rights principles contained within. After all, the documents that formed our government and state the core principles of our founders highlight the importance of international law and human rights.[54] Given that "world law and practice is moving steadily towards abolition of the death penalty," it is only a matter of time until a United States of America that is dedicated to human rights and willingly confines itself to the international laws it has signed (and those that it will sign), abandons capital punishment as the failed policy it is.

There are, of course, many significant barriers to the realization of pragmatic abolition. In the final section of the book, I outline and discuss these barriers and possible ways to overcome them. The barriers flow from responses by the experts about why capital punishment persists in the United States.

WHY CAPITAL PUNISHMENT PERSISTS IN AMERICA

> As you know, many of our allies have abolished the death penalty. In your opinion, why does the death penalty persist in the United States? That is, why do we still use this criminal sanction? Please list and briefly discuss the reason(s) you think the U.S. still practices capital punishment.

Given that the death penalty, as actually practiced in the United States, does not achieve its goals, is plagued by serious problems with its application, and is overwhelmingly opposed by those with great knowledge about it, why does the punishment persist? Is simple ignorance of the facts the reason, or is there more to it?

One question on the survey of capital punishment experts addressed was the issue of why states in the United States continue to practice capital punishment. The question was, "As you know, many of our allies have abolished the death penalty. In your opinion, why does the death penalty persist in the United States? That is, why do we still use this criminal sanction? Please list and briefly discuss the reason(s) you think the U.S. still practices capital punishment."

Death penalty experts responded with various reasons as to why they believe capital punishment persists in America today. There were seven main themes of responses to this question. They include reasons related to the following:

1) History and culture
2) Politics
3) Punishment generally
4) Public support
5) Crime rates in the United States
6) Religion
7) Government structure

America's History and Culture

First, 24 survey respondents listed and discussed historical and cultural reasons that explain why capital punishment persists in the United States. They noted America's long history of violence, including the frontier era of America, as well as America's culture of violence. They identified Americans' desire for blood, and explained that the death penalty is simply tradition in this country.

Respondents also noted the history and culture of the South, discussing issues such as prolonged slavery in the South which led to a high population of African Americans in the United States; racism; the southern culture; and connections between the death penalty, slavery, race, and lynchings in the United States. One respondent discussed "vigilante" attitudes present in the United States, and another mentioned that the United States is a young country that has not yet developed a full distrust in its government when it comes to killing citizens. Finally, one respondent speculated that the persistence of the death penalty may be explained by a backlash against the *Furman v. Georgia* decision and the abolitionist movement.

As one expert briefly explained: "The U.S. has a long culture of violence, individualism, and revenge that fits well with capital punishment." Another expert explained that America's "history and culture (especially in the South)" helps us understand why capital punishment persists in the United States, "which raises the question as to why the history and culture in Europe has not produced ongoing support for the death penalty."

Another expert suggested: "Culturally, we differ in so many ways from other western industrialized nations that it is difficult to compare them. We place tremendous value on individualism, and we hold the individual accountable. We are a country founded on violence that has grown through violence. And, we have the strong fundamentalist background that is blaming and punishing." He ended with: "The list goes on and on."

Similarly, there was the response that "our high levels of religious fundamentalism, our high levels of individuals, persisting racial prejudices." Another expert offered this: "There are probably too many reasons to name, but one that makes sense to me is that the United States is still a very young country and we have not lived through some of the atrocities that other countries, such as those in Western Europe have, that have convinced people to be distrustful of the government."

One death penalty expert provided a straightforward answer, pointing to the American South for his answer:

> The death penalty is today largely a "Southern thing." Northern states that still have it typically have had large movements of Southerners into it in the last hundred years. I'm not a Southerner; so, I have trouble understanding what makes the death penalty so attractive to them. I honestly don't think it is racism. I'm inclined to think, rather, that Southerners favor the death penalty for the same reason they murder each other more frequently than Northerners (and why they make better soldiers). They like bloodshed. There is no doubt one or more dissertations waiting to be written on this subject.

The respondent that mentioned the backlash against the *Furman* decision suggested:

> There are a variety of factors that drive the U.S. position on capital punishment which are quite different from what happened in Europe and other abolitionist regions. As many have noted, *Furman v. Georgia*, which held that the death penalty as then administered violated the 8th Amendment ban on cruel and unusual punishments, was (notwithstanding polls showing ambivalence during the 1960's on the subject) well ahead of the polity in the U.S. and created a backlash that arguably retarded the abolitionist movement.

An additional expert elaborated on the effect of slavery on capital punishment. She wrote: "The existence of slavery formalized and legitimated separate, unequal justice systems. The idea carried on after Abolition in laws passed by both Southern and non-Southern states giving African-Americans lesser access to justice, such as inability to testify against Euro-Americans or serve as jurors."

This respondent also noted other factors and events of U.S. history and culture relevant for why capital punishment persists:

Many cultures now and historically (e.g., France in the Middle Ages) have had a system of extralegal social control justified by repressive moral or religious tenets. The Appalachians are one American seat of this phenomenon—using "shivarees," "whipping bands," or "nightriders" to enforce churchgoing, martial fidelity, and other mores. The energy and rhetoric of this kind of social control contributes an irrational element into the ritual of punishment. But, in America, the punishments weren't usually fatal until post-Civil-War power struggles and/or a commercial rather than subsistence way of life injected acute economic and political competition into the mix. . . .

The Ku Klux Klan of the 1920s (not the terrorist group of the 1860s) played the morals card partly in order to inflame and capitalize on native Euro-Americans' fear of competition from "foreigners and Negroes." The Klan of this period committed rather few acts of violence; most of their clout was political. But their nationwide popularity nationalized and institutionalized both bigotry and sectarian self-righteousness, which still permeate our police, judicial, and penal procedures in spite of the absence of moral prescriptions in our Constitution.

The vigilante movement noted by one respondent was attributed back to the scholarship of Franklin Zimring who, in his book *The Contradictions of American Capital Punishment*, suggested that vigilantism in the South may best explain high execution rates in the South. This respondent wrote that Zimring's thesis has been "backed up with more recent research employing sophisticated multiple regression techniques [that] confirms the connections between the death penalty and slavery, race and lynching in the U.S."[55] Another expert noted Zimring's book, writing:

Frank Zimring's recent book *The Contradictions of American Capital Punishment* has probably the best analysis. Although the military, federal government, and 38 states do have the death penalty, it is important to note that the geographic and cultural distribution of executions is not nearly as widespread. Over 90% of post-*Furman* executions have occurred in states that had slavery in law or practice in 1860. The modern use of the death penalty is very deeply rooted in the history of slavery.

Other norms identified by experts important for explaining why capital punishment persists in the United States include a strong belief in individualism and responsibility, the "Cowboy mentality," and arrogance. The respondent who suggested the Cowboy mentality and arrogance also wrote: "We're Americans. We don't make mistakes." By this, it is assumed he meant that capital punishment persists because citizens don't think we make errors (either through continuing the punishment or executing the innocent).

Another expert explained: "The death penalty exists in the U.S. because of social norms and politicians. Our society has a desire to inflict suffering on others. There is a norm of individualism rather than group good. There is a desire for blood in our society. When things go wrong, there is usually a demand to punish someone." This expert linked this demand with America's "long history of violence" which he says is also "one of the reasons for the desire for handguns in this nation."

Finally, an additional expert wrote:

Capital punishment in the United States persists mostly for historical, political, ideological, religious, economical, and social reasons—having little to do with safety or practicality. Realistically, I consider capital punishment one of the biggest demons that the world has ever invented. Now, what is the driving force behind this demon? The most powerful single driving force is *indifference*.

Executions are brutal, vicious, expensive, irreversible, like an everlasting struggle against cancer that continues to get worse and worse. And, at the very bottom of its motive, there lies a mystery. As the harshest criminal sanction, capital punishment has been nicely coded by promising political language, which is designed to make lies sound truthful, government action logical and honorable, murder by the state legal (with a notion of legitimacy and justice), and to a fragile, feared, and mal-informed society, an appearance of global power and solidarity.

The executioners are part of the legal system and its laws, which are assumed to be unalterable, like the word of God. The executioners are serving the state, which has the power to absolve them from this demon. Yet, they do not even know why they are executing. The executioners accept the law almost as they accept the weather, which is, of course, unpredictable by nature. When questioned, the executioners are likely to [reply] with: 'respect for constitutionalism and legality'!!!

No one would support capital punishment if one were not driven on by some powerful demon whom s/he can neither resist nor understand.

Politics

Second, 13 survey respondents listed and discussed political reasons that explain why capital punishment persists in the United States. They listed politics, political figures, and the media fueling anger against "the enemy," and the political marginalization of liberals as reasons.

For example, one expert explained: "It is politically popular to support death, in all but a few states it is virtual political suicide to oppose it." Another expert suggested: "Politicians play the law & order/death penalty card very effectively (politics of fear)." Still another respondent wrote that the "push by politicians" explains the continuation of capital punishment: "In European nations, political parties control politics and strive to improve society regardless of the poll numbers. In the U.S., politicians push the death penalty as a simple solution to the crime problem. They do not care if it works or not. They only wish simple ideas to push on the public in their bids to be elected or reelected. This in turn increases the desire for capital punishment among the public."

Another expert exclaimed: "I feel that the death penalty persists in the United States for political reasons—the public is completely misinformed about the problems associated with capital punishment and politicians use that to their advantage—they are seen as 'tough on crime' if they are in favor of capital punishment [and] the public appreciates that." Still another expert wrote: "I think the [death penalty] is a political issue—those who oppose the [death penalty] are labeled as 'liberal' and 'soft on crime', etc. and are accused of coddling murderers. The U.S. occupies a unique position—promoting justice and democracy and fairness while at the same time executing its own citizens, often in the face of documented problems." He went on to say:

> The need or desire to be tough on crime has been around for decades, but there is an unwillingness to go out on a limb and admit that, perhaps, tough on crime policies may be counterproductive—if tough on crime isn't working, the instinct is to simply get tougher. Is there a way to step out of this mind set and address the real problems that affect crime in this country—poverty, unemployment, frustration/hopelessness?

One expert's response provides a possible answer to the question asked by the previous respondent: "For the last two decades the liberals/ progressives, who would be likely to lead the campaign to get rid of the death penalty, have been politically marginalized." This respondent implied that, without a strong presence of liberals or progressives to challenge and counter the dominant conservative voice in American politics, it is unlikely that the practice of capital punishment is likely to end anytime soon. Another expert would probably agree, as he explained that the death penalty "has become highly politicized because of intervention of U.S. Supreme Court since 1972, and certainly is much more conservative than Europe."

Still another expert suggested:

> There are numerous explanations/hypotheses for this. In today's political-cultural context, I think that crime (and now terrorism) has replaced communism as our enemy. Every culture has a sense of the other" that they cannot objectively or rationally assess and respond to. Politicians and the media fuel the public's anger and direct

our collective conscience against particular groups as responsible for our problems. I believe the need for reciprocity is fairly innate to humans as is sense of justice, but other countries have redirected those emotions towards other things. Individuals naturally feel outrage and a desire for retribution when an individual does something horrible. It is just as appropriate that such individuals suffer some negative consequences and that society be protected from them. I am not sure that the extreme of capital punishment is necessary or even [a] beneficial response.

A similar response was provided by an additional respondent, who wrote:

While I don't think that [capital punishment] is still used to intimidate and repress, it certainly is used to win elections, usually by discrediting the opposition. Paradoxically, a participatory rather than representative democracy has made public opinion easy to manipulate. The reason, I think, is that interest groups, identity politics, now rule. This situation does not foster discussion—and don't get me started on the spinelessness of most media. Occasionally in the past we've had a true party system based on issues, and at those moments it was possible for leaders (Lincoln, F. Roosevelt, Truman) to inject debate and apply a measure of principle.

Punishment

Third, 13 respondents listed and discussed reasons related to punishment generally that explain why capital punishment persists in the United States. They listed and discussed America's general punitiveness, our desire for vengeance or revenge and retribution, and the need by some for reciprocity and a sense of justice that the death penalty may provide. Another respondent noted the possible role played by the belief in deterrence. Finally, respondents noted possible skepticism about life sentences, a mistrust of indefinite incapacitation, and a lack of faith in rehabilitation as possible reasons why the death penalty persists.

Whereas one expert simply noted "our general punitiveness" as the reason why capital punishment persists in America, other experts were more specific. For example, one respondent simply said: "Vengeance—the death penalty allows US citizens to 'get even' with murderers. That is, we kill them to make ourselves feel better, not to bring closure, and no[t] to re-balance the moral order." Similarly, another expert reasoned: "Many citizens do believe in a strict retributive view that those who kill have forfeited that right to life." Another respondent added that capital punishment persists due to "continued support for retribution and deterrence (that is, death penalty viewed as 'just' . . . criminal gets what he/she deserves) and that it deters others." Each of these experts explained the persistence of capital punishment based on the justifications of capital punishment discussed in Chapter 4. Because the capital punishment experts overwhelmingly agreed that capital punishment fails to achieve deterrence, retribution, and incapacitation in practice, it is likely the experts who explained the persistence of capital punishment using these justifications simply believe that Americans are unaware of the ineffectiveness of the death penalty.

Another expert pointed out that "if the public had more confidence in the sentence of life without parole (really meaning LWOP . . . I never will get out of prison!), they would be less likely to support capital punishment." Similarly, an additional respondent suggested: "We mistrust government institutions, including courts and prisons, so we worry that convicted murderers will not be incapacitated indefinitely." Yet another expert suggested the reason, "lack of faith in rehabilitation [and d]istrust of government—will not impose alternative harsh punishment."

A final reason related to punishment was identified by one respondent. She wrote: "Creation of the large-capacity penitentiary such as those in New York, Pennsylvania, and Ohio had the unintended effect of identifying a 'criminal class,' whose presumed incorrigibility in some cases justified execution. The penitentiary then providing a fully bureaucratized 'procedure' and a remote location for carrying out executions."

Public Support

Fourth, 10 respondents listed and discussed public support as a possible reason why capital punishment persists in the United States. They listed the fact that the death penalty is endorsed by the public and the issue of an ignorant and misinformed public.

For example, one expert wrote: "The populace has endorsed it. In other countries, where it has been abolished (i.e., Canada & England) it is typically abolished by the elites (i.e., courts), while the citizens, as a whole, still generally support the sanction." Another expert answered: "Because it would seem that most people in the U.S. want the [death penalty] as a potential punishment for very serious criminals." And another respondent wrote:

> We continue to use capital punishment in the U.S. because the majority of the citizens support its use. It seems to me that our society does not see the administration of justice. Most criminals disappear into the prison or other parts of the justice mechanisms. When an execution occurs citizens see justice in operation and feel something tangible is being done to "dangerous" criminals. For the average citizen it validates the justice system.

It was agreed that public support plays a role in why capital punishment persists, but some experts suggested that the death penalty was supported by an ignorant or misinformed populace. For example, one expert wrote: "As Justice Marshall noted in *Furman*, people do not understand the reality of the death penalty (and politicians work to keep them in ignorance)." Another respondent agreed, saying: "I strongly believe in the Marshall hypothesis—If the public was fully informed about the problems associated with capital punishment, a majority would oppose it." Another expert suggested: "Public opinion continues to support it, and legislators in the U.S., unlike their counterparts in other countries, are unwilling to go against what is perceived as the public's wishes on this matter." This respondent added: "That the public is largely ignorant about the way capital punishment in this country is actually administered does not seem to matter." Another expert agreed, writing: "Simple: ignorance. Which side of the debate you're on is often like which baseball team you support: arbitrary [and] ignorant of the facts." One respondent noted that the death penalty was "held in place emotionally not rationally."

An additional expert provided some rationale for why Americans have continued to support capital punishment over the years, which is relevant for why it persists today. She wrote:

> After the Revolution, citizen dissent about the [death penalty] led to sequestered (instead of public) execution and to a series of "humane" methods of execution (e.g., electrocution instead of hanging). Over time, these compromises have satisfied the bloodthirsty and the squeamish alike, leaving only true [death penalty] opponents unsatisfied. And this group has usually been a minority in the United States as well as in countries such as Great Britain where a centralized government abolished the [death penalty] without majority public support. Our system of state-level penal authority has made it easier to sustain the [death penalty], as has the ever-growing control of interest groups over legislators and Congress members.

This respondent also discussed issues related to organized labor and its function in populist movements such as capital punishment abolition (which has not been strong in the United States). She explained:

> Labor conflict during the rise of industrial capitalism was also handled through both legal and extralegal execution, e.g., the trial of the Haymarket rioters (1886, Chicago) and the Ludlow massacre (1913, Colorado). A subtext here is unions' defining their membership as skilled workers and excluding day labor, immigrants, non-whites, and women. Such unions, which decisively triumphed over inclusionist unions at the start of WWI, paved the way for the entry of the few into

the middle class—not for formation of a working-class culture that could have been politically effective and populist, as it has been in some European countries.

Crime Rates

Fifth, five respondents listed and discussed issues related to high crime rates as possible reasons why capital punishment persists in the United States. They discussed America's high predatory murder rates, its high violent crime rates and homicide rates, and the fact that some may see it is necessary to control homicide. Another respondent specifically noted rising crime rates in the 1960s and 1970s.

One expert suggested that American states continue capital punishment because of "high rates of predatory (robbery, rape) murder & serial killing." He explained that: "Jurisdictions (states) that do not have capital punishment as an option have the lowest rates of these types of murder (with the exception of Michigan, Detroit in particular) and hence the least need for the sanction. Those jurisdictions with the highest rate of predatory murder use the death penalty most often."

Another expert agreed, saying: "My guess would be that the incidence of homicide has always been considerably higher in the United States than elsewhere in the developed world owing to the long 'frontier era' in the United States." Still another expert provided a similar response:

> Capital punishment has . . . always been seen as more necessary for controlling homicide in this country. Certainly the world-wide revulsion against the brutal history of Nazi Germany caused a universal reaction against the fundamental principle of state-sanctioned killing. The question is why this revulsion did not extend to the United States and cause the same abolition of capital punishment that occurred in other industrialized nations. One naturally looks for historical factors that set the U.S. apart. Aside from the prolonged frontier era . . . another factor was the prolonged slavery era that resulted, among other things, in quite a high proportion of black people in the population relative to other economically comparable nations. Perhaps another major factor in the important role of capital punishment in this nation was a perceived need to keep slaves or ex-slaves "under control."

Religion

Sixth, five respondents listed and discussed religion as a possible reason why capital punishment persists in the United States. This included American religion, Americans' religious beliefs, high religiosity, and our nation's fundamentalistic background.

For example, one expert noted that he was "convinced that religion, peculiarly enough, plays a supportive role, despite the fact that most main-line religions condemn (the church leaders may say one thing, but the congregation believes something entirely different)." Another expert suggested that "high religiosity might also have a role to play. While Jesus tells his follow[er]s to no longer follow 'the law of Moses,' i.e., the lex talionis, in the Gospel of Matthew, his evangelical followers today don't seem to have noticed." Still another expert pointed out that "support for the [death penalty] correlates strongly with religious beliefs. This is undoubtedly the course of much public support. Why the intellectual elite has not overridden the public, as in Europe, is another matter."

Government Structure

Seventh, three respondents listed issues related to our government structure, including federalism and local politics. For example, one expert explained that the "US is more democratic than Europe. High violent crime rates in [the] US lead [the] public to support [the] death penalty . . . public will can prevail in [the] US because of [federalism] (state control of administration of criminal justice)." Another expert wrote that capital punishment persists

> primarily because our legal system is driven by local politicians, as opposed to the national bureaucracies of other countries. In other countries, where public support for the death penalty is comparable to the United States, national leaders have moved beyond death—they know it is a bad idea, impossible to administer fairly, rarely used, ineffective, and really a distraction. But our system is driven by local prosecutors who do not see the big picture. They continue to sell death to the local people who end up on their juries.

And another expert wrote: "Because of a weak federal government, both legal and extralegal execution were allowed to be integral to forming local and state governments. Examples are the South Carolina Regulators (18th century), San Francisco vigilantes (1850s); Ku Klux Klan of the late 1860s."

Summary of Why Capital Punishment Persists in the United States

Death penalty experts believe that capital punishment persists in the United States for a variety of reasons, including historical reasons, political reasons, reasons related to American punitiveness and public support, our social norms, crime rates in the United States, religion, and due to the structure of our governments. The reasons offered by most of the experts revolved around our history and the political nature of capital punishment, suggesting that change to capital punishment practice will require dedicated and diligent work aimed at changing our basic values with regard to crime and criminal justice responses.

BARRIERS TO CHANGE

The reasons identified in this chapter by the experts that explain why capital punishment persists in the United States included reasons related to American history and culture; politics; punishment; public support; crime rates; religion; and government structure. Each of these can be considered a barrier to effectively bringing about change in America's capital punishment practice. I discuss each below.

America's History and Culture

To whatever degree killing—be it murder, abortion, war, or capital punishment—is normal for human beings (and especially Americans), one would expect support for capital punishment to remain high in the United States. We do have a long history of violence, although much older countries do, as well, and for longer periods of time (and most of these countries have lower rates of murder, abortion, involvement with war, not to mention executions). America's violent past seems unlikely to explain why many states retain capital punishment, especially since other older countries with far more violent pasts than our own have already abolished capital punishment. Thus, our frontier era, culture of violence, and "desire for blood" are likely unimportant to predicting the future of capital punishment in America.

However, the strength of tradition itself will be a significant barrier to overcome if abolition will occur in our lifetimes. That is, with each occasional execution, momentum toward persistence of capital punishment is constantly reinforced. With recent declines in the number of death sentences and executions in the United States, as well as stabilizing death row populations, there is hope for abolitionists that some of this momentum may be slowing. In my opinion, the best way to change our death penalty tradition is just to stop sentencing people and carrying out death sentences. In no time, a new tradition of not executing people will take over.

Four scholars reviewed the histories of nine abolitionist states—Michigan, Wisconsin, Maine, Minnesota, North Dakota, Hawaii, Alaska, Iowa, and West Virginia—and explained how legislators before 1972 abolished and have resisted efforts to reinstate capital punishment. In three other states—Massachusetts, Rhode Island, and Vermont—state courts found each system of capital punishment unconstitutional.[56] Their analysis of states without the death penalty verifies that a tradition of executions sustains capital punishment; evidence suggests abolition is easiest to achieve in states with less tradition of executions.[57] Specifically, "the history of the use of capital punishment gives rise to cultural traditions either supportive or nonsupportive of executions."[58]

One key point to remember when considering the future of capital punishment in the United States is that death penalty activity in America has been remarkably stable within states. Zimring explains: "All of the states that had abolished a death penalty by 1960 do not have a death penalty in 2003. All of the top twelve executing states in the 1950s resumed executing in the 1970s and 1980s, and the relatively small number of states that dominate execution statistics in the current era were high among the leaders half a century ago."[59] This means that strategies for change must be state specific and address issues that persist for some time (at least decades). However, executions have become more concentrated in fewer states, and there is less of a relationship between death sentences and executions, both of which may offer hope for those who want to see an end to capital punishment.

A very important point about America's culture that must be addressed when considering the future of capital punishment in the United States is pointed out by scholar Franklin Zimring. He shows how capital punishment has been symbolically transformed from a government sanction to a service for crime victims so that "an executing government is acting in the interest of victims and communities rather than . . . display[ing] governmental power and dominance."[60] This personal service function of the death penalty, Zimring argues, is unique to America and is of recent origin. Yet, it has its origins in our vigilante tradition, so that "those parts of the United States where mob killings were repeatedly inflicted as crime control without government sanction are more likely now to view official executions as expressions of the will of the community rather than the power of a distant and alien government."[61]

Three benefits of this transformation of executions into a "victim-service program" are 1) closure, 2) degovernmentalization of the death penalty, and 3) the symbolism of executions being linked "to a long American history of community control of punishment." Thus, capital punishment "becomes another public service, like street cleaning or garbage removal, where the government is the servant of the community rather than its master."[62]

Because citizens see capital punishment as a service to them and their communities rather than the most extreme form of governmental power (i.e., taking a human life), at least three outcomes are ensured. First, ironically, Americans are more likely to trust the government (and support executions) when it is taking a human life than they are to trust the government with far less serious responsibilities (e.g., taxation, regulation). This explains why support for the death penalty is high in the South even though people in this region are hostile to government power generally.[63]

Second, people will inevitably feel dissatisfied with the actual practice of capital punishment, given its rarity. Zimring explains: "When the expectation is established that only a death sentence will adequately recognize the suffering of victims and their families, this will guarantee unhappiness in more than 98 percent of all homicides."[64] Further, it is true that many—and probably most—families of murder victims do not feel a sense of closure upon the execution of their loved ones' killers.[65]

Nevertheless, citizens broadly claim to support capital punishment as a form of social control necessary to protect the community in which they live.[66] Zimring adds that "this mythology of local control can also create hostility to courts and judicial review, which can be seen as government restraint on the local power to punish."[67]

Third, the death penalty becomes a more salient and important political issue in the United States than in other countries.[68] This will likely make abolition more difficult in America, at least until our allegiance to vigilante justice wanes.[69]

Zimring cites "a strong tradition of vigilante values . . . found in all parts of the United States but . . . most powerful in the South and Southwest United States" to explain why capital punishment persists in this country.[70] Specifically, Zimring finds that the "states and the region where lynching was dominant show clear domination of recent executions, while those states with very low historic lynching records are much less likely than average to have either a death penalty or execution late in the twentieth century."[71] Zimring finds that the median number of executions in high lynching states is 24, versus zero in low lynching states. Zimring explains: "The statistical contrast between these two groups of states shows that they occupy the same extreme positions on the distribution of two distinct varieties of lethal violence in the United States separated by almost a century and the formal participation of government authority in the killing."[72]

It is important to note that Zimring views a history of vigilante justice (as measured by high levels of lynchings) as necessary but not sufficient to explain continued commitment and willingness to carry out executions currently.[73] Another factor that might also help explain higher rates of death sentences and executions in the South is the "culture of punishment" that is strongest there.[74]

The history and culture of the South, with its prolonged slavery, racism, racial discrimination and disparities, violent segregation and lynchings, civil rights struggles, and the vigilante attitudes that are more prevalent there, may better explain why capital punishment persists in the United States. Further, this may be one of the main barriers to overcome in order to bring about abolition of capital punishment in the United States.

The review of nine abolitionist states found that the makeup of a local population, including its degree of diversity, as well as demographic shifts in the population, plays some role in whether a state continues or abandons capital punishment.[75] It finds support for the "assertion that executions and population density are strongly associated. The tendency to execute racial and ethnic minorities characterizes the execution histories of the abolitionist states." Further, "the urge to execute dissipated as the relative size of minority populations declined."[76] Small, homogeneous, rural populations tend to mediate against executions, and states with "politically powerful minority populations that actively resists the reinstatement of capital punishment" are less likely to have capital punishment.[77] Further, organized resistance, especially by religious and civil rights groups, helps explain abolition by a state, especially when they expose biases in capital punishment practice:[78] "The role that religious elites play in exposing issues of racism and class bias to the general public and political elites cannot be overstated." This suggests that enlightening policy makers to the biased nature of capital punishment is likely to move the pendulum of death penalty practice toward abolition. Clearly, race correlates with vigilantism and ultimately with executions.

Zimring believes Americans have a strong allegiance to another value that competes with vigilantism—due process.[79] Zimring suggests that the death penalty happens when allegiance to due process loses out to vigilantism.[80]

I believe that appealing to the due process value can lead to strong negative public reactions to capital punishment. Opinion polls reviewed in this chapter show that when Americans learn of the realities of capital punishment (e.g., that death sentences are often imposed in violation of due process protections) they become less supportive of the death penalty and more supportive of a moratorium on executions to determine if the practice of the death penalty in their state is plagued by serious problems.

It may be possible to reframe the issue of capital punishment away from an issue of vigilante justice to an issue of human rights. Zimring shows how the issue of death penalty in Europe evolved over time from a state prerogative to a human rights issue.[81] The end of the death penalty in Europe was not brought about by a mass uprising or movement, nor was it led by a well-organized and motivated group or groups.[82] Rather, the historical circumstances of European nations led to its demise. According to Zimring: "The summary executions and death camps of the first half of the twentieth century may have had both the symbol and practice of execution less palatable to democratic governments in the second half of the century."[83] More specifically, it was elites who abolished capital punishment in Europe, even though the punishment was broadly supported by the masses.[84]

Today in Europe, the "orthodox belief . . . is that the death penalty is fundamentally a question about human rights and the proper limits of government power rather than merely a question of the costs and benefits of a particular punishment."[85] Another capital punishment historian, Roger Hood, agrees: "Most West European nations have come to recognize that, even in circumstances of war, capital punishment inflicted by the state is contrary to their commitment to maintain human rights."[86] For those that are skeptical of the appropriate meaning and/or importance of human rights as it relates to capital punishment, consider the statement that

> the great influence of the international law on human rights, at least where domestic or national courts are concerned, is essentially as a body of comparative law. Courts are rarely concerned with whether they are actually bound by the international authorities. But international law informs their appreciation of fundamental rights in a number of areas that impact upon death penalty litigation.[87]

In nations dedicated to human rights, national prerogatives do not decide the death penalty but rather "adherence to international human rights minimum standards" is more important.[88] European practice is consistent with international law. Table 6.8 outlines some key international laws as they pertain to capital punishment.[89]

Interestingly, the view in Europe that the death penalty was about human rights came after abolition, suggesting that a shift in the lens through which capital punishment is viewed in the United States will not lead to abolition.[90] Rather, it is likely that Americans will begin to see the death penalty as a human rights issue after it is eventually abolished. Although it is certainly true that nations that respect human rights tend to be abolitionist, the United States is an exception.[91]

Of course, the United States is a young country that has not yet developed a full distrust in its government when it comes to killing citizens, and Americans have not lived through some of the atrocities that other countries, such as those in Western Europe have (with the obvious exceptions of native Americans and African Americans). For these reasons, America may just not be quite ready to see the death penalty as a human rights issue. Perhaps the realities of America's "war on terror"—with all the

TABLE 6.8 International Law and the Death Penalty

1948—The United Nations (UN) adopted without dissent the Universal Declaration of Human Rights (UDHR). The Declaration proclaims the right of every individual to protection from deprivation of life. It states that no one shall be subjected to cruel or degrading punishment. The death penalty violates both of these fundamental rights.

1966—The UN adopted the International Covenant on Civil and Political Rights (ICCPR). Article 6 of the Covenant states that "no one shall be arbitrarily deprived of his life" and that the death penalty shall not be imposed on pregnant women or on those who were under the age of 18 at the time of the crime. Article 7 states that "no one shall be subjected to torture or to cruel, inhuman or degrading treatment or punishment."

1984—The UN Economic and Social Council (ECOSOC) adopted "Safeguards Guaranteeing Protection of the Rights of Those Facing the Death Penalty." In the same year, the Safeguards were endorsed by consensus by the UN General Assembly. The Safeguards state that no one under the age of 18 at the time of the crime shall be put to death and that anyone sentenced to death has the right to appeal and to petition for pardon or commutation of sentence.

1989—The UN General Assembly adopted the Second Optional Protocol to the ICCPR. Its goal is the abolition of the death penalty.

1990—The Protocol to the American Convention on Human Rights was adopted by the General Assembly of the Organization of American States. It provides for the total abolition of the death penalty, allowing for its use in wartime only.

1993—The International War Crimes Tribunal stated that the death penalty is not an option, even for the most heinous crimes known to civilization, including genocide.

1995—The UN Convention on the Rights of the Child came into force. Article 37(a) prohibits the death penalty for persons under the age of 18 at the time of the crime.

1999—The UN Commission on Human Rights (UNCHR) passed a resolution calling on all states that still maintain the death penalty to progressively restrict the number of offenses for which it may be imposed with a view to completely abolishing it.

2001—The UNCHR approved a European Union motion asking countries to halt executions as a step toward the eventual abolition of the death penalty.

2002—The Council of Europe's Committee of Ministers adopted Protocol 13 to the European Convention on Human Rights. Protocol 13 is the first legally binding international treaty to abolish the death penalty in all circumstances with no exceptions. When it was opened for signature in May 2002, 36 countries signed it.

Source: Death Penalty Defies International Human Rights Standards, by Amnesty International, 2006. Retrieved from http://www.amnestyusa.org/abolish/factsheets/international_h_r_standards. html

evidence of abuse of detainees, torture, secret prisons, extraordinary renditions, domestic spying without congressional approval and in violation of the law, and the killing and intense suffering of tens of thousands of innocent civilians at our hands—will make Americans become more respective of human rights and more skeptical of the federal government and the exercise of government power more generally. If so, this will put pressure on policy makers to end the most extreme use of government power available—the taking of a human life by the government.

This book has not portrayed capital punishment as a human rights issue; instead it has analyzed it as a criminal justice policy issue, which is consistent with how the issue is framed and viewed in this country by most.[92] Thus, the best way to currently understand the issue is whether it is a good criminal justice policy. In this book, I have shown that the experts do not think that capital punishment is a good criminal justice policy (because it does not achieve its goals and it is plagued by significant problems), and the empirical evidence supports this conclusion. However, I do not discount the importance of framing the death penalty as a human rights issue and even an issue relevant to foreign policy. Zimring suggests that capital punishment must be seen as a foreign policy issue—as in Europe—heightening the importance of human rights and international law in the debate.[93] He suggests that, until the death penalty becomes a human rights issue in the United States—an issue less of criminal justice policy and more of proper limits on government power—capital punishment will persist in the United States, especially in those states that have the strongest sense and tradition of vigilantism.

Politics

As shown in this chapter, the death penalty is also politically popular and a part of our culture reaching back even further than the founding of our nation. As long as rhetoric and irrationality rule in American politics and criminal justice, political figures and the media will continue to promote "feel good," easy solutions to complex problems. Further, as long as those who oppose capital punishment (especially on moral grounds) are politically marginalized, the conservative voice will continue to be the only one heard in debates over capital punishment.

The review of nine abolitionist states found that partisanship plays a role in whether capital punishment persists or is abolished: "Among politicians, Republicans tended to favor capital punishment while Democrats tended to favor abolition.... Positions on capital punishment depend on the strength of pro-death penalty sentiments in the community and the ability of organized political groups to punish politicians for taking an abolitionist stance."[94] This is one measure of public opinion that is likely relevant for the future of death penalty practice in the United States. Two relevant questions are 1) is pro-death-penalty sentiment amenable to change, and 2) can a politician with an abolitionist stance be protected from the onslaught of negative media coverage that is likely to typify his or her "soft on crime" views?

I addressed the former question above, suggesting that one way to modify pro-death-penalty opinion is to demonstrate the empirical realities of the administration of capital punishment in America. Polls indicate people are less supportive of the death penalty as they learn the facts. As for the second question, due to the politicization and media coverage of crime and criminal justice, politicians have little incentive to hold abolitionist stances to capital punishment.

Let me say this as clearly as possible: The main problem with the politicization and media coverage of crime and criminal justice is structural in nature.[95] That is, the mainstream media are owned by large corporations whose main purpose is not presenting and reporting objective facts, but rather generating profit. As long as "crime pays," we can expect media coverage to continue to reinforce punitive responses to crime. I think outreach to the media and media reform are two of the biggest challenges we face if we want to change any criminal justice policy, including capital punishment. To whatever degree it is possible to get the media to focus their stories on the realities of American capital punishment, the days of American capital punishment will likely be numbered.

As explained by the authors of the nine abolitionist states, mass media coverage of capital punishment directly impacts legislative outcomes.[96] As mass media outlets covered problems with capital punishment practice, including various biases, citizens became more aware of the realities of the death penalty: "The press is an interpreter of all murders, racism, and executions, providing a lens through which people can know about crime in their community."[97]

Punishment

It is unclear what role our strong belief in individualism and responsibility, the so-called Cowboy mentality and American arrogance, and revenge play in capital punishment. These factors likely have only indirect effects on the death penalty, but probably have more of a direct impact on supporting punitive solutions to problems generally (e.g., the "law and order" approach or the "crime control model"), of which capital punishment is one small part. It is unlikely that this needs to be overcome in order to achieve abolition of the death penalty, given how rarely the punishment is actually used.

I believe it should be possible to convince supporters to direct their punitive attitudes to alternatives to the death penalty, assuming supporters of capital punishment can be effectively shown that it is really not possible to largely increase the number of executions by American governments (given the unwillingness of prosecutors to seek it, jurors to impose it, and counties and states to pay for it). One way to do this may very well be to appeal to people's moral values, although in this book I have framed the important question as an empirical one.[98]

Franklin Zimring suggests that the beginning of the end of the death penalty in the United States has already begun, yet he believes the process "will be intense" and a "struggle."[99] He believes that "morally centered objections" and "morally committed activism" will be necessary to end the death penalty in America—perhaps along the lines of individuals such as Sister Helen Prejean and People of Faith Against the Death Penalty.[100] Zimring's suggestions for strategic objectives for abolitionists include making capital punishment "a major issue in every part of American public life," weakening "the moral confidence and sense of justice of death penalty supporters," and creating "a broad and morally committed community of activist opponents to the death penalty."[101]

Public Opinion

Were one to simply examine the findings from public opinion polls like those discussed in this chapter, one might suspect that capital punishment is likely to persist in the United States for some time because it is widely supported (but not deeply so). Yet, Zimring asserts that public opinion cannot explain the persistence of capital punishment in some states in the United States, nor can it explain state variation in executions.[102] Further, he says, public opinion is unlikely to end capital punishment.[103] In many European countries, for example, public opinion tended to favor capital punishment before, during, and even after its abolition.

The analysis of nine death penalty abolitionist states showed that public opinion, and particularly opinion of those who make key decisions with regard to policy (elites), ensures the continuation of capital punishment.[104] Specifically, it is "practical opinion that matters"—that is, even in abolitionist states citizens say they support the death penalty in the abstract but are in opposition to the state actually carrying out executions. In abolitionist states, legislators realize they cannot "win" on the death penalty, suggesting they know their citizens are practically opposed to capital punishment.[105] Further, in abolitionist states, "economic elites either viewed capital punishment as a nonissue, or viewed death penalty abolition as desirable."[106]

My personal view is that public support for capital punishment does not matter much in terms of the likely future of capital punishment in the United States. That is, other countries that have abolished capital punishment, including most if not all European countries, abolished the punishment through the actions of informed and motivated elites; when public opinion came around to abolition (in those countries where it did) it did so after abolition had already occurred. Certainly, I can envision a scenario where public outcry over capital punishment could lead to its end—either by the U.S. Supreme Court declaring it unconstitutional based on evolving standards of decency or more likely by legislative action at the state level—but I don't expect this to be the mechanism by which capital punishment is abolished in American states. Further, as long as the death penalty is supported largely by those ignorant or misinformed about the realities of capital punishment, it is unlikely that public opinion will shift much at all.

Americans should expect their elected officials to know and communicate the realities of capital punishment in the United States. Knowledge of the empirical realities of capital punishment necessarily leads down the path toward abolition. Public opinion will shift in favor of abolition once abolition becomes the reality and our elected officials communicate the empirical rationale for the policy decisions that lead to abolition.

Crime Rates

America's high crime rate may play some role in the continuation of capital punishment in America, especially our high predatory murder rates and high violent crime rates. Yet, nothing mandates executing violent criminals and even murderers. Other countries with high rates of violent crime and murder choose to deal with their violent offenders through alternative means such as life imprisonment or very long terms of incarceration. Further, the United States ranks nowhere near the top in terms of violent crime victimization according to international criminal victimization surveys.[107]

The review of nine abolitionist states found that the level and purpose of violence and crime rates play some role in whether a state maintains or abolishes capital punishment, although the relationship

> is not as straightforward, inevitable, or evolutionary as some suggest: The history of state-sanctioned violence among abolitionist states differs little from the histories of the states that continue to execute significant numbers of their citizens. . . . The primary factor that separated the violent cultural histories of Southern and Northern states was economic motivation. Violence in the North was motivated by pure and simple genocide, making way for incoming European settlers. Violence in the South was motivated by the need to politically control and exploit black labor, maintaining the sharecropper system. The task of Northern states ended with the near-total annihilation of Native Americans. Given the continued economic and political disenfranchisement of numerous African Americans, the task of the Southern

states continues. Thus, death penalty abolition in the Northern Central states of Michigan, Wisconsin, Minnesota, North Dakota, and Iowa cannot be explained by the cultural evolution of "civilized" Enlightenment ideals. One wonders what the laws of those states would be today if politically and economically viable Native American populations had survived into the twenty-first century.[108]

In terms of murder rates, the analysis of nine abolitionist states found that "closer scrutiny mediates against the notion that murder rates play a determining role in death penalty debates across the nation. . . . Since 1970, murder rates in abolitionist states reflect the maximum possible variation." Yet:

> heinous acts against children, women, and the elderly generally have considerable influence on capital punishment legislation. Political leaders, the public, and the press are understandably outraged by the occurrence of particularly brutal homicides . . . brutal homicides in any abolitionist state, no matter how rare or how common, become potential triggering events or opportunities to reinforce the notion that capital punishment is required to maintain social control.[109]

Franklin Zimring correctly asserts that the variation in capital punishment practice in the United States is not explained by crime rate variations.[110] Thus, supporters of capital punishment who claim that some states have more executions simply because there is more murder in their states may be mistaken.

Religion

The role that religion and Americans' religious beliefs play in capital punishment is interesting, according to the logic discussed by the capital punishment experts in this study. A few experts noted that Americans' religiosity helps account for why capital punishment persists in the country; so logically focusing on Americans' religious beliefs could possibly help bring about change in state death penalty activity.

Of particular importance to Christian Americans would be disparities between Old Testament and New Testament writings. Although a full treatment of religious issues is beyond the scope of this book, one significant analysis of religion and the death penalty cannot be ignored. The study focused on instances where the Bible either mandates, explicitly acknowledges, or implicitly implies a state-sponsored execution.[111] Author Scott Johnson writes: "People often cite specific verses of the Bible to justify a particular position on capital punishment, but these passages are frequently acontextual, failing to consider the significance of the passages containing these verses or the Bible as an entire document."[112] Because the Bible is more ambiguous on the death penalty than one might believe, both supporters and opponents can find evidence supporting their arguments in the Bible.

Consider that "the majority of biblical statements that support capital punishment are found in the Old Testament, more specifically the first five books of the Old Testament . . . the Pentateuch . . . the books of Genesis, Exodus, Leviticus, Numbers, and Deuteronomy." These are the oldest books of the Bible and they "clearly mandate the use of the death penalty for premeditated homicide."[113] They also allow for capital punishment for the crimes of blasphemy and sacrifice to false gods, dishonoring parents, disrespecting priests or elders, adultery, incest, and homosexuality!

The New Testament, a more recent testimony to God, "provides no overt statement in which Jesus or New Testament authors endorse the use of death as a punishment for crimes" and "also fails to reveal any overt rejection of capital punishment," although death was clearly used as a state-sanctioned punishment during this time.[114] Yet, the New Testament "also contains many passages that seem to refute the death penalty."[115] For example, the Bible at times argues against taking revenge and seems to advocate forgiveness. Jesus even says:

> "You may have heard that it was said, 'An eye for an eye and a tooth for a tooth.' But I tell you to resist an evil person . . . whoever slaps you on your right cheek, turn the other also. . . . You have heard that it was said, 'You shall love your neighbor and hate your enemy.' But I say to you, love your enemies, bless those who curse you, do good to those who hate you, and pray for those who spitefully use you or persecute you." (Matthew 5:38–45).

Perhaps the clearest example of ambiguity about the death penalty in the Bible comes in the form of the outcomes of people who committed murder in the Bible. Johnson identifies 22 murderers in the Bible; only 4 of them (18%) are executed by the state. Johnson explains: "It seems difficult to suggest that the Bible sincerely endorses state sponsored capital punishment, when so few murderers in the Scriptures receive the death penalty."[116]

Considering the lack of a clear mandate for executions in the Bible, death penalty scholar Robert Bohm poses an interesting question: How can people, "particularly people whose lives are governed by the Bible . . . endorse revenge, support or oppose capital punishment, and use the Bible as a basis of their support or opposition, when they know the Bible is ambiguous on the subject"?[117]

I believe that the nation's religious leaders could strongly impact (i.e. weaken) support for capital punishment if they simply told the truth about the punishment and how it seems to contradict their religious teachings. Whether this would impact death penalty practice is unclear.

Government Structure

American government structure—specifically federalism and local politics—plays an enormously important role in state capital punishment systems. Under the U.S. Constitution, states have the power to write and enforce their own laws. Similarly, under state constitutions, local governments have the authority to pursue their own priorities and set their own policies. Because of this, there is wide variation in capital punishment practice across regions of the country, states, and even within states (e.g., county-level variation in capital trials and death sentences). Thus, short of a U.S. Supreme Court decision striking down all death penalty laws, changing capital punishment practice will require state-by-state and county-by-county activity.

Certainly, abolitionists can learn lessons from states that have already abolished the death penalty. Based on the successes of those states that have abolished capital punishment, objectives should include overcoming tradition, changing public opinion, reaching out to and utilizing the mainstream media to tell the truth about the death penalty in America, organizing resistance among religious and civil rights groups (in part by reinforcing the perception of racial and class bias in capital punishment practice), and working with the political parties to discuss the empirical realities of capital punishment in the interest of informing policy. Abolitionists could also possibly gain some credibility among doubters if, simultaneous to their abolition efforts, they worked on creating and implementing efforts to reduce the levels of violence and crime rates in our society. As already noted briefly, heinous acts of violence—especially against the least protected members of our society—tend to reinforce support for, and the momentum of, capital punishment. Reducing such acts will assist abolition efforts. Efforts to abolish the death penalty should be included in larger efforts to reduce violence in American society.

CONCLUSION

Although the American public generally reports supporting capital punishment, their support appears largely based on misconceptions of the death penalty and ignorance of its realities. Further, public support is lessened when people are given alternatives to capital punishment, including life imprisonment without the possibility of parole. Logically, providing information about the realities of capital punishment to the American people will reduce support for the death penalty.

Simultaneously, the experts—those who teach and write about capital punishment—are overwhelmingly opposed to the death penalty. Further, they are universally unwilling to suggest death sentences as the most appropriate sentence for convicted murderers. This is logical given their strong beliefs, reported in earlier chapters, that capital punishment fails to meet its goals and that it is plagued by significant problems of bias, error, and inefficiency (all of which are supported by empirical evidence). The gap between American citizens and capital punishment experts is perhaps the most significant barrier to a future without capital punishment in America.

Other barriers identified in this chapter include America's history and culture, politics, American views of punishment generally, public support for capital punishment, crime rates in the United States, religious factors, and our government structure. As I explained in this chapter, many of these barriers are incapable of explaining why capital punishment has not yet been abolished. Nor should any of these barriers stand in the way of doing what is justified based on the empirical realities of capital punishment in the United States. The policy that is justified by the findings of this book is abolition of American capital punishment.

ENDNOTES

1. Bohm, B. (2003). *Deathquest II: An introduction to the theory and practice of capital punishment in the United States* (2nd ed.). Cincinnati, OH: Anderson.
2. Robinson, M. (2005). *Justice blind? Ideals and realities of American criminal justice* (2nd ed.). Upper Saddle River, NJ: Prentice Hall.
3. *Sourcebook of Criminal Justice Statistics.* (2006). Table 2.51.2005. Attitudes toward the death penalty for a person convicted of murder. Retrieved from http://albany.edu/sourcebook/pdf/t2512005.pdf
4. Death Penalty Information Center. (2006a). National polls. Retrieved from http://www.deathpenaltyinfo.org/article.php?scid=23&did=210#NP
5. Death Penalty Information Center. (2004). *Gallup poll: Public divided between death penalty and life imprisonment without parole.* Retrieved from http://www.deathpenaltyinfo.org/article.php?scid=23&did=1029
6. *Sourcebook of Criminal Justice Statistics.* (2006). Table 2.49.2005. Attitudes toward the penalty for murder. Retrieved from http://albany.edu/sourcebook/pdf/t2492005.pdf
7. Death Penalty Information Center. (2006). *News and developments—public opinion.* Retrieved from http://www.deathpenaltyinfo.org/newsanddev.php?scid=23

8. Death Penalty Information Center (2006b).

9. Bohm (2003); Haney, C. (2005). *Death by design: Capital punishment as a social psychological system*. New York: Oxford University Press.

10. Bohm (2003).

11. Death Penalty Information Center (2006b).

12. Death Penalty Information Center (2006a).

13. Death Penalty Information Center (2006b)

14. Death Penalty Information Center (2006a).

15. Young, R. (2002). Religious orientation, race and support for the death penalty. In J. Martinez, W. Richardson, & D. Hornsby (Eds.), *The Leviathan's choice: Capital punishment in the twenty-first century*. Lanham, MD: Rowman & Littlefield.

16. Cochran, J., & Chamlin, M. (2006). The enduring racial divide in death penalty support. *Journal of Criminal Justice, 34*(1), 85–99; Young, R. (2004). Guilty until proven innocent: Conviction orientation, racial attitudes, and support for capital punishment. *Deviant Behavior, 25*(2), 151–167.

17. One example comes from a study of Californians who supported the death penalty and thought it was a deterrent, cheaper than life imprisonment, and that life imprisonment without parole really did not mean life. See Haney (2005).

18. Death Penalty Information Center (2006a).

19. Sandys, M., & McGarrell, E. (1995). Attitudes toward capital punishment: Preference for the penalty or mere acceptance? *Journal of Research in Crime and Delinquency, 32*(2), 191–213.

20. Zimring, F. (2003). *The contradictions of American capital punishment*. New York: Oxford University Press.

21. Lifton, R., & Mitchell, G. (2000). *Who owns death? Capital punishment, the American conscience, and the end of executions*. New York: William Morrow, p. xii.

22. Pojman, L., & Reiman, J. (1998). *The death penalty: For and against*. Lanham, MD: Rowman & Littlefield.

23. Lifton & Mitchell (2000).

24. *Furman v. Georgia*, 408 U.S. 228, 261 (1972).

25. *Furman*, 408 U.S. at 263–264.

26. Cochran, J., & Chamlin, M. (2005). Can information change public opinion?: Another test of the Marshall hypothesis. *Journal of Criminal Justice, 33*, 573–584.

27. *Callins v. James*, 000 U.S. U10343 (1994).

28. Bohm, B. (1989). The effects of classroom instruction and discussion on death penalty opinions: A teaching note. *Journal of Criminal Justice, 17*, 123–131; Bohm, B. (1990). Death penalty opinions: Effects of a classroom experience and public commitment. *Sociological Inquiry, 60*, 285–297; Bohm, B., Clark, L., & Aveni, A. (1990). The influence of knowledge on death penalty opinions: An experimental test. *Justice Quarterly, 7*, 175–188; Bohm, B., Clark, L., & Aveni, A. (1991). Knowledge and death penalty opinion: A test of the Marshall

hypotheses. *Journal of Research in Crime and Delinquency, 28,* 360–387; Bohm, B., & Vogel, R. (1991). Educational experiences and death penalty opinions: Stimuli that produce changes. *Journal of Criminal Justice Education, 2,* 69–80; Bohm, B., & Vogel, R. (1994). A comparison of factors associated with uninformed and informed death penalty opinions. *Journal of Criminal Justice, 22,* 125–143; Bohm, B., & Vogel, R. (2002). *More than ten years after: The long-term stability of informed death penalty opinions.* Paper presented at the annual meeting of the Academy of Criminal Justice Sciences, Los Angeles; Bohm, B., Vogel, R., & Maisto, A. (1993). Knowledge and death penalty opinion: A panel study. *Journal of Criminal Justice, 21,* 29–45; Clarke, A., Lambert, E., & Whitt, L (2001). Executing the innocent: The next step in the Marshall hypotheses. *Review of Law and Social Change, 26,* 309–345; Cochran & Chamlin (2005); Ellsworth, P., & Ross, L. (1983). Public opinion and capital punishment: A close examination of the views of abolitionists and retentionists. *Crime and Delinquency, 29,* 111–169; Lambert, E., & Clarke, A. (2001). The impact of information on an individual's support of the death penalty: A partial test of the Marshall hypothesis among college students. *Criminal Justice Policy Review, 12,* 215–234; Longmire, D. (1996). Americans' attitudes about the ultimate sanction capital punishment. In Flanagan, T., & Longmire, D. (Eds.), *Americans view crime and justice: A national public opinion survey.* Thousand Oaks, CA: Sage; Lord, C., Ross, L., & Lepper, M. (1979). Biased assimilation and attitude polarization: The effects of prior theories on subsequently considered evidence. *Journal of Personality and Social Psychology, 37,* 2098–2109; Patenaude, A. (2001). May God have mercy on your soul! Exploring and teaching a course on the death penalty. *Journal of Criminal Justice Education, 12,* 405–425; Sandys, M. (1995). Attitudinal change among students in a capital punishment class: It may be possible. *American Journal of Criminal Justice, 20,* 37–55; Sarat, A., & Vidmar, N. (1976). Public opinion, the death penalty, and the Eighth Amendment: Testing the Marshall hypothesis. *Wisconsin Law Review, 17,* 171–206; Vidmar, N., & Dittenhoffer, T. (1981). Informed public opinion and death penalty attitudes. *Canadian Journal of Criminology, 23,* 43–56; Wright, H., Jr., Bohm, B., & Jamieson, K. (1995). A comparison of uniformed and informed death penalty opinions: A replication and expansion. *American Journal of Criminal Justice, 20,* 57–87.

29. Ellsworth & Ross (1983); Lord, Ross, & Lepper (1979).
30. Durham, A., Elrod, P., & Kinkade, P. (1996). Public support for the death penalty: Beyond Gallop. *Justice Quarterly, 13*(4), 322–341.
31. Bohm (2003).
32. For example, see Sarat & Vidmar (1976).
33. For example, see Vidmar & Dittenhoffer (1981).
34. For example, see Bohm (1989, 1990, 1991, 1992); Bohm et al. (1990, 1991); Bohm & Vogel (1994, 2002); Bohm et al. (1993).
35. Bohm (2003), p. 265.
36. Bohm (2003), p. 266.
37. Chamlin & Cochran (2005).
38. Haney (2005), p. 68.

39. Dow, D. (2002). How the death penalty really works. In D. Dow & M. Dow (Eds.), *Machinery of death: The reality of America's death penalty regime*. New York: Routledge; Haney (2005).

40. This respondent provided the following as citations for verification: Donohue, J., & Wolfers, J. (2005). Uses and abuses of empirical evidence in the death penalty debate. *Stanford Law Review, 58*, 791; Berk, R. (2005). New claims about executions and general deterrence: Déjà vu all over again? *Journal of Empirical Legal Studies, 2*(2), 303.

41. This respondent noted studies by David Baldus, Michael Radelet, Glenn Pierce, Margaret Vandiver, William Bowers, William Loftquist, Samuel Gross, and Robert Mauro.

42. This respondent was referring to the Governor's Council on Capital Punishment, which offered 10 proposals to create what it called "a fair capital punishment statute for Massachusetts that is as narrowly tailored, and as infallible, as humanly possible." The proposals included narrowing the list of death-eligible crimes, controlling prosecutorial discretion, providing high-quality defense attorneys, creating new procedures for bifurcated trials, creating special jury instructions pertaining to the use of human evidence, requiring scientific evidence to support guilt, heightening the burden of proof, requiring independent scientific verification of evidence, broadening authority for appeals courts to set aside death sentences, and creating a commission to study claims of innocence. See Massachusetts's *Governor's Council on Capital Punishment*. Retrieved from http://www.mass.gov/Agov2/docs/5-3-04%20MassDPReportFinal.pdf. The goal of creating a foolproof or perfect death penalty statute was seen by many as an impossible dream.

43. See Liebman, J., Fagan, J., & West, V. (2000). *A broken system: Error rates in capital cases, 1973–1995*. Retrieved from http://www.law.columbia.edu/instructionalservices/liebman/

44. This expert cited Greenberg, J. (1986). Against the American system of capital punishment. *Harvard Law Review, 99*, 1670.

45. Bedau, H. (2004). An abolitionist's survey of the death penalty in America today. In H. Bedau & P. Cassell (Eds.), *Debating the death penalty: Should America have capital punishment? The experts from both sides make their case*. New York: Oxford University Press, p. 34.

46. Bedau (2004), p. 47.

47. Haines, H. (1996). *Against capital punishment: The anti-death penalty movement in America, 1972–1994*. New York: Oxford University Press, p. 167.

48. Haines (1996), pp. 168–169.

49. Haines (1996), p. 193.

50. Hood, R. (2002). *The death penalty: A worldwide perspective* (3rd ed.). New York: Oxford University Press, pp. 25, 62.

51. For example, see Haney (2005); Miller, R. (2002). Reflections on the future of the death penalty. In J. Martinez, W. Richardson, & D. Hornsby (Eds.), *The Leviathan's choice: Capital punishment in the twenty-first century*. Lanham, MD: Rowman & Littlefield.

52. McAllister, P. (2003). *Death defying: Dismantling the execution machinery in the 21st century*. New York: Continuum International Publishing Group.
53. Haney (2005), p. 214.
54. For example, the Declaration of Independence states: "When in the Course of human events, it becomes necessary for one people to dissolve the political bonds which have connected them with another, and to assume among the Powers of the Earth, the separate and equal Station to which the Laws of Nature and of Nature's God entitle them, a decent respect to the opinions of mankind requires that they should declare the cases which impel them to the separation." Further, Article VI, clause 2 of the U.S. Constitution states: "This Constitution, and all the Laws of the United States which shall be made in Pursuances thereof; and all Treaties made, or which shall be made under the Authority of the United States, shall be the supreme law of the Land; and the Judges of every State shall be bound thereby, any Thing in the Constitution or Laws of any State to the Contrary notwithstanding." For more on this, see Wilson, R. (2003). The influence of international law and practice on the death penalty in the United States. In J. Acker, B. Bohm, & C. Lanier (Eds.), *America's experiment with capital punishment: Reflections on the past, present, and future of the ultimate penal sanction*. Durham, NC: Carolina Academic Press, p. 149.
55. This respondent provided the following as citations: Jacobs, D., Carmichael J. T., & Kent, S. L. (2005). Vigilantism, current racial threat, and death sentences. *American Sociological Review, 70*, 656; Messner, S. F., Baller, R. D., & Zevenbergen, M. P. (2005). The legacy of lynching and Southern homicide. *American Sociological Review, 70*(4), 633.
56. Galliher, J., Koch, L., Keys, D., & Guess, T. (2002). *America without the death penalty: States leading the way*. Boston: Northeastern University Press.
57. Galliher et al. (2002), p. 8.
58. Galliher et al. (2002), p. 209.
59. Zimring (2003), p. 85.
60. Zimring (2003), p. ix.
61. Zimring (2003), p. 89.
62. Zimring (2003), p. 62.
63. Zimring (2003), p. 84.
64. Zimring (2003), p. 56.
65. Zimring (2003), p. 60.
66. Zimring (2003), p. 109.
67. Zimring (2003), p. 111.
68. Zimring (2003), p. 127.
69. Zimring (2003), pp. 130–131.
70. Zimring (2003), p. 66.
71. Zimring (2003), p. 66.
72. Zimring (2003), p. 96. As noted by one of the respondents in this study, Zimring's main thesis has been replicated. Two recent studies show

relationships between (1) county-level lynchings and murder rates, and (2) state-level lynchings and executions. The authors of the second study suggest that executions have replaced lynchings as a means to deal with perceived racial threats. See Messner et al. (2005), p. 633; Jacobs et al. (2005), p. 656.

73. Zimring (2003), p. 98.
74. Zimring (2003), p. 116.
75. Galliher et al. (2002), p. 9.
76. Galliher et al. (2002), p. 217.
77. Galliher et al. (2002), pp. 211–212.
78. Galliher et al. (2002), p. 207.
79. Zimring (2003), p. 119.
80. Zimring (2003), p. 121.
81. Zimring (2003), p. 17.
82. For more on the state of capital punishment around the world, including Europe, Asia, Africa, South and Central America, the Middle East, the Carribean, and the Americas, see Hood (2002).
83. Zimring (2003), p. 18.
84. Zimring (2003), p. 23.
85. Zimring (2003), p. 25.
86. Hood (2002), p. 26.
87. Hodgkinson, P., & Schabas, W. (2004). *Capital punishment: Strategies for abolition.* Cambridge, UK: Cambridge University Press, pp. 39–40.
88. Zimring (2003), p. 25.
89. For more detailed information about international law as it applies to capital punishment in the United States and the world (e.g., the Universal Declaration of Human Rights, the European Convention on Human Rights, the International Covenant on Civil and Political Rights, the American Convention on Human Rights, the Second Optional Protocol to the International Covenant Aiming the Abolition of the Death Penalty, and the Protocol to the American Convention on Human Rights to Abolish the Death Penalty) see Bedau, H. (1997). International human rights law and the death penalty in America. In H. Bedau (Ed.), *The death penalty in America: Current controversies.* New York: Oxford University Press; Hodgkinson & Schabas (2004); Hood (2002); Wilson (2003).
90. Zimring (2003), p. 27.
91. Zimring (2003), p. 39.
92. Zimring (2003), p. 45.
93. Zimring (2003), p. 182.
94. Galliher et al. (2002), p. 214.
95. Robinson (2005).
96. Galliher et al. (2002), p. 9.
97. Galliher et al. (2002), p. 216.
98. Galliher et al. (2002), p. 214.
99. Zimring (2003), p. 141.

100. An example of an individual who challenges the death penalty on moral grounds is Sister Helen Prejean (see http://www.prejean.org/). An example of an organization that challenges the death penalty on moral grounds is People of Faith Against the Death Penalty (see http://www.pfadp.org/).

101. Zimring (2003), p. 194.

102. Zimring (2003), p. 11.

103. Zimring (2003), p. 193.

104. Galliher et al. (2002), pp. 8–9.

105. Galliher et al. (2002), p. 213.

106. Galliher et al. (2002), p. 214.

107. Paulsen, D., & Robinson, M. (2004). *Spatial aspects of crime: Theory and practice*. Boston: Allyn & Bacon.

108. Galliher et al. (2002), p. 208.

109. Galliher et al. (2002), pp. 209–210.

110. Zimring (2003), pp. 115–116.

111. Johnson, S. (2000). The Bible and the death penalty: Implications for criminal justice education. *Journal of Criminal Justice Education, 11*(1), 15–33.

112. Johnson (2000), p. 15.

113. Johnson (2000), p. 17.

114. Johnson (2000), p. 23.

115. Johnson (2000), p. 26.

116. Johnson (2000), p. 31.

117. Bohm (1999). *Deathquest: An introduction to the theory and practice of capital punishment in the United States*. Cincinnati, OH: Anderson, p. 182.

Index

Note: Page numbers followed by *f* indicate figures and by *t*, tables.